Money and Schools

For both aspiring and experienced education leaders in school budgeting, finance, and resource management courses, *Money and Schools* explains and demonstrates the relationship between money and equality of educational opportunity in a way that is clear, precise, and engaging. Grounded in research and best practices, this book provides a broad overview of school finance, budgeting, and resource allocation, an understanding of the underlying economic, social, legal, and political principles that drive how schools are funded, as well as a detailed examination of day-to-day funding operations. Rich pedagogical features include chapter opening challenges, chapter drivers, point/counterpoint discussions, case studies, and recommended resources. This accessible and engaging book offers strong connections to real-world experiences and detailed information on pre-K–12 funding history, concepts, and current operations.

New to this edition:

- Coverage of environmental sustainability and other emerging trends in this unprecedented uncertainty of schools' economic and social environment.
- Updates to references and overall funding changes since the previous edition.
- Revised end-of-chapter activities and additional resources that are aligned with the key concepts and content of each chapter.
- Updated supplemental downloads, including editable PowerPoints.

R. Craig Wood is Professor of Educational Administration and Policy at the University of Florida, USA.

David C. Thompson is the Skeen Endowed Chair in Education and Professor and Department Head of Educational Leadership at Kansas State University, USA.

Faith E. Crampton is President and CEO of Crampton & Associates, an education consulting firm, who retired as Associate Professor of Education Finance and Policy at the University of Wisconsin-Milwaukee, USA.

Money and Schools

Seventh Edition

R. Craig Wood, David C. Thompson, and Faith E. Crampton

Routledge
Taylor & Francis Group

NEW YORK AND LONDON

Seventh edition published 2019

by Routledge
52 Vanderbilt Avenue, New York, NY 10017

and by Routledge
2 Park Square, Milton Park, Abingdon, Oxon, OX14 4RN

Routledge is an imprint of the Taylor & Francis Group, an informa business

© 2019 Taylor & Francis

First edition published by Eye on Education 1998
Sixth edition published by Routledge 2015

Library of Congress Cataloging-in-Publication Data
Names: Wood, R. Craig, author.
Title: Money and schools/by R. Craig Wood, David C. Thompson, and
Faith E. Crampton.
Description: Seventh Edition. | New York: Routledge, 2019. | David C.
Thompson is listed as the primary author on the title page of the fifth
edition. | "Sixth edition published by Routledge 2015"–T.p. verso.
Identifiers: LCCN 2018059782 | ISBN 9781138327634 (Hardback) |
ISBN 9781138327665 (Paperback) | ISBN 9780429449147 (eBook)
Subjects: LCSH: School budgets–United States–Handbooks, manuals, etc. |
Schools–United States–Accounting–Handbooks, manuals, etc. |
Education–United States–Finance–Handbooks, manuals, etc.
Classification: LCC LB2830.2 .T56 2019 | DDC 371.2/060973–dc23
LC record available at https://lccn.loc.gov/2018059782

ISBN: 978-1-138-32763-4 (hbk)
ISBN: 978-1-138-32766-5 (pbk)
ISBN: 978-0-429-44914-7 (ebk)

Typeset in Sabon
by Deanta Global Publishing Services, Chennai, India

For eResources, please visit: http://www.routledge.com/9781138327665

Brief Contents

Contents

PART II
Operationalizing School Money   **105**

4   School Funds: Accountability, Performance, and Professionalism   107

Figures

Tables

About the Authors

Dr. R. Craig Wood is one of the leading scholars in the field of financing public education in America. He is currently Professor of Educational Administration and Policy at the University of Florida. His career has spanned public school classroom teacher, school district chief financial officer, and assistant superintendent for finance for school districts across the nation. Prior to his present position he was a professor of educational administration at Purdue University. He is one of the most prolific authors in America regarding the funding of public education. His publication record includes more than 250 book chapters, monographs, law reviews, and scholarly peer-reviewed journal articles including the American Education Finance Association's *Annual Yearbooks* and the Education Law Association's *Handbook of School Law* series. His authored and co-authored books include *Money & Schools* (seven editions), *Education Finance Law* (four editions), *Fiscal Leadership for Schools*, and *Principles of School Business Management* (three editions). He serves on the editorial boards of *Education Law Reporter, Journal of Education Finance*, and *Education Law & Policy Review*. He has published his education finance research in such journals as the *Journal of Education Finance*, the *Kentucky Law Review*, the *Saint Louis University Public Law Review*, the *University of Arkansas Law Review*, the *Brigham Young University Education and Law Journal, Educational Considerations, School Business Affairs, Planning & Changing*, and the *Education Law and Policy Review*. He has delivered keynote addresses to a variety of national and international education research conferences during his career. He has presented at numerous national academic conferences over the years, including in England and South Africa. He has conducted education finance litigation workshops for the National Conference on State Legislatures and the National Association of Attorneys General. He has served as the lead expert witness involving state constitutional challenges to financing public education in many states. He has served as the lead expert witness for charter schools regarding funding. He has consulted with over two dozen state legislatures regarding the financing of public education and many school districts. He is a past President of the American Education Finance Association as well as its Executive Director. He is the past President of the Education Law Association housed at Cleveland Marshall College of Law, Cleveland, Ohio. He is also the past President of the National Education Finance Academy and received its Lifetime Achievement Award in 2017. He holds an Ed.D. and M.A. Ed. in Educational Administration from the Virginia Polytechnic Institute and State University and a B.S. *cum laude* from Campbell University in North Carolina.

Dr. David C. Thompson's professional career has spanned the roles of classroom teacher, high school principal, superintendent of schools, and the professoriate. He is a specialist in education finance litigation. His prolific publication record encompasses numerous book chapters, monographs, and refereed journal articles. A frequently invited author in respected circles, he has published chapters in four consecutive *American Education Finance Association Yearbooks* and has been widely published in the *Journal of Education Finance*, the *NOLPE Handbook of School Law*, West's *Education Law Reporter*, books by the Association of School Business Officials International (ASBO), and many others. He has served on numerous boards, including the Authors' Committee of West's *Education Law Reporter*, is currently legislative editor for the *Journal of Education Finance*, has written an invited review of school finance litigation for West's *Education Law Reporter*, and is past chair of the Board of Editors for the scholarly journal *Educational Considerations*. His textbooks include *Fiscal Leadership for Schools: Concepts and Practices*, *Principles of School Business Management*, *Education Finance Law: Constitutional Challenges to State Aid Plans*, *Money and Schools*, *Saving America's School Infrastructure*, and *Funding Public Schools in the United States and Indian Country*. He also served as author, editor, and consultant to the Core Finance Data Task Force's 2003 total rewrite of the U.S. Department of Education's authoritative handbook *Financial Accounting for Local and State School Systems*. His consulting work has included advisement to more than 20 state departments of education, state legislatures, attorneys general, and litigants in school finance. His research has been presented to numerous organizations, including the American Education Finance Association, Education Law Association, National Center for Education Statistics, National Education Association, National Conference of State Legislatures, and the National Association of Attorneys General, along with other keynote addresses to large audiences. His scholarly work has been cited by the U.S. Supreme Court. He also served as Founding Director of the University Council for Educational Administration's (UCEA) Center for Education Finance at Kansas State University and the University of Florida from 1989 to 2006. He is the recipient of numerous awards and recognitions, including the UCEA Award for Sustained and Meritorious Service. In 2013 he was inducted into the Kansas State University Academy of Fellows. He is a Distinguished Research Fellow in the National Education Finance Academy (NEFA), and in 2013 was awarded the Lifetime Achievement Award by the NEFA. Dr. Thompson holds the Skeen Endowed Chair in Education and has been Department Head of Educational Leadership at Kansas State University since 1994.

Dr. Faith E. Crampton's professional career has spanned public education, senior administrative positions in state government, senior research and policy positions in national education and legislative organizations, and graduate faculty positions in public and private research universities. Currently, she is a consultant serving as

President and CEO of Crampton & Associates, a firm specializing in rigorous, results-oriented research and policy analysis. She is past President of the Fiscal Issues, Policy, and Education Finance Special Interest Group of the American Educational Research Association and a past member of the Board of Directors of the American Education Finance Association and the University Council for Educational Administration Center for Education Finance. She has held graduate faculty appointments in education finance and policy at the University of Oregon, University of Rochester, and University of Wisconsin-Milwaukee. Outside academe, she has served as a senior researcher with the National Education Association, a senior policy analyst and consultant for the National Conference of State Legislatures, and Deputy Director of the Ohio Student Loan Commission. She has published widely in leading journals such as the *Journal of Education Finance, Journal of Educational Administration, Educational Considerations, National Association of Secondary School Principals Journal, Journal of School Business Management, Journal of the Council of Educational Facility Planners International, Multicultural Learning and Teaching, School Business Affairs*, and West's *Education Law Reporter* in addition to authoring numerous monographs, reports, book chapters, and policy briefs. Also, she has served as executive editor of the scholarly journal *Educational Considerations*, consulting editor for *The Professional Educator*, collaborating scholar with the National Center for the Twenty-First Century Schoolhouse, and editorial staff member of the *Journal of Education Finance* and *Journal of Women in Educational Leadership*. In 2003, she published the groundbreaking book *Saving America's School Infrastructure*, with a foreword by the late Senator Edward M. Kennedy. She has presented scholarly papers and given invited presentations to national and international research and policy organizations, such as the American Education Finance Association, American Educational Research Association, British Educational Management and Administration Society, Center for Budget Policy and Priorities, Council of Educational Facilities Planners International, Council of State Governments, Education Commission of the States, Education Writers Association, The Finance Project, NAACP, National Conference of Professors of Educational Administration, National Conference of State Legislatures, National Education Association, National Education Finance Academy, North Central Regional Educational Laboratory, Organizations Concerned about Rural Education, and University Council for Educational Administration. In 2012, she was honored as a Distinguished Research Fellow by the National Education Finance Academy. Dr. Crampton began her career as a public school teacher.

Preface

OVERVIEW

Welcome to the seventh edition of this book! To our contemporaries who used the earlier editions, we welcome you back as friends and colleagues. To new users, we offer you a special welcome to this new edition and hope you will be able to satisfy your interest in school finance and resource utilization through this longstanding and time-tested book. As was true with each of the previous six editions, we have again attempted to shed new light on the critical needs of the field in a way that is clear, precise, and engaging. Our reasoning for this approach is simple—we believe that how schools are funded is of critical importance in today's world of high-stakes accountability, and we believe that effective educational leaders must be highly connected to the relationship between money and the aims of education *and* highly responsive to public perceptions about how fiscal resources are utilized. In our view, the topic is vibrant and the need for clarity and preciseness cannot be overstated.

WHO WE ARE

Our approach in this book is due in meaningful part to who we are as authors. Our own personal histories as practitioners and university professors permeate the entire book, reflecting how we believe new generations of school leaders should be prepared. Who we are therefore says a great deal about what readers should expect from this seventh edition of *Money and Schools*. Plainly put, we are very experienced scholars and public school practitioners, and we believe the impact of our collective history is important to readers' willingness to accept what we say in this book. We are scholars given our work in major research universities, carrying out scholarly agendas and teaching courses in educational leadership, specifically involving issues related to school finance. It is equally important that we have deep and extensive practitioner roots. Collectively, we have served as superintendents, assistant superintendents, school business managers, chief financial officers, grant managers, principals, and classroom teachers in public school systems across the United States. We have also provided extensive consulting work on behalf of school districts, and for more than three decades we have been involved in legal battles in numerous states as expert witnesses on behalf of plaintiffs or defendants seeking objective analysis of funding for schools. The especially critical aspect of our professional histories is that we have not written this book solely from a theory base, nor have we used the book as a bully pulpit to advance any political views about how national, state, or local units of government should fund schools at a combative point in history. Instead, who we are relates to this book at the most basic level by virtue of the fact that we are practitioners who have done the things our readers are most interested in—we've built budgets, cut budgets, raised taxes, faced angry constituents, hired and fired staff, experienced the accountability and student achievement wars, and so on. As a result, we believe our readers' experience with this book will be enhanced by knowing us for who we are— *for the most part, we are school people like most of our readers.*

THE CURRENT CONTEXT

As we go to press with this seventh edition, the context of schooling and its funding is in a state of flux. Roilings at the federal level are having great impact on school districts across the nation, as the U.S. Department of Education's fascination with deregulating many aspects of schools has been taken to new and unprecedentedly disruptive heights. Many states are pressing forward with reforms containing measures that more and more are tied to state funding for schools. School leaders are also facing new challenges under conditions requiring schools to do more with scarce resources. Although our profession has always believed that education is a high-stakes enterprise in which all children deserve the best opportunity regardless of individual circumstance, the result of new demands and greater uncertainty has been to engage leaders at a higher level of understanding about just how critical effective leadership is to guaranteeing universally coveted pupil performance outcomes.

The current context demands that school leaders must be highly effective. To that end, a critically important skill is understanding the relationship not only between *opportunity and money* but also between *outcomes and money*. Effective school leaders, then, are key to meeting state and federal mandates for the academic success of all students. As a result, the context of this seventh edition of *Money and Schools* is that federal law demands equality of educational outcomes for all children; that school performance accountability expectations at the state level continue to increase even while fiscal resources may be stagnant or diminished; and that the education profession itself must embrace rigorous performance accountability. In sum, this environment *absolutely* demands school leaders who understand the complex nature of schooling and the relationship of money to equal opportunity and outcomes.

WHAT'S NEW IN THIS EDITION?

Based upon positive feedback from our many reviewers and textbook adopters, we have maintained the overarching structure and design found in the previous edition. This includes an opening challenge, chapter drivers, highly conversational language, point/counterpoint discussions, case studies, web resources, and recommended resources—all in a structure based on translating theory and research into best practice. The first half of the book, therefore, continues to be devoted to understanding the underlying economic, social, legal, and political principles that have long driven how schools are funded, while the second half of the book is devoted to detailing the operational implementation of policy—that is, theory and research into best practice.

Changes to this new seventh edition largely center on critically reviewing and revising all content on the basis of absolute currency, analyzing continuing or emerging trends, and explicating the nearly unprecedented uncertainty of schools' economic and social environment. More specifically, these actions by the authors resulted in the following changes to this edition:

- *Carefully parsed text*, often significantly rewritten in both content and form.
- *Cutting-edge research* written into the text itself on the impacts of money on student learning outcomes.
- *New and expanded chapter-by-chapter annotations* that point readers to current resources, many of which are available online, and that explain key concepts in greater detail.
- *Elimination of some text data and figures* that either no longer fit current economic trends or that tend to become dated too quickly—notwithstanding, the text is still heavily data-driven since a deep grasp of school funding requires familiarity and comfort with fiscal data.
- *Addition of many new comprehensive tables*, along with expanded and updated tables that were carried forward from the previous edition. Where appropriate, 50 state tables are provided for easy cross-state comparisons.
- *Addition of many new, visually appealing graphs and charts* that distill complex information into an easy-to-understand format.
- *New concepts that have gained traction* since the last edition of this book, such as environmental sustainability.
- *Updated, parsed, and enhanced web resources and recommended resources* that are carefully aligned with the key concepts and content of each chapter. In addition, these features provide helpful support for the portfolio exercises. Most of the recommended readings are available online.
- *Updated PowerPoints* available for download. This feature is fully manipulable by professors so that chapter-tailored presentations can be created that cover the text material, as well as allowing for customization to any given state in the United States.
- *Updated downloads* that include several chapter-based interactive figures from the text for *what-if* scenarios—e.g., salary costing and enrollment forecasting, along with other figures from the text that can be projected in large detail on a screen.

Finally, the chapter on site-based leadership has been eliminated since that trend has largely faded. The book is now shorter, but with a new Chapter 12 focused on reviewers' request that more discussion be included on the controversial topic of school choice. As before, the book concludes with positive words about the future, as—in the end—we as authors deeply believe in public education and the democratic ideal, and we will never be dissuaded from the American dream despite the fury of opposing anti-democratic and dictatorial forces. We wish the same for you.

WHO SHOULD READ THIS BOOK

From its title, it is clear that this book is meant for both broad and specialized audiences. Choosing this book indicates that readers have a connection to schools that causes them to demonstrate a high level of interest in the costs of education. Specifically, this book reaches out to school administrators, classroom teachers, school boards, and laypersons—including politicians—in the broader public. Although that sounds like everyone, each of these audiences has a different value for the book. Administrators will find that the material confirms their existing knowledge, reminds them of things not considered recently, and extends their knowledge by engaging recent federal and state reform movements. We've also long advocated that the first group of people who should know more about school funding is classroom teachers. Teachers often complain about limited school budgets and instinctively understand that new requirements are stretching inadequate dollars even thinner, but they usually have little knowledge of how school budgets work—for example, sources of revenue and permissible expenditures. We also believe that school board members will benefit from this book—while it is popular to bash school boards as insensitive to the financial shortcomings of schools, it is altogether too easy to forget that boards are asked to make difficult and unpopular decisions, usually without being professionally trained in recognizing education's needs—a reality made more complex by increasingly stringent federal and state accountability requirements. Finally, laypeople and politicians can benefit from this book, in that we are all taxpayers. So, in the end, this book truly is for nearly everyone, subject only to the limitations on what the book does and does not try to do.

WHAT YOU SHOULD EXPECT FROM THIS BOOK

This seventh edition continues to be organized into three broad parts: An overview of funding concepts, an overview of daily funding operations, and a look into the future. Moving through these parts is like an inverted pyramid, starting with the broad social context of schools and continuing into specialized examinations of various elements of school budgeting in each individual chapter.

At the broadest level, it is important for everyone to understand that money and achievement are related (Chapter 1). It is also critical to know that education's current condition is a product of a long history that involves the interplay of complex aspects of our cultural and governmental heritage (Chapter 2). The next logical step is to review sources of revenue and expenditure (Chapter 3), in that people's frustrations and misunderstanding of school budgets often can be traced back to these complex issues. After this broad overview, the book launches into a detailed view of daily funding operations. We keep the focus on our audience, however, seeking readability without the clutter of academic jargon. We begin with the view that accountability, regulation, and ethics are the watchwords for the future, so that understanding the flow of money into schools and its proper handling is the basis for all good decision-making (Chapter 4). School budget planning (Chapter 5) is next addressed from the perspective of how budgets are built, with subsequent chapters looking in greater detail at the major elements of budget construction. Specifically, budgeting for human resources (Chapter 6), budgeting for instruction (Chapter 7), and budgeting for student activities (Chapter 8) cut across wise budgeting behaviors at both district and school levels. The same can be said about budgeting for school infrastructure (Chapter 9), budgeting for transportation and food service (Chapter 10), and the need to budget for liability and risk management (Chapter 11). Finally, a look to the future is essential (Chapter 12) because schools continue to face radical change—threatening changes in attitudes and social/economic structures.

Acknowledgments

As we have remarked in each of the previous six editions of *Money and Schools*, no book is ever written without the valuable assistance of others. This again proved true in this new and remarkably different seventh edition. Much credit for all that is good about this book goes not only to each of us as co-authors, but particularly also to manuscript reviewers and resource people trusted for their ability to discern and clarify a variety of issues that might have escaped us during the writing stage.

The authors wish to thank the following people who contributed in important ways leading to this seventh edition. In particular, the authors are grateful to reviewers of the previous six editions, whose advice continues to strongly influence this latest iteration:

Appreciation is also afforded to the students we serve. In this seventh edition, Angie Messer (graduate assistant and doctoral candidate, Kansas State University) brought her recent experience in formal school leadership to bear on updating various case studies, and Karen Low (Skeen graduate assistant and doctoral candidate, Kansas State University) was integral to updating many tables and graphs. And to all our students and beyond and especially to their professors—we are humbly grateful for the long-standing acceptance of our work by the field, whose opinions we value most of all.

Schools, Values, and Money

THE CONTEXT OF PUBLIC EDUCATION TODAY

It is apparent to virtually all education stakeholders today that the context of public education in the United States is experiencing dramatic change. Indeed, this newest edition of *Money and Schools* argues that change is roiling not just U.S. public education, but that many sectors of global society are likewise being relentlessly restructured on a massive scale equal to extraordinary events from the past that reshaped the fate of entire nations. Further, the pace of change shows no signs of slowing. Consequently, any study of money and schools needs to immediately be seen in the following light: That is, schools are not only highly vulnerable to today's economic, political, and social dynamics, but rather schools are among the first targets of intentional social reengineering—so much so that some observers fear the stability of U.S. public education is in danger.

These bold assertions represent the culmination of a broad range of policy issues that have been raised at all levels of society over the past several decades. Although some may cling to a vision of an ideal past and posit that educational and social issues will be resolved only with a return to the good old days, others have sounded an alarm based on their perception of the emergence of an adversarial culture where shared values of civility, tolerance, social justice, and the common good have been replaced by aggressive social reordering meant to either create a new reality or restore some remembered reality. In the political domain, it is easy to discern how recent national and state elections have evidenced these culture wars as extremist candidates and commentators across both ends of the sociopolitical spectrum accuse one another of singlehandedly destroying the America they know and love. The breakdown of civility appears deliberate in election results so tightly drawn as to divide the nation along bitter ideological lines wherein challenging the outcomes of national, state, and even local elections through litigation or threat of various rebellion is not uncommon. At their roots, these rifts represent diametrically opposed views of the role of government in society, often beginning with the provision and funding of a robust system of public education.

School leaders are not spared this turmoil, and taking on the mantle of leadership virtually ensures a baptism by fire. As an integral part of today's society, public schools serve many masters and aspire to many goals, chief among them is preparing future generations of young people for living and working in a global context. Yet, because the splinterings in social values are now so protracted and bitter, education today is especially caught between divisive demands that dispute and propound the mission of schools from opposite ends of sociopolitics. The dilemmas arising are profound. For example, what are public schools becoming—can it even be known? For that matter, where did schools come from, and what does that say about what schools are today? Of critical importance are contentious questions arising from stakeholders at all levels, ranging from local communities to the nation's capitol: What should schools be doing? What are schools capable of doing? These questions do not exist in a vacuum; often, the answers are the subject of inflamed debates encompassing the full spectrum of human differences. Unfortunately and with increasing frequency, these debates end in gridlock, and it is the children who attend public schools who are the losers.

At the federal level, these struggles are starkly illustrated by the two most recent renewals of the Elementary and Secondary Education Act[1] of 1965 (ESEA); first, the *No Child Left Behind Act*[2] of 2001 (NCLB), and the more recent *Every Student Succeeds Act*[3] of 2015 (ESSA). Politics have long been described as a pendulum, and in large part ESSA represented a reaction against the prescriptive requirements of NCLB which many states considered not only onerous under the dreaded Adequate Yearly Progress (AYP) measure, but also tantamount to a federal unfunded mandate. For example, by 2014 NCLB had come under major attack, with 42 states receiving federal waivers from its rigorous (some might say burdensome) pupil achievement benchmarks.[4] In addition, over time there had developed a strong parental backlash against what was perceived as NCLB's excessive standardized testing, which some asserted led teachers to "teach to the test" at the expense of other critical aspects of the curriculum.[5] As a result, ESSA represented a pendulum swing in the war over federal control vs. state discretion. That war has been so intense that even a set of voluntary academic standards, national in scope and jointly developed by the National Governors Association and the Council of Chief State School Officers in 2009 referred to as the Common Core State Standards,[6] met with both resistance and criticism by education and legislative/political constituencies, as well as the popular media. As further evidence of schism, of the 46 states that originally adopted the Common Core, eight have since officially repealed or withdrawn, while 22 other states have revised or renamed them.[7]

These challenges raise a worrisome specter: Where is public education headed? These are unsettling issues facing an increasingly unpredictable future—issues that current and new generations of school leaders must address. As a result, the balance of this chapter sets the stage for the critical importance of schools and money in these challenging times. In brief, adequate and equitable support for public schools is absolutely essential, if for no other reason than the individual and collective wellbeing of the nation and world depends on preparing each new generation to take the economic, political, and social reins of leadership if democracy is to survive. To that end, this book sets out a view of schools and money grounded in research and best practices, while being ever-mindful of the social and political context in which truth finds itself today. That said, the journey begins with the context of public education because that setting is where school money is gained and spent.

WHAT ARE SCHOOLS BECOMING?

The context of public education today is likely the crux of all that is to come as far into the future as can be seen. Repeated often in this chapter and throughout the entire book is this chapter's burning question: Where might public schools be headed? Although the question is too complex to fully answer here, it is useful to raise because the answer is so basic to understanding schools and money. To answer that question, it is key to first consider the history of public schools in the United States, followed by a discussion of what schools should be doing vs. what they are capable of doing. Only then can the thorny question of the effect of money on schools have real meaning.

Where Did Schools Come From?

The history of American education begins with the establishment of schools in the original colonies approximately 400 years ago. Massachusetts was the first state to enact a law requiring town leaders to determine if children were receiving adequate religious and occupational training. Similar laws followed in several other colonies, so that by 1720 laws mandating some amount of schooling were in place in the states of Connecticut, Maine, New Hampshire, and Vermont.[8] These laws were destined to be broadened as the idea of enlightened self-government was added to the defense for public education, giving birth to the now familiar democratic principles argued by Thomas Jefferson, William Penn, and other founders of the new nation.

The fierce independence of colonists and, later, settlers of the vast western territories were additional powerful contributors to the evolving structure of public schools. The original colonies were fiercely independent, even to the point of deciding separately whether they each would give financial support to the American Revolution. In the post-war era, the early Congress struggled with lack of funds to pay war debts, much of which stemmed from intense resistance to centralized government, and it was a harbinger of a politically mistrustful future in which the early nation saw a bitter war of contrasting ideologies, such as those of Hamilton and Jefferson regarding establishment of a strong federal government. Westward expansion, with its attendant geographic isolationism, only exacerbated the independent streak of early Americans, shaping strong local views on how schools should be organized. Yet, at the same time, the nation's make-up was shifting dramatically in other ways relating to soaring immigration, the establishment of large cities, and growing sentiment against child-labor abuse. Through a long series of complex events, the Common Schools Movement arose under early advocates like Horace Mann, so that public education somewhat like the structure of schools today began to emerge by 1840.

Probably the most striking features of public schools in the early nation were the frequency in which they were established and the localism characterizing them. Westward expansion led to the creation of a multitude of tiny one-room schools. Although no one knows how many schools existed in the nation before a trend toward school consolidation began, the number had to be at least equal to the number of towns in the states and territories at any given time. The only meaningful way to understand the staggering proliferation of schools is to look to the first formal attempts to tally public schools, with U.S. Department of Education data showing that in 1929 there were 238,306 elementary schools; 149,282 one-teacher schools; and 23,930 secondary schools—a total of 411,518 schools—all within slightly more than 119,000 school districts! These data go far in explaining the fiercely local nature of schooling, and speak forcefully to why today one can still find schools only two or three city blocks apart, each with low enrollments. After all, if there were more than 100,000 school districts, it stands to reason that there was a multitude of preferences for how schooling should be carried out, especially because states did not seek to regulate schools until well into the twentieth century.

The evolution of public schools in the United States is, of course, far more complex than is presented here, but these broad historic roots mirror many current realities. Just as children internalize some of the same values taught during their own upbringing, the customs and culture of local communities are deeply held values that still affect the nature of schools, and the devotion of Americans to the creation and preservation of local traditions through public schools is unequaled. The unquenchable desire for local control is expressed by the constant fear of many modern rural school districts, as citizens leap to charge, "as the school goes, so goes the town." Indeed, any experienced school leader can recall countless community members' anguish as they fret, "If the school goes, the post office and the churches will follow close behind." In brief, schools are the heart of the community in many people's minds. Consequently, local tradition produces a fierce struggle at any cost to save schools, and the entirety of the war over education—be it budgets, taxes, or curriculum—is rooted in the tradition of local control and resistance to outside interference.

What Should Schools Be Doing?

Where schools came from is part of the answer to what schools are becoming, but another aspect of the question about what schools are becoming is wrapped up in the sub-question: What *should* schools be doing?

Although the United States has come a long way from the political and social isolationism of the past, the insular nature of schools still stands as a reminder of the great difficulty of trying to reach real consensus on what schools should be about. Almost daily, news reports chronicle some new dispute about schools, ranging from threats to withdraw fiscal support to impassioned calls for reform related to some perceived breakdown in effectiveness. It is not uncommon for school leaders to lose their jobs due to arguments over what schools should be doing. School board members may find themselves subject to recall when communities are deeply split over some aspect of schooling, and legislators of all stripes are subjected to tremendous pressures from interest groups specifically organized to force or prevent changes in what schools are doing. Immunity to pressure is impossible, in large part because people believe that schools are critical to the nation's future.

Historic opinions on what schools should do have centered mostly on issues relating to morality, democracy, and equality. Intense interest among the early colonists in preparing children for a morally upright life through religious education was noted previously. Leaders like Thomas Jefferson, Horace Mann, and many others weighed in, broadening the scope of education by arguing that an enlightened citizenry is the most effective curb on tyranny. More recently, concerns for equality of educational opportunity and social justice have been added to the aims of schooling. The landmark *Brown v. Board of Education*[9] decision in 1954, overturning the race-based doctrine of separate but equal, was clear evidence of expanding concern for equality in education and all other aspects of the human condition. The Civil Rights Act of 1964 and the expansive civil rights laws that followed likewise had enormous educational impacts, giving rise to a massive body of federal and state case law and statutes controlling far-reaching concepts, including gender equity, rights of children with disabilities, and rights of citizens under equal access provisions.

Unsurprisingly, these wars still rage with increasing energy and sophistication. Such ideological conflict provides a window on current views regarding what schools should be doing, especially in context of the operational meaning of equality of educational opportunity and social justice. While little disagreement exists about education as an engine for economic productivity, ensuring equal access to educational opportunity quite oppositely provides fertile ground for disputes involving equity. Critics today charge that many pupils do not have access to economic-enhancing opportunities such as technology or higher education, which is then posited to ensure the perpetuation of disadvantaged populations far into the future—a position instantly attacked by opponents who forcefully invoke local control, e.g., the choice to exceed or offer only a minimally adequate education program. Even greater disagreement currently exists about the role of education with regard to morality, particularly when powerful parent groups believe some issues infringe upon personal or religious beliefs, such as teaching human sexuality or evolution vs. creationism and intelligent design. And even more, the broader issue around attempts to ensure uniformity across schools related to social and academic equality seems to produce the greatest conflict regarding what schools should be about. The questions appear reasonable and addressable, but merely raising the issues provokes battles. For example, is it the role of schools to provide only a minimum level of educational opportunity, or is it education's role to provide exactly the same educational opportunities to all children? Or, is it the role of schooling to provide equal educational outcomes? And the question of who knows best produces some of the greatest conflict. There are no simple answers because the long-held tradition of local control of education collides with more modern, expansive, and nuanced conceptions of social justice and absolute freedom. Some advocates for equal opportunity assert that localism has inherently led to racially and economically segregated schools, while the opposing side argues that the world has gone crazy in its attempts to suppress individual freedoms. This debate is carried out on multiple levels—e.g., courts struggle with lawsuits over school funding; legislatures receive intense pressure from special interest groups of all stripes; and taxpayers revolt. Meanwhile, school boards, teachers, administrators, and children are caught in an interminable tug-of-war that ultimately results in diminished resources due to costly litigation and lack of cooperation. In the end, there is no one voice speaking for what schools should be doing because the many voices are a cacophony of different and conflicting aims.

What Are Schools Capable of Doing?

A critical, although often overlooked, component of the current debate is objective and realistic consideration of what schools are truly *capable* of doing. Depending on whom one asks, answers range from "nothing" to "everything." Those at one end of the political scale see public schools as a failed social experiment, a wasteful government monopoly that should be forcibly dismantled through privatization that nurtures competition, entrepreneurialism, and individualism. At the opposite end of the spectrum are those whose faith in the potential of public schools to enhance social justice and equality of educational opportunity is just as unshakable. Still others look back with nostalgia (perhaps through a rosy lens) to a time when schools reflected their own "traditional" values and focused on teaching basic skills while regarding enrichment as optional. Still others who felt excluded or even bullied as children recall those times less fondly and vow to ensure that their children have a better educational experience in a more inclusive school environment. With such diversity among so many deeply committed voices, it is hard to find much common ground, especially since the only commonality is that all fervently believe schools are the major vehicle to *their* essential outcomes. The question as to what schools are actually capable of doing only becomes more difficult: That is, can schools achieve the aims of all and, importantly, at what cost? This generates countless subquestions, to which data offer only partial insight. For example: Beliefs are strongly held, but what truly is the evidence on the effect of money in schools? What truly happens when schools receive more money? Do schools truly need more money? What will happen if schools receive less money? The answers are complex and nuanced and often entirely elusive.

What Is the Effect of Money on Schools?

An ongoing and contentious debate turns on whether money can have any agreed-upon measurable effect on pupil achievement. Because K–12 public education in the United States has been increasingly driven (for better or worse) by the results of high-stakes testing,[10] the question of the relationship between money and educational outcomes has become central to funding debates at local, state, and national levels. However, after nearly a half-century of research, definitive answers remain elusive. Because teaching and learning are complex human endeavors affected by many factors within and outside the classroom, it is not surprising that it is hard to isolate the effect of a single variable, e.g., spending levels, on pupil achievement. Nonetheless, researchers have grappled with this question for decades and, given the intensity of current policy debates about raising academic achievement while holding down costs, it is likely that this line of inquiry will persist. As such, it is helpful to chronicle the history of this line of research and the accompanying controversy regarding its application to schools.

The history of such research, often referred to as production-function studies, offers a fascinating journey. To begin, the methodology itself is controversial. Production-function methodology is based on the application of a private sector manufacturing model that equates education to a factory assembly line, whereby the components of learning are reduced to three variables: Inputs, throughputs or process, and a single output (see Figure 1.1). However, due to the difficulty in quantifying educational processes such as pedagogy, production-function studies have narrowly focused on inputs, many of which are directly or indirectly related to money, with the outcome focused on a single achievement test score on a standardized instrument.[11] As a result, from its earliest applications in the 1960s, the production-function model has been attacked not only for appropriateness of the use of a manufacturing model to education, but also for its failure to include variables that reflect what educators consider an essential component: The educational process itself.

Production-function studies are often traced to the Coleman Report,[12] a study that was funded by the federal government as part of the Civil Rights Act of 1964. The research focused on questions of racial inequality in schools, using indicators of quality such as curriculum, teacher qualifications, resources, and standardized test scores. The central findings affirmed that, a decade after the *Brown* decision, there still existed significant segregation in schools and race-based disparities in educational offerings and opportunity. However, it was a more general set of findings that engendered the controversy that still surrounds this research approach today; that is, the impact of a child's home environment, e.g., parental education and parental attitudes toward education, dwarfed the effects of school-related factors and resource levels.

FIGURE 1.1 Model of Production Function

Response to the Coleman Report by the research community was swift and dramatic. Many critiques of the study's methods and interpretation of results ensued and still endure today.[13] A spate of counter-studies sprang up, typified by the Summers and Wolfe study[14] which examined 627 sixth-grade students in the Philadelphia schools, finding that certain variables such as better teacher preparation, presence of high achievers, and smaller class size did have a positive effect on achievement. Another approach emanated from the Effective Schools Movement, which has been characterized by some as an ideological protest against the Coleman Report. This body of research sought to identify traits of effective schools that could be emulated to boost achievement; however, it relied more on qualitative research methods which are difficult to replicate and with results that suffer a lack of generalizability.

Of greatest importance to this discussion, though, is that a narrower application of the production-function model ensued that focused far more sharply on the relationship of money (either direct expenditure or indirect expenditure, e.g., teacher salaries) to pupil achievement. This approach has persisted from the 1970s up to today, although it continues to yield results that are inconsistent, conflicting, and counterintuitive. This is largely due to methodological issues, poorly conducted studies, researcher bias, and failure to include or quantify process variables that are essential if one claims to be using a production function approach.[15] Even overarching studies of production function research (referred to as meta-analyses), conducted in the late 1980s and 1990s, have yielded similar conflicting results.[16]

Amid such uncertainty, more recent research has emerged that is radical in its critique of the production function model as an appropriate and practical application for measuring the impact of fiscal resources on educational outcomes. Although achievement scores remain the focus, this new approach addresses one of the key shortcomings of the statistical technique (referred to as multiple regression) commonly used in production function research; that is, multiple regression analysis allows only one educational output, e.g., a test score, to be analyzed at a time. This, of course, is unrealistic. In the real world of educational testing, students are generally tested in at least two subjects (reading and mathematics) and more frequently in a range of subjects, including, for example, science and social studies. A small number of studies have begun using a more sophisticated technique referred to as canonical analysis, which allows for the inclusion of multiple education outcomes in the model.[17] In addition, to open the "black box," other researchers are engaging in theory building that provides a foundation for evaluating the impact of investments in education.[18] These represent emergent research routes, but the early results have been promising, and, as such, may prove more useful to answering not only the question of whether or not money matters, but also when and how does it matter?

What Happens When Schools Get More (or Less) Money?

Unfortunately, no longitudinally systematic studies of these two questions have been conducted. Furthermore, it is unethical to conduct experimental studies wherein resources are intentionally withheld from one setting in order to compare it to another setting. As a result, researchers are left in large part with anecdotal data and single case studies; although these are informative, they cannot be generalized to all schools. Under these conditions, a more realistic third question may be of greater importance to school leaders: What should schools do when they receive *more*, or *less*, money?

Regarding the first question, it is important to note that rarely in the history of taxpayer funding have schools received dramatic windfalls of new money. A more common scenario is incremental funding increases of a few percentage points. Although every new dollar is important, it is difficult for schools to make dramatic changes or undertake significant reforms without truly substantial new funds. As such, school boards often decide during the process of approving an annual budget to simply allocate any new funds using their best judgment. Budget hearings are open to the public in most states, so hypothetically anyone can provide input. Some districts may engage staff and community in more formal mechanisms such as listening sessions or focus groups. However, most districts do not have extensive formal plans for how to allocate new funding; consequently, they risk allocating these monies haphazardly, often in response to internal or external pressures. Ideally, such decisions should flow from district and school strategic plans which have prioritized in advance how new funds will be allocated if they become available. In addition, as will be seen in Chapter 6 on budget planning, districts can prepare for this scenario by using an approach like Planning, Programming, Budgeting, and Evaluation Systems (PPBES), a comprehensive approach that prioritizes the district's educational goals and objectives and accompanying expenditures: i.e., when new funds become available, the school board will have a formal and thoughtful blueprint to follow.

The equally interesting counter-question is raised when asking what would happen if schools were to receive less money. Here too there is no body of research literature upon which to draw, although there tends to be more case studies that can be instructive. For example, in a five-state study of school districts that had suffered significant reductions in state aid, researchers found that school districts tended to reduce funding in four areas:[19]

- Personnel and instruction, resulting in increases in class size;
- Early childhood education (Pre-K and kindergarten);
- Elective courses such as art, music, physical education, science, technology, foreign languages, and advanced/advanced placement courses;
- Extracurricular activities, like athletics and drama.

In some cases, courses and programs were completely eliminated. Or, in the case of extracurricular activities, schools began charging hefty fees for pupil participation. In many states, schools have limited or no ability to charge fees for required academic programs or transportation. Also, under federal law they cannot reduce or eliminate services to pupils with disabilities. However, faced with aid reductions, districts in more legislatively permissive states promptly faced the temptation to increase revenues by adding fees, even to core academics.

Reasonably, school districts face difficult and unpleasant decisions when they receive less money. No matter what they cut or eliminate, someone in the community will be upset. Nonetheless, districts should consider the same approach to receiving less money as they would with the opposite scenario; that is, the use of strategic education and fiscal planning found in approaches like PPBES to guide them in setting priorities for budget reductions. Granted, nothing will make budget cuts less wrenching for schools and communities, but a rational, thoughtful approach may minimize the pain.

On balance, very few schools are ever faced with excess funds. Also on balance, most schools are not faced with immediate financial ruin, although increases in funding have become far more difficult to secure and their distribution increasingly more contentious. In addition, it is a reality that accountability, both achievement-based and fiscal efficiency-driven, has become a bludgeon in the hands of state legislatures and governors, as states have demanded sweeping reforms while courts have ruled on a wide array of issues under the aegis of equality of educational opportunity—all while simultaneously being met with threats of legislative revolt against judicial power. These types of events serve to underscore this chapter's message of intense competition for fiscal resources, as well as the chapter's focus on an increasingly fragmented society that is unwilling to support more funding for schools without hard evidence of greater cost-effectiveness and pupil achievement.

WHERE PUBLIC SCHOOLS MAY BE HEADED

Aptly titled *Schools, Values, and Money,* this chapter deliberately set a context for hard topics that will be discussed throughout the remaining chapters—primarily by providing a brief history of public schools, along with frank assessment of the current and complex social, economic, and political environments in which PreK–12 education finds itself today. The message has been that a free, common public school system has been part of the fabric of this nation for more than 150 years, serving as a key building block in the foundation of democratic society. And the chapter contained a warning: If public schools are to remain a vibrant part of democracy, it is essential to adequately and equitably fund schools so that they can deliver on the promise of equality of educational opportunity and upward mobility which heretofore has been the centerpiece of the American dream. The chapters that follow delve into the many facets of schools and money, ranging from budgeting for the core function of instruction to the supporting role of student activities, infrastructure, and auxiliary services.

To return to the question of where public schools may be headed: Schools must promote their virtues, take the lead in performance accountability, and engage their constituents. If school leaders fail, it is clear where education is headed—into a world that includes ever-expanding alternatives to public schools and concomitant loss of support for public education.

POINT–COUNTERPOINT

POINT
The wars over school funding prove that everyone knows money matters because everyone battles to control the money. If elected officials and private citizens are frustrated by poor test scores, the answer is to step up to the plate and spend more on schools—to remain the world's leader will require spending at the level of other advanced nations.

COUNTERPOINT
Money doesn't matter because the data show that money thrown at schools disappears with no visible impact on learning. Schools are reckless in how they spend money, and the only thing that happens with increased spending is that overpaid teachers and administrators get more big salary bumps. Schools spend money on things that are the responsibility of absent or irresponsible parents who think schools are society's caretaker. Spending more money on education won't buy good parenting, so it's time for schools to deliver the fundamentals and get out of the parenting business.

Questions

- Which of these views is closest to your own? Explain.
- Which of these views is closest to the views in your community? Explain.
- What has happened to both funding and achievement levels in your state and school district in recent years? Is there a relationship between them? Explain.
- Have there been attempts in your district or state to cut funds? If yes, provide some examples and describe the events that followed.
- Could existing funding in your school or district be used more effectively? If yes, provide some examples.

CASE STUDY

As a newly hired high school principal, you were surprised when the superintendent asked to speak with you about the upcoming local tax referendum. As the conversation unfolded, you learned that two previously supportive school board members had raised concerns at a recent board meeting about the tax referendum in which local voters would be asked to approve an increase in property taxes to maintain programs such as PK–12 gifted education, Advanced Placement (AP) courses, an increase in guidance/

career counselor staffing at all grade levels, and district-wide technology upgrades. The rationale behind the bond issue was to sustain the district's history of educational excellence as demonstrated by the following: The high number of National Merit Scholars produced by the district; the district's mean SAT/ACT scores were well above the national average; and more than 80% of the district's graduates pursued postsecondary education.

The superintendent explained that the two board members had been contacted by a local taxpayer organization which presented them with data showing local district spending had outpaced the Consumer Price Index (CPI) inflation rate for the last decade and that the district's property taxes were the highest in a ten-county area and sixth highest in the state. In addition, the taxpayer association maintained that the educational programs that would benefit from the tax increase served only a small percentage of the student body. Furthermore, they asserted that over the past few years district residents had been hit hard by a sluggish economy. There had been layoffs from a local plant closing, and those with jobs were not seeing wage increases. Given these conditions, they asserted that taxpayers could not afford even a small increase in property taxes.

The bottom line, the superintendent confessed, was how to protect the district's goals in the face of these data. Not only might the district lose the referendum and have to reduce the scope of these programs, but defeat might embolden the taxpayer organization to recall those board members who had supported it, leading to the election of new board members whose main goal would be to reduce taxes at the expense of educational quality. As the superintendent put it, "politics are becoming pretty ugly here."

The superintendent then explained your role in the referendum. Given these new developments, the superintendent was charging each principal with developing a specific outcome-oriented plan for his or her school that would justify the tax increase and—importantly—identify any potential damage resulting from a failed referendum. Although the referendum vote was still four months away, moving ahead now mattered because a concerted effort would be needed to carry the message to the board and the community.

Below is a set of questions. As you respond, consider the content of this chapter and apply your new knowledge to the situation:

Questions

- What observations about the community can you draw from this case study?
- What questions or concerns about the tax referendum are likely to be raised by the community?
- What data will be needed to justify a tax increase in a community like this one?
- How will you go about carrying out your charge?
- How does this school district and community compare to yours?

PORTFOLIO EXERCISES

- What are your own beliefs and values about what schools are capable of doing vs. what they should be doing? Research and write an essay in which you identify and describe your beliefs and values on these topics. Share your essay with classmates, to be followed by class or online discussion where you compare and contrast your views with those of others.

- As an individual or in small groups, identify and interview key stakeholders in your community on their views about the relationship between money and achievement. Select persons from different sectors of the community: For example, a school board member, a business owner, a teacher, a member of the clergy, an administrator, a retired person, a student, a local elected official, a parent, and so forth. Compare and contrast their views.

- In your school district, what department and/or individuals are responsible for assessing academic performance? These might include central office and school site personnel such as directors of assessment or curriculum, principals, and counselors. Ask those involved about district and school performance profiles and trends and determine how the district and individual schools go about raising pupil achievement when needed. Ask if any formal attempt is made to link money and achievement, and, if so, how? Present the results to your classmates for discussion.

- Is your community supportive of schools? Why or why not? Research recent news coverage and social media in your community, taking note of attitudes and opinions expressed about schools, school funding, and school performance. Analyze your findings to determine your community's support level for education.

NOTES

1 P.L. 89–10, Elementary and Secondary Education Act of 1965.
2 P.L. 107–110, No Child Left Behind Act of 2001.
3 P.L. 115–141, Every Student Succeeds Act of 2015.
4 Michele McNeil, "NCLB Waivers: A State-by-State Breakdown," *Education Week*, February 25, 2014, http://www.edweek.org/ew/section/infographics/nclbwaivers.html.
5 See, for example, Alexander Russo, "When Parents Yank Their Kids Out of Standardized Tests," *The Atlantic Monthly*," November 14, 2013, https://www.theatlantic.com/education/archive/2013/11/when-parents-yank-their-kids-out-of-standardized-tests/281417.
6 For further information, see "Common Core State Standards Initiative," http://www.core-standards.org.

7   Alison DeNisco, "Common Core No More? New York and 21 Other States Revise or Rename K12 Standards," *District Administration* (November 2017), https://www.districtadministration.com/article/common-core-no-more-new-york-and-21-other-states-revise-or-rename-k12-standards.

8   Although innovative for their time, early colonial schools bore little resemblance to the public schools of today. For instance, females, African Americans, and Native Americans were generally excluded. The curriculum was decidedly religion-based, and tuition was charged limiting education to those who could afford it. See, Carl F. Kaestle, "Victory of the Common School Movement," *Historians on America* (Washington, DC: U.S. Department of State, 2008) 22–29.

9   374 U.S. 483 (1954).

10 See, e.g., Dianne Ravitch, *Reign of Error* (New York: Alfred A. Knopf, 2013).

11 Another outcome that has been used is high school graduation.

12 James S. Coleman, Ernst Campbell, Carol Hobson, James McPartland, Alexander Mood, Frederic Weinfeld, and Robert York, *Equality of Educational Opportunity* (Washington, DC: U.S. Government Printing Office, 1966).

13 Chief among criticisms have been nonresponse and stratification of variables resulting in noncomparable data, errors in data entry, and misinterpretation of interaction effects. Simply put, nonresponse refers to the misleading impression of a very large data set when in fact the number of respondents was far smaller than intended, raising questions of generalizability. Stratification refers to data being examined in separate sets, perhaps wrongly constructed, so that effects of variables such as race, religion, and so forth might have been exaggerated or misleading. Errors in data entry plague all large data sets and may make the results suspect. Finally, misinterpretation of interaction effects refers to a lack of sophistication in research design, in which causal relationships are inferred that were not really verified by the data.

14 Anita Summers and Barbara Wolfe, "Do Schools Make a Difference?" *American Economic Review* 67 (September 1977): 639–652.

15 Throughput or process variables are sometimes referred to as the "black box" in the production function model. See, e.g., Jennifer King, "Illuminating the Black Box: The Evolving Role of Education Productivity Research," in *Education Finance in the New Millennium*, edited by Stephen Chaikind and William J. Fowler, Jr., 121–138 (Larchmont, NY: Eye on Education, 2001).

16 See, e.g., Eric A. Hanushek, "The Impact of Differential Expenditures on School Performance," *Educational Researcher* 18 (May 1989): 45–51, 62; and Larry Hedges, Richard Laine, and Rob Greenwald, "Does Money Does Matter: A Meta-Analysis of Studies of the Effect of Differential School Inputs on Student Outcomes," *Educational Researcher* 23 (April 1994): 5–14.

17 See, e.g., Robert C. Knoeppel and James S. Rinehart, "Explaining the Relationship between Resources and Student Achievement: A Methodological Comparison of Production Functions and Canonical Analysis," *Educational Considerations* 35 (Spring 2008): 29–40.

18 See, e.g., Faith E. Crampton, "Spending on School Infrastructure: Does Money Matter?" *Journal of Educational Administration* 47 (Spring 2009): 305–322.

19 Jeff Bryant, *Starving America's Public Schools* (Washington, DC: Campaign for America's Future, 2011). http://www.ourfuture.org/report/2011104111/starving-america-s-public-schools.

WEB RESOURCES

American Association of School Administrators, www.aasa.org

American Federation of Teachers, www.aft.org

Council of Chief State School Officers, www.ccsso.org

National Association for Elementary School Principals, www.naesp.org

National Association of Secondary School Principals, www.nassp.org

National Education Association, www.nea.org

National School Boards Association, www.nsba.org

RECOMMENDED RESOURCES

Baker, Bruce. *Does Money Matter in Education?* Washington, DC: Albert Shanker Institute 2016.

BenDavid-Hadar, Iris. "Education, Cognitive Development, and Poverty: Implications for School Finance Policy." *Journal of Education Finance* 40, 2 (Fall 2014): 131–155.

Coleman, James S., Ernst Campbell, Carol Hobson, James McPartland, Alexander Mood, Frederic Weinfeld, and Robert York. *Equality of Educational Opportunity.* Washington, DC: U.S. Government Printing Office, 1966.

Crampton, Faith E. "Spending on School Infrastructure: Does Money Matter?" *Journal of Educational Administration* 47 (Spring 2009): 305–322.

Darling-Hammond, Linda, Soung Bae, Channa M. Cook-Harevy, Livia Lam, Charmaine Mercer, Anne Poldolsky, and Elizabeth Leisy Stosich. *Pathways to New Accountability through the Every Student Succeeds Act.* Palo Alto, CA: Learning Policy Institute, 2016.

DeNisco, Alison. "Common Core No More? New York and 21 Other States Revise or Rename K12 Standards." *District Administration* (November 2017). https://www.districtadministration.com/article/common-core-no-more-new-york-and-21-other-states-revise-or-rename-k12-standards.

Dynarski, Mark. *It's Not Nothing: The Role of Money in Improving Education.* A Brookings Report. Washington, DC: Brookings Institution, 2017. https://www.brookings.edu/research/its-nothing-the-role-of-money-in-improving-education.

Hanushek, Eric. *Every State's Economic Future Lies with School Reform.* Report, American Enterprise Institute (May 2018).

Hanushek, Eric. "What Matters for Student Achievement: Updating Coleman on the Influence of Families and Schools." *Education Next* (Spring 2016). educationnext.org

Hedges, Larry, Richard Laine, and Rob Greenwald. "Does Money Does Matter: A Meta-Analysis of Studies of the Effect of Differential School Inputs on Student Outcomes." *Educational Researcher* 23 (April 1994): 5–14.

Jakee, Keith and Erin Keller. "The Price of High-Stakes Educational Testing: Estimating the Aggregate Costs of Florida's FCAT Exam." *Journal of Education Finance*, 43, 2 (Fall 2017): 123–151.

Kaestle, Carl F. "Victory of the Common School Movement." In *Historians on America*, 22–29. Washington, DC: U.S. Department of State, 2008.

Kaplan, Leslie S. and William A. Owings. "The Unaddressed Costs of Changing Student Demographics". *Journal of Education Finance*, 39, 1 (Summer 2013): 15–46.

Knoeppel, Robert C. and James S. Rinehart. "Explaining the Relationship between Resources and Student Achievement: A Methodological Comparison of Production Functions and Canonical Analysis." *Educational Considerations* 35 (Spring 2008): 29–40.

McMahon, Walter W. "Financing Education for the Public Good: A New Strategy." *Journal of Education Finance* 40, 4 (Spring 2015): 414–437.

Olugbenga, Ajilore. "Estimating the Spillover Effects of School District Demographics on Per-Pupil Spending." *Journal of Education Finance* 39, 2 (Fall 2013): 101–114.

Ravitch, Dianne. *Reign of Error.* New York: Alfred A. Knopf, 2013.

Thompson, David C., R. Craig Wood, and David S. Honeyman. *Fiscal Leadership for Schools: Concepts and Practices.* New York: Longman, 1994.

Yeh, Stuart S. "The Cost Effectiveness of 22 Approaches for Raising Student Achievement." *Journal of Education Finance* 36, 1 (Summer 2010): 38–75.

Zimmerman, Jonathan. *Whose America? Culture Wars in the Public Schools.* Cambridge, MA: Harvard University Press, 2005.

CHAPTER 2

Funding Schools:
A Policy Perspective

CHAPTER DRIVERS

Please reflect upon the following questions as you read this chapter:

- What is the scope of education finance in America?
- How are education and economics related?
- What is the structure of school governance in America?
- From where do schools derive financial support?
- What constitutes adequate and equitable funding for schools?
- Can schools at once serve economics, equality, productivity, and liberty?

A MORE EXPANSIVE VIEW

The previous chapter ended with a warning that there is a growing belief in the United States that public education's performance is at best lackluster, if not suffering a crisis. Clearly, research on linkages between achievement and school funding levels is mixed, but there is more to it than pure economics. At the same time, it is never as simple as a bottom line because the whole discussion revolves around fiscal variables in tandem with other social and political principles that cannot be ignored if society is to preserve a civil democracy.

There are additional social, political, and economic issues that complicate and drive how school leaders should act and react in today's political climate. The benefits and costs of public education are never as easy as looking only at growth in revenue and spending—society must also examine the broader scope of funding schools from a policy perspective. The concept of *investment* in education vs. an attitude of *expenditure control* is important too because spending should take into account the value of education to the economy and to society itself. Certainly, a critical part of spending on children's education is affected by whether federal, state, and local governments are appropriately sharing the duty to fund schools. Issues of adequate and equitable funding are therefore a major concern for educators, politicians, and taxpayers. The debate concerning money and schools is more than thinking about test scores: It also includes weighing the ethics of civic responsibility, at least until society no longer chooses to pursue opportunity, equality, and liberty for everyone—without exception.

WHAT IS THE SCOPE OF EDUCATION FINANCE IN AMERICA?

Every textbook on education finance in the last 50 years has noted that education is big business. Although people are used to hearing about enormous costs for all aspects of society, the demands of life today on human and fiscal resources are truly gigantic. Americans know that the nation is deeply in debt, but the sum of $21.6 trillion in late 2018 is unfathomable.[1] This abstract number has more meaning if restated as *each* citizen's share of the national debt totaled nearly $66,000 in 2018, adjusted for inflation. Figures 2.1, 2.2, and 2.3 illustrate these soaring patterns and reveal that federal expenditures are mostly social programs meant to transfer wealth. In contrast to the national debt, however, funding for public schools is mostly paid on a current basis, meaning that revenues must meet expenditures. Inasmuch as most government spending goes to domestic and international programs, including schools, the scope of public finance in the United States is very large. Under these conditions, it is unsurprising that Chapter 1 was titled Schools, Values, and Money.

Revenue Growth for Schools

Skyrocketing growth in school revenue has long been evident, even in earlier times when needs were simpler. Although good data collection did not begin until the early twentieth century, revenues from 1920 to 2015 reflect the increasing importance of education in the nation (see Table 2.1). In 1920, total revenue for K–12 schools was $970 million. By 1930, revenues had grown to $2.09 billion. An important observation is that despite the costs of World War I, school revenue rose steadily, due partly to the need for training a fighting force and partly due to postwar prosperity. It is further important to note that the revenues seen in this section are in current dollars; that is, they are unadjusted for inflation.

School revenue expansion experienced only brief lags over the ensuing years, with the first 30 years of the last century witnessing rapid growth. Only the Great Depression slowed the pattern, as from 1930 to 1940 school revenue grew only slightly from $2.09 to $2.26 billion. Even yet, the increase was remarkable in light of the economic turmoil in the nation.

The surge in money for schools resumed with the recovery spurred by World War II. Between 1940 and 1950, revenue more than doubled to $5.4 billion. The pattern continued from 1950 to 1960, triggered by the launch of the Soviet satellite *Sputnik I* and giving rise to a national education agenda under the *National Defense Education Act*[2] (NDEA) in 1958. NDEA led to unequaled funding growth in both

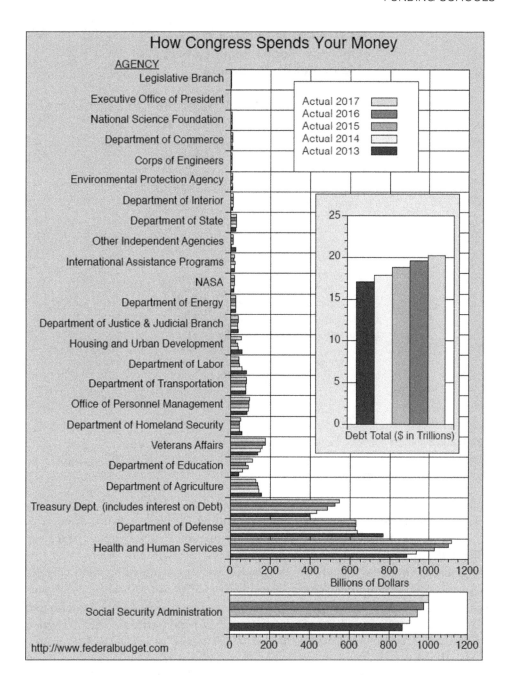

FIGURE 2.1 Federal Expenditures: 2013–17

Source: National Debt Awareness Center. "How Congress Spends Your Money." www.federalbudget.com.

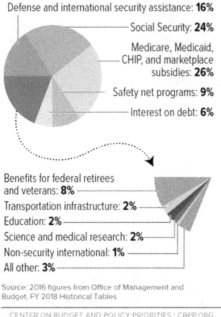

FIGURE 2.2 Where Do Our Federal Tax Dollars Go?

Source: Center on Budget and Policy Priorities. Federal Fiscal Year 2016 Data. https://www.cbpp.org/research/federal-budget/policy-basics-where-do-our-federal-tax-dollars-go

K–12 and higher education as new federal funding directed at math, science, and foreign languages fueled an era in which an information economy began to replace a fading industrial economy.

Global competition brought on by *Sputnik* was accompanied by rapid change in the social order of the United States, especially from 1950 to 1970. The nation's population, toughened by economic depression and wars, moved out of rural America to the cities. Two events forever changed education and its fiscal patterns. The first was the 1954 landmark court case *Brown v. Board of Education*[3] in which the U.S. Supreme Court ruled that racial segregation in schools was unconstitutional. The second event was the profound social upheaval of the 1960s, including the War on Poverty led by former President Lyndon Johnson. *Brown* reshaped the fundamental nature of public schools, with massive desegregation costs, while the War on Poverty marked the beginning of a long list of federal entitlements to schools through the *Elementary and Secondary Education Act*[4] (ESEA) of 1965, whereby the federal share of school revenues nearly doubled by 1968. Although the federal government had long tried to aid schools, these two events sparked a revolution that would alter the face of American education. While these events did not account for all growth in school funding during

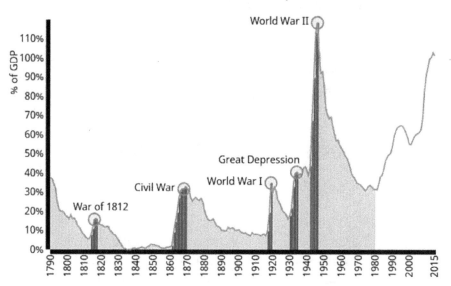

U.S. Government Debt, 1790-2015

FIGURE 2.3 History of U.S. Government Spending, Revenue, and Debt (1790–2015)

Source: Metrocosm. http://metrocosm.com/history-of-us-taxes/

that time, the era from 1950 to 1970 remains unmatched as revenues grew to $14.7 billion by 1960 and to $44.5 billion by 1970. Although inflation and rapid enrollment growth of the postwar baby boom must be taken into account, revenue grew at historic rates during these years of social progress and economic prosperity.

The era from 1970 to 1980 was marked by dramatic education and social reform, including passage of the groundbreaking federal law *The Education for All Handicapped Act*[5] of 1975, ensuring that all children with disabilities, some of whom had been excluded from public school, would receive a free and appropriate education in the least restrictive environment. In addition, many states' systems for funding schools were ruled unconstitutional by state courts and spending for education soared. By 1980, school revenues neared $106 billion. Although public education's share of the gross domestic product (GDP) began to waver in 1980, revenue growth continued because redistribution of wealth and funding increases followed the court-ordered restructuring of many state school finance systems. The resiliency of school revenues was also evident in the economic slump of the 1980s, more than doubling to $223 billion in 1990 and continuing through the roaring economy of the 1990s to more than $401 billion in 2001. In amazing fashion, revenues reached nearly $648 billion by the 2014–15 school year.

Although these data show that education prospered, another view is worthwhile because there were at least three factors that affected growth in school revenue over time. First, the data speak only to national totals, with each state facing different social and economic situations tied to its fiscal ability and voter preference. Second, some data suggest that schools' ability to serve may have been weakened despite fiscal growth, especially during the economic downturns of the new millennium.

TABLE 2.1 Revenues for Public Elementary and Secondary Schools by Source of Funds for Selected Years: 1920–2015

School Year	Total	Federal	State	Local
1919–20	$970,121	$2,475	$160,085	$807,561
1929–30	2,088,557	7,334	353,670	1,727,553
1939–40	2,260,527	39,810	684,354	1,536,363
1949–50	5,437,044	155,848	2,165,689	3,115,507
1959–60	14,746,618	651,639	5,768,047	8,326,932
1969–70	40,266,922	3,219,557	16,062,776	20,984,589
1979–80	96,881,164	9,503,537	45,348,814	42,028,813
1989–90	208,547,573	12,700,784	98,238,633	97,608,157
1993–94	260,159,468	18,341,483	117,474,209	124,343,776
1994–95	273,149,449	18,582,157	127,729,576	126,837,717
1995–96	287,702,844	19,104,019	136,670,754	131,928,071
1996–97	305,065,192	20,081,287	146,435,584	138,548,321
1997–98	325,925,708	22,201,965	157,645,372	146,078,370
1998–99	347,377,993	24,521,817	169,298,232	153,557,944
1999–2000	372,943,802	27,097,866	184,613,352	161,232,584
2000–01	401,356,120	29,100,183	199,583,097	172,672,840
2001–02	419,501,976	33,144,633	206,541,793	179,815,551
2002–03	440,111,653	37,515,909	214,277,407	188,318,337
2003–04	462,026,099	41,923,435	217,384,191	202,718,474
2004–05	487,753,525	44,809,532	228,553,579	214,390,414
2005–06	520,621,788	47,553,778	242,151,076	230,916,934
2006–07	555,710,762	47,150,608	263,608,741	244,951,413
2007–08	584,683,686	47,788,467	282,622,523	254,272,697
2008–09	592,422,033	56,670,261	276,525,603	259,226,169
2009–10	596,390,664	75,997,858	258,863,973	261,528,833
2010–11	604,228,585	75,549,471	266,786,402	261,892,711
2011–12	597,885,111	60,921,462	269,043,077	267,920,572
2012–13	603,769,917	55,860,888	273,215,485	274,693,545
2013–14\2\	623,649,738	54,505,981	288,637,122	280,506,635
2014–15	647,679,130	55,002,853	301,529,692	291,146,585

Source: Table 235.10. Digest of Education Statistics 2017. Washington, DC: NCES, Institute for Education Sciences, U.S. Department of Education, 2017. https://nces.ed.gov/programs/digest/d17/tables/dt17_235.10.asp?current=yes

Third, schools underwent vast demographic changes during the last half of the twentieth century alone: i.e., school districts that provided inferior facilities and funding for many minority children and excluded students with disabilities were suddenly required to serve all students regardless of cost in order to ensure equality of educational opportunity.

While some may argue that these historic changes inadequately account for the increases in school revenue, two points are key to an accurate view of the social and economic context of money and schools. First, since Americans have long regarded education as the engine for economic and social mobility, they have fought hard for good schools under strong local control. Second, Americans have historically directed vast resources to schools, a fact that underscores how much they value education because people resist paying for what does not have personal value. But as critics have noted, the United States, which once touted its educational system as the best in the world, now believes its students are falling behind other nations in academic achievement, while spending on education continues to grow. These critics ask whether the public will continue funding a school system that it sees as losing ground to global competitors. A more constructive approach, though, takes the long view that sees education as an investment in the future, rather than as a waning social enterprise.

EDUCATION AND ECONOMICS

Debate over the value of education has not been limited to recent fears about achievement test scores. For years, researchers have held that education makes contributions to national economic and social wellbeing as well as global competitiveness, and so there have been efforts to quantify the value of schooling.

Economics Defined

It is hard to reduce the complex field of school finance to a simplistic economic discussion. However, it is useful to think of economics as the production, allocation, and consumption of goods and services for the satisfaction of human needs and wants. Economics is thus interested in goods and services in relation to supply and demand. Rogers and Ruchlin captured it well: "Economics is concerned with two primary phenomena, desires and resources, which lead to a confrontation ... because desires are infinite, whereas resources are finite."[6] Economics in a society where commodities must be bought thus means that some goods and services will be scarce or unequally available, while others are plentiful and less valued.

This presents challenges for a capitalist democracy like the United States. Capitalism needs markets, while democracy seeks equal access to commodities that aid freedom and promote economic productivity and social mobility. Conflict arises because education in a capitalist democracy must be purchased, raising issues regarding the funding and fair distribution of schooling to people in varying economic and social circumstances.

Education as an Economic and Social Good

Because economics deals with goods and services and the supply of commodities, it has a direct relationship to funding public schools. One of the key relationships is that education produces human capital, contributes to economic health, and drives the economic and social welfare of entire nations. These benefits accrue both to individuals and to society as a whole; therefore, they are central to understanding whether education is an investment or an expense.

Education and Human Capital

In the 1980s, a series of national reports on the condition of American education served as a reminder of enduring beliefs that education produces human capital. Researchers have long explored the link between economic prosperity and education, holding that while linkages are not fully explained, education and economics are highly interdependent. Economists including John Kenneth Galbraith, Milton Friedman, and Theodore Schultz have all found positive relationships, arguing that the historic elements of land, capital, and labor must be redefined to include human capital. According to Schultz, "Human capital has the fundamental attributes of the basic economic concept of capital; namely, it is a source of future satisfactions, or of future earnings, or both of them. What makes it human capital is the fact that it becomes an integral part of the person."[7]

By this view, education takes on real worth. Whereas ownership of land, capital assets, and costs of unskilled labor were the old bases of economics, the addition of human capital sees unskilled labor as a true *cost*, while the expense of creating skilled workers is an *investment*. Because capital is used to create new wealth, human capital is an important step in knowing whether education is an expense or an investment because creating highly skilled workers is a tool for stimulating economic growth.

Education and National Economic Health

The justification for capitalism is freedom to create private wealth in a free market. Justification for democracy is based partly in the limitations of a survival-of-the-fittest economy. Thus a capitalist market in a democratic society demands opportunities. Applied to education, schooling in a private market would serve only those able to buy it. The ultimate test of the idea that education enhances human capital has played out in the United States, as one of the most powerful generators has been universal access to education so that more people can create a greater store of private wealth (education), and—in turn—sell their skills in an open market at higher wages. This threshold of opportunity believes that education leads to valuable individual and societal benefits. Rather than seeing competition and higher labor costs hurting production, access to education at public expense has been seen to create a stronger economy, a higher quality of life for individuals and families, and a more stable society.

Belief in a link between economics and education has been strong in the nation's history over the last century. In 1918, the Commission on Reorganization of Secondary Education declared the need to prepare students for work as one of its seven cardinal principles.[8] In 1951, the Ten Imperative Needs of Youth, issued by the National

Association of Secondary School Principals, gave emphasis to job training.[9] In 1955, the United States Chamber of Commerce said, "People who have a good education produce more goods, earn more money, buy and consume more goods, read more magazines and newspapers, are more active in civic and national affairs, enjoy a higher standard of living, and in general, contribute more to the economy."[10] Many recent national reports also have confirmed a deep belief in the direct link between economic and social productivity and schools.

Whether there is proof of a link between education and national economic health seems less arguable when comparing developed and developing nations. Few would argue that education widely dispersed does not aid economic and social goals. As the World Bank noted long ago:

> The emphasis in low-income countries is on development of low-cost basic education. ... In middle-income countries, where first-level education is already widely available, educational quality is emphasized and with it the expansion of facilities to meet the needs of an increasingly sophisticated economy. ... As absorptive capacity ... grows, the priority shifts toward providing higher level technical skills, as well as developing skills in science, technology, information processing, and research.[11]

In sum, education is an economic engine that creates jobs in local communities *and* provides employers with skilled workers who, in turn, stimulate the local economy as consumers.

Education and Individual Benefits

Another way of judging whether education is an investment or an expense rests in the individual benefits of schooling. Individuals are prime beneficiaries because others are excluded from direct and equal use of each person's unique skills. Individuals benefit by greater social mobility, better pay, higher status, and more cultural opportunities. Benefits spill over to society because salaries return to the economy as affluence leads to more consumerism. Better educated individuals are also healthier, see less unemployment, are more open to change, and work more efficiently.

Individual benefits are indeed dramatic. Figure 2.4 shows earnings of workers by educational level, ranging from high-school dropout to doctoral degree. Figure 2.4 shows that workers with higher levels of education consistently earn higher wages. Projecting to a lifetime of work, it is clear that education has a powerful impact on individuals' finances and quality of life. In addition to higher wages, those with higher levels of education are less likely to be unemployed. Figure 2.5 offers an additional perspective by comparing unemployment by education level from 1992 to 2018, and the trend is stark: A high school drop-out is three times more likely to be unemployed than a college graduate.

Social and Economic Efficiencies of Education

It is unreasonable to say that the *spillover* effects of education do not benefit all of society. To argue that only a minimum education is needed is to miss a fourth step in

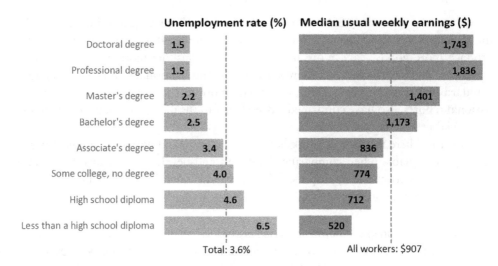

FIGURE 2.4 Education Pays: Earnings and Unemployment Rates by Educational Attainment

Source: U.S. Department of Labor. Bureau of Labor Statistics. "Employment Projections." Current Population Survey https://www.bls.gov/emp/chart-unemployment-earnings-education.htm

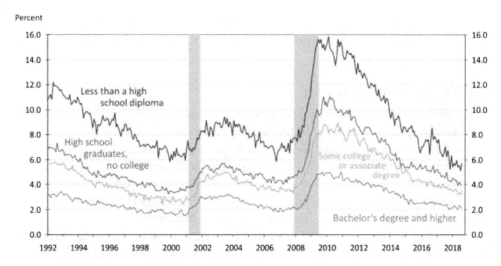

FIGURE 2.5 Unemployment Rates for People 25 Years and Over by Educational Attainment: 1992–2018

Source: U.S. Department of Labor. Bureau of Labor Statistics. "USA Unemployment Rate: Various Levels of Education."

assessing the worth of schooling because society and the economy would suffer greater costs were it not for efficiencies inherent to public education.

The *exclusion principle* is the basis for arguing against broad social services by claiming that high spending for schools is inefficient. The issue is whether social spending (including schools) yields positive returns or whether it drains money while returning low achievement scores. This view ignores that social services are meant to ward off even greater social misfortune and that spending for public aims is actually more efficient because charities would have to pay such costs absent of taxes. Such a view also ignores the reality that it is inefficient (impossible) to provide all such services on a charitable basis.

The exclusion principle sees individuals as the sole beneficiaries of an expenditure or a good or service. Implicit is that exclusion is at least neutral in its impact on others and economically efficient for the recipient. In other words, for the exclusion principle to work, depriving others of a benefit cannot result in harm, and the cost needs to be attractive to the beneficiary. However, highway taxes are a good example of the fallacy in application of the exclusion principle. It might be argued that failure to provide public roads would not cause unreasonable harm to others. But even if one were to accept that premise, applying the exclusion principle to roads leads to economic *inefficiencies* because most people could not provide their own roads due to cost. Analogously, relying on charities for critical social services is automatically inefficient and introduces the risk that society would stop providing services exempt from the force of taxation. In other words, many key services are efficiently produced in the public sector at relatively minimal individual cost, so that small sacrifices by many make up a large collective benefit.

Like many tax-based services, education's efficiencies compete in capitalist democracy. For example, arguments to privatize schools to improve performance and enhance personal choice weigh against the fact that education does not neatly fit the exclusion principle. Critics falter if they claim that children are the sole beneficiaries because spillover in social mobility, higher pay, socioeconomic status, employment, cultural opportunities, and other benefits show that taxing and spending for schools improves society as a whole. Likewise, democracy requires an informed citizenry, and most people could not privately pay for education at any level. For many reasons, the benefits of investing in public schools cannot be reached by any exclusionary mechanism.

Returns on Educational Investment

Chapter 1 recapped a more skeptical view of spending for public schools, allowing that critics have had much to say when attacking productivity. Achievement truly is a formidable challenge, and it is reasonable for taxpayers to ask if spending more money on schools is efficient when other educational alternatives exist.

Many studies have examined this cost–benefit question. Return on educational investment studies can be grouped into at least two types. The first type has examined relationships between education and economic growth, while the second type has examined returns on investment to individuals and society. Often, the latter group is referred to as rate-of-return studies.

Education and Economic Growth

As said earlier, Americans have long embraced education's impact on individual prosperity. But it is equally valid to evaluate education's effect on national economic prosperity. Such studies generally have examined changes in gross national product (GNP) to estimate the impact of education; that is, the added value of human capital.

As a public policy, measuring return on investment (ROI) in a society that provides about one-half trillion dollars annually for public K–12 schools is reasonable. Answering the resulting questions is more difficult. Although researchers always seek exact quantification, they are sometimes forced to settle for estimates. Presently, no way exists by which to measure the exact output on educational investment relative to dollar inputs, so researchers have estimated *residual effect* on the economy.

A residual effect can be likened to a sum and its parts, where several values are joined to conclude that the whole is greater than the sum of parts. Such an analogy illustrates the approach taken by some researchers in assessing the dynamic contribution of education to the economy. Economics has usually regarded growth as a function of changes in land, labor, and physical capital. If one variable changes, production changes in response; that is, changes in GNP depend on changes in land, capital, and labor. The equation fails, though, in relation to changes in the educational stock of employees (i.e., human capital) because labor traditionally did not include a value for worker qualifications. Failing to account for human capital has resulted in an unexplained residual effect. In other words, solving the equation results in the analogy of the sum and its parts, as land, labor, and capital sum to *less* than 100% of dynamic increase in GNP—leaving the unexplained residual to be attributable to human capital.

Respected studies have long supported the idea of residual effect. Schultz argued that people acquire a stock of knowledge and skills that is useless until put to work. As worker knowledge grows, productivity increases. Schultz looked at the distribution of education by years of schooling and the cost at each level after adjusting for increases in length of the school year over time.[12] He found that the 'stock of education' as measured by the cost of producing that same education had increased from $180 billion in 1929 (adjusted to 1956 prices) to $535 billion in 1957. He also found that only $69 billion in costs could be tied to the 38% growth in the size of the labor force. He next imputed that the remaining $286 billion represented a net increase in the stock of education. At the same time, labor income grew $71 billion beyond where it would have been if earnings had stayed constant at 1929 levels, with the $71 billion termed residual. Schultz concluded that the increase in education per person from 1929 to 1957 explained 36% to 70% of residual economic growth—in essence, he found that the economy improved by 36% to 70% as a consequence of investing in schools.

Denison took a different approach as he studied the impact of 20 variables in the United States from 1909 to 1957. Using changes in worker age, gender, hours, and more, he calculated increases in labor productivity and found a residual of 0.93%, with 0.67% attributable to education—a net effect attributing 23% of increased productivity to schooling. In a later study, Denison showed that increases in education explained 33% of growth in GNP from 1973 to 1981. Another Denison study examined the economies of nine Western nations, concluding that the value of education was highest for the United States.[13]

Rate-of-Return Studies

The impact of education can be seen at smaller levels by assessing the relative value of schooling at elementary, secondary, and postsecondary levels. These studies have followed two models: Calculating the *present discounted value* (PDV) of education, and calculating *individual rates of return* (IRR) for schooling. Both methods imply that consumer decisions about how much education to buy have an effect on personal income.

The PDV method takes the actual present value of schooling and multiplies it by a discount rate to estimate a future value. PDV is similar to a price deflator that holds dollars constant for purchasing power over time. For example, the average teacher salary in 1970 in then-current dollars was $8,626. By 2016, the figure had risen to $58,064.[14] Although seniority and advanced degrees accounted for some of the increase, a large part of the change is due to inflation.[15] The price deflator analogy helps in understanding the PDV method of assessing the worth of education to an individual.

The IRR method has also been used. Its advantage is in not having to set an accurate discount rate by substituting a zero interest rate; that is, what is education worth in *today's* market? The IRR method examines the cost of each level of education compared to benefits at each level. The principle is that the higher the expected income and the lower the cost, the higher the consequent rate of return. Figure 2.5 earlier showed weekly earnings based on dropping out, completing high school, completing some college or an associate degree, and completing college. The differential was real at each level of attainment: i.e., the IRR was highly favorable.

Of course, the cost varies for different levels of education. Elementary schooling costs the least, mostly because facility costs are lower than for specialized programs in high schools. But there are other costs that affect the profitability of higher units of schooling. For instance, in advanced nations child labor is nonexistent. Yet as children grow, the cost of education should include loss of earnings from being in school instead of in the workforce. Similarly at postsecondary levels, costs are increased by tuition and living expense. Also, more years of postsecondary education do not yield uncapped earnings because career choice affects income. For example, the income of a teacher with a doctoral degree will never match that of a physician although they both have the same years of formal education. Also, some societies value some professions more than others and pay professionals at highly variable rates.

Some recent studies have tested return on elementary education, but those studies have been largely confined to developing nations. In such cases, even a few years of schooling offer big returns on investment. Far more studies have examined returns on secondary schooling. Becker studied returns in the twentieth century, finding an IRR for high school graduates of 16% in 1939, 20% in 1949, and 28% in 1958.[16] His estimates were close to Schultz's, who estimated the return on high school at 25%. Other studies have agreed, with the added note that human capital has grown at the same time.

Returns on postsecondary education have become murkier. Career choice has a strong impact on earnings, and higher levels of education reach a point of diminishing returns where more school does not yield more income. There is an argument that the United States is overinvested in higher education, creating a glut of overqualified people because the job market cannot keep up with the supply of graduates. Postsecondary studies show returns on undergraduate degrees varying by career field, with graduate degrees more dependent on field. Yet despite variation, all returns on education are large because when the options are weighed, evidence shows that poorly educated people are left behind as social and economic standards spiral at dizzying speed.

Education and Socioeconomic Investment

That many services are best provided at public expense is absolute from an efficiency view. Other benefits accrue too, including freedom, lower crime, less demand for other types of public support, and socioeconomic mobility. These benefits have led scholars to claim that society pays these costs to stem an adverse tide, while investment in education reverses the tide and actually pays dividends.

At the most basic level, the greatest return is the survival of democracy itself. Democracy is government by consent, with the freedom to decide to be led and to choose one's leaders. Such decisions require defenses against abuse, namely, a level of thinking and literacy to prevent class warfare and greed and to foster informed voter behavior. Liberals and conservatives alike have embraced this view—long ago, Adam Smith noted in *The Wealth of Nations*[17] that education is necessary to prevent people from becoming incapable of self-enlightenment and devoid of all charity. Thomas Jefferson, a champion of public schools, argued that "if a nation expects to be ignorant & free, in a state of civilization, it expects what never was & never will be."[18]

Relationships among education, democracy, and self-reliance thus cannot be overestimated, and from these roots flow other benefits as people are empowered to lead productive lives. Much research, for example, points to reduced crime and reduced need for welfare due to education. If the cost of schools is high, the cost of crime is higher because that money could have better uses. Economists and criminologists take a dim view of how society squanders resources, arguing that locking up millions of citizens misses the investment mark when comparing the United States to other developed countries; that is, those nations opting to incarcerate residents usually have the lowest welfare spending, while those nations supporting welfare spending typically have the lowest incarceration rates.[19] And it has long been known that far too many prisoners are juveniles, so that when the cost of schools is compared to the cost and outcomes of jails the loss to society is enormous. The proposition is irrefutable—money is always better spent on education and job training than prisons. Perhaps the greatest accolade for investing in education was given by Alfred Marshall:

> We may then conclude that the wisdom of expending public and private funds on education is not to be measured by its direct fruits alone. [O]ne new idea, such as Bessemer's chief invention, adds as much to England's productive power as the labour of a hundred thousand men. All this spent during many years in opening the means of ... education to the masses would be well paid for if it called out one more Newton or Darwin, Shakespeare or Beethoven.[20]

Whether American society will ever truly embrace such grand expressions seems doubtful. Voters are less willing to invest uncritically in schools, and trends in education legislation have focused more on market models seeking immediate results. In 2011, the nonpartisan Center for American Progress (CAP) released the first-ever attempt to quantify achievement in every school district in the nation, with discouraging findings that spoke to both policy and trends. Updated in 2014,[21] CAP's findings and recommendations pointed to the need to reinvigorate beliefs in public schools. Among its 2014 pronouncements were the following:

- Low educational productivity remains a pressing problem, with billions of dollars lost in low-capacity school districts;
- Some of the most affluent districts also show a worrying lack of productivity;
- Spending priorities in some districts are misplaced;
- State efforts and methods for improving fiscal effectiveness are widely varied;
- States have often failed to prioritize fiscal equity, with visibly large funding gaps;
- State budget practices are at times inconsistent and opaque.

Tellingly, CAP's recommendations especially focused on fiscal variables, arguing strongly that state legislatures should build educational systems around incentivized productivity models and that legislatures should encourage smarter, fairer approaches to student-based funding policies. Overall, where society, policy, and schools go next is an open question—a question that requires some understanding of basic school governance structures.

THE STRUCTURE OF SCHOOL GOVERNANCE IN AMERICA

Even ancient civilizations often had good education systems for their day. The Greeks viewed education as the cornerstone of democracy, holding that the mark of a free man was the ability to read, write, think, and speak. Americans today are likely to argue that this nation's founders foresaw an entitlement to education when they declared that the right to life, liberty, and the pursuit of happiness are secure only in a republic governed by an intelligent people. Surely, today's American would say, the nation's founding documents have always guaranteed everyone the educational wherewithal for self-governance. America's education system today, however, does not even remotely resemble its past. As a result, it is helpful to trace the structure of school governance in the United States in order to grasp its complex and sometimes arcane funding systems that span federal, state, and local levels. " *direct quote #2*

Brief Historical Roots of American Education

Only a quick glance at American history is needed to picture the struggles of settlers in a vast wilderness. Simply surviving in a new way of life was hard enough without the trouble of creating broad government services. In the earliest days of the nation, little in the way of schooling occurred because settlers were busy feeding themselves and protecting their personal safety. And there was little motivation for schooling because the skills needed to survive under those conditions had little to do with books.

Whatever schooling did occur in early America was the province of the home or church. But some concern for education was evident early on, as the first school law was enacted in Massachusetts in 1642, requiring children to be taught to read in order to understand religion and to learn a vocation. Formal interest began to grow, and in

1647 Massachusetts passed *Ye Old Deluder Satan Act* to guide the teaching of morality to children by reading the Bible. As the colonies grew, compulsory education for morality gained popularity, with Connecticut, Maine, New Hampshire, and Vermont passing similar laws by 1720.

As nations move beyond survival mode, they seek higher order such as formal education systems. Toward the end of the eighteenth century, interest in formal schooling had taken shape in most colonies. Although education for morality had been the aim of early laws, the War of Independence in 1776 raised new concerns for education in a young nation that had chafed under British rule. The war inspired calls for enlightened government, and Thomas Jefferson, the great champion of liberty, was among the loudest voices calling for an end to ignorance through education for the common people. In a radical shift from centuries of elitist political control, Jefferson argued that ordinary citizens must be taught to elect good leaders and to keep guard on government. These skills, he said, could only be developed by education for the commoner—a new idea in a world inexperienced in self-determination.

Notwithstanding, government-sponsored schooling progressed slowly for many years after the Revolutionary War. Caught up in westward expansion, Americans had no time for luxuries like schooling. Nor was there much desire, as liberal education had left a distaste with colonists whose experiences associated schooling with aristocracy. Moral and economic education could be taught at home and, in the mind of the colonist, morally literate and politically wise voters were a luxury that must wait.

Survivalism and expansionism did not last forever. Not everyone wanted to go west, and some were too poor to go. Great cities sprang up in the early 1800s, populated by droves of immigrants. These groups were both the beginning and the result of industrialization in the new nation because they provided the labor on which industry could be built. As cities grew, more industry arose, fueling a need for more labor, which in turn caused cities to grow again. As the cycle fed itself, industry began to recognize that not all growth was good because the throngs of workers lacked skills. The solution was to call for a new role for education by demanding vocational schooling. Although industrialists argued about whether education solved a need or whether it increased labor costs, the effect was to add economics to education's emerging role.

Rapid growth, especially in cities, had the effect of increasing demand for formal education systems. Although the nation had opened its doors in order to encourage expansion, the speed was unexpected. Immigration skyrocketed—from 1820 to 1840 the nation grew by only 751,000, while from 1840 to 1850 more than 1.7 million people entered the country; more than 16 million immigrants came to the United States between 1840 and 1900. The nation was ill prepared to deal with the influx, and social problems became severe as unskilled immigrants clustered in cities. Rural Americans migrated to industrial centers too because they either had tired of frontier life or had failed. From 1820 to 1900, the U.S. population grew from 10 million to 76 million, resulting in cities beset with problems of poverty and illiteracy.

Solutions had to be found. While educating for morality and self-government was still important, leaders like Horace Mann and Henry Barnard argued that education for economic productivity was needed too. Under their leadership, the roots of a uniform public school system emerged in the Common Schools Movement. Spurred by immigration, the movement reached its peak between 1840 and 1880. Although driven by education for economic productivity, it held a fourth thread that would embed itself in the mind of America. Because it had its roots in people who had fled injustice in other lands, the movement embraced not only commitment to morality, self-determination, and economics, but also commitment to justice and equality.

The Common Schools Movement was nothing short of miraculous. It laid the basis for refinements that would deeply shape the nature and scope of American schools. One refinement forever altered the face of education. Although much of the nation's prosperity was due to a favorable business climate, an unsavory aspect of industry before 1900 was the use of child labor. Although the United States had followed the European model of exploiting children, industrialization bore labor unions, which in the last half of the nineteenth century sought to improve wages of adults with the side effect of lobbying against child labor. The Common Schools Movement was jointly benefited because child labor laws had the effect of removing children from the workforce, leaving schools to become a caretaker.

By the turn of the twentieth century, public education barely resembled colonial schools. Although the resemblance was small, the roots were deep. For example, education for morality had moved from religion to humanism based on the views of reformers, but the expectation that schools would build character remained. Likewise, as the nation won its freedom, education for self-governance held strong in the name of democracy. As industry and commerce grew, education for economics was spurred by immigration, setting the stage for calls for reform that critics would issue throughout the twentieth century. In sum, schools had put down roots in a nation that had become vast and diverse, taking on a role that reformers still struggle with today because the wars over morality, democracy, economics, and equality still rage.[22]

Development of School Organization in America

The history of schooling in the United States had a powerful impact on educational governance that is still seen today. For instance, people often clustered on the basis of religious, political, or ethnic heritage which led to strong views about education and how it should be governed. Early New England developed as a religious state, with strong regulation and taxation for schools. Religious groups opposing state control also settled the middle colonies, including Maryland, New Jersey, and Pennsylvania. In still another model, middle and southern colonies leaned toward the view that public schools were for paupers, thereby rejecting state control or tax support. Such attitudes were deeply rooted and are still evident in geographic regions notable for the supply or absence of private schools and where state school funding approaches may show sympathy for such historical views.

Westward expansion also led to unique school governance designs. Scholars have decried the problems of following educational history due to settlers' fierce resistance to control. Katz captured the tension well:

> The conflicts between the democratic localists and the bureaucrats often assumed the atmosphere of an undeclared guerrilla war of sabotage and resistance, as local school districts refused to comply with state regulation and parents refused to comply with the state's representative, the teacher. Insofar as most of the resistance came from inarticulate people, it is the hardest and most maddening aspect of nineteenth century educational history to document. That it existed is, however, beyond doubt, as the frustrated testimony of local and state reformers testifies in almost every document they wrote.[23]

Although reformers tried to standardize educational systems, years passed before the designs emerged that exist today. As the population shifted westward, political preferences took shape as people settled and built schools. Intolerance led dissidents to leave when local traditions did not reflect their will. Aided by long distances in sparsely settled lands, the result was creation of thousands of tiny isolated schools serving equally isolated settlements.

Table 2.2, showing the number of school districts from 1870 to 2015, makes several points. First, citizens today can find schools that seem inordinately close together, but which hark back to times when travel was difficult, making neighborhood schools a necessity. Second, in earlier times each small town had its own school, a truly vast number given all the towns that lived and died. Third, the number of school districts has been far greater than for any other duplicate units of government because school district boundaries in many states are not coterminous with other governments such as counties. Fourth, while no one knows the highest number of school districts that existed before the turn of the twentieth century, the number far exceeded the 117,108 districts found in 1940. Finally, the relationship between growing state control and the number of districts is clear, as more than 117,000 districts in 1940 fell to slightly more than 13,600 in 2015.

Although thousands of school districts have closed over the years, organizational uniformity never followed. The U.S. Constitution permits wide latitude by leaving control of schools to individual legislatures subject to state constitutional language. States have answered by creating school systems differing greatly in structure, operation, control, and fiscal support. The effect has been to create state systems rooted in local control, although earlier discussion suggested that local control is weakening as legislatures have adopted education reform agendas in recent decades. But the picture is still best described as a patchwork quilt, as education is state-specific in many ways (see Table 2.3), i.e., the data reveal wide structural diversity in the 50 states as late as 2016, with the number of school districts ranging from one in Hawaii to over 1,000 in California, Illinois, Ohio, and Texas. But most importantly, the struggle over schools has persisted—a struggle not only regarding the aims of education and who is in control, but also about who is responsible for costs and at what level they should be funded.

TABLE 2.2 Number of Public School Districts in Selected Years: 1869–70 through 2014–15

School Year	Regular Public School Districts	Total, All Schools	Total Schools, with Reported Grade Span	Schools with Elementary Grades		Schools with Secondary Grades
				Total	One Teacher	
1869–70	n.a.	116,312	n.a.	n.a.	n.a.	n.a.
1879–80	n.a.	178,122	n.a.	n.a.	n.a.	n.a.
1889–90	n.a.	224,526	n.a.	n.a.	n.a.	n.a.
1899–1900	n.a.	248,279	n.a.	n.a.	n.a.	n.a.
1909–10	n.a.	265,474	n.a.	n.a.	212,448	n.a.
1919–20	n.a.	271,319	n.a.	n.a.	187,948	n.a.
1929–30	n.a.	248,117	n.a.	238,306	148,712	23,930
1939–40	117,108	226,762	n.a.	n.a.	113,600	n.a.
1949–50	83,718	n.a.	n.a.	128,225	59,652	24,542
1959–60	40,520	n.a.	n.a.	91,853	20,213	25,784
1970–71	17,995	n.a.	89,372	65,800	1,815	25,352
1979–80	15,944	87,004	n.a.	n.a.	n.a.	n.a.
1989–90	15,367	83,425	81,880	60,699	630	23,461
1999–2000	14,928	92,012	90,538	68,173	423	26,407
2000–01	14,859	93,273	91,691	69,697	411	27,090
2001–02	14,559	94,112	92,696	70,516	408	27,468
2002–03	14,465	95,615	93,869	71,270	366	28,151
2003–04	14,383	95,726	93,977	71,195	376	28,219
2004–05	14,205	96,513	95,001	71,556	338	29,017
2005–06	14,166	97,382	95,731	71,733	326	29,705
2006–07	13,856	98,793	96,362	72,442	313	29,904
2007–08	13,838	98,916	97,654	73,011	288	30,542
2008–09	13,809	98,706	97,119	72,771	237	29,971
2009–10	13,625	98,817	97,521	72,870	217	30,381
2010–11	13,588	98,817	97,767	73,223	224	30,681
2011–12	13,567	98,328	97,357	73,000	205	30,668
2012–13	13,515	98,454	97,331	73,037	196	30,623
2013–14	13,491	98,271	97,290	73,223	193	30,256
2014–15	13,601	98,176	97,601	73,420	165	30,528

Note: n.a. = not available.

Source: Digest of Education Statistics 2016. Table 214.10. Washington, DC: NCES, Institute for Education Sciences, U.S. Department of Education, 2016.

TABLE 2.3 Number of Operating Public Schools and Districts, Student Membership, and Pupil/Teacher Ratio, by State or Jurisdiction: School Year 2015–16

State or Jurisdiction	Number of Operating Schools	Number of Operating Districts	State Level		
			Student Membership	Teachers	Pupil/ Teacher Ratio
United States	98,456	18,328	50,327,015	3,151,497	16.0
Alabama	1,509	180	743,789	40,766	18.2
Alaska	508	54	132,477	7,832	16.9
Arizona	2,284	692	1,109,040	47,944	23.1
Arkansas	1,088	289	492,132	35,804	13.7
California	10,303	1,163	6,226,737	263,475	23.6
Colorado	1,862	265	899,112	51,798	17.4
Connecticut	1,369	205	537,933	43,772	12.3
Delaware	223	50	134,847	8,962	15.0
District of Columbia	228	64	84,024	6,789	12.4
Florida	4,322	76	2,792,234	182,586	15.3
Georgia	2,297	223	1,757,237	113,031	15.5
Hawaii	290	1	181,995	11,747	15.5
Idaho	744	159	292,277	15,656	18.7
Illinois	4,175	1,052	2,041,779	129,948	15.7
Indiana	1,921	418	1,046,757	57,675	18.1
Iowa	1,349	345	508,014	35,687	14.2
Kansas	1,320	317	495,884	40,035	12.4
Kentucky	1,541	186	686,598	41,902	16.4
Louisiana	1,390	179	718,711	58,469	12.3
Maine	611	267	181,613	14,857	12.2
Maryland	1,437	25	879,601	59,414	14.8
Massachusetts	1,862	408	964,026	71,969	13.4
Michigan	3,468	902	1,536,231	84,181	18.2
Minnesota	2,478	564	864,384	55,985	15.4
Mississippi	1,076	157	487,200	32,175	15.1
Missouri	2,424	567	919,234	67,635	13.6
Montana	823	490	145,319	10,412	14.0
Nebraska	1,085	284	316,014	23,308	13.6
Nevada	662	19	467,527	22,702	20.6
New Hampshire	490	299	182,425	14,770	12.4
New Jersey	2,588	694	1,408,845	114,969	12.3
New Mexico	884	158	335,694	21,722	15.5
New York	4,824	989	2,711,626	206,086	13.2
North Carolina	2,603	297	1,544,934	99,355	15.5

(Continued)

State or Jurisdiction	Number of Operating Schools	Number of Operating Districts	State Level		
			Student Membership	Teachers	Pupil/ Teacher Ratio
North Dakota	518	222	108,644	9,195	11.8
Ohio	3,619	1,103	1,716,585	101,742	16.9
Oklahoma	1,800	605	692,878	42,452	16.3
Oregon	1,242	221	576,407	29,086	19.8
Pennsylvania	3,019	784	1,717,414	120,893	14.2
Rhode Island	313	64	142,014	10,631	13.4
South Carolina	1,248	102	763,533	50,237	15.2
South Dakota	698	168	134,253	9,638	13.9
Tennessee	1,859	146	1,001,235	66,488	15.1
Texas	8,826	1,232	5,301,477	347,329	15.3
Utah	1,033	152	647,870	28,348[4]	22.9
Vermont	314	357	87,866	8,338	10.5
Virginia	2,133	222	1,283,590	90,255	14.2
Washington	2,427	330	1,087,030	57,942	18.8
West Virginia	744	57	277,452	19,664	14.1
Wisconsin	2,255	465	867,800	58,185	14.9
Wyoming	370	60	94,717	7,653	12.4

Note: The textbook's authors show Table 2.3 as NCES's data. However, the authors are aware based on their expertise and residence that some NCES data do not agree with their personal knowledge: e.g., Colorado actually had 178 school districts; Florida had 67 districts; Kansas had 286 districts; and Wisconsin had 464 districts in the year of record. The authors cannot account for the discrepancy.

Source: U.S. Department of Education, National Center for Education Statistics, Common Core of Data (CCD), "Public Elementary/Secondary School Universe Survey," 2015–16, Provisional Version 1a, "Local Education Agency Universe Survey," 2015–16, Provisional Version 1a, and "State Nonfiscal Survey of Public Elementary/ Secondary Education," 2015–16, Provisional Version 1a.

School organization has also been affected by other trends. Chapter 12 at the end of this textbook speculates on the state of P–12 education, including latest trends along with an eye to the foreseeable future. While the variables affecting school governance are too plentiful to explore in a school finance text, competition for enrollments is among the most impactful struggles that can be attached to this current discussion. Particularly the advent of school choice, especially in the form of charter schools and virtual schools, has caused visible shifts in the delivery, enrollments, and configurations of districts. An ever-changing landscape, charter schools exist in most states with fiscal support often equal to traditional public schools, even though their aim typically is to secure exemption from most state statutes, rules, and regulations. Likewise, states have seen rapid growth in virtual education, again with many states having some form of distance learning for pupils at elementary and secondary levels. In brief, public schools now compete with traditional private school vendors as well as internal competitions often involving charter and virtual variations. If it has been a struggle to arrive at today's school organization, the end of such struggles is nowhere in sight as sociopolitical and demographic variables continue to shape the future.

SOURCES OF FISCAL SUPPORT FOR SCHOOLS

Despite positive links between economics and education and almost surely hampered by wars over how to organize educational services, fiscal support for schools has faced a difficult path, mostly in regard to who should bear the costs. Although education has long attracted federal, state, and local policymakers, the types and amounts of support from each level of government have varied. In fact, how schools are funded today is a direct result of how federal, state, and local policymakers have accepted (or denied) responsibility for education.

Federal Support for Schools

Most Americans are probably unsure about the current extent of federal involvement in funding public schools. But most people would say that even if the level of support is questionable, the federal government has had a profound impact on schools. That answer would correctly depict the federal government's role in education, as it has exercised influence in a great many ways.

Beginning with the Northwest Ordinance of 1787 surveying lands and granting the sixteenth section of each township for educational uses, the federal government embarked on an early mission to aid schools in the name of national interest. One goal was promoting national defense. A second was aiding higher education, and a third was influencing economic and social issues via education. An additional, but indirect, goal has evolved by appointing federal judges, who in turn have impacted rulings on lawsuits involving education. At times these goals have overlapped, making the federal role greater than otherwise would have been true.

Although scholars often advocate for a stronger federal role in education, they are agreed on why the federal role has been limited. Many of the nation's founders opposed a strong national government, and even Alexander Hamilton, the lone federalist sympathizer at the Constitutional Convention in 1787, did not argue for a strong federal role in education. Resistance to central government was so high that only two years after the Constitution was ratified, Congress passed a set of amendments, known as the Bill of Rights, which had profound impacts on education. The Tenth Amendment was key to education because its curbs on federalism spoke to the framers' intent by stating, "The powers not delegated to the United States by the Constitution, nor prohibited by it to the States, are reserved to the States respectively, or to the people."[24] With these words, the doctrine of sovereign limits was formed such that the federal government was denied a direct role in education because the Constitution is silent; that is, by default, education is a state responsibility.

Despite Tenth Amendment limits, Congress has devised a long history of federal influence on education in other direct and indirect ways. Direct authority has been derived by two means. The first has been through the powers of Congress in Article 1 of the Constitution which requires Congress to provide a strong national defense—a duty Congress has used to send large sums of money to schools. The second has been by creative interpretation of Article 1, Section 8 known as the General Welfare Clause, which gives Congress the power to "lay and collect taxes, duties, imposts and excises,

[and] to pay the debts and provide for the common defense and general welfare of the United States." National defense has given Congress an easy way to be involved in education, but—more importantly—Congress and the courts have construed the general welfare clause to allow broad federal interest in schools, especially in social and economic issues. Aiding that path has been Congress's indirect influence, as it has used persuasive ways such as withholding federal funds from programs unrelated to schools unless states embrace federal education goals.

Federalism and Defense Education

Education for defense has a long history, with its beginnings generally marked by establishment of the U.S. Military Academy in 1802. Designed to train military leaders, the academy gave rise to other defense colleges: The Naval Academy in 1845, the Coast Guard Academy in 1876, and the Air Force Academy in 1954. The Reserve Officer Training Corps (ROTC) also was created at universities so that future leaders could marry civilian education with military training. Other aid followed, some of which was meant to enhance defense or to help veterans reenter civilian life.

Although a full list of federal interests in defense education is too lengthy to include here, a sample gives the flavor and breadth. In 1918, the *Vocational Rehabilitation Act* provided disabled veterans with job training, and similar aid to World War II veterans was given in 1943.[25] In 1944, Congress created the *Serviceman's Readjustment Act*, known as the GI bill,[26] providing educational benefits to millions of returning veterans. In 1941, a change to the *Lanham Act* gave federal aid to construct and operate schools in areas impacted by federal facilities. In 1950, Congress passed legislation enhancing this aid, a program that sent millions of dollars to local school districts that lost tax base to military installations.[27] After World War II, the military established American schools overseas for the children of deployed soldiers. These schools continue today as Department of Defense Schools (DODS).

Some of the largest outlays for defense education were sparked by cold wars and the technology race. In 1950, Congress created the National Science Foundation in part to train more mathematics and science teachers. In 1958, the *National Defense Education Act* (NDEA) was passed to further improve education in math, science, and foreign languages in response to the launch of the Soviet satellite *Sputnik I*.[28] The NDEA also provided higher education loans and job training for defense occupations. More recently, Congress extended the GI bill to persons entering the military after 1985.[29] Many other programs followed: The *Education for Economic Security Act* of 1984 reflecting new thinking on defense in the modern world;[30] a continuing interest typified by the *National Defense Authorization Act* of 2000;[31] the *Higher Education Relief Opportunities for Students Act* of 2001 providing financial waivers to deal with student and family situations resulting from the September 11, 2001 terrorist attacks;[32] and the *Higher Education Relief Opportunities for Students Act* of 2003 dealing with financial aid to address student and family situations resulting from wars and national emergencies.[33]

Federalism and Higher Education

A corollary to defense has been federal aid to higher education. Typically, there is an effort to separate federal interest in general higher education through the debut of the federal government in nonmilitary higher education affairs as marked by the *Morrill Act* of 1862[34] which established agricultural and mechanical colleges via land grants or payments to states. A second *Morrill Act* followed in 1890.[35] Some of these schools became state land grant universities, with missions of research, teaching, and service in a practical tradition.

Federal interest in higher education did not end with the Morrill Acts. The 1935 *Bankhead Jones Act* made grants to states for agricultural experiment stations,[36] a program that spilled over to public schools through the *Agricultural Adjustment Act* of 1938 authorizing farm commodity supports, which later developed into school lunch and milk programs.[37] The 1950 *Housing Act* authorized loans to construct college housing.[38] Likewise, the *Higher Education Facilities Act* of 1963 granted aid for classrooms, libraries, laboratories, and other facilities.[39]

The vast social reforms of the 1960s led the federal government to plunge deeper into various aids and entitlements under the *Civil Rights Act* of 1964,[40] often with aid for higher education. The Civil Rights Act funded in-service training in higher education, especially for desegregation. Grants like the Health Professional Educational Assistance Amendments provided scholarships for needy students;[41] likewise, the *Higher Education Act* of 1965 funded community service and teacher training programs and created the National Teacher Corps and graduate fellowships aimed at aiding disadvantaged groups.[42] A long list of federal education programs over the last several decades similarly reflects contemporary concerns: The *Taxpayer-Teacher Protection Act* of 2004, increasing the amount of loans that may be forgiven for qualified math, science, and special education teachers who serve in high-poverty schools for five years;[43] the *Student Grant Hurricane and Disaster Relief Act* of 2005, waiving repayments for students receiving federal loans if they were residing in, employed in, or attending an institution of higher education in a major disaster area;[44] and the *Hurricane Education Recovery Act* of 2005, providing aid to states affected by Hurricane Katrina to restart schools and more.[45] Very recently, new federal aid was granted to additional natural disaster victims,[46] a practice Congress appears to be permanently adopting. Countless other federal avenues exist, such as the Public Service Loan Forgiveness Program[47] controlled by the U.S. Department of Education which has the power to lessen the burden of repaying student loans for such service as AmeriCorps, Peace Corps, and a host of other public service opportunities. Although education has defaulted to the states, the federal government has managed to support both K–12 and higher education in aggressive ways.

Federalist Interest in Justice and Education

Federal concern for economic and social issues has not been neatly severable from other federal aims, but it has been the most pervasive and lasting of all federal goals for education. Particularly for K–12 schools due to the Tenth Amendment's silence on education, overlap between federal programs has been most visible, as Congress has had to be creative in order to exert influence. As noted, the legal basis for federal intervention rests in the general welfare clause, which has been held to grant broad powers up to the point of Congressional free will unless overturned by courts. In *United States v. Butler*,[48] the U.S. Supreme Court ruled that the general welfare clause could be broadly construed unless Congress acted arbitrarily—a judgment made on a case-by-case basis. A further test came in *Helvering v. Davis*,[49] as the Court held that the general welfare clause was not confined to the Constitutional framers' intent, but could shift with needs of the nation.

Brown v. Board of Education,[50] of course, changed the entire nature of schools by ruling that segregation denies equal opportunity. But it was still not until the Civil Rights Act[51] of 1964 that the federal government aggressively entered the field of education. As history reveals, the events that followed would have a lasting effect by sparking a massive influx of federal aid into a variety of programs aimed at fundamental fairness in the nation's schools.

Although the list of federal interests is vast, two further Congressional acts especially accounted for the changing federal role in schools—the *Elementary and Secondary Education Act*[52] (ESEA) of 1965 and the *Education of the Handicapped Act*[53] of 1975. Much of the ESEA was aimed toward disadvantaged children because the law was an outgrowth of the Civil Rights Act. ESEA made grants to K–12 school programs for low-income children and for libraries, textbooks, and materials. ESEA also aided educational centers, strengthened state education agencies, and provided funds for research and training. The original ESEA had more than 40 entitlements, each addressing specific interests of Congress.

The most far-reaching provisions of ESEA lay in Title I's funding for supplementary services for low income and culturally disadvantaged children. Children qualified if they met certain criteria such as the $2,000 family income limit. Entire schools could qualify for Title I status based on threshold numbers of qualifying children in a single school. Schools qualified on three criteria: Number of low-income families; number of children receiving Aid to Families with Dependent Children (AFDC); and a formula tied to statewide expenditure per pupil. Title I grew rapidly from $746.9 million in 1965 to its peak of $3 billion in 1980. In 1981, Congress repealed the ESEA in response to former President Reagan's drive to streamline bureaucracy and to stem the erosion of state control that was said to have occurred under a liberal Congress. Congress then passed the *Education Consolidation and Improvement Act*[54] (ECIA), which reauthorized the ESEA but aimed to reduce federal involvement by collapsing programs. Title I was continued as Chapter 1, but was changed to provide more local discretion via block grants. More than 40 other programs were collapsed into Chapter 2 while new provisions relating to administration were made under Chapter 3, reducing the role of the federal government and returning many powers to the states. ECIA did allow several other programs to remain freestanding, including Vocational Education, Education of the Handicapped, National School Lunch, Higher Education, Impact Aid, Title VII Bilingual Education, and Title IX Women's Educational Equity.

Congress also extended its reach by passing the *Education for all Handicapped Children Act*[55] (EHA) in 1975 in response to intensive litigation seeking to ensure the rights of children with disabilities. The driver behind PL 94–142 was the 1972 *PARC*[56] lawsuit. Although many states provided some special education services, provisions were often minimal, permissive, or nonexistent. Held for plaintiffs, *PARC* unleashed a series of lawsuits aimed at forcing states to provide services to all children. With Congressional passage of the EHA, states failing to provide services were denied federal aid to schools. To help states provide services, Congress appropriated $300 million and authorized itself to fund up to 40% of special education costs. Although federal support has never met the 40% goal, federal aid and pressure by courts have discouraged states from denying services. Special education law has long been under scrutiny and constant revision, including renaming to the *Individuals with Disabilities Education Act* (IDEA) and amendments such as those in the *No Child Left Behind Act*[57] and the current *Every Student Succeeds Act.*[58]

In brief, strong federal interest in K–12 education continues today. These efforts show that while the federal government has no direct duty to education, it has taken great interest and at times has seized a central role. The only reasonable conclusion is that if the K–12 services funded in part by the federal government were left to local or state units of government, the loss would be enormous—an impact equal to $55 billion (8.5%) of school districts' revenues in Fiscal Year 2015 (see Table 2.4).

State Support for Schools

In the absence of a federal duty, states have had to create state aid schemes to fund schools or face telling patrons that they must raise local taxes to pay for services. As will be extensively developed later in Chapter 3, tax base variability has been so great that virtually all states have now assumed significant responsibility for funding schools, albeit reluctantly in some cases.

Although public K–12 education has become a state legislative duty, its funding has been contentious, with huge and still unsettled shifts in the balance of power between local and state governments. In this striking fiscal interplay, states have moved (on average) from funding only 16.5% of school costs in 1920 to 46.6% in 2015. But importantly, averages can obscure large individual variations.

Table 2.4 illustrates how the three levels of government share school costs. Obviously the federal role is quite limited. Given that the U.S. Constitution grants plenary powers to states, a major portion of school costs now fall to the states, but Table 2.4 suggests that (on average) the states have shifted a sizable cost share to local school districts. Closer examination shows that although slow to accept major responsibility, over time many states have assumed genuinely greater proportions of these costs out of necessity *and* because courts have found a duty to fund schools implied or expressed in individual states' constitutions. But as indicated, states have accepted their funding roles quite unevenly, as (on average) in 2015 states and local school districts shared funding education relatively equally, with each contributing about 46%. Across states, though, the percentage varied greatly—from 24.9% (Illinois) to 90.1% (Vermont). A major take-away from Table 2.4 is that while it is relatively simple to describe how the federal government has aided schools, in contrast there are 50 states, each with its own constitution, and consequently a nearly equal range of ways to fund public education.

Nevertheless, each state today grants some school aid. Amounts and method depend on economic and political factors. The first factor is likely the taxable wealth of each local school district. Generally speaking, state legislatures try to equalize school funding by granting more aid to poorer districts; but this can be politically difficult.

TABLE 2.4 Revenues for Public Elementary and Secondary Schools by Source of Funds and State or Jurisdiction: 2014–15

State or Jurisdiction	Dollars (in Thousands)				Distribution by %		
	Total	Federal	State	Local	Federal	State	Local
United States	$647,679,130	$55,002,853	$301,529,692	$291,146,585	8.5	46.6	45.0
Alabama	7,435,758	835,012	4,129,101	2,471,644	11.2	55.5	33.2
Alaska	2,935,538	347,699	2,037,616	550,223	11.8	69.4	18.7
Arizona	9,860,167	1,277,021	4,345,427	4,237,720	13.0	44.1	43.0
Arkansas	5,283,244	608,559	2,720,257	1,954,428	11.5	51.5	37.0
California	74,395,627	7,148,875	42,525,283	24,721,469	9.6	57.2	33.2
Colorado	9,764,525	723,032	4,452,824	4,588,670	7.4	45.6	47.0
Connecticut	11,376,740	480,791	4,661,930	6,234,018	4.2	41.0	54.8
Delaware	2,077,887	181,122	1,199,264	697,501	8.7	57.7	33.6
District of Columbia	2,251,430	218,044	†	2,033,386	9.7	†	90.3
Florida	26,789,374	3,192,508	10,661,588	12,935,279	11.9	39.8	48.3
Georgia	18,772,155	1,888,388	8,485,440	8,398,327	10.1	45.2	44.7
Hawaii	2,699,827	259,391	2,381,547	58,888	9.6	88.2	2.2
Idaho	2,294,497	246,320	1,491,161	557,016	10.7	65.0	24.3
Illinois	27,304,004	2,264,000	6,787,531	18,252,473	8.3	24.9	66.8
Indiana	12,103,344	988,205	6,787,225	4,327,914	8.2	56.1	35.8
Iowa	6,463,514	475,848	3,460,804	2,526,863	7.4	53.5	39.1
Kansas	6,225,153	556,947	4,001,451	1,666,755	8.9	64.3	26.8
Kentucky	7,453,976	856,715	4,093,058	2,504,203	11.5	54.9	33.6
Louisiana	8,927,289	1,307,850	3,875,345	3,744,095	14.7	43.4	41.9
Maine	2,737,132	192,628	1,077,156	1,467,348	7.0	39.4	53.6
Maryland	14,521,045	821,418	6,316,683	7,382,943	5.7	43.5	50.8

(Continued)

TABLE 2.4 Continued

State or Jurisdiction	Dollars (in Thousands)				Distribution by %		
	Total	Federal	State	Local	Federal	State	Local
Massachusetts	17,197,389	903,425	6,726,216	9,567,749	5.3	39.1	55.6
Michigan	19,452,849	1,785,600	11,706,291	5,960,957	9.2	60.2	30.6
Minnesota	12,183,690	699,165	8,131,825	3,352,701	5.7	66.7	27.5
Mississippi	4,550,410	672,385	2,324,855	1,553,170	14.8	51.1	34.1
Missouri	10,927,026	979,787	3,555,885	6,391,354	9.0	32.5	58.5
Montana	1,805,295	219,405	863,889	722,001	12.2	47.9	40.0
Nebraska	4,168,349	343,356	1,350,595	2,474,399	8.2	32.4	59.4
Nevada	4,522,125	416,393	1,621,778	2,483,954	9.2	35.9	54.9
New Hampshire	2,992,501	166,235	1,000,374	1,825,892	5.6	33.4	61.0
New Jersey	28,489,659	1,191,041	11,989,910	15,308,708	4.2	42.1	53.7
New Mexico	3,986,781	557,590	2,771,343	657,848	14.0	69.5	16.5
New York	62,517,215	2,831,810	25,938,520	33,746,884	4.5	41.5	54.0
North Carolina	13,681,971	1,662,823	8,543,954	3,475,194	12.2	62.4	25.4
North Dakota	1,578,414	158,647	926,792	492,974	10.1	58.7	31.2
Ohio	24,516,266	1,850,536	11,179,287	11,486,443	7.5	45.6	46.9
Oklahoma	6,261,170	717,590	3,090,488	2,453,092	11.5	49.4	39.2
Oregon	7,077,486	565,086	3,678,010	2,834,391	8.0	52.0	40.0
Pennsylvania	28,983,071	2,003,649	10,764,800	16,214,622	6.9	37.1	55.9
Rhode Island	2,444,422	199,039	990,389	1,254,995	8.1	40.5	51.3
South Carolina	8,891,519	855,168	4,198,817	3,837,534	9.6	47.2	43.2
South Dakota	1,420,613	211,164	431,422	778,027	14.9	30.4	54.8
Tennessee	9,428,987	1,127,603	4,258,683	4,042,701	12.0	45.2	42.9

Texas	56,127,791	6,085,723	22,787,667	27,254,401	10.8	40.6	48.6
Utah	5,127,846	450,732	2,798,042	1,879,073	8.8	54.6	36.6
Vermont	1,758,461	105,353	1,584,246	68,862	6.0	90.1	3.9
Virginia	15,624,013	1,012,211	6,240,351	8,371,451	6.5	39.9	53.6
Washington	13,606,501	1,036,795	8,301,015	4,268,691	7.6	61.0	31.4
West Virginia	3,525,371	362,449	2,027,143	1,135,779	10.3	57.5	32.2
Wisconsin	11,197,990	840,933	5,139,509	5,217,548	7.5	45.9	46.6
Wyoming	1,961,721	120,788	1,116,909	724,024	6.2	56.9	36.9

Source: Digest of Education Statistics 2017. Table 235.20. Washington, DC: NCES, Institute for Education Sciences, U.S. Department of Education https://nces.ed.gov/programs/digest/d17/tables/dt17_235.20.asp?current=yes

Another factor is the amount of federal school aid flowing to a state, such as federal impact aid. In some states, the amount of land exempt from local taxation due to federal installations is high; in such cases, state aid is valuable, but high impact aid may moderate state aid amounts. A key factor is the operation of political philosophy. For example, some states have adopted equalization aid formulas that inversely link local wealth and state aid. Other states have chosen minimum foundation plans to help school districts reach a base support level before leaving the balance of costs to local taxpayers. Only a few state legislatures have even proposed full state funding (see Chapter 3 for a full discussion of aid formulas). A factor of enormous importance has been the force of law via school funding lawsuits. The overall result is that state school finance formulas are an interplay of political, legal, and economic realities. In brief, the level and type of state aid to schools have developed unevenly, resulting in the widely varied mix of federal, state, and local revenues seen today in each school district.

The fragmentation brought about by state plenary authority restrained only by politics and courts and surges in federal interest has left a patchwork effect in terms of how each state funds schools. It is unfortunate that such variability has developed because—to whatever extent money buys quality—the value of an education may be equally variable across states since the range of revenues, expenditures, and programs is great. Although it can be argued that fiscal ability and needs and costs genuinely differ among states, it is difficult to conclude that wide expenditure differences per pupil are really a result of careful analysis of educational needs. Inversely, it is also difficult for school leaders to explain why spending for schools should increase when the public often is convinced that pupil achievement is unsatisfactory. And it is ultimately most difficult to explain these realities when expenditure levels differ greatly not only across states, but also across school districts within single states as well. But regardless of these disparities, the record shows an increasing state role in funding K–12 schools over time—it only remains to be seen whether recent attempts by states to take greater control of education will also result in a larger state funding role.

Local Support for Schools

Although citizens are often aware of state aid, their tax bills lead them to see education as a local enterprise. This arises from the fact that schools are visible in every community and have been seen as locally controlled from the earliest days of the nation. It is difficult to live and work today without being aware of the turmoil surrounding local school boards, the high profile of local school leaders, and the tensions around local school property taxes. As discussed earlier, states have taken a much larger role in education, especially via accountability mandates. But since not all states have assumed equal responsibility for school funding, it is important to further explore local cost-share issues in order to gain a complete view of school funding.

Table 2.1 indicated that schools have become less insular over time. Beginning in 1920 with the first national reporting of costs, 83% of the total $970 million funding fell on local districts. The first big shift came in 1940, as the local share of the $2.26 billion dropped to 68%. By 1970, the local share of the $40.27 billion available to schools had dropped to 52%. By 1990, the local share made up 47% of the

$208.5 billion cost for public schools. Table 2.4 shows that by 2015, the local share stood at about 45% of the total amount available for K–12 education.

Although the proportion of local spending fell over the last century, the picture is somewhat unstable. It is true that local support for schools in the nation's early days was high as a percent of total costs compared to today. But by many accounts, real local dollars have not declined, either in total or in aggregate burden. Locally, taxpayer dollars have increased due to inflation and as a result of increased costs due to other factors such as expanded programs arising either from local choice or in response to mandates. Likewise, aggregate tax burden has not declined and actually may have increased, as the additional dollars needed in modern school organizations have soared and as other governmental units have increased taxes too. Though *municipal overburden* was coined to depict demand on urban taxpayers by multiple taxing units such as cities, counties, police and fire departments, central water and sewer systems, schools, and other services, tax levels in rural and urban settings alike have led critics to charge that there has been very little taxpayer relief.

A second issue of local responsibility lies in seeing the differing realities of K–12 funding in the 50 states. States have been free to create funding systems to meet their constitutional duty except for the pressure of politics which can force similarities among states, and the demand by courts to fund schools in compliance with state constitutional mandates. Thus, school finance reform has occurred over time; but despite such events, experience in individual states has not led to equal shifts in local districts' cost shares. At the end of the day, tax burdens are still very different among states, and national averages do not speak loudly to those differences.

A third issue of local responsibility rests in the basic nature of how local cost shares are set. School districts typically derive revenue from a local *tax base*. Although some states tax more than one type of object for school purposes, most states rely on *real property* to define a district's tax base. This means that real estate is often the main source of tax revenue at the local level. No two school districts contain exactly the same property values, so that highly unequal *tax capacity* may be evident from one district to another. A simple illustration makes this clear. Urban properties are often valuable, with businesses, homes, and land bringing high prices. Rural property may be less so because it may consist mostly of open land. Unless rural land has other value such as natural resources, urban areas may have much higher *property wealth*. That wealth, or *assessed valuation*, is typically the basis for deriving school revenue by assessing a tax against each property. State statutes define assessed valuation and collections. For example, an acre of urban land might sell for millions of dollars depending on location, but in a rural area a one-acre home site might sell for $30,000—perhaps $3,000 if remotely located. A *tax rate* of 10 *mills*[59] on a $1,000,000 urban acre would yield $10,000 in school tax revenue, while the remote home site would yield only $30—a vast difference, with implications for the ability of a local district to provide adequate funding for schools.

Even the implications are complex. These data might suggest rural disadvantage and unfairly high urban wealth, while the opposite may be true. For example, it is certain that one aspect of an urban area is population density. Thus, high property wealth spread over a large population may actually yield lower *per capita* wealth. The urban condition may bring higher costs associated with economically disadvantaged groups and tax base competition (i.e., municipal overburden). Some urban property owners are absentee individuals or businesses, with no community loyalty or interest other than taking profits without reinvesting, potentially driving down urban prices through blight. Rural conditions are complex too. Although rural property may be less costly, ownership rests in fewer hands, which results in a heavier per capita tax burden. Also, the lack of urban issues in rural areas does not always result in lower costs, as smaller populations lead to higher per-pupil costs due to diseconomies of scale. And low income is not a unique urban reality; in fact, some rural areas have a higher incidence of poverty than some cities.

A fourth feature of local responsibility is actually a complication of how local school districts set the cost share and—to some extent—the level of overall spending. This phenomenon takes several forms and is made more complex by how school district budgets are determined, the interdependency of tax bases, and intergovernmental competition. The concept of municipal overburden was raised earlier, and the broader concept of *tax overburden* applies in some way to almost all school districts, including rural areas. A byproduct of tax overburden is the hostility encountered by many local school districts when seeking to increase funding through increases in local property taxes. In addition, in many states the community must vote on school budgets. And even though some states allow *local option leeway* (i.e., giving school boards the option of additional local tax effort for schools), voter approval of this highly visible tax is still required. As state aid plans limiting voter leeway have come into existence and as overall tax burdens have grown, voter approval has become harder to obtain. Another complicating factor in some states is the issue of *fiscal dependence* where local school budgets are submitted to a higher authority in tandem with budgets of other tax units such as cities and counties. In these circumstances, fiscal dependency creates problems because local school districts may have trouble securing adequate revenue when competition for a finite tax pool includes multiple units of local government.[60] In brief, local school district budgets can be constrained in multiple ways.

The issues driving local responsibility and ability to pay for schools are so numerous that it is difficult to tell from percentages alone why the local share in a particular state has declined or increased. What is clear is that school districts differ in ability to pay and that experience among the states varies widely. It is also clear that if local districts depended entirely on local tax bases, unconscionable disparities would follow. And finally, it is clear that the federal, state, and local partnership is both variable and essential. Education has long been a partnership in America—the real issue is refinement of that partnership in ways that enhance fiscal adequacy and equity for every child.

WHAT CONSTITUTES ADEQUATE AND EQUITABLE FUNDING FOR SCHOOLS?

The importance of adequate and equitable funding is heightened by the sweeping scope and costs of public schools, changing demographics, and links between education and economic and social progress. Even though research cannot quantify the link between achievement and money, there is a longstanding belief that society must guard against underinvesting in schools in order to avoid destructive economic and social consequences. In this uncertain context, policymakers have been challenged to fund education at an appropriate level.

The result has been unending debate about money and schools. While some debates deal with what schools mean to different segments of society, perhaps the greatest issue is over how school money is distributed. Much of the struggle arises because there will never be enough money to address every educational and societal need, so that distribution becomes even more critical. By all accounts, the noise has escalated due to greater eagerness to pursue confrontational remedies such as legal challenges to state school finance formulas. Some researchers are quick to assert that more money makes better schools, arguing that education distributes economic and social opportunity and that equal opportunity depends entirely on the quality of public schools. They further contend that despite the lack of a perfect link between money and outcomes, school quality is powerfully affected by purchased resources such as qualified teachers and modern facilities. They draw a bright line that challenges people who argue for the irrelevance of money, pointing out that those same people still want more money spent on the education of their own children. Under these conditions, litigants have aggressively sought fair and adequate funding, believing that how states fund education has a direct effect on social and economic justice.

Origins of School Funding Challenges

For more than 100 years, the financing of public schools has been a deep concern for courts and policymakers. Although school finance as a discipline only emerged during the early twentieth century, issues of school taxation have been a flashpoint since the earliest days of the nation. Likewise, schools have long been the object of intense conflict regarding equality of educational opportunity as it relates to discrimination, and it is easy to link discrimination to disparities in funding across and within schools, districts, and states.

The history of school finance litigation has played out in federal and state courts. At the federal level, litigation has focused on interpretation of the U.S. Constitution in regard to federal responsibility for education, hoping to read a *guaranteed right* into the Constitution. At the state level, litigation has focused on both the *constitutional* and *statutory* demands of each state. State constitutional interpretations have been swayed by the times and attitudes of courts, particularly whenever there were wide variances among states in constitutional and statutory provisions. In both federal and state cases, litigants have sought rulings on the meaning of equal opportunity and have sought to test the strength of states' constitutional and statutory language involving schools. Traditionally, federal challenges have followed two claims: Education as a *fundamental right,* and *the equal protection* of the law. In kind, state constitutional challenges have followed three claims: Education as a *fundamental right*, the *equal protection* of laws, and the *education articles* of state constitutions. Each of these can be traced from their federal and state origins into modern school finance litigation strategy.

Federal Origins

Although school finance litigation is now largely seen as state-specific, the federal case predates all other strategy. Plaintiffs first sought equality in funding by seeking a favorable U.S. Supreme Court ruling as the supreme law of the land. The logic was that if a ruling were favorable, states would be subject to federal law.

Bringing a federal lawsuit was a reasonable act. Equality had been important since the days when the colonial charters first sought freedom from British rule. Equality was key in the Bill of Rights, and the Fourteenth Amendment to the Constitution guaranteed equality under federal law. The Fourteenth Amendment was critically important because its provisions applied to the individual states:

> No State shall make or enforce any law which shall abridge the privileges or immunities of citizens of the United States; nor shall any State deprive any person of life, liberty, or property, without due process of law; nor deny to any person within its jurisdiction the equal protection of the laws.[61]

A federal case for school funding fairness was laid in a series of lawsuits testing the limits of equality under the U.S. Constitution. Earlier cases had laid other groundwork, including over-turning racial segregation, wherein the practical implications included the costs and organization of public schools. The next reasonable step was to bring a suit alleging that unequal funding for schools is also an impermissible inequality under law.

The strategy was actually an extension of judicial sympathy that already existed for other established fundamental rights. In addition to named rights in the Constitution, the Supreme Court had previously ruled for other rights so basic that they could not be denied except by due process of law. The importance of establishing a fundamental right to education could not be overstated, in that *fundamentality* meant that these rights must be protected at all costs. Plaintiffs therefore were seeking to link school funding and equal rights under the Fourteenth Amendment's equal protection clause. This line of thinking produced two litigation thrusts. One thrust came from defining unequal treatment of *suspect classes*: i.e., school funding litigation might prevail if plaintiffs could show that money was tied to a protected social class in schools. The second thrust came from seeking ways in which some other fundamental right might be established by nexus to unequal funding. In brief, the strategy was perilous—if neither a fundamental right to education nor a suspect class (e.g., poor people) could be established, lawsuits would have to focus elsewhere—such as on individual state constitution education clauses.

The Early Federal Case

Although federal racial equality litigation actually spanned many decades, it was in *Brown v. Board of Education*[62] in 1954 that equality of educational opportunity found a footing as the U.S. Supreme Court overturned the 'separate but equal' education provisions that had allowed racially segregated schools. Overturning the entire social and economic history of the nation, the Court held that separate but equal was inherently unequal and that education was vital to the health and wellbeing of the nation. The Court stated that:

> [Education] is perhaps the most important function of state and local governments. … It is the very foundation of good citizenship. … In these days, it is doubtful that any child may reasonably be expected to succeed in life if he is denied the opportunity of an education. Such an opportunity, where the state has undertaken to provide it, is a right that must be made available to all on equal terms.

Emboldened by *Brown*, reformers turned to fiscal inequality, believing that the same analysis might apply to funding public schools because it was easily proposed that money and educational opportunity varied based on residence in school districts of wildly unequal wealth. Of value to this theory was a line of argument that unequal district wealth equaled wealth discrimination, so that the happenstance of residence could be established as a wealth-based suspect class. By this logic, wealth-disadvantaged children by accident of residence in poor school districts were a perfect case in point.

The first federal suit took form in Virginia in *Burruss v. Wilkerson*[63] in 1969. Plaintiffs based their claims on the Fourteenth Amendment, arguing that state aid was not sent to school districts on the basis of educational need. The United States District Court, however, held that whereas "deficiencies and differences are forcefully put by plaintiffs' counsel … we do not believe they are creatures of discrimination by the State … We can only see to it that the outlays on one group are not invidiously greater or less than that of another." The court added, "the courts have neither the knowledge, nor means, nor the power to tailor the public moneys to fit the varying needs of these students throughout the state." The tone of *Burruss* foretold much of the potential failure of a federal case. Over the coming years, plaintiffs repeatedly heard the same logic, often as federal courts drew on the words of previous court decisions to express their own limitations. The near lone exception came in 1972 in *Van Dusartz v. Hatfield*[64] as a Minnesota federal court held that wealthy districts not only had greater revenue per child but also enjoyed lower tax rates—conditions linked to the child's residence. *Van Dusartz* was hardly the rule, though, as other federal courts complained that their hands were tied by a lack of judicially manageable standards. Equality in federal court was stated negatively, in that absence of money was not the same as discrimination.

San Antonio v. Rodriguez

Application of the federal concept was argued before the U.S. Supreme Court in 1973. In *San Antonio Independent School District v. Rodriguez*[65] the Court overturned plaintiffs' claims that the state of Texas must be neutral in aiding schools. Additionally, the Court overturned the claim that education was of fundamental interest to the state. *Rodriguez* was on appeal to the U.S. Supreme Court, where plaintiffs were arguing that the Texas funding system violated federal equal protections by discriminating against a suspect class of poor and that students making up that class were denied a right to equal education. The Court rejected the suspect class argument, however, as it saw only students living in poor school districts, rather than being poor themselves. The Court noted that individual income did not correlate with district wealth and that even if the link were strong, the Court's view of wealth suspectness was limited to absolute deprivation. Because no child was absolutely deprived of an education, fiscal inequalities were of only relative difference.

The Court also rejected education as a fundamental right. Plaintiffs had argued that education was so prerequisite to other rights that it created a nexus to other established rights. The Court disagreed, seeing no link between education and other rights. Although the Court criticized the disparities in Texas schools, only a *rational basis* was required to defend the state education finance formula absent invidious discrimination. A rational basis could be found in the Texas goal of promoting local control, and the Court refused to intervene in a complex political arena.

Subsequent Federal Litigation

Although *Rodriguez* had a chilling effect on new federal lawsuits, other cases were brought, especially in light of the fact that the Supreme Court did not close the door to future claims. Three cases illustrate the importance of the federal courts in defining a federal role in educational equality.

Thirteen years after *Rodriguez*, plaintiffs in Mississippi sued in *Papasan v. Allain*[66] for equal protection on revenue disparity based on Section Sixteen lands lost during the Civil War. Although the state provided aid to offset losses in affected school districts, by 1981 state funds were only $0.63 per pupil compared to $75.34 per pupil in districts where land had not been taken. Though the case was dismissed in federal district court, the Fifth Circuit Court held on appeal in *Papasan* that although the Eleventh Amendment to the U.S. Constitution did not bar equal protection claims, *Rodriguez* was the appropriate standard regarding fiscal disparity. The U.S. Supreme Court affirmed, but it also sent the case back for development. *Papasan* was thus notable for two reasons. First, the complaint was narrowly taken, never drawing the issue of fundamentality. Second, in remanding to the lower court, the Supreme Court noted that unreasonable government action would attract the Court's interest, leaving open a small window of federal interest in school funding.

A second important case arose in Texas as the U.S. Supreme Court ruled in *Plyler v. Doe*[67] that refusal by a state to educate illegal aliens could invoke federal equal protections. Although the Court stopped short of declaring education a fundamental right, it approved a higher level of scrutiny in cases of absolute educational deprivation. The Court pointed to its hesitancy to forestall any attempt in the federal courts, as it stated:

> Education provides the basic tools by which individuals might lead economically productive lives to the benefit of us all. In sum, education has a fundamental role in maintaining the fabric of our society. We cannot ignore the significant social costs borne by our Nation when select groups are denied the means to absorb the values and skills on which our social order rests.

The third important federal case came in *Kadrmas v. Dickinson Public Schools*,[68] as plaintiffs in North Dakota alleged that fees for bus service denied equal protection because the plaintiff child could not afford to pay for transportation. The U.S.

Supreme Court held for the defendant state, but its five–four vote was a bare majority and indicated the unsettled nature of federal education claims. The Court warned that *Rodriguez* was not the last word in that there were nuances that deeply interested the Court. The minority opinion expressed this well:

> The Court ... does not address the question whether a state constitutionally could deny a child access to a minimally adequate education. In prior cases this Court explicitly has left open the question whether such a deprivation of access would violate a fundamental constitutional right. That question remains open today.

Although *Rodriguez* has been said to close off hope for a successful federal claim, the record disagrees. Federal courts are sympathetic to judicially unmanageable standards, and they are inclined to defer to legislative prerogative. Likewise, the nation's highest court is reluctant to declare education a fundamental right. But it is also clear that the Supreme Court takes interest in education, as over time it revisits and refines its rulings. More recently, plaintiffs have attempted to overturn state education finance formulas arguing racial intent and thus discrimination against minority children.[69] But again, these attempts have failed for the same reasons. In the end, it is clear that the case for school finance reform has had to turn to state courts to find meaningful and systematic success.

State Origins

Development of a state case for equalizing money in schools has followed the federal path—i.e., there has been significant overlap of both timeline and nature of claims. Indeed, lawsuits were often brought simultaneously in state and federal courts in the early days. For example, *Burruss* and *Rodriguez* were both filed in federal court in the 1960s, and the California case of *Serrano v. Priest*[70] actually ended at the California Supreme Court level in 1971 before the U.S. Supreme Court had ruled in *Rodriguez* in 1973. The nature of claims also overlapped, as state cases like *Serrano* made complimentary federal and state constitutional claims. But while success on the federal front was unlikely, state litigation occurred far more frequently and with greater success.

Serrano v. Priest

The first state education finance distribution formula constitutional challenge to gain attention was *Serrano v. Priest*,[71] as the California Supreme Court ruled in what would become a model for state school finance litigation. Plaintiffs sought a ruling for a fundamental right to education, wealth as a suspect class, and federal and state equal protections. Plaintiffs charged that the state education finance formula created disparity and that these differences impacted the quality of schools. Plaintiffs also charged that some taxpayers paid higher tax rates and received a poorer education. The net sum of such finance schemes, plaintiffs alleged, was to make the quality of education dependent on local property wealth.

In a sweeping victory for plaintiffs, the state supreme court overturned the California school funding formula, holding that it violated both the federal Fourteenth

Amendment and the state constitution's equal protection clause. This ruling ran counter to every trend. The state supreme court was harsh in its view of unequal opportunity:

> We have determined that this funding scheme invidiously discriminates against the poor because it makes the quality of a child's education a function of the wealth of his parents and neighbors. Recognizing, as we must, that the right to an education in our public schools is a fundamental interest that cannot be conditional on wealth, we can discern no compelling state purpose necessitating the present method of financing.

The fact that the federal claim would be later overturned in *Rodriguez* did not weaken the impact of *Serrano* at the state level because it meant that state courts might not adopt the same posture as federal courts; that is, state law can be stricter than federal law. *Serrano* provided a blueprint for state litigation by its success on state-level fundamentality and equal protection claims, and it showed that state constitutions might be vulnerable in ways unavailable at the federal level. Many states immediately saw *Serrano* as a harbinger of the future. As a result, an explosion of school finance reform litigation followed in other states, along with many states acting ahead of anticipated lawsuits. Since *Serrano's* time, nearly every state has faced a lawsuit regarding its school finance formula and whether it meets the state constitutional standard. Not unexpectedly, such challenges have met with varying degrees of success and failure.

Subsequent Failures in State Litigation

The case for state-level litigation challenging school finance formulas did not enjoy sudden and sustained success. Although a full accounting of the history of litigation is beyond the scope of this book, a few early cases illustrate that the state-level record included significant failures.[72]

Shortly after *Serrano*, the Michigan Supreme Court held in *Milliken*,[73] a ruling that changed in a relatively short time. The original ruling was for plaintiffs and was modeled on *Serrano*, but the victory was short-lived because the state supreme court experienced a change of sitting judges—a change that ended in reversal of the ruling. The new court vacated the prior decision, saying the evidence did not show that equal protection of children in low-wealth districts was violated. Of particular importance was the issue of a link between fiscal inputs and pupil achievement, so that additional money could not be shown to provide more equal outcomes.

After *Rodriguez*, the Arizona Supreme Court held for the defendant state in *Shofstall*.[74] The court had been asked whether the state's school funding statute violated the state equal protection clause and the *general and uniform* provision in the state's constitution. The court interpreted 'general and uniform' to mean that the state would set a minimum school year, certify personnel, and approve course requirements and standards. Although the court found a fundamental right to education, it saw legislative redress as the solution to political problems; that is, school funding.

The Illinois Supreme Court ruled on behalf of the state in the contemporary case of *Blase*.[75] Plaintiffs had based their claims on the state constitution's strong wording, which said, "the State shall provide for an efficient system of high quality public educational institutions and services [and that] the State has the primary responsibility for financing the system of public education." Plaintiffs wanted the state to provide no less than 50% of costs, along with other strict equality provisions. The state supreme court rejected this view, ruling that the language expressed only a goal rather than a specific command.

A challenge in Washington State illustrates a stunning defeat for plaintiffs in *Northshore v. Kinnear*,[76] as the plaintiffs' case failed despite all elements of victory seemingly in place. Plaintiffs' claims included a charge that the state had disobeyed a provision of its constitution, which read, "it is the *paramount* duty of the state to make *ample* provision for the education of *all* children," and that the state had failed to provide a *general and uniform system* of public schools [emphasis added]. Although Washington was seen as one of the states having the most forceful constitutional language, the state supreme court nonetheless denied all claims, noting that even if the state were only one school district, spending per child would still depend on geography, climate, terrain, social and economic conditions, transportation, special services, and local choices. The strength of language regarding ample provision was viewed unfavorably, as the court noted, "constitutionally speaking, the duty or function is the same as any other major duty or function of state government."

Despite continual suits in state courts over many years, it is important to emphasize the still unsettled condition of state constitutional obligations to the financing of public schools. In nearly all states that have experienced school finance litigation, plaintiffs have prevailed at times while defendant states have prevailed at others. Although there have been numerous plaintiff victories, a realistic view recognizes that failure is always possible when plaintiffs engage in high stakes constitutional litigation.[77]

Subsequent Successes in State Litigation

Although plaintiffs have lost cases at the state level, it is true that victories have dramatically affected how schools are financed. A few important state cases wherein the plaintiffs prevailed following *Serrano* illustrate the volatile context of school funding litigation.

The blueprint for funding reform was aided by a key victory soon after *Serrano*, as the state supreme court in New Jersey ruled in *Robinson v. Cahill*.[78] The state court reviewed a lower court's holding for plaintiffs wherein it was charged that the state aid formula violated federal and state equal protections and denied a fundamental right to education because tax revenue varied by district wealth and was not equalized. The court denied fundamentality and wealth suspect class, stating that such findings would have the unintended effect of changing the most basic political structures. But the court still overturned the school funding scheme by turning to the education article of the state constitution, which demanded a *thorough and efficient* system of schools—a requirement unmet due to lack of equalization in revenues and thereby violating the state's equal protection clause.

Other plaintiff victories followed in the next few years. One of the more expansive state supreme court rulings came in Wyoming in *Washakie*[79] as the court found that poor districts showed a pattern of less revenue due to low assessed valuation. The court upheld plaintiff arguments that the quality of education was related to money. The court cut to the core, stating, "until equality of financing is achieved, there is no practicable method of achieving equality of quality." The Wyoming Supreme Court based its decision on the fact that certain provisions of the state constitution were more demanding than federal equal protections and that education was of such compelling interest to the state that it was among the protected fundamental rights. Unlike most courts, the Wyoming court embraced wealth as a suspect class, saying, "the state has the burden of demonstrating a compelling interest ... served by the challenged legislation and which cannot be satisfied by any other convenient legal structure."

The still unsettled nature of state school finance litigation was again illustrated in Texas in a series of cases that came before the state supreme court over the years. Failing in *Rodriguez*, plaintiffs turned to the Texas Supreme Court, which ruled in their favor in *Edgewood*[80] in 1988. The court ordered the state legislature to create a remedy within a specific time period—a duty that the legislature had difficulty meeting, consequently forcing the case to return for judicial review. These same issues moved through subsequent decisions,[81] with the courts repeatedly reviewing the efforts to improve equity and adequacy, in part by recapturing local revenues from the state's wealthier school districts for redistribution to poorer schools. Not surprisingly, such solutions were contentious, so that in 2001 high-wealth school districts sued under *West Orange-Cove*,[82] claiming that a state-imposed property tax lid meant to limit funding disparities was unconstitutional. Plaintiff intervenors joined hundreds of school districts to the case and reshaped the basic nature of the suit, with the outcome being that the trial court in 2004 held that the system of property taxation did not allow meaningful discretion and was thus unconstitutional.[83] Still unresolved, a taxpayer coalition filed a new suit[84] regarding legislative changes in response to *West Orange-Cove*, in addition to recent cuts in state aid. The case was heard in 2013 and reheard in 2014, with a state high court ruling[85] in 2016 finding the state system satisfied the reasonableness test.

Plaintiff victories are further illustrated by two other key cases in Kentucky and New Jersey, both of which provide insight on the prospects of school funding challenges. One of the central plaintiff wins that recently led states to revise both academic systems and their finance formulas was the Kentucky Supreme Court's ruling in *Rose*[86] in 1989. In a case that shook the nation, the Kentucky court held that the system of common schools was not efficient and found for a fundamental right to education—a conclusion arising when the state's schools were underfunded and inadequate in educational programs—observations that caused the court to order a complete overhaul of the educational system with massive new funds. Simultaneously, the New Jersey case of *Abbott v. Burke*[87] in 1990, a multi-decade continuation of the original 1973 *Robinson* case, stirred national interest as that state's school aid formula was again overruled because it did not meet the needs of poor urban districts and because the formula still violated the state's thorough and efficient clause. Although the court later found the level of fiscal resources to finally meet adequacy standards—a finding only after subsequent cases,[88] New Jersey's experience represents serial litigation that by its very nature continues interminably in various forms as in 2011 when plaintiffs again triumphed in *Abbott XXI*[89] by forcing the state to restore funding reductions to the *Abbott* districts that came as the result of a revenue shortfall due to a weak state economy. Even yet, New Jersey's battle continues, as the governor sought in 2017 to override collective bargaining agreements and teacher seniority layoff laws[90] and as an administrative petition[91] was filed in 2018 alleging that on average plaintiff districts had received less than 50% of state aid entitlement granted a decade earlier.

After decades of litigation, several conclusions are possible. First, while winless in federal court, plaintiffs have won in states for various reasons, as the central question has been whether the state aid formula conformed to state constitutional mandates. Second, it must be understood that the judicial picture will continue to evolve. Third, as each decade of the twenty-first century arrives, the beat goes on as illustrated in Table 2.5 where case after case is filed and as plaintiffs win and lose on the merits. And fourth, whether the defendant states or plaintiffs win, success depends on having an excellent legal team, a structurally sound state aid formula, and data-driven evidence to support plaintiff claims.[92] And plaintiffs need money to pay legal fees.

TABLE 2.5 Summary of Plaintiff Win/Loss Record 1973–2017

Plaintiff Win	State Win	Pending Lawsuit	No Filing
Alaska	Alabama	Arizona	Hawaii
Arizona	Arizona	Arkansas	Mississippi
Arkansas	Colorado	Delaware	Nevada
California	Connecticut	Florida	Utah
Connecticut	Florida	Iowa	
Idaho	Georgia	Kansas	
Kansas	Illinois	New Mexico	
Kentucky	Indiana	New York	
Louisiana	Louisiana	North Carolina	
Maryland	Maine	Pennsylvania	
Massachusetts	Michigan	Tennessee	
Montana	Minnesota	Washington	
New Hampshire	Missouri		
New Jersey	Nebraska		
New Mexico	Oklahoma		
New York	Oregon		
North Carolina	Rhode Island		
North Dakota	South Dakota		
Ohio	Texas		
Pennsylvania	Virginia		
South Carolina	Washington		
Tennessee	Wisconsin		
Texas			
Vermont			
West Virginia			
Wyoming			

Source: School Funding.Info. "Overview of Litigation History: Summary of School Funding Court Cases (1973-2017)." New York: A Project of the Center for Educational Equity at Teachers College. (2018) http://schoolfunding.info/litigation-map/

EQUALITY, PRODUCTIVITY, AND LIBERTY IN PUBLIC EDUCATION

Schools face a very difficult situation when trying to satisfy all stakeholders. Some elements of society pursue education solely for economic gain; others see schooling as a primary tool to redress social injustice. Still others view schools as a place where the principles of liberty should reign, though there is strong disagreement about whether liberty means freedom to achieve based on ability, or whether freedom is only realized once schools have enabled the less fortunate. In all instances, a common thread is the demand for educational outcomes—however defined—a demand that is becoming ever more strident.

Maintaining—or even establishing—adequate and equitable fiscal support for America's schools has become exceedingly complex. As costs have risen, taxpayer burdens have grown at the same time that costs for other social services have skyrocketed. Attitudes about adequate funding for schools are a morass of desires, resentments, and mandates.[93] On one hand, the dollars are so vast that it is hard to imagine that revenues are inadequate and that to ask for more stretches the limits of reason, particularly as education is only one of many essential government functions. On the other hand, the depth of need reflects increasing demands on schools from all quarters. And at the same time, the success of public school is relentlessly questioned.

The struggle comes not so much from whether people want the benefits of schooling, but rather from how to distribute education in ways that respect the common good while respecting individual freedom to accept or reject educational benefits or to obtain them from non-public sources. Hence the movement toward charter and virtual schools, as well as vouchers and other privatization. It is exactly this tension that is mirrored in schools: It is a tension among economics, equality, productivity, liberty, and democracy. And it is in exactly this context that all education finance policy will continue to be made.

POINT–COUNTERPOINT

POINT

The endless struggle over school funding in states and courts is divisive and wasteful. Common sense says that children have unequal needs, and common sense should tell politicians to quit squabbling over school aid plans because we have the technical knowledge to do what is right. The controversy is only a ruse to distract from the underlying agenda—those with money do not want to share it, and to fund schools fairly in the face of a political machine is suicidal for politicians. It is simply easier to window-dress justice than to face a political take-down.

COUNTERPOINT

The endless history of school finance litigation has produced a set of rabid reformers, all of whom believe that no amount of funding will eliminate the perceived equality gap. The real issue is that existing resources are poorly managed, and any new money will be misused too. Public schools are inefficient takers. Plaintiffs in school finance regularly play on race and class and try their case in the media ahead of entering the courtroom because their sole mission is to drive new money to schools regardless of demonstrable benefit. If schools really are underfunded, the only solution is to combine existing and new funding with structural reform in performance-based systems that are tightly benchmarked to pupil achievement.

- Which of these entrenched perspectives on school funding best represents your own view? Explain.
- Do any arguments presented by either side make sense? Why?
- How can states redress the legitimate issues in this discussion, while funding all the other services that states normally provide in a fair and equitable manner?

CASE STUDY

As the new assistant superintendent for finance in your school district, you sensed an undercurrent at last night's school board meeting. Several board members seemed intently interested in recent media reports that the state might take renewed interest in school size and efficiency and that school district consolidation might be a hot topic in the upcoming legislative session. Having seen the same news reports, you already knew that a legislative committee had been created to explore slashing taxes as an economic stimulus, especially given the mood in the nation and since the next year would be an election year. You are new to your position, but you are savvy enough to realize that some issues can drive headlines in a heartbeat, and you speculated privately that these issues of tax reduction, fiscal efficiency, and reelection might be just such a storm in the making.

At this morning's administrative cabinet meeting, the superintendent immediately went to the specter of consolidation. She briefed the cabinet on national and regional trends, including a short synopsis of mandatory and permissive consolidation legislation on the books in all 50 states. She observed that several nearby states had already jumped on the consolidation bandwagon. While she framed today's session as an awareness event, it was clear this would be an ongoing priority at administrative and board levels.

Predictably, the superintendent asked to meet with you afterward to begin further analyzing the district's position and how it might benefit or lose under various scenarios. She asked you to form an expert task force to extensively map data on surrounding school districts, including enrollment, staffing, and facility facts, and to rank the findings in comparison to your own district. Most important, she said, would be to assess whether consolidation would help or harm your district: i.e., neither she nor you were worried that your district might be targeted for elimination, but rather that your district might well be regarded as capable of absorbing pieces of any wide-scale reorganization. To that end, she indicated that the board wished to see an evaluation of the impact of consolidation, including estimates of budget impact. She concluded by indicating that your task force should also examine surrounding states' profiles and experiences and draw findings helpful to your own situation. Your study, you learn, will be used in lobbying your local legislative representatives, the state school board association, and other power brokers in the state capital.

- What concerns do you believe will be immediately voiced by the community once this topic becomes public?
- How does this district's profile compare to your own in terms of these issues?
- What would be the local reaction in your school district if consolidation of any kind were proposed?

PORTFOLIO EXERCISES

- Research the history of financing schools in your state (your state department of education is likely to be a good source of information). Identify important issues such as the history of school district formation and reorganization, major state initiatives related to the financing of schools, and the relative autonomy (degree of centralization or decentralization) of educational decision-making permitted by your state legislature over time.
- Identify the major organizations in your state that have direct or indirect influence on educational policymaking at state and local levels. State the nature of their influence and reflect on the degree of impact they have on funding schools.
- Obtain a copy of the organizational chart in your school district and trace the formal authority and power structure.
- If there has been school finance litigation in your state, list and describe the relevant court cases. Using what you have learned in this chapter, analyze whether or not these cases have improved the equity and adequacy of the state school finance system.

NOTES

1 The federal fiscal year begins October 1 and ends September 30. For a current overview of spending see, U.S. Debt Clock, www.usdebtclock.org.

2 20 U.S.C. 401 et seq.

3 374 U.S. 483 at 493 (1954).

4 PL 89–10, 20 U.S.C. 2701 et seq.

5 PL 94–142, 20 U.S.C. 1499 et seq.

6 Daniel C. Rogers and Hirsch S. Ruchlin, *Economics and Education* (New York: Free Press, 1971), 5.

7 Theodore Schultz, "The Human Capital Approach to Education," in *Economic Factors Affecting the Financing of Education*, edited by Roe L. Johns, Irving J. Goffman, Kern Alexander, and Dewey H. Stollar (Gainesville, FL: National Educational Finance Project, 1970), 31.

8 U.S. Bureau of Education, "Cardinal Principles of Secondary Education," A Report of the Commission on Reorganization of Secondary Education, Bulletin, no. 35 (Washington, DC: Department of the Interior, U.S. Government Printing Office, 1918).

9 National Contest Committee of the National Association of Secondary School Principals, "National Contests for Schools 1951–52," *NASSP Bulletin* 35 (October 1951): 5–10.

10 Chamber of Commerce of the United States of America, *Education as an Investment in America* (Washington, DC: 1955), 31.

11 Habte Aklilum, *Education and Development: Views from the World Bank* (Washington, DC: World Bank, 1983) 8.

12 Theodore Schultz, "Education and Economic Growth," in *Social Forces Influencing American Education*, 16th Yearbook of the National Society of Education, edited by Nelson B. Henry and Paul A. Witty (Chicago: University of Chicago Press, 1961), 63.

13 Edward F. Denison published a series of studies examining these concepts. See, *The Sources of Economic Growth in the United States and the Alternatives Before Us* (New York: Committee for Economic Development, 1962);*Why Growth Rates Differ* (Washington, DC: Brookings Institution, 1967); *Why Growth Rates Differ: Postwar Experience In Nine Western Countries* (Washington, DC: Brookings Institution, George Allen & Unwin Ltd, 1968); *Accounting for United States' Economic Growth, 1929–1969* (Washington, DC: Brookings Institution, 1974); *Accounting for Slower Economic Growth: The United Sates in the 1970s* (Washington, DC: Brookings Institution, 1979).

14 U.S. Department of Education, *Digest of Education Statistics 2016*, "Estimated Average Annual Salary of Teachers in Public Elementary and Secondary Schools, by State: Selected Years, 1969–70 through 2015–16," Table 211.60 (Washington, DC: Institute of Education Sciences, National Center for Education Statistics, 2016), https://nces.ed.gov/programs/digest/d16/tables/dt16_211.60.asp

15 Edwyna Synar and Jeffrey Maiden, "A Comprehensive Model for Estimating the Financial Impact of Teacher Turnover," *Journal of Education Finance* 38, 2 (2012): 130–144.

16 Gary Becker, *Human Capital: A Theoretical and Empirical Analysis, with Special Reference to Education* (New York: National Bureau of Economic Research, 1964).

17 Adam Smith, *An Inquiry into the Nature and Causes of the Wealth of Nations* (New York: Modern Library, 1937), 734–735.

18 Thomas Jefferson, letter to Charles Yancey, January 6, 1816, page 7.

19 David Downes and Kirstine Hanson, "Welfare and Punishment in Comparative Perspective," in *Perspectives on Punishment: The Contours of Control*, edited by Sara Armstrong and Lesley McAra, 133–154 (Oxford, UK: Oxford University Press, 2006).

20 Alfred Marshall, "Education and Invention," in *Perspectives on the Economics of Education*, edited by Charles S. Benson (Boston: Houghton Mifflin, 1961), 83.

21 Center for American Progress. "Return on Educational Investment 2014: A District-by-District Evaluation of U.S. Educational Productivity." July 9, 2014. https://www.americanprogress.org/issues/education-k-12/reports/2014/07/09/93104/return-on-educational-investment-2/

22 Gail Robinson. "From Charters to Common Core, There's a Ceasefire in NY's School Wars." September 19, 2018. https://citylimits.org/2018/09/19/from-charters-to-common-core-new-york-sees-a-truce-in-the-school-wars/

23 Michael B. Katz, "From Voluntarism to Bureaucracy in American Education," in *Power and Ideology in Education*, edited by Jeremy Karabel and A. H. Halsey (New York: Oxford University Press, 1977), 394.

24 U.S. Const. Amend. X.

25 PL 78–16.

26 PL 78–346.

27 PL 81–815 and PL 81–874.

28 PL 85–865.

29 PL 95–525.

30 PL 98–377.

31 PL 106–398.

32 PL 107–122.

33 PL 108–76.

34 7 U.S.C. 301 et seq.

35 7 U.S.C. 321 et seq.

36 PL 74–182, 7 U.S.C. 17.

37 PL 75–430, 35 U.S.C. 1281.

38 PL 81–475.

39 PL 88–204.

40 PL 88–352.

41 PL 89–290.

42 PL 89–239.

43 PL 108–409.

44 PL 109–67.

45 PL 109–148.

46 See, e.g., PL 115–123 known as the Bipartisan Budget Act of 2018, granting assistance to students and schools impacted by Hurricanes Harvey, Irma, and Maria and the 2017 California wildfires. An additional $2.7 billion was directed to help K–12 school districts and schools as well as institutions of higher education (IHEs) in their recovery efforts.

47 A program created under PL 110–84 (2007) College Cost Reduction and Access Act.

48 56 S. Ct. 312 (1936).

49 57 S. Ct. 904 (1937).

50 347 U.S. at 493.

51 PL 88–352.

52 PL 89–910.

53 PL 94–142.

54 PL 97–35

55 PL 94–142.

56 *Pennsylvania Association of Retarded Citizens (PARC) v. Pennsylvania*, 343 F. Supp. 279 (1972).

57 PL 107–110 (2001).

58 PL 114–95 (2015).

59 A mill equals 1/1,000 of a dollar. Therefore, 1 mill (.001) equals $1 tax revenue per $1,000 assessed value (AV). The formula is AV × mills = tax yield. Therefore, assuming the urban acre in the example is valued at $1,000,000 × 0.010 = $10,000 tax yield. Likewise, $30,000

× 0.010 = $300. In the remote parcel, $3,000 × 0.010= $30. This does not consider fractional assessment, a practice in many states that takes only a portion of the market value of a piece of property, thereby yielding depressed revenue or perversely forcing a higher tax rate to generate enough revenue.

60 See, e.g., Carlee Poston Escue, "Adequate Yearly Progress as a Means of Funding Public Elementary and Secondary Education for Impoverished Students: Florida Funding," *Journal of Education Finance* 37, 4 (Spring 2012): 347–373.

61 U.S. Const. Amend. XIV, Sec. 1.

62 *Brown v. Board of Education* 347 U.S. 483.

63 *Burruss v. Wilkerson*, 310 F. Supp. 572 (1969).

64 *Van Dusartz v. Hatfield*, 334 F. Supp. 870 (Minn. 1971).

65 *San Antonio Independent School District v. Rodriguez*, 411 U.S. 1 (1973).

66 *Papasan v. Allain*, 478 U.S. 265 (1986), 756 F.2d 1087 (5th Cir. 1985).

67 *Plyler v. Doe*, 457 U.S. 202 (1982).

68 *Kadrmas v. Dickinson Public Schools*, 487 U.S. 450, 108 S. Ct. 2481 (1988).

69 R. Craig Wood, "A Critique of the Federal Challenge to Financing Public Education Along Racial Lines in *Lynch v. Alabama*: How the Plaintiffs, the Defendants, and the Federal District Court Erred in Examining the Funding of Public Education in Alabama," *Education Law and Policy Review* 1 (Spring 2014): 123–171.

70 *Serrano v. Priest*, 487 P.2d 1241 (1971).

71 487 P.2d 1241 (1971).

72 For an overview of school finance litigation trends, see, R. Craig Wood, David C. Thompson, John Dayton, and Christine Kiracofe, *Education Finance Law: Constitutional Challenges to State Aid Plans, An Analysis of Strategy*, fourth ed. (Dayton, OH: Education Law Association, 2015). To follow regular updates to school finance litigation in the 50 states, see http://schoolfunding.info

73 *Milliken v. Green*, vacated, 212 N.W.2d 711 (Mich. 1973), 203 N.W.2d 457 (Mich. 1972).

74 *Shofstall v. Hollins*, 515 P.2d 590 (Ariz. 1973).

75 *Blase v. Illinois*, 55 Ill. 2d 94, 302 N.E.2d 46 (Ill. 1973).

76 *Northshore v. Kinnear*, 530 P.2d 178 (Wash. 1974).

77 See, e.g., R. Craig Wood and William E. Thro, "Originalism and the State Education Clauses: The Louisiana Voucher Case as an Illustration," *Education Law Reporter* 302 (April 2014); Carlee Escue, William Thro, and R. Craig Wood, "Some Perspectives on Recent School Finance Litigation," *Education Law Reporter*, vol. 268, no. 2, August 18, 2011, 601–618.

78 *Robinson v. Cahill*, 287 A.2d 187 (N.J. Super. 1972), aff'd as mod., 303 A.2d 273 (N.J. 1973).

79 *Washakie County School District v. Herschler*, 606 P.2d 310 (1980).

80 *Edgewood v. Kirby*, 761 S.W.2d 859 (Tex. 1988).

81 *Edgewood Indep. Sch. Dist. v. Kirby*, 804 S.W.2d 491 (Tex. 1991), 777 S.W.2d 391 (Tex. 1989).

82 *West Orange-Cove Consolidated ISD v. Nelson*, 107 S.W.3d 558 (2001).

83 *Neeley v. W. Orange-Cove Consol. Indep. Sch. Dist.*, 176 S.W.3d 746 (Tex.2005).

84 *Texas Taxpayer and Student Fairness Coalition v. Scott*, Cause No. D-1-GN-11–003130, Travis County District Court, 200th Judicial District. (2013).

85 *Morath v. The Texas Taxpayer and Student Fairness Coalition*, Supreme Court of Texas. No. 14-0776 (Tex. May 12, 2016).

86 *Rose v. Council for Better Education*, 790 S.W.2d 186 (Ky. 1989).

87 *Abbott v. Burke*, 575 A.2d 359 (N.J. 1990).

88 *Abbott v. Burke*, 971 A.2d 989, (N.J. 2009), 693 A.2d 417 (N.J. 1997), 575 A.2d 359 (N.J. 1990); *Robinson v. Cahill*, 303 A.2d 273 (N.J. 1973).

89 *Abbott v. Burke* (M–1293–09), May 24, 2011.

90 *Abbott v. Burke,* (M–378) Order filed January 31, 2107.

91 *Hallion et al. v. Harrington,* Petition of Appeal, January 11, 2018.

92 For example, see R. Craig Wood and George Lange, "Selected State Education Finance Constitutional Litigation in the Context of Judicial Review," *Education Law Reporter* 207, no. 1 (May 4, 2006): 1–16; R. Craig Wood and George Lange, "The Justiciability Doctrine and Selected State Education Finance Constitutional Challenges," *Journal of Education Finance* 32, 1 (Summer 2006): 1–21; George Lange and R. Craig Wood, "Education Finance Litigation in North Carolina: Distinguishing *Leandro,*" *Journal of Education Finance* 32, 1 (Summer 2006): 36–70; R. Craig Wood and Alvin Schilling, "An Examination of *Abbeville v. South Carolina:* Constitutional Challenge in Financing Public Elementary and Secondary Education," *Education Law Reporter* 220, 2 (August 23, 2007): 453–470; John Dayton and R. Craig Wood, "School Funding Litigation: Scanning the Event Horizon," *Education Law Reporter* 224, 1 (November 29, 2007): 1–19; William Thro and R. Craig Wood, "The Constitutional Text Matters: Reflections on Recent School Finance Cases," *Education Law Reporter* 251, 2 (February 18, 2010): 510–532; R. Craig Wood, "Justiciability, Adequacy, Advocacy, and the 'American Dream,'" *Kentucky Law Journal* 98, 4 (2009–2010): 739–787; Faith E. Crampton and David. C. Thompson, "The Road Ahead for School Finance Reform: Legislative Trends 2011 and Beyond," *Journal of Education Finance* 37, 2 (Fall 2011): 185–204; David C. Thompson and Faith E. Crampton, "The Impact of School Finance Litigation: A Long View," *Journal of Education Finance* 27 (Winter 2002): 783–816; R. Craig Wood and David C. Thompson, "Politics of Plaintiffs and Defendants," in *Money, Politics, and Law*, eds. Karen DeMoss and Kenneth K. Wong (Larchmont, NY: Eye On Education, 2004), 37–45.

93 R. Craig Wood and R. Anthony Rolle, "Improving 'Adequacy' Concepts in Education Finance: A Heuristic Examination of the Professional Judgment Research Protocol," *Educational Considerations* 35, 1 (Fall, 2007): 51–55.

WEB RESOURCES

Association of School Business Officials, www.asbointl.org

Bureau of Labor Statistics, www.bls.gov

Center on Budget and Policy Priorities, www.cbpp.org

Council of the Great City Schools, www.cgcs.org

Education Law Center, www.edlawcenter.org

National Association of State Budget Officers, www.nsbo.org

National Center for Education Statistics, U.S. Department of Education, www.nces.ed.gov

National Conference of State Legislatures, www.ncsl.org

National Education Association, www.nea.org

National Education Finance Conference, www.nationaledfinance.com

National Governors Association, www.nga.org

U.S. Department of Education, www.ed.gov

RECOMMENDED RESOURCES

Alexander, Nicola A. and Hyunjun Kim. "Adequacy by Any Other Name: A Comparative Look at Educational Spending in the United States and the Republic of Korea." *Journal of Education Finance* 43, 1 (Summer 2017): 65–83.

Apple, Michael. *Official Knowledge: Democratic Education in a Conservative Age.* New York: Routledge, 2000.

Baker, Bruce and Mark Weber. "Beyond the Echo-Chamber: State Investments and Student Outcomes in U.S. Elementary and Secondary Education." *Journal of Education Finance* 42 1 (Summer 2016): 1–27.

Billger, Sherrilyn M. and Frank D. Beck. "The Determinants of High School Closures: Lessons from Longitudinal Data throughout Illinois." *Journal of Education Finance* 38, 2 (Fall 2012): 83–101.

Condron, Dennis J. "The Waning Impact of School Finance Litigation on Inequality in Per Student Revenue During the Adequacy Era." *Journal of Education Finance*, 43, 1 (Summer 2017): 1–20.

Dewey, John. *Democracy and Education.* New York: McMillan, 1916.

Gándara, Denisa and Robert K. Toutkoushian. "Updated Estimates of the Average Financial Return on Master's Degree Programs in the United States." *Journal of Education Finance* 43, 1 (Summer 2017): 21–44.

Goldstein, Dana. *The Teacher Wars.* New York: Anchor Books, 2014.

Houck, Eric A., R. Anthony Rolle, and Jiang He. "Examining School District Efficiency in Georgia." *Journal of Education Finance* 35, 4 (Spring 2010): 331–357.

Husted, Thomas and Lawrence Kenny. "The Political Economy of Education Finance: The Case of Texas." *Journal of Education Finance* 40, 1 (Summer 2014): 1–16.

Kozol, Jonathan. *Death at an Early Age.* New York: Houghton-Mifflin, 1967.

Kozol, Jonathan. *Savage Inequalities.* New York: HarperCollins, 1992.

Lockridge, Courtney and Jeffrey Maiden. "The Tangible Impact of School Finance Litigation." *Journal of Education Finance* 39, 4 (Spring 2014): 344–369.

McGrath Ellison, Jessica, William Owings, and Leslie S. Kaplan. "State Fiscal Effort and Juvenile Incarceration Rates: Are We Misdirecting our Investment in Human Capital?" *Journal of Education Finance* 43, 1 (Summer 2017): 45–64.

Nguyen-Hoang, Phuong. "School District Income Taxes and School Inputs: The Case of Ohio." *Journal of Education Finance* 40, 1 (Summer 2014): 38–59.

Owings, William A., and Leslie S. Kaplan. "The Alpha and Omega Syndrome: Is Intra-District Funding the Next Ripeness Factor?" *Journal of Education Finance* 36, 2 (Fall 2010): 162–185.

Owings, William A, Leslie S. Kaplan, and Monique Volman. "Education in the U.S. and the Netherlands: An Equity Comparison and a Few Big Questions." *Journal of Education Finance* 42, 2 (Fall 2015): 145–163.

Pittner, Nicholas A., Melissa M. Carleton, and Cassandra Casto. "School Funding in Ohio: From DeRolph to the Evidence-Based Model (EBM) and Beyond." *Journal of Education Finance* 36, 2 (Fall 2010): 111–142.

Ravitch, Diane. *The Death and Life of the Great American School System: How Testing and Choice are Undermining Education.* New York: Basic Books, 2010.

Saleh, Matthew. "Modernizing San Antonio Independent School District v. Rodriguez: How Evolving Supreme Court Jurisprudence Changes the Face of Education Finance Litigation." *Journal of Education Finance* 37, 2 (Fall 2011): 99–129.

Salmon, Richard G. "The Evolution of Virginia Public School Finance: From the Beginnings to Today's Difficulties." *Journal of Education Finance* 36, 2 (Fall 2010): 143–161.

Springer, Matthew G., Matthew J. Pepper, and Bonnie Ghosh-Dastidar. "Supplemental Educational Services and Student Test Score Gains: Evidence from a Large, Urban School District." *Journal of Education Finance* 39, 4 (Spring 2014): 370–403.

Ullrich, Laura D. and Matthew N. Murray. "A Constrained Bureaucratic Model of Behavioral Responses to School Finance Reform." *Journal of Education Finance* 42, 4 (Spring 2017): 386–413.

Whitehead, Alfred North. *The Aims of Education and Other Essays.* New York: The Free Press, 1933.

Basic Funding Structures

THE CONTEXT OF FUNDING SCHOOLS

The journey so far has made it clear that the context of funding public schools is highly complex, largely due to the turbulent political, economic, and social environment in which education operates. Unlike the private sector, the goal of government is to provide for the public good rather than to pursue profit. Simply stated, the goal of a private sector business in a capitalist system is to offer products or services that consumers are willing to buy at a price that will yield a profit for business owners and investors. If products or services are overpriced, demand will be weak, or if a competitor offers a better/cheaper version, the business must adapt or fail. In contrast, public goods like education historically have relied upon tax revenues for survival, albeit from a sometimes resistant citizenry. At the same time, public schools compete with other government-funded services for limited tax revenues. Furthermore, depending on state statutes, public schools increasingly compete for tax dollars with nonprofit and for-profit entities through the expansion of charter schools owned by education management organizations (EMOs) and vouchers, allowing students to choose private, nonprofit, and religious schools. Given such context, the crux of this chapter becomes clear: Public schools are increasingly called upon to face competition and to improve the efficiency with which they expend tax revenues. Although businesses have a straightforward understanding of the products they sell, there is no broad societal agreement on what education's products should be. Rather, education's outcomes are multidimensional and often subject to disagreement as to their relevance, importance, or priority. In addition, education's stakeholders, (parents, communities, and taxpayers) often lack a clear understanding of the mix of local, state, and federal tax revenues that support public schools, so that some never get beyond the unhappy feeling that the taxes they pay for schools are too high—regardless of the actual dollar amount.

Although the topic of education's funding sources is complex, a working grasp of the issues can be gained by reviewing the sources and types of revenue used to support schools. Relatedly, a deeper understanding of school funding context comes by considering the elements of school funding formula fairness as it has developed over the last century in response to legislative and litigative pressures. Finally, it is important to grasp the current and prospective status of school funding by exploring how states actually fund schools. In brief, the politics of schools, values, and money go hand in glove with state-by-state revenue sources and school funding systems.

WHAT IS THE OVERARCHING TAX SYSTEM?

A consistent theme in this textbook is that revenue for schools is a source of genuine conflict in many states and communities. The roots of this struggle arise from disputes over what schools should do and the unavoidable fact that school revenue is derived predominantly from taxation, some of which involves little or no direct input from taxpayers. Although other revenue sources exist, it is unrealistic to think that taxes are less than the lion's share of school resources or that taxes will be replaced soon by some new pool of money.

The history of taxation is extensively detailed in many sources. Taxes are essential to support the myriad public services required by a civilized society. As seen in the previous chapter, a strong national defense, interstate highways, stable social benefits, and intergovernmental revenue-sharing are among the indispensable services funded by federal taxation. State tax revenues provide many comparable services, albeit for their specific citizenry, such as state highways and social safety net programs, along with oversight of each state's natural resources such as parks, lakes, and rivers. City streets, police and fire protection, and local parks are among the local tax benefits enjoyed by citizens. Of especial importance, local taxes provide many highly visible services, including a significant contribution to school costs. The overarching tax system therefore has three principal players in the form of *federal*, *state*, and *local* units of government.[1] Each plays a different role, although overlap is common; and each level of government has a relationship to schools in some varying proportion.

What is the Federal Tax System?

Today's federal tax system is far removed from the nation's awkward early attempts to create a federal tax structure. Federal tax revenues today support a wide range of programs, from national defense to environmental protection. Many taxes (see Figure 3.1) are used to finance these key services. Of these, individual income tax revenues comprise 47% and payroll tax revenues 33%. Corporate income tax revenue is a distant third at 11%, though the latter represents a significant shift (−2%) since the last edition of this textbook.

Ironically, in a nation born of suspicion toward central government, the federal tax system today is both massive and complex; it also is the object of frequent criticism across the political spectrum. Fiscal conservatives argue that federal taxes are too high and bemoan the complexity of the tax system. Budget hawks advocate for simplifying the tax code and granting tax cuts to the private sector to stimulate the economy and create jobs. In addition, they are often critical of social programs, including education, along with the levels of tax revenues dedicated to them. At the other end of the spectrum are political liberals and progressives who assert that the federal tax system is regressive and needing a major redesign to tax those with the greatest ability to pay, be they individuals or corporations, so that all pay a fair share. In general, such views are more tolerant of a complex tax system, asserting that complexity is an integral part of a robust and fair tax system. In addition, they advocate for tax-funded social safety nets as a public good that reinvests and repays immediate and intergenerational benefits to individuals and the nation.

At its most elemental level, the debate over federal taxation is rooted in efforts to limit the role of central government. Historically a nation of tax protesters, Americans have always fought federal taxation. Numerous attempts at centralized taxation dating

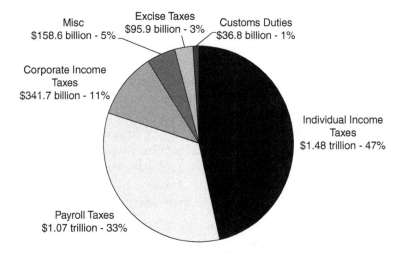

Federal Tax Revenue 2015: $3.18 Trillion

Misc
$158.6 billion - 5%

Excise Taxes
$95.9 billion - 3%

Customs Duties
$36.8 billion - 1%

Corporate Income
Taxes
$341.7 billion - 11%

Individual Income
Taxes
$1.48 trillion - 47%

Payroll Taxes
$1.07 trillion - 33%

FIGURE 3.1 Federal Tax Revenue by Type of Tax for Fiscal Year 2015 (projected)

Source: National Priorities Project. "Federal Revenue: Where Does the Money Come From?" https://www.nationalpriorities.org/budget-basics/federal-budget-101/revenues/

from the 1600s were bitterly opposed by the colonists and underlay the Revolutionary War in 1776. Even the war itself was a target of tax protest, marking the first instance of a budget deficit as the new nation struggled to pay war debt. Early presidents and Congressional leaders were themselves mostly anti-tax, leading to a weak federal tax system that depended mostly on tariffs and customs for the first 125 years of nationhood. Repeated efforts to establish a federal income tax failed or were rescinded shortly after passage into law, including a lawsuit in which the U.S. Supreme Court invalidated an 1894 income tax law on the grounds that the federal Constitution did not expressly authorize Congress to collect such a tax.[2]

However, the many needs of a growing nation caused an early impoverished Congress to create the structure that eventually became the tax system that exists today. In 1909, Congress proposed the Sixteenth Amendment to the U.S. Constitution, granting itself the power to "lay and collect taxes on incomes, from whatever source derived, without apportionment among the States, and without regard to any census or enumeration." The amendment was finally ratified in 1913, whereupon Congress imposed a tax of 1% on personal incomes which subsequently was expanded and modified in numerous ways on many occasions in order to meet a broad range of federal policy goals. Administration of federal tax laws emanating from ratification of the amendment eventually evolved into the large federal agency now known as the Internal Revenue Service, collecting sums of money that most people find incomprehensible. By 2021, federal tax collections are projected to total $4.57 trillion, up $1.32 trillion since the last edition of this text (see Table 3.1).

Although the federal tax system and its revenues have expanded over time, the path has been far from smooth. Even in times when Congress has faced voter pressure to reduce taxes, people have continued to expect a strong national defense, a sound retirement system, safe highways, and more. Education has been a beneficiary of federal funding, although the federal role has been limited because the Tenth Amendment left education to the individual states. Still, federal involvement in education and its funding have a long history, as the federal government became involved as early as 1787 through the Northwest Ordinance which granted land to states for educational purposes. As seen in Chapter 1 earlier, the list of federally aided education programs is long and includes programs like special education, school meals, and vocational education to name just a few. In brief, although the federal role has often been indirect, the dollars have not been trivial, as federal funds for elementary and secondary education in 2016 through the U.S. Department of Education totaled $82 billion,[3] a sum excluding other federal agency programs that directly or indirectly benefit schools such as the U.S. Department of Agriculture's child nutrition programs (school breakfast, lunch, and afterschool snacks); Health and Human Services Head Start program; and the U.S. Department of Labor's youth employment and training programs.

What is the State Tax System?

An important aspect of taxation in the United States has been the simultaneous development of multiple tax systems. States have played a key role in the nation's history, so much so that even today issues of states' rights are debated vigorously in many forums.

TABLE 3.1 Summary of Receipts, Outlays, and Surpluses or Deficits (–): 1789–2021 in millions of dollars

Year	Total		
	Receipts	Outlays	Surplus or Deficit (–)
1789–1849	1,160	1,090	70
1850–1900	14,462	15,453	–991
1910	676	694	–18
1920	6,649	6,358	291
1930	4,058	3,320	738
1940	6,548	9,468	–2,920
1950	39,443	42,562	–3,119
1960	92,492	92,191	301
1970	192,807	195,649	–2,842
1980	517,112	590,941	–73,830
1990	1,031,958	1,252,993	–221,036
2000	2,025,191	1,788,950	236,241
2001	1,991,082	1,862,846	128,236
2002	1,853,136	2,010,894	–157,758
2003	1,782,314	2,159,899	–377,585
2004	1,880,114	2,292,841	–412,727
2005	2,153,611	2,471,957	–318,346
2006	2,406,869	2,655,050	–248,181
2007	2,567,985	2,728,686	–160,701
2008	2,523,991	2,982,544	–458,553
2009	2,104,989	3,517,677	–1,412,688
2010	2,162,706	3,457,079	–1,294,373
2011	2,303,466	3,603,056	–1,299,590
2012	2,449,988	3,536,951	–1,086,963
2013	2,775,103	3,454,647	–679,544
2014	3,021,487	3,506,114	–484,627
2015	3,249,886	3,688,292	–438,406
2016 estimate	3,335,502	3,951,307	–615,805
2017 estimate	3,643,742	4,147,224	–503,482
2018 estimate	3,898,625	4,352,222	–453,597
2019 estimate	4,095,054	4,644,309	–549,255
2020 estimate	4,345,701	4,879,818	–534,117
2021 estimate	4,571,990	5,124,248	–552,258

Source: Adapted from Office of Management and Budget. "Historical Tables: Table 1.1 "Summary of Receipts, Outlays, and Surpluses or Deficits (–) 1789–2021. (2018). https://obamawhitehouse.archives.gov/omb/budget/ Historicals

People feel strongly about the relationship of government to its constituents, and the authority of states has been jealously guarded.

The extensive tax nature ascribed to the federal government is also true of state tax systems. The dissimilarity, though, is the number of variations on tax themes, as there are 50 states but only one federal government. As a result, each state's tax system has been affected by unique social, economic, and political factors, and further shaped by the relationship of states to the federal government.

As discussed earlier, colonial tax systems predated federal efforts to levy taxes. In fact, the system of elected representation to Congress guaranteed that states would fiercely guard their autonomy, as the U.S. Constitution granted to the states all powers not reserved to Congress itself. Differences in geography, climate, economy, and preferences further ensured that states would approach taxation differently. Many of the earliest colonial government structures were purposely aimed at thwarting a strong federal seat of power, starting with the Virginia legislature's defiance in 1619 of the Virginia Company's attempts to revoke certain freedoms. By 1700, all colonies had written charters guaranteeing liberties—all born of conflict between the Crown and independent-minded colonialists.

Not surprisingly, colonial—and later state—systems of taxation were tightly linked to local politics and economies. As the need for revenue expanded with the population, the New England colonies favored taxing personal property, land, and houses in the belief that every person's taxpaying ability was different and that everyone should pay. Concentrated wealth in the South meant only a few persons would bear the brunt of taxation, so a revenue system based on exports and imports was developed to shift taxes away from the wealthy. Other taxes, such as poll and faculty taxes, were used as early primitive forms of income tax.[4] The middle colonies picked up this system and made additional refinements. Colonies also ran lotteries or invented other special revenue sources.

It cannot be overstated how stringent state curbs on federal power were deliberate. The U.S. Constitution gave the federal government only limited power to levy taxes for the purpose of paying debts and for the general welfare of the nation. States, however, were granted full (plenary) powers, including control of local government; chartering of towns; building of roads and bridges; protection of civil liberties; and, of course, care of the federal government via representation in Congress. Such responsibility was not free to states, however. By the end of the Civil War, colonial-style tax systems were no longer adequate given these broad responsibilities and a growing population, and the answer seemed to be state authority to tax all property—both real and personal. However, widespread tax evasion was rampant, in that land, buildings, and livestock were visible while other property such as bonds, notes, and negotiable instruments was easily concealed. The unintended effect was the shifting of the tax burden to property owners who could not hide their wealth.

Around 1880, study commissions began seeking ways to improve state tax systems, especially administration of the property tax. This resulted in the creation of tax equalization boards, efforts to improve property assessments, prosecution of tax evasion, and refinement of tax requirements on various property types. Efforts still

TABLE 3.2 State Reliance on Major Tax Sources: 2015

State	Property	General Sales	Individual Income	Corporate Income	Other Taxes (a)
U.S.	31.1%	23.5%	23.5%	3.7%	18.2%
Ala.	17.2%	29.9%	22.6%	3.5%	26.9%
Alaska	57.2%	8.9%	0.0%	8.8%	25.1%
Ariz.	29.8%	39.1%	15.8%	2.9%	12.4%
Ark.	18.1%	37.0%	23.1%	4.1%	17.6%
Calif.	24.8%	21.8%	34.1%	3.9%	15.3%
Colo.	30.1%	26.3%	25.4%	2.7%	15.5%
Conn.	38.4%	15.3%	30.8%	2.6%	12.9%
Del.	18.0%	0.0%	26.6%	9.0%	46.4%
Fla.	35.7%	34.2%	0.0%	3.2%	26.9%
Ga.	32.0%	25.6%	27.0%	2.8%	12.7%
Hawaii	17.6%	36.9%	22.8%	0.8%	21.8%
Idaho	28.1%	25.8%	26.0%	3.8%	16.3%
Ill.	36.4%	17.7%	21.6%	5.5%	18.9%
Ind.	25.4%	28.7%	25.4%	3.6%	16.9%
Iowa	33.0%	22.6%	24.1%	3.1%	17.2%
Kans.	32.8%	31.5%	17.7%	3.6%	14.3%
Ky.	20.7%	19.5%	32.1%	5.4%	22.3%
La.	22.0%	38.5%	16.2%	1.4%	22.0%
Maine	40.2%	18.9%	22.6%	2.5%	15.8%
Md.	26.6%	12.6%	37.6%	2.9%	20.3%
Mass.	35.6%	13.5%	33.6%	5.2%	12.1%
Mich.	34.5%	23.2%	23.4%	3.0%	16.0%
Minn.	25.8%	17.3%	31.8%	4.5%	20.6%
Miss.	26.5%	31.2%	16.2%	4.9%	21.2%
Mo.	27.2%	26.5%	28.1%	2.3%	15.9%
Mont.	37.3%	0.0%	28.3%	4.0%	30.4%
Nebr.	37.5%	22.6%	23.4%	3.6%	12.9%
Nev.	23.4%	39.7%	0.0%	0.0%	36.9%
N.H.	65.7%	0.0%	1.6%	9.3%	23.4%
N.J.	46.1%	15.3%	22.2%	4.3%	12.0%
N.M.	18.6%	37.4%	16.0%	2.9%	25.2%
N.Y.	30.9%	16.7%	32.0%	7.0%	13.4%
N.C.	25.1%	24.9%	29.4%	3.5%	17.1%
N.D.	13.3%	23.2%	7.7%	2.7%	53.1%
Ohio	28.8%	27.6%	26.9%	0.5%	16.2%

(Continued)

TABLE 3.2 Continued

State	Property	General Sales	Individual Income	Corporate Income	Other Taxes (a)
Okla.	18.3%	33.0%	22.5%	2.7%	23.5%
Ore.	32.2%	0.0%	41.6%	4.0%	22.2%
Pa.	29.9%	16.9%	25.8%	4.7%	22.7%
R.I.	43.2%	16.8%	21.2%	3.1%	15.7%
S.C.	33.0%	24.1%	22.3%	2.3%	18.4%
S.D.	36.0%	40.5%	0.0%	0.1%	23.4%
Tenn.	26.4%	40.7%	1.4%	6.5%	25.0%
Tex.	42.0%	36.3%	0.0%	0.0%	21.7%
Utah	26.9%	24.3%	29.1%	3.4%	16.3%
Vt.	43.8%	10.4%	19.5%	3.1%	23.1%
Va.	34.1%	13.7%	31.9%	2.2%	18.2%
Wash.	29.6%	45.9%	0.0%	0.0%	24.5%
W.Va.	21.7%	17.3%	25.6%	2.5%	32.9%
Wis.	34.7%	19.6%	26.3%	3.8%	15.6%
Wyo.	36.7%	28.0%	0.0%	0.0%	35.3%
D.C.	31.7%	18.5%	26.3%	6.3%	17.2%

Source: Tax Foundation. "Facts and Figures 2018: How Does Your State Compare?" Table 8. Washington, DC (2018). https://taxfoundation.org/facts-figures-2018/

met with limited success as equalization proved unpopular and tax evasion and resistance were impossible to eliminate. The numerous woes of property tax administration ultimately led to many recommendations that states should abandon the property tax in favor of other tax bases. Faced with such problems, states began to rely less on property, and by 1920 several states had adopted both individual and corporate income tax plans. Although the property tax at the state level was never completely eradicated, the majority of states now have additionally enacted income taxes, as well as other taxes on commercial transactions such as sales and excise taxes (see Table 3.2).

Over the last century, growth in state taxes has been phenomenal. The earliest records dating from 1902 indicate that state legislatures were levying only small property taxes and other miscellaneous taxes, while now they assess and collect a much wider range of taxes, with substantial revenues from sales, gross receipts, and income taxes (see Table 3.2). Table 3.3 portrays the sum and source of state tax collections—a truly astounding growth record when compared to the $156 million collected in 1902 and measured in 2018 at an astounding $929.9 billion only 106 years later.

State aid to K–12 schools today constitutes, on average, about 35.4% of state budgets,[5] in large part because the U.S. Constitution prevents the federal government from assuming a direct educational role. These funds make up the lion's share—and the arguments and litigations that rage—around the complex state aid formulas discussed later in this chapter.

TABLE 3.3 State Government Tax Collections by Total and Source 2016

Geographic area name	Year	Meaning of Tax Type	Amount ($1,000)
United States	2016	Total Taxes	929,891,144
United States	2016	Property Taxes	18,291,411
United States	2016	Sales and Gross Receipts Taxes	441,289,331
United States	2016	General Sales and Gross Receipts Taxes	292,411,243
United States	2016	Selective Sales and Gross Receipts Taxes	148,878,088
United States	2016	Alcoholic Beverages Sales Tax	6,612,056
United States	2016	Amusements Sales Tax	7,588,813
United States	2016	Insurance Premiums Sales Tax	20,448,622
United States	2016	Motor Fuels Sales Tax	43,855,057
United States	2016	Pari-Mutuels Sales Tax	121,148
United States	2016	Public Utilities Sales Tax	13,291,415
United States	2016	Tobacco Products Sales Tax	18,009,890
United States	2016	Other Selective Sales and Gross Receipts Taxes	38,951,087
United States	2016	License Taxes	53,903,812
United States	2016	Alcoholic Beverages License	638,031
United States	2016	Amusements License	549,250
United States	2016	Corporations in General License	5,608,277
United States	2016	Hunting and Fishing License	1,595,245
United States	2016	Motor Vehicle License	25,548,818
United States	2016	Motor Vehicle Operators License	2,596,698
United States	2016	Public Utilities License	1,249,473
United States	2016	Occupation and Business License, NEC	14,702,043
United States	2016	Other License Taxes	1,415,977
United States	2016	Income Taxes	391,758,772
United States	2016	Individual Income Taxes	344,732,255
United States	2016	Corporations Net Income Taxes	47,026,517
United States	2016	Other Taxes	24,647,818
United States	2016	Death and Gift Taxes	5,133,756
United States	2016	Documentary and Stock Transfer Taxes	9,169,576
United States	2016	Severance Taxes	7,720,876
United States	2016	Taxes, NEC	2,623,610

Source: U.S. Census Bureau. American FactFinder. State Government Tax Collections: 2016. Excerpted from https://factfinder.census.gov/faces/tableservices/jsf/pages/productview.xhtml?src=bkmk

What is the Local Tax System?

What many people think of as local taxes are, in reality, state taxes; that is, local governments, including school districts, have no taxing authority except by state statutory permission. Hence, the local property tax, often a major funding source for schools, is actually a tax that the state has delegated to local governments. In addition to state aid, school districts in most states rely on local property tax revenues for a portion of funding even though they likely share that tax base with other local governmental units like counties, cities, and even the state itself. States may also allow localities to levy a local sales tax.

Though federal and state units of government have tended to be centrally structured, local government is often more fragmented to include multiple jurisdictions such as counties, cities, school districts, villages and townships, as well as special taxing districts for entities like public libraries and sanitation systems. Because local governmental units are created and controlled by the state, they are limited in what they can tax and the level of that taxation. Yet the amount of tax revenues collected by localities is not insignificant (see Table 3.4). In 2016, they collected over $1 billion, of which $487 million was property tax revenue. The sales tax accounted for nearly $677 million in local revenues. Other noteworthy local taxes include those on individual income and corporate income.

TABLE 3.4 State and Local Government Finance by Level of Government and State 2016

Description	State and Local Government Amount	State Government Amount	Local Government Amount
Revenue[1]	$3,401,787,688	$2,136,454,470	$1,802,160,151
General revenue[1]	$3,008,099,919	$1,909,321,839	$1,635,605,013
Intergovernmental revenue[1]	$690,198,339	$637,167,820	$589,857,452
From Federal Government	$690,198,339	$621,508,922	$68,689,417
From State government[1]	$0	$0	$521,168,035
From local governments[1]	$0	$15,658,898	$0
General revenue from own sources	$2,317,901,580	$1,272,154,019	$1,045,747,561
Taxes	$1,599,449,033	$922,855,839	$676,593,194
Property	$503,238,675	$15,945,411	$487,293,264
Sales and gross receipts	$558,846,627	$441,124,499	$117,722,128
General sales	$376,911,326	$291,472,708	$85,438,618
Selective sales	$181,935,301	$149,651,791	$32,283,510
Motor fuel	$45,126,322	$43,731,888	$1,394,434
Alcoholic beverage	$7,256,064	$6,613,628	$642,436
Tobacco products	$18,446,621	$17,981,249	$465,372
Public utilities	$27,628,474	$13,069,580	$14,558,894
Other selective sales	$83,477,820	$68,255,446	$15,222,374
Individual income	$376,297,498	$343,620,739	$32,676,759
Corporate income	$54,259,322	$46,201,841	$8,057,481
Motor vehicle license	$27,501,605	$25,566,382	$1,935,223
Other taxes	$79,305,306	$50,396,967	$28,908,339

[1] Duplicative intergovernmental transactions are excluded.

Source: United States Census Bureau. "2016 State & Local Government Finance Historical Datasets and Tables. Washington, DC (2018). https://www.census.gov/data/datasets/2016/econ/local/public-use-datasets.html

TABLE 3.5 State-by-State Taxpayer Burden Rank by Tax Source

State	Overall Index Rank	Corporate Tax	Individual Income Tax	Sales Tax	Property Tax
Alabama	35	22	22	49	12
Alaska	3	26	1	5	38
Arizona	21	13	18	47	6
Arkansas	39	39	30	44	22
California	48	32	50	41	13
Colorado	18	18	15	39	14
Connecticut	44	31	37	27	49
Delaware	15	50	34	1	20
Florida	4	19	1	29	10
Georgia	36	10	42	28	23
Hawaii	27	14	31	23	16
Idaho	20	25	23	26	3
Illinois	29	36	16	35	45
Indiana	9	23	10	9	4
Iowa	40	48	33	19	39
Kansas	23	38	19	31	19
Kentucky	33	27	29	14	36
Louisiana	42	40	27	50	30
Maine	28	41	26	8	41
Maryland	43	20	46	18	42
Massachusetts	22	35	12	12	46
Michigan	12	8	14	11	21
Minnesota	46	43	45	25	28
Mississippi	24	24	20	38	35
Missouri	16	5	28	24	7
Montana	6	12	21	3	9
Nebraska	25	28	24	13	40
Nevada	5	33	1	42	8
New Hampshire	7	45	9	2	44
New Jersey	50	42	49	46	50
New Mexico	34	24	35	40	1
New York	49	7	49	43	47
North Carolina	11	3	13	20	32
North Dakota	30	16	36	34	2
Ohio	45	47	47	30	11
Oklahoma	32	9	38	36	15

(Continued)

TABLE 3.5 Continued

State	Overall Index Rank	Corporate Tax	Individual Income Tax	Sales Tax	Property Tax
Oregon	10	34	32	4	18
Pennsylvania	26	44	17	21	33
Rhode Island	41	30	39	22	43
South Carolina	37	15	41	32	24
South Dakota	2	1	1	33	25
Tennessee	14	21	8	45	29
Texas	13	49	6	37	37
Utah	8	4	11	17	5
Vermont	47	37	44	16	48
Virginia	31	6	40	10	31
Washington	17	46	6	48	27
West Virginia	19	17	25	15	17
Wisconsin	38	29	43	7	26
Wyoming	1	1	1	6	34
District of Columbia	(47)	(26)	(43)	(34)	(45)

Source: Tax Foundation. "Facts and Figures 2018: How Does Your State Compare?" Washington, DC (2018). https://taxfoundation.org/publications/facts-and-figures/

Like other units of local government, schools depend on a mix of revenue sources, and that mix varies across states. In general, schools rely on approximately equal proportions of state aid and local property taxes, with federal aid a distant third place. This represents a striking evolution from the Common Schools Movement days in the nineteenth century when schools were almost completely reliant on the local property tax.

Tax System Summary

School districts draw on key revenue sources—federal, state, and local—each with advantages and disadvantages. First, federal aid is limited in scope and often targeted to specific purposes. Second, state aid has become increasingly important, as states have responded to school finance reform and litigation. Third, school districts in many states still depend on the local property tax to fund a meaningful ratio of their budgets, such that in 2015 the average mix of school district revenues was 46.6% state, 45.0% local, and 8.5% federal (see Table 2.4 in the previous chapter), although state-by-state differences in ratios and taxpayer burden are vast (see Table 3.5[6]). Fourth, schools usually have been unable to tap tax bases other than property, as most states do not permit schools to tax sales, income, or other kinds of wealth. The net sum is that schools are still primarily supported by state and local taxation, with limited but helpful federal assistance.

In brief, the overarching tax system in the United States is made up of federal, state, and local tax structures, with the federal system relying heavily on the individual income tax and providing only a small portion of school district monies. State tax systems rely primarily on revenues from individual income and general sales taxes, with the lion's share of state aid to schools dependent on the social, economic, and political environment in each state. At the local level, tax systems derive a large percentage of revenue from real property taxation, with a large portion going to schools—a reality that has caused the property tax to be (incorrectly) seen as the school tax. From this flows the observation that revenues available to schools are three-fold in most cases: i.e., sales and income taxes (through state aid) and property taxes (through the local level). Finally, it is clear that schools compete at all levels for tax revenue because there are practical limits on the amount of taxes that can be generated—i.e., those same dollars must be apportioned among the many worthy governmental programs that serve the public good.

STATE FUNDING FOR SCHOOLS

Having learned that taxation is the fount of school monies, the next step is to understand how state aid distribution formulas work. This issue goes much deeper than tax systems, as it defines the heart of resource fairness and equal educational opportunity. If the *amount* of money flowing to schools is important to the academic success of children, then it follows that *how* money flows from the state to local districts is equally critical.

The final part of this chapter therefore speaks to operationalizing *adequacy* and *equity* in school funding. The first goal is to understand how states distribute aid to school districts. The second goal is to understand the principles of fair aid formulas and other mechanisms for distributing funds. The third goal is to consider fairness in context of having enough money to effectively carry out the aims of education. In other words, all the remaining topics in this book have no real-world impact if school revenues are inadequate or inequitable.

THE DEVELOPMENT OF STATE SCHOOL AID FORMULAS

In most states, the ad valorum (real estate) property tax is a major source of local revenue for schools. At the same time, virtually no school district in the nation is entirely at the mercy of its local tax base for funding education. Variations in size of the local tax base across any state, often expressed as the measure of school district wealth, are so extreme that even the most fiscally conservative state lawmaker probably recognizes a role for state aid. Indeed, most states have tried to develop state school aid schemes that speak to some basic elements of adequacy and equity. State aid formulas thus attract attention at federal, state, and local levels, although states have been the principal actor in designing and implementing aid formulas, both by choice and by force of litigation.

Under these conditions, state aid formulas are legislative policy mechanisms used to redress natural disparities in educational opportunity that would occur if schools were entirely reliant on their respective local taxable wealth. It is not hard to imagine the size of such disparity absent state aid intervention, as most states have wide extremes of local wealth, i.e., tax capacity. A fairly common case is a public utility power plant located in a low enrollment school district that creates vast wealth per pupil in the form of taxable property. In contrast, another district in the same state having similar enrollment size may have only marginal agricultural property for its tax base. Disparities in wealth per pupil in such cases can easily be 100:1 or greater, meaning that the property-wealthy district can raise $100 for every $1 raised in the property-poor district under equal tax rates! The example in Figure 3.2 is quite common, with the wealthiest district able to raise $25 million locally, five times more than the poorest district—all at a uniform tax rate of 100 mills (or $100 per $1,000 of assessed property valuation)—albeit ignoring the fact that a property-poor district politically cannot tax itself at such a high rate. The choice is vastly different tax rates to levy the same amount of revenue per pupil, *or* vastly different revenue per pupil. Any number of variations on this example can be

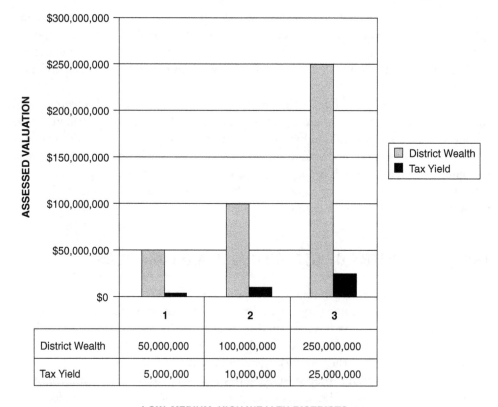

	1	2	3
District Wealth	50,000,000	100,000,000	250,000,000
Tax Yield	5,000,000	10,000,000	25,000,000

LOW, MEDIUM, HIGH WEALTH DISTRICTS

FIGURE 3.2 Tax Capacity at 100 Mills Uniform Effort

imagined to fit any state's profile. For example, urban school districts often have less per-pupil property wealth than nearby affluent suburbs due to their higher enrollments and lower tax bases. In sum, a state school aid formula's purpose is to reduce or eliminate tax base differences by offsetting the effects of taxable wealth disparity on equal educational opportunity.

Americans have never been enthusiastic about paying taxes. Part of the reluctance has been cultural, but real problems have plagued tax administration, further aggravating an already sensitive situation. As discussed earlier, tax evasion has hounded all levels of government because some people have refused to pay taxes and—in the more modern case—tax bases have eroded because people have managed to legally reduce or avoid taxes. The many tax problems faced by government led to extensive studies of tax fairness and administration, so that technical knowledge about good tax systems grew rapidly during the first half of the last century.

Growth of the nation's schools, along with growth in state responsibility for education, also led to state interest in providing at least some aid so that by 1890 states were providing nearly $34 million to schools, or about 24% of total revenue. A goodly portion of that aid was sparked by the new concept of educational program equity that followed on the heels of the first state studies that had revealed vast disparities arising from local tax base reliance. Although state aid predates the work of Cubberley,[7] he is credited with the dramatic rise in interest in state aid via his 1906 monograph that set the tone for the future. Cubberley's thesis was simple by today's standard, but it was deeply profound for his time: i.e., he argued that all the children of the state are equal and entitled to equal advantages. In studying several states, Cubberley concluded that few, if any, shared this philosophy because educational quality varied greatly while rising or falling in tandem with local property wealth.

Cubberley's work sparked a growth industry as other scholars undertook similar studies. Updegraff's[8] work in 1922 provided another step extending this line of thinking. Studying rural schools in the state of New York, he argued that state aid should vary by local wealth and in relationship to local tax effort. Where Cubberley had shown the need for aid and birthed the concept of equality, Updegraff introduced the ideas of equalization and reward for tax effort; that is, districts could receive more state aid by taxing themselves to a greater extent. The next major advance came in 1923 in the work of George Strayer and Robert Haig.[9] Accepting all that had already been done, Strayer and Haig took another giant leap by advocating that concepts of equality and equalization should also result in a measure of minimum educational opportunity. Their view obligated the state to go beyond merely providing money; rather, they urged that the state must require some metric of program equality. Additionally, they argued that such a program should be available under uniform tax effort. The result was a foundation aid program, whereby the state would guarantee a fiscal foundation on which local districts could build.

Still another significant step was taken by Paul Mort[10] in 1924. Mort extended the minimum program concept by defining the weighted pupil, arguing that educational programs must have different costs in order to be equal. For example, small enrollment schools cost more due to diseconomies of scale. His contribution was to press how states determine aid to districts, arguing that aid should vary along multiple criteria based on estimating true program costs rather than just distributing aid in a supposedly neutral fashion.

The ideas of these early researchers were widely utilized as states struggled to conceptualize how they should aid schools. One last major breakthrough was less enthusiastically received, however. Henry Morrison,[11] writing in 1930, was so disturbed by the extremes in quality of educational programs that he argued for abolishing all school districts in favor of a complete state takeover. This was not radical in his view because he believed that since states had the ultimate duty to control education, inequality could not be resolved until tax base and program control were state affairs. Obviously, his thinking ran counter to local control—a sentiment that endures today despite the uniformity that comes with a statewide funding system.

The creation of state aid plans clearly had basic fairness in mind by seeking ways to make educational opportunity more equal through the use of money. States worked at developing aid plans using these criteria, with each plan uniquely reflecting their educational, fiscal, and political philosophies and realities. For example, states taking an aggressive view of state responsibility for education developed school aid plans that made the state a fuller funding partner. Conversely, states favoring local control tended to devise aid plans that left considerable local freedom to exceed educational minimums. These realities were the basis for the development of state aid plans that fall into several general types, based on what states envisioned as fair. Known broadly as grant-in-aid plans, over the years these aid schemes have become further refined as flat grants, equalization grants, multi-tier grants, and full state funding grants.

Flat Grants

The earliest form of state aid, known as the flat grant, was a flat sum of money per unit, such as pupil or teacher, paid to school districts without concern for a local cost-share or local ability to pay. This plan was justified as distributionally neutral. Critics, however, argued that taxable wealth disparity remained unchanged and that aid amounts were often too low to make any difference. Flat grants proved popular, however—at the beginning of the twentieth century, 38 states were using them to aid public schools. Popularity fell only as school finance litigation escalated in the 1970s. Long outmoded, no state now relies solely on flat grants as the principal finance scheme, although they are still used for other purposes or in multi-tier combinations.

The operation and impact of a flat grant is shown in Figure 3.3. The figure shows that while a $1,000 flat grant per pupil would be welcomed in low, medium, and high wealth districts alike, its impact is unrelated to local ability to pay for schools. Naturally it would be most needed in the low wealth district, as it would increase the total available revenue per pupil.

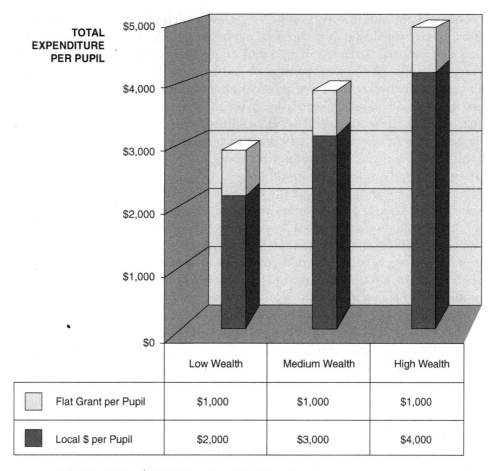

TOTAL EXPENDITURE PER PUPIL

	Low Wealth	Medium Wealth	High Wealth
Flat Grant per Pupil	$1,000	$1,000	$1,000
Local $ per Pupil	$2,000	$3,000	$4,000

FIGURE 3.3 Effect of a $1,000 Per-Pupil Flat Grant

The issue, though, is that a flat grant has zero impact on equalization; that is, wealth-based inequalities are untouched while revenue in all districts goes up by $1,000; alternatively, the district might choose to reduce local tax effort by that same $1,000 so that children are still no better off dollar-wise. While the net sum of a flat grant to poor districts is to have no favorable effect on equalization, the net sum for wealthy districts is enrichment unrelated to educational need or tax equity. Although flat grants represented a welcome step forward in their day in terms of states actively participating in education's costs, flat grants did nothing reduce property tax base inequalities.

Equalization Grants

Equalization plans have included a wide variety of state aid formulas seeking to grant school aid inversely to local ability to pay. Largely in response to the non-equalizing effect of earlier aid plans, equalization grants were designed to bring revenue and expenditure levels closer together in rich and poor districts, or at least to better equalize poorer districts' opportunity to spend at the same level as wealthier districts. Although many kinds of equalization grants have come into being, all such plans aim to boost state aid to those local districts with lesser tax capacity. However, differing political philosophies have shaped aid formula designs in the 50 states, primarily by virtue of two decisions facing legislatures: First, whether the state should set expenditure levels and tax rates; or, second, whether the state should let districts set their own tax-and-spend limits. Major equalization plans arising from these philosophy debates became known as *foundation plans* and *resource accessibility* plans.

Foundation plans were originally based on a minimum support concept. This meant several things. First, a foundation plan is politically and factually attractive in that equality is perceived by requiring a uniform minimum expenditure level and a uniform minimum tax rate in each school district throughout the state. Second, the state requires districts to provide a minimum standard educational program. Third, a foundation plan permits local leeway to engage in higher local spending by allowing additional local tax effort. Fourth, the minimum program is equalized because the amount of state aid is inversely related to local ability to pay for schools. However, to be truly effective, the minimum required expenditure level must be meaningful, and the state cost-share must be high enough to encourage local effort above the minimum. Foundation plans have long been the most popular form of equalization aid, with the vast majority of states using them today as the primary method to distribute state aid (see Table 3.6). Blended schemes exist too, as states may opt to use a foundation in combination with other aid programs.

Resource accessibility plans seek to equalize school monies by taking a different approach. While foundation plans historically focused on statewide minimum tax rates and expenditure levels, resource equalization plans have meant to empower districts to make their own fiscal and program decisions, unhindered by local wealth barriers. This means that variability in programs and expenditures is acceptable so long as availability of revenue is not the reason for variability; i.e., while foundation plans seek minimum equality, resource accessibility plans seek to balance wealth inequalities (ability to pay) in each district through aid formulas that adjust for tax base differences. The result has been various *percentage equalizing* plans, and these plans have been further refined to include variations such as *guaranteed tax base* (GTB), *guaranteed tax yield* (GTY), and *district power equalization* (DPE). Each of these plans uses a different approach to the problem of unequal resources. Percentage equalizing plans guarantee a constant percentage of budget from the state based on local ability to pay, with the local district setting costs and programs. GTB and GTY equalize revenues by promising districts the same tax capacity as all other districts. DPE carries the resource accessibility concept to its ultimate potential (recapture of excess revenue capacity) by requiring districts with wealth greater than the state's per-pupil guarantee to remit excess revenues to the state for redistribution through the formula to poorer districts. Compared to the popularity of foundation plans, far fewer states

TABLE 3.6 Basic State Aid Plans 2018

State	Formula	Notable Adjustments (may be in base aid or add-ons)
Alabama	Foundation	Grade-level weighted classroom unit; declining enrollment/growth; special education; at-risk; ELL; preschool.
Alaska	Foundation	Basic need determined by school size; area cost differential; special education; vocational; intensive needs; declining enrollment/growth; debt service.
Arizona	Equalization	Basic aid equalized on base support, transportation, capital outlay; sparsity/density; technical education; special education; at-risk; preschool.
Arkansas	Foundation	Density/sparsity; declining enrollment/growth; debt service; enhanced transportation; charter schools; special education; at-risk; matching grants; ELL; gifted; career/technical.
California	In transition	Transitioning to local control funding formula requiring performance accountability; density/sparsity; grade-level differences; declining enrollment/growth; debt service; transportation; charter schools; special education; at-risk; ELL; technical education; preschool.
Colorado	Foundation	Additional funding for special education; ELL; gifted; at-risk; preschool; transportation; technical education; declining enrollment/growth; charter schools.
Connecticut	Foundation	Weights for poverty, ELL; declining enrollment/growth; debt service; charter schools; special education; at-risk; technical education; preschool.
Delaware	Flat Grant/ Equalization	Declining enrollment/growth; debt service; transportation; charter schools; special education; at-risk; ELL; gifted; technical education; preschool.
Florida	Equalization	Basic formula accounts for variations in tax base, program costs, cost of living, sparsity/density; transportation; debt service; special education; at-risk; ELL; gifted; technical education; preschool.
Georgia	Foundation	Basic formula calculated on 18 program weights; additional funds for density/sparsity; declining enrollment/growth; transportation; charter schools; special education; at-risk; ELL; gifted; technical education; preschool.
Hawaii	Near-Full Funding	Economic disadvantage; ELL; gifted; transience; grade level; declining enrollment/growth; debt service; transportation; special education; at-risk.
Idaho	Foundation	District size/grade-level; density/sparsity; declining enrollment/growth; transportation; charter schools; special education; ELL; technical education.
Illinois	Foundation/ Flat Grant	Base aid plus evidence-based funding; declining enrollment/growth; grade-level differences; at-risk; ELL; special education; gifted; debt service; transportation; charter schools; special education; technical education; early childhood.
Indiana	Foundation	Base formula consists of basic tuition support, honors grant, special education grant, vocational grant, complexity grant.

(Continued)

TABLE 3.6 Continued

State	Formula	Notable Adjustments (may be in base aid or add-ons)
Iowa	Foundation	Density/sparsity; declining enrollment/growth; special education; at-risk; ELL gifted.
Kansas	Foundation	Density/sparsity; declining enrollment/growth; debt service; transportation; at-risk; ELL; technical education; preschool.
Kentucky	Foundation	At-risk; special education; transportation; grade-level differences; declining enrollment/growth; debt service; technical education; preschool.
Louisiana	Foundation	Base formula weights for low income; ELL; technical education; special education; gifted; economy of scale; density/sparsity; declining enrollment/growth; charter schools; preschool.
Maine	Foundation	Density/sparsity; grade-level differences; debt service; transportation; charter schools; special education; at-risk; ELL; gifted; technical education; preschool.
Maryland	Foundation/ Guaranteed Tax Base	Declining enrollment/growth; debt service; transportation; preschool.
Massachusetts	Foundation	Grade-level differences; debt service; transportation; charter schools; special education; at-risk; ELL; preschool.
Michigan	Foundation	Density/sparsity; charter schools; special education; at-risk; ELL; technical education; preschool; STEM.
Minnesota	Foundation	Density/sparsity; grade-level differences; declining enrollment/ growth; transportation; charter schools; special education; at-risk; ELL; gifted; preschool.
Mississippi	Foundation	Declining enrollment/growth; transportation; charter schools; special education; at-risk; gifted; technical education.
Missouri	Foundation	Declining enrollment/growth; transportation; charter schools; special education; at-risk; ELL.
Montana	Foundation/ Guaranteed Tax Base	Grade-level differences; declining enrollment/growth; debt service; transportation; district/school size; special education; at-risk; gifted.
Nebraska	Foundation	Declining enrollment/growth; transportation; special education; at-risk; ELL; preschool.
Nevada	Foundation	Density/sparsity; grade-level differences; district/school size; declining enrollment/growth; transportation; charter schools; special education; at-risk; gifted; ell; technical education; preschool; STEM.
N. Hampshire	Foundation	Infrastructure; charter schools; special education; at-risk; ELL; technical education; STEM.
New Jersey	Foundation/ Equalization	Declining enrollment/growth; debt service; transportation; grade-level differences; ELL; security aid; special education; at-risk; preschool; gifted; vocational.
New Mexico	Foundation	Density/sparsity; district/school size; declining enrollment/ growth; debt service; transportation; instructional materials; special education; ELL; gifted; preschool.

(Continued)

State	Formula	Notable Adjustments (may be in base aid or add-ons)
New York	Foundation	Base aid indexed to pupil needs and regional cost factor; grade-level differences; declining enrollment; debt service; transportation; charter schools; special education; at-risk; ELL; technical education; preschool; regional services.
N. Carolina	Multiple grants	Basic aid comprised of position/dollar/categorical allotments; low SES; small/isolated schools; transportation; special education; at-risk; ELL; gifted; technical education; preschool.
N. Dakota	Foundation	Density/sparsity; district/school size; declining enrollment/growth; transportation; special education; at-risk; ELL; technical education; regional education associations.
Ohio	Foundation	Declining enrolment/growth; debt service; transportation; charter schools; special education; at-risk; ELL; gifted; technical education; preschool; vouchers; literacy; graduation bonus; third grade reading proficiency bonus.
Oklahoma	Foundation	Density/sparsity; district/school size; declining enrollment/growth; transportation; charter schools; special education; at-risk; ELL; gifted; technical education; out-of-home placement weights.
Oregon	Multiple grants	Base aid is general purpose grants, transportation grants, high cost disability grants, facility grants. Density/sparsity; grade-level differences; declining enrollment/growth; small high school grants; special education; virtual schools; education service districts; charter schools; special education; at-risk; ELL; technical education.
Pennsylvania	Foundation	Grade-level differences; debt service; transportation; special education; gifted; technical education; Ready to Learn block grants.
Rhode Island	Foundation	Declining enrollment/growth; debt service; transportation; charter schools; special education; at-risk; ELL; technical education; preschool; consolidation.
S. Carolina	Foundation	Grade-level differences; transportation; special education; at-risk; technical education; preschool.
S. Dakota	Foundation	Base aid tied to salary schedule/PTR ratio/enrollment. Density/sparsity; transportation; special education ELL.
Tennessee	Foundation	Grade-level differences; debt service; transportation; charter schools; special education; ELL; gifted; technical education.
Texas	Foundation/ Guaranteed Yield	Density/sparsity; declining enrollment; debt service; transportation; charter schools; special education; at-risk; ELL; gifted; technical education; preschool; tax compression aid.
Utah	Foundation	Density/sparsity; grade-level differences; district/school size; declining enrollment; debt service; transportation; special education; at-risk; gifted.
Vermont	Near-Full Funding	Density/sparsity; grade-level differences; declining enrollment; transportation; special education; at-risk; ELL; technical education; preschool.

(Continued)

TABLE 3.6 Continued

State	Formula	Notable Adjustments (may be in base aid or add-ons)
Virginia	Foundation	Density/sparsity; transportation; special education; at-risk; ELL; gifted; preschool; technical education; preschool; prevention, intervention and remediation; remedial summer school; technology.
Washington	Foundation	Density/sparsity; grade-level differences; debt service; transportation; charter schools; tribal compact schools; special education; at-risk; ELL; gifted; technical education preschool.
W. Virginia	Foundation	Density/sparsity; enrollment growth; transportation; special education; ELL; gifted; preschool.
Wisconsin	Guaranteed Tax Base	Density/sparsity; high poverty; transportation; special education; at-risk; ELL; gifted; technical education.
Wyoming	Foundation	Density/sparsity; grade-level differences; declining enrollment/growth; debt service; transportation; charter schools; special education; at-risk; ELL; gifted; technical education.

Source: Interpreted from Verstegen, Deborah. "A Quick Glance at School Finance: A 50-State Survey of School Finance Policies and Programs (2018)." https://schoolfinancesdav.files.wordpress.com/2018/09/survey18-vol-i1.pdf

have adopted resource accessibility formulas, and most states adopting some version of these plans have modified the politically unpopular features or combined them with a foundation plan in a two-tiered funding system. No state today uses true DPE. The overarching observation is that equalization plans have served a very useful purpose, in that school finance reform in the 1970s gave impetus to self-scrutiny by states, with resultant improvement of overall equalization.

The operation and impact of a foundation plan is shown in Figure 3.4. The figure illustrates a uniform tax rate and a $5,000 per-pupil expenditure target or *foundation level*. The low-wealth district can raise only 20% of the target using local tax effort, and so the state provides 80%. Conversely, the wealthiest district is able to raise 100% of the target at the uniform minimum tax rate. Countless variations on this scheme are possible as well. Some states provide local option leeway above the minimum expenditure, and the leeway may or may not qualify for state aid depending on the structure of the aid plan. Recapture can be built in by setting the statewide tax rate high enough to produce more revenue than wealthy districts can legally spend per pupil if expenditure caps are in place. The possible variations are too numerous to illustrate here, but the impact of aid inversely related to local ability to pay is clearly the point of any equalization formula. However, equalization plans can be costly to states, both in terms of actual dollars when setting adequate resource levels and in political terms because concepts like low aid, zero aid, or recapture can prove politically unpalatable to property-wealthy communities.

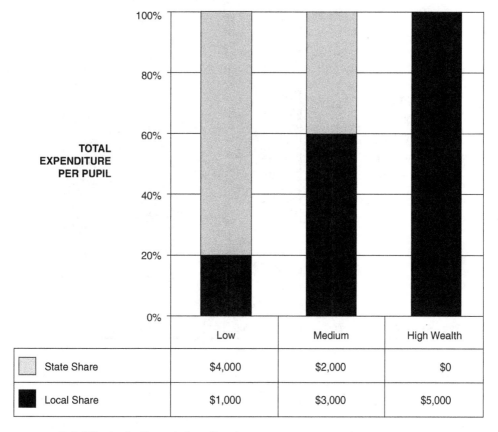

**FOUNDATION PLAN UNDER UNIFORM TAX RATE WITH
A STATE COST-SHARE RATIO 0–80%**

		Low	Medium	High Wealth
▨	State Share	$4,000	$2,000	$0
■	Local Share	$1,000	$3,000	$5,000

FIGURE 3.4 Effect of a Foundation Grant

Multi-Tier Grants

To make state aid equalization plans more palatable to some constituencies, policy-makers have sometimes created formulas by combining parts of two or more plans. For example, a state might enact a foundation program combined with a percentage equalizing formula (DPE, GTB, or GTY) that offers greater local budget leeway to appeal to a broader range of school districts, similar to the two-tiered plan described in the last section. Other variations might include capping the matching feature of a percentage equalizing grant to keep costs down; equalizing it at the same aid ratio as the foundation amount to better perfect equity features and to encourage local effort; or equalizing the percentage equalizing grant up to a certain point (another form of capping to control costs). Other types of aid, such as a flat grant, could also be attached to the basic formula structure.

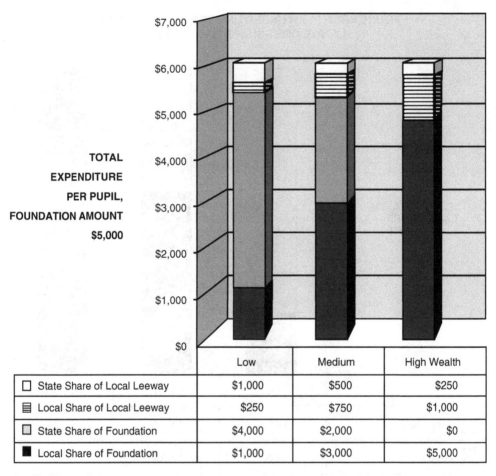

	Low	Medium	High Wealth
☐ State Share of Local Leeway	$1,000	$500	$250
☷ Local Share of Local Leeway	$250	$750	$1,000
☐ State Share of Foundation	$4,000	$2,000	$0
■ Local Share of Foundation	$1,000	$3,000	$5,000

FIGURE 3.5 Effect of a Foundation Grant with Equalized Local 25 Percent Option Leeway

Figure 3.5 illustrates a state aid formula that combines a foundation of $5,000 per pupil with a 25% local option leeway aided at the same aid ratio as the base amount. In this example, districts can choose to spend up to $6,250 per pupil, but they must voluntarily tax themselves for the portion identified as the local share of the local leeway option. The state's aid ratio, however, is guaranteed up to the maximum per-pupil expenditure level, so choosing to increase local tax effort means more state aid. Of course, districts can choose not to make the extra tax effort and forego additional aid. Politically motivated strategies also can be built into these designs. For example, the local leeway option may reflect a concession to high-wealth districts because without it this group of districts would receive no state aid. Similarly, in low wealth districts the local leeway might be advertised as nearly free money. Such strategies are sometimes used as compromise measures by state lawmakers to gain buy-in from a majority of the state's school districts in order to enact coveted reforms in the state funding system.

Full State Funding Grants

Often regarded as a threat to local control, adoption of full state funding has been exceedingly rare. The rationale for full state funding formulas is state acceptance of plenary responsibility for education. Operationally, full state funding is simple: It places all the resources of a state within reach of every child by converting that portion of the local property tax earmarked for local school support to a statewide tax so that it can be pooled at the state level and redistributed as aid to schools without regard to local property wealth. As a result, individual districts no longer have local discretion to spend more or less than other districts. In addition, recapture, widely viewed as politically deadly, is required in full state funding because a uniform statewide property tax rate will yield varying amounts from communities based on their property wealth, with some communities generating revenue in excess of state-mandated education expenditure levels. As such, full state funding radically departs from the other state aid plans in this chapter.

With these stipulations, Vermont has come closest to adopting full state funding, while Hawaii's single school district structure has created a de facto kind of full state funding. As seen earlier in Table 2.4, in 2014–15 Vermont provided 90.1%[12] of school district expenditures, while Hawaii provided 88.2%. Discussion around Table 2.4 earlier showed a much lower overall national picture, however, as the U.S. average for state aid was about 46% in 2015, with Illinois holding the lowest spot at 24.9% and with four other states providing one-third or less cost share.

Figure 3.6 illustrates a full state funding plan, albeit oversimplified because it lacks vertical equity adjustments or additions (see next section). Each district spends

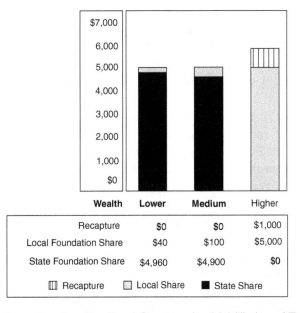

	Wealth	Lower	Medium	Higher
Recapture		$0	$0	$1,000
Local Foundation Share		$40	$100	$5,000
State Foundation Share		$4,960	$4,900	$0

▥ Recapture   ☐ Local Share   ■ State Share

FIGURE 3.6 Full State Funding Per-Pupil Grant under 20 Mills Local Tax Effort with Recapture Provision

$5,000 per pupil, with the local share funded by a uniform tax effort of 20 mills. The low property-wealth district can raise only $40 per pupil in local revenue, while the high property-wealth district's tax yield per pupil exceeds the required uniform expenditure per pupil. The result is that the state provides enough aid to less wealthy districts so that they too are able to spend $5,000 per pupil when combined with their local tax effort. At the same time, the state finances this plan in part with funds recaptured from the wealthiest districts.

ADJUSTMENTS AND ADDITIONS TO BASIC AID FORMULAS

Discussion so far has considered general (basic) state aid, but with no provision for formula vertical equity adjustments based on pupil differences. Although *horizontal equity*,[13] defined as the equal treatment of equals, requires all children to be funded as equals, everyone is not in the same place in that most children need extra resources to be successful in school. Hence, state school funding systems must incorporate mechanisms for *vertical equity*,[14] or the appropriately unequal treatment of unequally situated children. Broadly speaking, equity adjustments fall into the two categories of *need equalization* and *cost equalization*.

Need Equalization

State and federal law guarantees that every child is entitled to an education appropriate to his or her needs.[15] Need speaks to vertical equity, i.e., differences among children who are unequally situated by virtue of circumstance beyond their control. Although there is no universal agreement on the definition of educationally disadvantaged, research often references children who are at risk of academic failure. Among these need-based definitions are children from low income families; those with certain disabilities; racial/ethnic minority groups; English language learners; children in urban schools; and children from families with low parental education attainment.[16] Consequently, need equalization is a critical component of state school funding systems. A range of financial aid programs has sprung up around need equalization, of which the most common are special education, compensatory education, bilingual education, and early childhood education. Today most states provide at least some extra financial support to these programs, usually in the form of categorical aid or weightings within the per-pupil basic aid plan.

Special education has been the most visible and most costly of the various need equalization programs. Although special education has existed for many decades, it took on new meaning in the 1970s with enactment of federal legislation and aggressive litigation surrounding the rights of children with disabilities to be educated in the least restrictive environment. Although other need equalization may receive only modest redress in some states, the needs of special education children have been the center of intense advocacy, with every indication of continuing far into the future as a powerful political and legal force.

States generally fund special education in much the same way as other need equalization programs, but the mandated nature of special education has resulted in close governmental monitoring, particularly because special education funding involves a disproportionate mix of federal, state, and local monies wherein the federal government is a large contributor. States themselves usually fund special education through pupil weightings, categorical aids, cost reimbursement, or census.[17] States using weighting factors often load pupils by type or severity of need incidence. In reality, though, states often pay only a portion of districts' actual costs, leaving local units to fund the rest after federal and state aid is exhausted. All 50 states in some fashion aid special education services.

In contrast, the purpose of compensatory aid is to redress social and economic inequality by earmarking extra funding for income-disadvantaged children. The federal government has long had an interest in compensatory education aid through a range of programs, e.g., Title I funding, free and reduced-price school meals and after-school snacks, and Head Start. Most states provide some level of aid for compensatory education.

With rapid growth in new immigration, aid to bilingual education has become increasingly important to states and local school districts. Various court rulings have stressed the value of bilingual programs, and civil rights legislation has pressed to overcome language barriers. States have consequently created bilingual programs or have risked lawsuits or loss of federal funding. While enthusiasm among states has been varied, most states have provided some level of aid for English language programs.

Finally, numerous studies have indicated that there is a significant return on investment in preschool programs, particularly for low income and special needs children, that accrue to both schools and society.[18] Because federal Head Start funding allows only a small percentage of children to enjoy access to quality early childhood education, states have had to become involved in either supplementing Head Start or providing funding to school districts for pre-K services. While most states provide some type of early childhood education, only a handful provides such programs to all deserving children. Political interest and support, though woefully inadequate compared to need, appears to be growing as state-funded preschools served over 1.5 million children during the 2016–17 school year, a number never before reached. In that increase, the vast majority (86%) were four-year-olds, primarily because state-funded preschool continues to be a program predominantly for that age group.[19] Similarly, recognizing that third grade reading proficiency is a crucial marker for later academic success, many governors have increased state prioritization of early childhood education by dedicating additional funding to pre-K and early interventions—e.g., in 2018, at least 11 governors named early learning initiatives in their State of the State addresses. [20]

Cost Equalization

The differing economic, demographic, and geographic profiles of the 50 states have resulted in tailored cost equalization adjustments and additions to state school funding systems. Cost equalization in state aid typically takes two forms. One form recognizes that different costs may arise due to diseconomies of scale, while the second attempts to compensate districts for market-based cost differentials. For example, higher costs may stem from the price of urban life. Conversely, rural districts may face higher costs when trying to attract and retain staff. Similarly, rural districts may face higher costs related to transportation over sparsely populated but geographically large school district territory in terms of square miles.

Cost equalization is handled most often through categorical aid or pupil weightings attached to basic or general aid, such as adding weighting factors like enrollment density or sparsity and declining or increasing enrollment factors. A few states have tried with limited success to create education cost indices tied to market-based cost differences (a market basket approach) within the state, but in many instances a lack of detailed data, along with the complexity of constructing a valid index and political sensitivities, has served as a deterrent to widespread adoption.

WRAP-UP

The discussion in this chapter has illustrated that states have many complex goals when creating school aid formulas. At the most basic level, state aid formulas are an effort to redress local tax base inequalities, i.e., high vs. low property wealth—rich vs. poor districts. Such inequality, if unabated, would result in unacceptable disparities in number, type, and quality of educational programs and, hence, equality of educational opportunity. The first goal of general or basic aid formulas, then, is to make adequate funding available to all districts *through the use of state resources*. Other goals are equally important. Among them are the need to address special human conditions, to reflect the unique problems of individual states, and to convince taxpayers that their voices matter and that their tax dollars are not wasted. At the same time, state aid formulas must satisfy the legal mandates in state constitutions, state statutes, and the U.S. Constitution. In addition, state policymakers must be attuned to political philosophies as they try to build state aid plans that neither infringe on local control nor are too weak to be effective.

Table 3.7 lays out an 'ideal' set of policy principles that most scholars would agree conform to state-of-the-art school finance theory. Although ideal, the road to enacting such a school aid formula would be very hard in many states given competing needs and desires across America's 13,584 public school districts.[21] Table 3.6 earlier attempted to accumulate a brief overview of how the 50 states currently fund schools—but it must be emphasized that the task of accurately compiling such a resource is complex and risk-laden given the countless nuances that comprise school funding in the twenty-first century—i.e., school aid plans do not lend themselves well to summarization, and experts in each state will wonder why one or more variables were not included in a brief distillation. Still, all data in this chapter show that schools today are funded at historic levels and that aid formulas are trying to benefit children in every corner of the nation—no doubt brought about by the combined force of politics, litigation, and many good intentions.

TABLE 3.7 Elements of a Right School Aid Formula

Elements	A Right School Aid Formula
Equity—all children horizontally and vertically aided by educational need category	***Foundation amoun**t—a right school aid formula* contains an expenditure floor and an expenditure cap for general fund. Horizontal equity demands uniform base expenditure per pupil and equalized tax effort for pupil and taxpayer equality to offset local wealth variations. All instructional, support, and operating expenses are co-equal within the base formula, including transportation, capital outlay, and infrastructure. Vertical equity demands sensitivity weights, including sparsity, density, special education and gifted education, vocational/career/technical education, and special needs to include low income/at-risk, English Language Learners, and unique variables like extraordinary costs such as dramatic enrollment shifts. Formula must be tied to current year realities. Any local leeway provision must be fully equalized, and maximum range above the unadjusted per-pupil base must be tightly controlled. A shift to a new aid formula should not result in loss of baseline funding to any school district.
Adequacy— expenditure per pupil tightly tied to accurate, comprehensive costs	***Adequacy**—a right school aid formula* provides an adequate level of funding from combined state, local, and federal sources to fully fund the true costs of all instruction and program supports in the school district. True costs are determined by comprehensive cost studies utilizing longitudinal expenditure data and market-driven data in context of pupil performance data. Again, a shift to a new aid formula should not result in loss of baseline funding to any school district.
Efficiency— comprehensive range of educational programs provided by highly qualified classroom and support personnel in all schools under a state-level unitary control and funding system	***Efficiency**—a right school aid formula* provides an efficient funding system that satisfies all elements of equity and adequacy and does so by guaranteeing state resources. The state recognizes and accepts its primary duty to provide a unitary education system, where unitary means all children in all locations have full and free access to equal educational programs. An efficient funding system must be based on multiple revenue sources representing the state's true economic base and must be tied to multiple sources in order to weather natural economic fluctuations in economy segments. Boundary studies should inform both program and cost evaluations.
Stability—stable, predictable revenue sources and streams, multiply tied to state economic strengths and state/ local/ federal partnership principles	***Stability**—a right school aid formula* requires a predictable, steady mix of resources to enable school districts to engage in short, intermediate, and long-range planning and investment in educational programs in order to produce expected pupil achievement outcomes. This cannot be done with single source or volatile revenue bases. A stable system takes into account that the state has primary responsibility for funding schools, followed by highly equalized local contributions, with consideration for any available federal partnership. Sound school finance principles strongly expect a broad-based progressive state tax scheme, meaning a first preference for the statewide income tax; a second preference for the statewide property tax; a third preference for the local property tax; and a least preference for the sales tax. Often referred to as a three-legged stool, these three revenue sources (income, property, sales taxes) are regarded by virtually all respected school finance experts as best able to withstand economic fluctuations that threaten school formula stability.

(Continued)

TABLE 3.7 Continued

Elements	A Right School Aid Formula
Accountability— rigorous formula monitoring using nationally accepted measurements of performance on the formula's elements	***Accountability**—a right school aid formula* should regularly measure performance on equity and adequacy using accepted school finance statistical measures and should continuously evidence a positive trend line on each of the five principles and their respective sub-elements.

Source: Thompson, David C. "A Policy Brief on Kansas School Finance." Presented to the Governor and Special Task Force on School Finance, Kansas Statehouse (October 2016). Based and expanded on Faith E. Crampton and Terry N. Whitney, Principles of a Sound State School Finance System (Denver, CO, and Washington, DC: Foundation for State Legislatures, 1996).

POINT–COUNTERPOINT

POINT

States today face many tax-funded obligations, of which public schools are only one. Of all these, schools should be the absolute priority—if necessary, at the expense of other social programs—given how poorly funded schools eventually translate into higher remedial social service costs.

COUNTERPOINT

When states experience revenue shortfalls, all state spending—including for public schools—must be cut because states cannot and should not engage in deficit spending. In terms of priorities, schools are no more important than any other program or service the state funds. It is only fair that schools take their share of losses in state aid to help balance the state's budget.

- In your opinion, which state services are most important to fully fund in a budget shortfall? Why?
- How do states come to experience budget shortfalls, and what should they do to address and prevent such situations?

CASE STUDY

As one of the more established superintendents in your state, you have been asked to testify next month before a legislative interim committee studying school finance. You are no stranger to state politics, and it has long been your belief that your state's school funding formula is outdated and deficient in some important ways. More specifically, you have spoken out in the past in favor of increasing state aid in the belief that it is inadequate if school districts are to meet new, more rigorous state standards. You have further lobbied for increased vertical weightings to the state funding system that would increase funding to students who might have difficulty reaching those standards without additional help, like tutoring. As you have considered the invitation to testify, it has occurred to you that you will be questioned closely because you know that some members of the interim committee will represent school districts that would not benefit from your views.

As you prepare for your testimony, you run through the possible viewpoints you might face. Certainly, your own school board will want you to advocate positions favorable to your district—i.e., a fairly well-to-do community whose children perform well on state assessments. Your district has one of the highest graduation rates in the state, and the vast majority of your high school graduates pursue postsecondary education. Relatedly, your state allows school districts to raise additional property tax revenues for program enhancements without seeking voter approval, and your district currently levies at the maximum allowed in order to fund exemplary curricular and cocurricular programs that might have to be cut if the state changed or eliminated this option. At the same time, other types of school districts will advocate for their needs. For example, many of the small, rural school districts face stagnant or declining enrollments and are experiencing challenges in offering just the state's basic mandated curriculum under the current funding system. You know those districts want an across-the-board increase in per-pupil state aid, and they have recently lobbied for more transportation aid because of rising fuel costs. The state's urban school districts, on the other hand, face crowded classrooms and crumbling infrastructure. You know those districts have been lobbying for added state aid for class size reduction, as well as new aid for school construction and modernization. And of course, there are the many districts resembling yours, i.e., doing well and mostly wishing for new money to do more good things for children, but they are generally reluctant to rock the boat in the state capital.

The agenda for next month's legislative committee meeting devotes an hour to your testimony. You know the committee has already heard from experts on the elements of good school aid formulas. Your testimony will conclude the information gathering phase, after which public comments will be taken. The committee's goal is to recommend changes to the state funding system in the upcoming legislative session.

Below is a set of questions. As you respond, consider your learning throughout this chapter and apply your knowledge and views to the situation:

- What will be the major talking points in your upcoming legislative testimony?

- How will you go about satisfying the expectations of your school district while taking into consideration the needs of other school districts in the state?
- Using your own state's school aid formula as a basis, what would you recommend to the legislative committee? What counterarguments could you expect from legislators, other school districts, and general critics of education spending; and how would you respond?

PORTFOLIO EXERCISES

- Obtain documents explaining the state aid formula in your state (these are often available through your state department of education and online). Identify the type of general or basic aid formula used in your state. Identify state revenue sources used to fund education (e.g., income taxes, sales taxes, lottery profits, etc.). Identify from these documents, if possible, your state's policy goals and priorities with regard to aid to local school districts.
- Identify how your state aid formula addresses pupil and taxpayer equity as well as adequacy. Consider how horizontal equity is addressed, and identify any adjustments or additions to base aid to address vertical equity. Identify the amounts of money allocated to general aid, categorical aid, pupil weighting, and need or cost adjustments. Determine whether there has been any recent research on the equity or adequacy or your state's funding system and examine the results.
- Interview leaders of educational organizations (e.g., school board, parent-teacher associations, teachers' unions, administrators, state agencies, professional associations) to learn what they perceive as the strengths and weaknesses of your state's school funding system. Ask what needs to be done to improve any weaknesses they perceive.
- Watch for meetings addressing school funding you can attend. These might include legislative committee meetings, legislative issues town meetings, teacher association meetings, local school board meetings. Take notes on the issues and attitudes expressed, and try to identify the most influential players. Take note of any changes proposed to financing schools.
- Compare how your state funds education to other states in your region. Consider the numbers of pupils to be educated, dollars legislatively appropriated, choice of state aid formula design, and revenue (tax) sources for education. Assess which states appear to provide the greatest degree of equity and adequacy in their funding systems.

NOTES

1 In addition, many states have what are termed 'intermediate' units of government. The types of intermediate units vary greatly across states along with their powers to tax (or lack thereof) and responsibilities. One of the most common intermediate units in the United States is the county. For further information, see the National Association of Counties, www.naco.org.

2 *Pollock v. Farmers Loan & Trust Co. Supreme Court of the United States,* 158 U.S. 601; 15 S.Ct. 912 (1985).

3 *Digest of Education Statistics 2016,* "Federal Support and Estimated Federal Tax Expenditures for Education, by Category: Selected Fiscal Years 1965 through 2016." Table 401.10. https://nces.ed.gov/programs/digest/d16/tables/dt16_401.10.asp?current=yes

4 A poll tax, also referred to as a "head tax," was levied per individual, generally as a matter of convenience in colonial times when the individual voted. It, however, was later used to discriminate against African-American voters, primarily in the South, although it affected all voters too poor to pay the tax. The 24th Amendment ratified in 1964 outlawed its use in federal elections. A faculty tax was an early form of income tax whereby individuals were taxed a flat amount based upon their profession.

5 National Association of State Budget Officers, "Summary: NASBO State Expenditure Report." (2017), p4. https://higherlogicdownload.s3.amazonaws.com/NASBO/9d2d2db1-c943-4f1b-b750-0fca152d64c2/UploadedImages/Issue%20Briefs%20/State_Expenditure_Report_Summary_FY15-17.pdf

6 Table 3.5 illustrates the burden of state and local taxes by state. It should be noted that a low number illustrates less tax burden, while a higher number reflects a greater tax burden.

7 Elwood P. Cubberley, *School Funds and Their Apportionment* (New York: Columbia Teachers College, 1906).

8 Harlan Updegraff, *Rural School Survey of New York State: Financial Support* (Ithaca, NY: Author, 1992).

9 George D. Strayer and Robert M. Haig, *The Financing of Education in the State of New York,* Vol. 1 (New York: Macmillan, 1923).

10 Paul Mort, *The Measurement of Educational Need* (New York: Columbia Teachers College, 1924).

11 Henry C. Morrison, *School Revenue* (Chicago: University of Chicago Press, 1930).

12 Appropriations in this high aid state appear to have declined since the last edition of this textbook. A new book indicates state aid is expected to be 83.6% of general fund costs for FY 2019. See forthcoming David C. Thompson, R. Craig Wood, S. Craig Neuenswander, John M. Heim, and Randy D. Watson (eds). *Funding P-12 Schools in the 50 States and Indian Country.* National Education Finance Academy (2019).

13 Robert Berne and Leanna Stiefel, *The Measurement of Equity in School Finance* (Baltimore, MD: Johns Hopkins University Press, 1984), 406.

14 Ibid.

15 Caveat: Federal and state laws guarantee children with disabilities an education to meet their individual needs. Each state constitution, in some manner, guarantees each child an education as defined by the controlling language, applicable court rulings, and state statutes.

16 See, e.g., Randall S. Vesely, Faith E. Crampton, Festus E. Obiakor, and Marty Sapp, "The Role of States in Funding Education to Achieve Social Justice," *Journal of Education Finance* 34 (Summer 2008): 56–74.

17 Census based funding is based on a fixed percentage of total district enrollment set by the state, not the actual number of students identified as having special needs in a particular district. See, William T. Hartman, "The Impact of Census-Based Special Education in

Pennsylvania," *Journal of Special Education Leadership* 14, no. 1 (2001): 4–12. www.csef-air.org/publications/related/jsel/hartman.html.

18 See, e.g., Clive Belfield, "Does It Pay to Invest in Preschool for All? Analyzing Return-on-Investment in Three States?" NIER Working Paper (New Brunswick, NJ: Rutgers University Press, 2006), http://nieer.org/resources/research/DoesitPay.pdf.

19 National Institute for Early Education Research. "The State of Preschool 2017. NIEER (2018). http://nieer.org/wp-content/uploads/2018/04/YB2017_Executive-Summary.pdf

20 Education Commission of the States. "Education Trends: Governors' Top Education Priorities in 2018 State of the State Addresses." Denver, CO: NCSL (2018).

21 National Center for Education Statistics. *Digest of Education Statistics: 2017 Tables and Figures*. Table 214.10. "Number of Public School Districts and Public and Private Elementary and Secondary Schools: Selected years, 1869-70 through 2015-16." Washington, DC: NCES (2018). https://nces.ed.gov/programs/digest/d17/tables/dt17_214.10.asp?current=yes

WEB RESOURCES

Alexander, Kern. *Education Today: Issues and Experts*. "Investing in Education." (2016). https://www.youtube.com/watch?v=2Sj1GgLmdks#action=share

Alexander, Kern. *The Rise and Decline of the Public School Ideal in America: Politics, Law and Finance*. Distinguished Lecture Series. Kansas State University (2016). https://mediasite.k-state.edu/mediasite/Play/841a8f7ce5f24b6bbe4181c453b760a51d?playFrom=16996&autoStart=true

Council of State Governments, www.csg.org

Education Commission of the States, www.ecs.org

National Association of State Budget Officers, www.nasbo.org

National Conference of State Legislatures, www.ncsl.org

National Education Finance Academy, https://www.nationaledfinance.com

Tax Foundation, www.taxfoundation.org

Thompson, David C. *Education Today: Issues and Experts*. "On School Finance." (2015). https://www.youtube.com/watch?v=PGF0MU2-Ick#action=share

U.S. Census Bureau, www.census.gov

U.S. Department of Education, National Center for Education Statistics, http://nces.ed.gov

U.S. Office of Management and Budget, www.whitehouse.gov/omb/budget

RECOMMENDED RESOURCES

Bourdeaux, Carolyn and Nicholas Warner. "School Districts' Expenditure Responses to Federal Stimulus Funds." *Journal of Education Finance* 41, 1 (Summer 2015): 30–47.

Conlin, Michael and Meg Jalilevand. "Systemic Inequities in Special Education Financing." *Journal of Education Finance* 41, 1 (Summer 2015): 83–100.

Crampton, Faith E. and Terry N. Whitney. *Principles of a Sound State School Finance System*. A monograph of the Education Partners Project. Denver, CO, and Washington, DC: Foundation for State Legislatures, 1996.

Daberkow, Kevin S. and Wei Lin. "Constructing a Model of Lottery Tax Incidence Measurement: Revisiting the Illinois Lottery Tax for Education." *Journal of Education Finance* 37, 3 (Winter 2012): 267–286.

Davis, Matthew, Andrea Vedder, and Joe Stone. "Local Tax Limits, Student Achievement, and School-Finance Equalization." *Journal of Education Finance* 41, 3 (Winter 2016): 289–301.

DeLuca, Thomas A. "Do Countywide LEAs Allocate Expenditures Differently from Community-centric LEAs?: Evidence from National Center for Education Statistics Common Core Data." *Journal of Education Finance* 40, 3 (Winter 2015): 222–252.

Driscoll, Lisa G. and Richard G. Salmon. "Challenges Confronting Public Elementary and Secondary Education in the Commonwealth of Virginia." *Journal of Education Finance* 38 (Winter 2013): 230–254.

Ely, Todd L. and L. Fermanich. "Learning to Count: School Finance Formula Count Methods and Attendance-Related Student Outcomes." *Journal of Education Finance* 38, 4 (Spring 2013): 343–369.

Evans, Chad and Joel R. Malin. "The Relationship Between Magnet Status and Neighborhood Home Values in Chicago." *Journal of Education Finance* 43, 1 (Summer 2017): 84–103.

Fahy, Colleen. "Education Funding in Massachusetts: The Effects of Aid Modifications on Vertical and Horizontal Equity." *Journal of Education Finance* 36, 3 (Winter 2011): 217–243.

Fahy, Colleen A. "Fiscal Capacity Measurement and Equity in Local Contributions to Schools: The Effects of Education Finance Reform in Massachusetts." *Journal of Education Finance* 37, 4 (Spring 2012): 317–346.

Finch, Maida A., Peter Goff, and Eric Houck. "Opting Out of the Bill: Voluntary Adequacy Funding in Maryland." *Journal of Education Finance* 42, 1 (Summer 2016): 28–48.

Halcoussis, Dennis, Kenneth Ng, and Nancy Virts. "Property Ownership and Educational Discrimination in the South." *Journal of Education Finance* 35, 2 (Fall 2009): 128–139.

Knight, David S. "Are High-Poverty School Districts Disproportionately Impacted by State Funding Cuts?: School Finance Equity Following the Great Recession." *Journal of Education Finance* 43, 2 (Fall 2017): 169–194.

Larkin, Brittany, Christine Kiracofe, and Spencer Weiler. "The Good, the Bad, and the Alarming: Commentary on the 2017 State of the States Submissions." *Journal of Education Finance* 43, 3 (Winter 2018): 217–219.

Malin, Joel R. "The Prediction of States' PK–12 Funding Effort and Distribution Based on Their Ideological Makeups." *Journal of Education Finance* 42, 2 (Fall 2016): 220–242.

National Association of State Budget Officers. *Summaries of Fiscal Year 2019 Proposed and Enacted Budgets* (Washington, DC, 2018).

Ramirez, Al, Dick M. Carpenter II, and Maureen Breckenridge. "Exploring the Impact of Inadequate Funding for English Language Learners in Colorado School Districts." *Journal of Education Finance* 40, 1 (Summer 2014): 60–79.

Reinagel, Tyler P. "Budget Stability, Revenue Volatility, and District Relations: Determinants of Georgia ELOST Distribution to Municipal School Districts." *Journal of Education Finance* 40, 2 (Fall 2014): 156–174.

Rolle, R. Anthony and Oscar Jimenez-Castellanos. "An Efficacy Analysis of the Texas School Funding Formula with Particular Attention to English Language Learners." *Journal of Education Finance* 39, 3 (Winter 2014): 203–221.

Silverman, Robert Mark. "How Unwavering is Support for the Local Property Tax?: Voting on School District Budgets in New York, 2003–2010." *Journal of Education Finance* 36, 3 (Winter 2011): 294–311.

Steinberg, Matthew P. and Rand Quinn. "A Tale of Two Decades: New Evidence on Adequacy and Equity in Pennsylvania." *Journal of Education Finance* 40, 3 (Winter 2015): 273–299.

Sweetland, Scott R. "An Assessment of the Adequacy of Ohio School Funding: New Performance Standards and Alternative Measurements of Adequacy." *Journal of Education Finance* 41, 2 (Fall 2015): 124–144.

Sweetland, Scott R. "An Exploratory Analysis of the Equity of Ohio School Funding." *Journal of Education Finance* 40, 1 (Summer 2014): 80–100.

Thompson, David C., R. Craig Wood, and David S. Honeyman. *Fiscal Leadership for Schools: Concepts and Practices* (New York: Longman, 1994).

Thompson, David C, R. Craig Wood, S. Craig Neuenswander, John M. Heim, and Randy D. Watson (eds). *Funding P-12 Schools in the 50 States and Indian Country* (National Education Finance Academy, 2019).

Verstegen, Deborah A. "Leaving Equity Behind?: A Quantitative Analysis of Fiscal Equity in Nevada's Public Education Finance System." *Journal of Education Finance* 39, 2 (Fall 2013): 132–149.

Verstegen, Deborah A. and Robert C. Knoeppel. "From Statehouse to Schoolhouse: Education Finance Apportionment Systems in the United States." *Journal of Education Finance* 38, 2 (Fall 2012): 145–166.

CHAPTER 4

School Funds: Accountability, Performance, and Professionalism

CHAPTER DRIVERS

Please reflect upon the following questions as you read this chapter:

- What is fiscal accountability?
- What are the purposes of accounting?
- What are the fiduciary responsibilities of school districts and school leaders?
- How does the accounting process help establish accountability?
- How do revenue, expenditure, and audit structures assist in tracking money?
- What ethical standards should guide school leaders' professionalism in handling money?

SCHOOL FUNDS ACCOUNTABILITY

Americans today, with wide-ranging views on the value of education, are increasingly involved in schools. At the same time, the issues faced by federal, state, and local governments are extraordinarily complex as every governmental agency tries to meet the demands of constituents. Public schools are part of the fabric of larger society, and patrons have the power to cause lasting change by either force or resistance. Many school leaders have learned the hard way that the public is becoming bolder when disagreeing with what administrators have long regarded as routine policy in budgeting, curriculum, and even the daily operations of schools. This chapter is therefore a discussion of fiscal accountability, performance, and fiduciary trust because the best-laid educational plans mean nothing without a sound financial plan—a plan based on the highest ethical and professional accounting standards.

This chapter goes to the specific elements of implementing school budgets—i.e., the operational aspects of putting money to work in schools. Money is an issue of accountability, performance and trust because only a very few people in any school district really understand the complex expectations to which administrators and others are held when handling public funds and the spiraling demands for pupil outcomes. Consequently, new and experienced school leaders alike must be thoroughly versed in the concepts of fiscal accountability and the fiduciary trust. Simultaneously, this chapter reviews the receipt of revenue and restrictions on expenditure and provides a panoramic view of how money flows through a school district from beginning to end. Finally, this chapter describes the code of ethical standards for handling public monies. Many school leaders have difficulty in this arena—usually due to ignorance of good practice and a lack of sufficient training. In sum, the complexity of appropriate stewardship is still far less complex than facing the consequence of mishandling public funds.

For many individuals, the concept of accountability for school money is intimidating. Truly, there is no defense for people who do not take time to fully grasp the weight of accountability because all aspects of education suffer irreparable harm when accountability measures are not followed; that is, failure to establish good fiscal accountability results in distrust of everyone involved. As a consequence, this chapter begins with the concept of accountability itself, followed by deeper discussions of how money flows through schools.

FISCAL ACCOUNTABILITY

Accountability is a constant in public education circles. This does not mean too much accountability exists, but rather that the word is applied to a wide scope of activities ranging from curriculum and achievement to mapping bus routes and winning ballgames. As a result, accountability is variously defined, and its definition is made more elusive by a lack of precise tools to measure what people hope to achieve when they demand accountability. In the discipline of education finance, accountability has clearer meaning. Fundamentally, accountability in fiscal terms means that those responsible for any activity involving money must provide evidence of appropriate care as conservators, which includes the wise use of all resources. Importantly, the scope of fiscal accountability continues to expand so that wise use is being constantly redefined and increasingly includes pupil performance outcomes.

Fiscal accountability can be understood on numerous levels. At its root, it describes the practice of sound business principles when handling money regardless of whether the source is public or private. This definition can be traced over many centuries. Growth in schools in the United States forced formal recognition of the importance of good business practice in education, with the first known business manager's position created in 1841 when the schools in Cleveland, Ohio hired a manager to care for the accounting functions of the school district. The ever-increasing complexity of managing the millions of dollars characterizing virtually every modern school district has added greatly to needs for accountability awareness because the rising price of education dramatically increases the need for confidence that good business procedures are in place.

More broadly, accountability also has come to mean wise use of all resources entrusted to the care of the school district. This includes not only the accounting function, but also the decision-making process by which funds are spent for instructional and support services. Most patrons would agree that spending for things that hold little chance of helping children learn is not a wise business practice, yet the issues discussed in this textbook suggest that proving wise resource utilization does not come easily. In other words, an increasingly distrustful public is no longer satisfied with simple evidence of good accounting procedures, as many citizens now additionally ask pointedly sophisticated questions about whether increasing teachers' pay or creating new programs is worthwhile from the perspective of *both* fiscal and educational accountability. Visibly protracted struggles over which programs enjoy funding or are eliminated stand as proof of emerging applications of accountability, as do legislative and local debates on the relationship between funding and pupil achievement. This latter issue reached historic proportions with the passage of the *No Child Left Behind Act*[1] of 2001, which mandated states to require schools to increase academic performance standards, commonly referred to as *adequate yearly progress* or face increasingly harsh sanctions for both the state and underperforming schools and districts. While generally agreed that the *Every Student Succeeds Act*[2] (ESSA) of 2015 returned power and flexibility to grassroots states, in reality ESSA maintained the focus on pupil performance that had grown pervasively since the original federal interest found many years earlier in the ESEA of 1965. The topics of resource decision-making, fiscal accountability, and performance outcomes are therefore concepts repeatedly raised in this book, particularly in later chapters when addressing the act of budgeting for educational programs.

Fiduciary Responsibilities

Central to the concepts of professionalism, accountability, and performance is the role of the school leader as *fiduciary*. The origin of the word, *fiducia*, is Latin for "trust." As a noun, a fiduciary is a *trustee*. Trusteeship is itself an intriguing term, having serious weight attached by virtue of *trust* as its etymology. More specifically, fiduciary responsibility carries many pointed elements, inclusive of "the power and obligation to act for another [often called the beneficiary] under circumstances which require total trust, good faith and honesty."[3] A fiduciary is required to place the beneficiary's interests above self. Such gravity needs no development except to underscore the weighty language. For purposes of this textbook, a person having fiduciary responsibility is someone placed in charge of any kind of asset and in whom others—the community, in the case of public schools—have placed trust, so much so that the fiduciary's own personal reputation and professional livelihood depend on public confidence and support in wise use and conservatorship. Under these conditions, the level of trust is enormous—indeed, it is hard to imagine a more serious charge than that of a fiduciary, and the responsibility for millions of dollars entrusted to schools and their leaders is staggering. Adding performance outcomes to that seriousness only deepens expectations for the leader's competence and ingenuity.

Clearly, then, as accountability has risen to new levels of public scrutiny, so have the duties and responsibilities of persons with fiduciary obligations. The duties of a fiduciary from the particular perspective of a school leader have been identified for many years. The fiduciary role touches school boards, administrators, teachers, staff, policymakers, and laypersons to varying degrees; that is, anyone who comes in contact with any kind of school resources in some manner. The duties have been identified as the following:

- *Planning:* The process of looking to the future, identifying resources and needs, and creating a master plan to follow;
- *Decision-making:* The process of choosing among options, knowing that setting a course of action is not easy to reverse and that making choices precludes other options;
- *Organizing:* The process of preparing a plan for identifying needed human and fiscal resources and a sequence of events to reach a set of stated goals;
- *Directing:* The process of accepting responsibility to see that plans are implemented and carried out;
- *Controlling:* The process of monitoring progress against the original goals so that errors can be corrected during the implementation phase;
- *Evaluating:* The ultimate responsibility for determining if goals were met and whether resources were wisely used.[4]

These responsibilities are directly applicable to financing schools. For example, school leaders, teachers, and other staff have a shared responsibility for making schools successful so that only the individual's level of involvement differs. As a rule, instructional staff perform these duties in ways related to teaching and learning, although school site councils, decentralized budgeting, salary negotiations, and other aspects of shared decision-making have expanded formerly centralized fiduciary roles. Building principals, school superintendents, and chief finance officers, as well as local boards of education, have more hands-on control of financial resources, although their control may be significantly limited by laws governing resource utilization and shared decision-making. At the same time, state and local policymakers are very involved in establishing financial guidelines and controls, in many instances providing primary leadership for increased accountability. As said earlier, laypeople are increasingly involved too, particularly in approving or rejecting budgets, serving on site councils, and either directly or tacitly controlling planning activities through democratic processes. Indeed planning, organizing, directing, controlling, and evaluating are no longer discrete functions, as these critical duties now involve interactions among multiple vested interest groups.

Although roles may drive individual or group levels of direct involvement in budget matters, interest in the fiduciary trust relating to schools and money always comes to the same end. Ultimately, the fiduciary trust relates to fulfilling the primary mission of schools—an accountability and performance question; that is, are schools doing what is expected of them? The fiduciary path to answering this question answers a second query: What are the essential fiduciary duties associated with schools? The bulleted list as follows indicates that meeting schools' primary mission is a multifaceted task:

- General management;
- Office management;
- Personnel management;
- Staff development;
- Collective negotiations;
- Legal control;
- Financial planning and budgeting;
- Fiscal accounting and financial reporting;
- Cash management;
- Fiscal audits and reports;
- Payroll management;
- School activity and student body funds;
- Purchasing and inventory;
- School insurance and risk management;
- Plant security and property protection;
- School property management;
- School plant maintenance;
- School plant operations;
- Educational facility planning;
- School construction management;
- Debt service and capital-fund management;
- Information management and technology;
- School transportation services;
- School food services;
- Grants and contracts;
- School–community relations.

The Purposes of Accounting

Though not widely understood, the accounting process is *the* vehicle by which a substantial part of accountability is carried out. Although insufficient alone to satisfy school effectiveness under the meaning of performance accountability, the accounting process serves a critical function by managing the single resource (money) that controls the purchase of all other human and material resources used to carry out the educational mission. Importantly, emerging developments suggest that linkages will be increasingly established between the financial data examined in accounting and other forms of public calls for accountability.[5] In other words, tying school money to student learning outcomes is no longer a question—it has become reality and a harbinger of infinite future increase.

Broadly speaking, most people view accounting as a tool used in business to report profits and losses and to detect financial wrongdoing. Though accurate, that view is incomplete because it does not capture the full range of benefits gained from the accounting cycle, nor does it acknowledge that financial accounting equally applies to nonprofit and governmental entities. In addition, in the case of elementary and secondary education, accountability and funding and pupil learning are joined through a school district's budget. Consequently, a budget is the *fiscal expression of the educational philosophy* of a school district and its schools; that is, a budget is the implementation of the district's *educational plan.* By creating a budget, school districts identify how money will be spent to achieve written educational goals. Only by accounting for how the budget is spent can it be known whether—in fiscal terms—the district is satisfying its performance expectations. These realities establish five key purposes for the accounting function, all of which mean to keep the organization focused on its mission.

The first purpose of accounting is to establish procedures by which all fiscal activities in a school district can be accumulated, categorized, reported, and controlled. Each of these terms has specific meaning and value. Accumulating transactions sets up a method of data collection in one location (a set of books)[6] that allows people to view the school district's fiscal transactions. Categorizing transactions separates the various fiscal activities by similarities; it implies that grouping transactions will provide useful analysis about where money is going. Reporting transactions makes the results of activities known. Controlling transactions is essential because resources are finite, while needs are infinite.

The second purpose of accounting is to provide a means to judge progress toward goals. This is a cornerstone of the accountability and performance issue, as schools increasingly must show wise use of resources beyond traditional methods that have relied on standardized tests or locally constructed achievement measures. The accounting function can provide a tool for assessing progress in several ways, and new directions are constantly being sought, particularly given increasingly fiery debates on school funding policy. One way in which the accounting function is able to assess educational attainment is by tracking the financial condition of a school district. For example, the accounting function monitors changes in balances of all funds and accounts. To illustrate, if only 10% of instructional supply money remains by the end of the first month of the school year, the accounting function will flag a serious problem unless there has been a decision to spend this amount to capture some benefit such as bulk purchasing or strategic investment in instruction. Performance budgeting is discussed later—an activity aided by the accounting function that assists in evaluating progress on academic goals by tying fiscal information to pupil achievement data. The accounting function therefore helps to assess whether expenditures and programs are in proper alignment.

The third purpose of accounting is complementary by providing hard evidence to the state that schools are meeting required educational responsibilities specified in statute and regulations. Accounting helps the state in other ways, as the state education agency is required to evaluate whether school districts (as legal arms of the state) are fulfilling the state's constitutional duty to educate children. Every state has an inescapable duty to education, and accountability data—including financial data—are indicators by which states may judge and be judged. In addition, states' interests have increased as state aid to schools has soared, with many states now demanding extensive reporting of school revenues and expenditures on which state and local policy decisions ultimately may be based. In addition, states themselves face accountability in the form of federal reporting to qualify for federal grants and aid, as well as to meet compliance with federal laws relating to educational equity.

The fourth purpose of accounting is to aid in budget preparation. The task of building a budget at district and school levels requires historical data for baseline purposes. Indeed, budgeting is the act of placing money on lines in the total budget for the express purpose of carrying out the district's educational plan. The process is bidirectional: The accounting function is satisfied in part by budgeting, and the act of budgeting satisfies accounting data. Specifically, accounting establishes both initial and end products by creating the funds and line items to which budget allocations are made, while the process of executing a budget creates data needed to carry out the accounting cycle and to establish a baseline for the next budget cycle.

The fifth purpose of accounting is to ensure proper handling of money and to guard against abuse of the fiduciary trust. Given the public's general distrust of government, this aspect of the accounting function is crucial to many issues discussed in earlier chapters. One direct outcome of this distrust is suspicion aimed at public officials, including school leaders, making it critical for schools to observe the highest standards of transparency and integrity. Nearly everyone can relate to instances of real or alleged abuse of public trust, and media reports speculating about misuse of public money have become a daily reality. A critical aspect of the accounting function is to provide *proof* that public confidence is deserved. Accounting is thus a powerful tool for carrying out educational planning, control, and stewardship through budget structures and organization, while the budget itself is the companion vehicle on which accountability rests. Accounting provides a major accountability feature when it does the following:

- *Creates a complete record* of all financial transactions at district and school levels;
- *Summarizes financial activities* of the schools in reports required for proper, effective, and efficient administration;
- *Provides information* used in budget preparation, adoption, and execution;
- *Provides safeguards* on use of money and property, including protection against waste, inefficiency, fraud, and carelessness;
- *Creates a longitudinal record* to aid administrators, teachers, boards, and laypersons in program decision processes.

ALLOCATION IN EDUCATION BUDGETS

The previous section identified reasons and benefits of accountability structures for tracking money, but it did not examine what happens when money comes into a school district. The question of how budgets are allocated actually has several embedded questions that are discussed in greater detail in later chapters. For example, questions arise regarding how to determine amounts of money to be assigned to budget lines during the budget-building process. These issues are highly interwoven within the accounting and budgeting functions. The first issue for examination, however, is the overall revenue structure for a typical school district.

Fund Structure

School districts receive money from multiple sources, primarily other federal, state, and local governments. But regardless of how revenue sources are designed in a given state, certain accounting principles apply that make it possible to record revenues and expenditures. For accounting and accountability purposes, the overarching record system is known as the *fund structure*.[7] Within the fund structure are the broad categories of *governmental* funds, *proprietary* funds, and *fiduciary* funds. Each of these must be defined in order to grasp how revenues are allocated at any level.

As a preface to examining each operational fund's purpose, it must be understood that the fundamental point is that schools operate under a system of *fund accounting*. Fund accounting is a term describing how the types of revenue and expenditure are organized and reported for (in this case) an educational organization. Fund accounting's main value is based in the requirement that each fund may be used only for specific purposes and that the various separate funds in the total fund accounting system should not be commingled. By way of specific example, school districts must credit state transportation aid only to the transportation fund for exclusive use in transportation-related expenditures as defined by the state accounting code. Analogously, special education money may only be credited to the special education fund. Thus, the purpose of fund accounting is to recognize distinct or *segregated* fiscal operations, to track revenues and expenditures by function, and to provide accountability according to intended use.

Governmental Funds

The broad fund structure is made up of one or more individual funds. Governmental funds comprise most of the various fund types in school districts, receiving most of the actual money receipted and expended by schools. Generally, school districts operate four types of governmental funds. While the eventual fund structure is broken down further than these four funds suggest, the broad fund structure is comprised of the following:

- *General fund*: All money not reserved to other funds is placed in the school district's general fund—hence its name, implying a general use fund. The general fund is the largest of all funds in a district because most current annual instructional expenses are paid from it, including teacher and administrator salaries, teaching supplies, insurance, and utilities.
- *Special revenue fund*: Money restricted to specific use, such as compensatory programs or special education, is placed in various named special revenue funds. The purpose is to earmark monies to ensure they are spent only for specified purposes.
- *Capital projects fund*: A capital projects fund allows deposit and expenditure of money from a variety of sources (usually bond revenues) used to finance long-lived assets such as buildings, durable equipment, and land. A capital projects fund is distinct from other annual operating funds such as capital outlay and debt service funds, which might also be used to buy some long-lived assets.

- *Debt service fund*: A debt service fund allows receiving and expending money to amortize long-term debt, including bond issues for school infrastructure or major equipment purchases. Bond issues usually require establishment of debt service funds, with a separate fund established for each bond issue.

Proprietary Funds

Not all money received by school districts is governmental, thus requiring a separate accounting. The convention for receiving and expending the most common types of nongovernmental monies is the creation of separate *proprietary* funds. Proprietary funds often involve fees for services and may be used to create a method of internal billing; as implied by the name, these are monies generated and owned differently than governmental money, with the latter being the property of the state or other taxing unit. In contrast, proprietary funds are created to fit local needs and ways of doing business using non-tax dollars. They are further identified as either *enterprise* or *internal service* funds, a distinction clarified as follows:

- *Enterprise funds*: These funds handle money from non-tax activities such as athletics, school newspapers, and student bookstore operations. The idea is that these activities are like private enterprises, with services provided in exchange for fees, and may be self-supporting. As a result, enterprise revenues and expenditures are maintained separately.
- *Internal service funds*: Large school districts often produce goods or services within the organization that are purchased and consumed by other parts of the same organization. Examples include central printing or maintenance. Such districts may create an internal charge-back system, which also assists in tracking the utilization, cost, and profitability of these various services.

Fiduciary Funds

Not all revenues fall neatly into either governmental or proprietary funds. One type of revenue of growing importance to school districts is money received from external nongovernmental sources such as business partnerships, major gifts, endowments, donations, and other benevolent trusts. Although the vast majority of districts are too small to have extensive fiduciary funds, a structure is available in case the opportunity arises. Such funds are known as *fiduciary* funds.

Quite expectedly, districts managing fiduciary funds are trustees rather than owners, as the name implies. Appropriate revenue is deposited to a named fiduciary fund, and expenditures are controlled by an agreement detailing the purpose of the fund, how the fund is to be managed, and the disposition of proceeds if the agreement is dissolved. In general, fiduciary funds include two basic types:

- *Trust funds*: These may be of several different types. In all cases, however, the school district has trusteeship and acts as the fund's manager. A pension trust fund is a common type and may exist when the district offers local pension benefits in addition to, or in lieu of, a state retirement system. Pension funds, as described here, are highly state-specific as state statutes govern the creation and administration of such funds. An investment trust fund is another type and is used to account for the external portion (the part that does not belong to the school district) of investment pools operated by the district. Again, investment funds are generally highly regulated by state statute and vary among the 50 states. Private-purpose trust funds are the final type: These may include nonexpendable trusts where the principal amount must remain intact, with the earned interest available for school district benefit. Similarly, an expendable trust fund may be set up, wherein both the principal and earned interest are available for school district use. Again, it is stressed these types of funds vary from state to state and are closely regulated by state statutes.

- *Agency funds*: Finally, agency funds are monies held in trusteeship by a school district for individuals, private organizations, or other governments. Examples include accounting for student activities or taxes collected for another unit of government. A common use of agency funds has included setting up a central payroll fund to reduce the number of accounts needed for payroll transactions to the various entities in a school district—for example, teachers, administrators, support staff, and food service workers. Under one central agency fund, all data on wages, fringe benefits, tax withholding, and workers' compensation may be more efficiently monitored and administered.

An Intermediate Overview

The executive view of accounting for school leaders says it is critical to grasp that there is a *structure* for school money that allows it to be *receipted, expended,* and *tracked* according to its intended purpose. The total *accounting system* is first made up of various *funds*. School districts in all states operate *governmental* funds made of up a *general* fund and *special revenue* funds, and most districts also have *capital project* and *debt service* funds. Similarly, all districts use *proprietary* funds to some extent, especially for common operations such as *enterprise* activities, and many school districts also have *internal service* funds. Far fewer districts will have extensive *fiduciary* funds. Ultimately, pursuant to state statutes, the local board of education is the final *custodian* for all funds maintained by the district, and building administrators are often charged with administering *school activity* funds. School boards typically delegate by charging the superintendent of schools and his or her staff to manage such funds. Policymakers and higher units of government rely on fund accounting to direct the flow of school money, including state aid, and to judge the impact of educational and tax policy decisions. Ultimately, the community depends on fund accounting to ensure educational experiences for children and to protect the public fiduciary trust. In brief, accounting through fund accounting is a critical component of accountability in all its forms.

TRACKING SCHOOL MONEY

To more fully understand fiscal accountability, the focus turns now to the examination of how money is handled by the fund structure once it is received by the school district. The twin concepts of *revenue* and *expenditure* are key starting points.

The *accounting cycle* is a third key concept. These underpinnings are foundational to the actual budget process discussed in later chapters; that is, the process by which resources are assigned in the budget to educational uses.

Revenue Structure

For accounting purposes, a district's financial affairs can be conceptualized as a two-dimensional plane—*revenue* and *expenditure*—even though it was explained earlier that the budget is a three-sided expression of the school district's educational plan. The three-sided view is often referred to as the budget triangle, where accountability for program planning is linked to revenue and expenditure. But for present purposes, a two-dimensional view is more useful by thinking first about revenue as money going *into* schools, as contrasted to expenditure, which is that same money going back *out* in support of teaching and learning.

The revenue side of school funding generally involves a three-tiered classification. The first tier is the *fund*, as already discussed in this chapter. The second tier is the *source* of revenue. The third tier is the *type* of revenue. These concepts are interrelated.

The earlier discussion about *fund* structure reenters now in that revenue received must be recorded to one of the funds operated by the school district. For example, revenue earmarked for transportation must be deposited to the transportation fund, and revenue for any other restricted or categorical purpose must be recorded to its appropriate special fund. Revenue not reserved for special funds is usually placed in the general fund.

When actual budgeting behaviors are presented in later chapters, it will be evident that the revenue side of a budget requires placing each revenue receipt on a budget line along with noting its source. While each state's department of education has its own budget forms, the practice is universal: Placing money on a source line in the revenue side of the budget is required because it allows the school district to report fiscal data to the appropriate state agency and to establish lobbying positions during legislative sessions; that is, fund accounting is required by law, and part of the reasoning behind such requirement is that accounting data reveal a great deal of information along with requiring a desired level of uniformity. Regardless of the state in which a school district is located, three revenue sources apply to school budgeting and accounting:

- *Local and intermediate sources* include money raised by the school district, usually from local property taxes. Intermediate sources include money from governmental units that exist in many states which stand between the local district and the state, such as cities and counties.
- *State sources* include money raised within the state where the district is located: Generally referring to state aid, but excluding funds that are passed through the state from the federal government.
- *Federal sources* include direct federal aid or state flow-through money, usually categorical aid.[8]

Type of revenue refers to both source and use. Local revenues often include property tax, tuition, student transportation fees, investment earnings, student organization fees, and revenue from textbook rentals. Intermediate and state revenues may include grants-in-aid and revenue in lieu of taxes under tax exemptions or tax abatements granted by other taxing units. Types of revenue from federal sources include unrestricted grants-in-aid received either directly from the federal government or as restricted grants from the federal level distributed through the state. Figure 4.1 illustrates how fund, source, and type of revenue come together to express the revenue side of a school district's budget. In Figure 4.1, the *fund* is the general fund. *Sources* include local, intermediate (county in this illustration), state, federal, and other. *Types* include, for example, ad valorem property taxes levied and a personal property tax on recreational vehicles.[9] Source codes are part of the system for reporting to the federal government.[10] Importantly, budget documents in the various states may look quite different from Figure 4.1 because of differences in the underlying tax scheme, but these essential elements of fund accounting apply universally to all states.

GENERAL	Code 06 Line	12 mo. 2016-2017 Actual (1)	12 mo. 2017-2018 Actual (2)	12 mo. 2018-2019 Budget (3)
UNENCUMBERED CASH BALANCE JULY 1	01		#N/A	#N/A
Cancel of Prior Yr Enc	03			
REVENUE: 1000 LOCAL SOURCES 1300 Tuition				
1312 Individuals (Out District)	30			
1320 Other School District/Govt Sources In-State	40			
1330 Other School District/Govt Sources Out-State	45			
1410 Transportation Fees (Reimbursement)	47			
1510 Interest on Idle Funds	48		XXXXXXXXXX	XXXXXXXXXX
1700 Student Activities (Reimbursement)	50			
1900 Other Revenue From Local Source 1910 User Charges (Reimbursement)	55			
1980 Reimbursements	60			
1985 State Aid Reimbursement**	65			
1990 Miscellaneous	67			
2000 COUNTY SOURCES 2600 Other County Revenue	66	XXXXXXXXXX		
2800 In Lieu of Taxes IRBs/Rental Excise	85	XXXXXXXXXX	XXXXXXXXXX	XXXXXXXXXX
3000 STATE SOURCES 3110 General State Aid	95	#N/A	#N/A	CK LINE 175
3130 Mineral Production Tax	115			
3140 Supplemental General State Aid	116	XXXXXXXXXX	XXXXXXXXXX	XXXXXXXXXX
3205 Special Education Aid	120	#N/A	#N/A	0
3221 KPERS Aid	125	#N/A	XXXXXXXXXX	XXXXXXXXXX
3223 Capital Outlay State Aid	130	XXXXXXXXXX	XXXXXXXXXX	XXXXXXXXXX
3226 Extraordinary Need State Aid***	132	XXXXXXXXXX	#N/A	XXXXXXXXXX
4000 FEDERAL SOURCES 4820 PL 382 (Exclude Extra Aid for Children on Indian Land and Low Rent Housing) (formerly PL 874)	145			0
5000 OTHER 5208 Transfer From Authorized Funds****	165	0	XXXXXXXXXX	XXXXXXXXXX
RESOURCES AVAILABLE	170	#N/A	#N/A	#N/A
TOTAL EXPENDITURES & TRANSFERS	175	#N/A	0	#N/A
EXCESS REVENUE TO STATE	200	XXXXXXXXXX	XXXXXXXXXX	XXXXXXXXXX
UNENCUMBERED CASH BALANCE JUNE 30 *	190	#N/A	#N/A	XXXXXXXXXX

FIGURE 4.1 Sample Revenue Side of a Budget

The system of revenue structure is important because it is used to allocate money to all the different funds comprising a school district's total budget. To summarize, revenues are thus first classified by fund and source, and then broken into governmental, proprietary, and fiduciary groups for further distinction by fund, source, and type. Not all of these distinctions are apparent in Figure 4.1, which only shows governmental general fund revenue, but Figure 4.1 illustrates that the very first step to creating an educational plan is receiving and depositing revenue so that an expenditure plan can be built—a plan in the case of Figure 4.1 that takes into consideration the school district's three-year historical revenue trends when setting a new year's budget.

Expenditure Structure

In contrast, expenditure structure is significantly more complex than the revenue side. Revenue sources typically fit into only three categories, while expenditures are broken into many different classifications. Simply said, this means that school districts have only a few sources of revenue, while in contrast they have many expenditure categories that detail their actual expenses.

Budget documents in every state classify educational expenditures using a program budgeting format. Expenditures are classified by *fund*, *function*, and *object*, and may be further broken down by *project*, *instructional level*, *operational unit*, *subject matter*, and *job classification*. States and local school districts vary in the amount of detail they provide, although states generally specify a minimum amount of coding that districts must use. Such a classification scheme permits accumulation of data that may be used for a variety of purposes, the very first of which is tracking expenditures for program accountability. Each level in the expenditure classification scheme has discrete codes hierarchically arranged to track expenditures from broad to narrow. For example, although the general fund is very broad, object codes break functions into various sub-codes for more detailed reporting and analysis.

Extensive detail of how expenditures can be broken down is again beyond the scope of this discussion. For general purposes of understanding expenditure structure, however, the following statements describe how coding moves from the broad to the specific:

- *Fund*: Expenditures are first classified as an expenditure from a governmental fund, proprietary fund, or fiduciary fund. The reason for starting with the fund is sensible: Since revenue is first assigned to a fund on the basis of use in support of some educational activity, it is sensible that expenditures must be assigned to the corresponding fund—for example, Code 01 to designate an expense to the general fund;
- *Function*: Expenditures can be classified by function, which refers to the general activity for which a purchased good or service is acquired. Function describes the areas of instruction, support services, operation of noninstructional services, facilities acquisition and construction, and debt service. These codes track expenditures more closely by identifying functions carried out—for example, Code 2300 to designate an expenditure for general administration support services within the general fund;

- *Object*: Finally, expenditures are classified by object, or the item or service acquired. This includes nine major object categories (numbered 100–999), which can be further subdivided. Major categories include areas such as salaries, employee benefits, purchased professional and technical services, purchased property services, and supplies. For example, Code 310 might designate a board-level salary expense within the general fund.

Figure 4.2 illustrates this complex structure. Figure 4.2 is the expenditure side of a sample school district's general fund budget document. Assume the district has received and deposited revenue to each of its operating funds. Assume also that the budget process is complete and that a budget has been legally adopted—a procedure explored further in later chapters. Now the school district has authority to spend money. Importantly, several other things are in place. Figure 4.2 reflects expenditure classification as follows. The *fund* is the general fund. *Functions* in the general fund

GENERAL	Code 06 Line	12 mo. 2016-2017 Actual (1)	12 mo. 2017-2018 Actual (2)	12 mo. 2018-2019 Budget (3)
UNENCUMBERED CASH BALANCE JULY 1	01		#N/A	#N/A
Cancel of Prior Yr Enc	03			
REVENUE: 1000 LOCAL SOURCES 1300 Tuition				
1312 Individuals (Out District)	30			
1320 Other School District/Govt Sources In-State	40			
1330 Other School District/Govt Sources Out-State	45			
1410 Transportation Fees (Reimbursement)	47			
1510 Interest on Idle Funds	48		XXXXXXXXXX	XXXXXXXXXX
1700 Student Activities (Reimbursement)	50			
1900 Other Revenue From Local Source 1910 User Charges (Reimbursement)	55			
1980 Reimbursements	60			
1985 State Aid Reimbursement**	65			
1990 Miscellaneous	67			
2000 COUNTY SOURCES 2600 Other County Revenue	66	XXXXXXXXXX		
2800 In Lieu of Taxes IRBs/Rental Excise	85	XXXXXXXXXX	XXXXXXXXXX	XXXXXXXXXX
3000 STATE SOURCES 3110 General State Aid	95	#N/A	#N/A	CK LINE 175
3130 Mineral Production Tax	115			
3140 Supplemental General State Aid	116	XXXXXXXXXX	XXXXXXXXXX	XXXXXXXXXX
3205 Special Education Aid	120	#N/A	#N/A	0
3221 KPERS Aid	125	#N/A	XXXXXXXXXX	XXXXXXXXXX
3223 Capital Outlay State Aid	130	XXXXXXXXXX	XXXXXXXXXX	XXXXXXXXXX
3226 Extraordinary Need State Aid***	132	XXXXXXXXXX	#N/A	XXXXXXXXXX
4000 FEDERAL SOURCES 4820 PL 382 (Exclude Extra Aid for Children on Indian Land and Low Rent Housing) (formerly PL 874)	145			0
5000 OTHER 5208 Transfer From Authorized Funds****	165		0 XXXXXXXXXX	XXXXXXXXXX
RESOURCES AVAILABLE	170	#N/A	#N/A	#N/A
TOTAL EXPENDITURES & TRANSFERS	175	#N/A	0	#N/A
EXCESS REVENUE TO STATE	200	XXXXXXXXXX	XXXXXXXXXX	XXXXXXXXXX
UNENCUMBERED CASH BALANCE JUNE 30 *	190	#N/A	#N/A	XXXXXXXXXX

FIGURE 4.2 Sample Expenditure Side of a Budget

GENERAL EXPENDITURES	Code 06 Line	12 mo. 2016-2017 Actual (1)	12 mo. 2017-2018 Actual (2)	12 mo. 2018-2019 Budget (3)
1000 Instruction				
100 Salaries				
110 Certified	210			
120 NonCertified	215			
200 Employee Benefits				
210 Insurance (Employee)	220			
220 Social Security	225			
290 Other	230			
300 Purchased Professional and Technical Services	235			
400 Purchased Property Services	237			
500 Other Purchased Services				
560 Tuition				
561 Tuition/other State LEA's	240			
562 Tuition/other LEA's outside the State	245			
563 Tuition/Priv Sources	250			
590 Other	255			
600 Supplies				
610 General Supplemental (Teaching)	260			
644 Textbooks	265			
650 Supplies (Technology Related)	267			
680 Miscellaneous Supplies	270			
700 Property (Equipment & Furnishings)	275			
800 Other	280			
2000 Support Services				
2100 Student Support Services				
100 Salaries				
110 Certified	285			
120 NonCertified	290			
200 Employee Benefits				
210 Insurance (Employee)	295			
220 Social Security	300			
290 Other	305			
300 Purchased Professional and Technical Services	310			
400 Purchased Property Services	313			
500 Other Purchased Services	315			
600 Supplies	320			
700 Property (Equipment & Furnishings)	325			
800 Other	330			
2200 Instr Support Staff				
100 Salaries				
110 Certified	335			
120 NonCertified	340			
200 Employee Benefits				
210 Insurance (Employee)	345			
220 Social Security	350			
290 Other	355			
300 Purchased Professional and Technical Services	360			
400 Purchased Property Services	363			
500 Other Purchased Services	365			

FIGURE 4.2 (Continued)

GENERAL EXPENDITURES	Code 06 Line	12 mo. 2016-2017 Actual (1)	12 mo. 2017-2018 Actual (2)	12 mo. 2018-2019 Budget (3)
600 Supplies				
640 Books (not textbooks)				
and Periodicals	370			
650 Technology Supplies	375			
680 Miscellaneous Supplies	380			
700 Property (Equipment & Furnishings)	385			
800 Other	390			
2300 General Administration				
100 Salaries				
110 Certified	395			
120 NonCertified	400			
200 Employee Benefits				
210 Insurance (Employee)	405			
220 Social Security	410			
290 Other	415			
300 Purchased Professional				
and Technical Services	420			
400 Purchased Property Services	425			
500 Other Purchased Services				
520 Insurance	430			
530 Communications				
(Telephone, postage, etc.)	435			
590 Other	440			
600 Supplies	445			
700 Property (Equipment & Furnishings)	450			
800 Other	455			
2400 School Administration				
100 Salaries				
110 Certified	460			
120 NonCertified	465			
200 Employee Benefits				
210 Insurance (Employee)	470			
220 Social Security	475			
290 Other	480			
300 Purchased Professional				
and Technical Services	485			
400 Purchased Property Services	490			
500 Other Purchased Services				
530 Communications				
(Telephone, postage, etc.)	495			
590 Other	500			
600 Supplies	505			
700 Property (Equipment & Furnishings)	510			
800 Other	515			
2500 Central Services				
100 Salaries				
110 Certified	730			
120 NonCertified	735			
200 Employee Benefits				
210 Insurance	740			
220 Social Security	745			
290 Other	750			
300 Purchased Professional and Technical Services	755			
400 Purchased Property Services	760			

FIGURE 4.2 (Continued)

GENERAL EXPENDITURES	Code 06 Line	12 mo. 2016-2017 Actual (1)	12 mo. 2017-2018 Actual (2)	12 mo. 2018-2019 Budget (3)
500 Other Purchased Services	765			
600 Supplies	770			
700 Property (Equipment & Furnishings)	775			
800 Other	780			
2600 Operations & Maintenance				
100 Salaries				
120 NonCertified	520			
200 Employee Benefits				
210 Insurance (Employee)	525			
220 Social Security	530			
290 Other	535			
300 Purchased Professional and Technical Services	540			
400 Purchased Property Services				
411 Water/Sewer	545			
420 Cleaning	550			
430 Repairs & Maintenance	555			
440 Rentals	560			
460 Repair of Buildings	565			
490 Other	570			
500 Other Purchased Services				
520 Insurance	575			
590 Other	580			
600 Supplies				
610 General Supplies	585			
620 Energy				
621 Heating	590			
622 Electricity	595			
626 Motor Fuel (not schoolbus)	600			
629 Other	605			
680 Miscellaneous Supplies	610			
700 Property (Equipment & Furnishings)	615			
800 Other	620			
2601 Operations & Maintenance (Transportation)				
100 Salaries				
120 NonCertified	622			
200 Employee Benefits				
210 Insurance (Employee)	623			
220 Social Security	626			
290 Other	628			
300 Purchased and Professional Technical Services	630			
400 Purchased Property Services	632			
500 Other Purchased Services	634			
600 Supplies				
610 General Supplies	636			
620 Energy				
621 Heating	638			
622 Electricity	640			
626 Motor Fuel (not schoolbus)	642			
629 Other	644			
680 Miscellaneous Supplies	646			
700 Property (Equipment & Furnishings)	648			
800 Other	650			

FIGURE 4.2 *(Continued)*

GENERAL EXPENDITURES	Code 06 Line	12 mo. 2016-2017 Actual (1)	12 mo. 2017-2018 Actual (2)	12 mo. 2018-2019 Budget (3)
2700 Student Transportation Serv				
2720 Supervision				
100 Salaries				
120 NonCertified	652			
200 Employee Benefits				
210 Insurance	654			
220 Social Security	656			
290 Other	658			
600 Supplies	660			
730 Equipment	662			
800 Other	664			
2710 Vehicle Operating Services				
100 Salaries				
120 NonCertified	666			
200 Employee Benefits				
210 Insurance	668			
220 Social Security	670			
290 Other	672			
442 Rent of Vehicles (lease)	674			
500 Other Purchased Services				
513 Contracting of Bus Services	676			
519 Mileage in Lieu of Trans	678			
520 Insurance	680			
626 Motor Fuel	682			
730 Equipment (Including Buses)	684			
800 Other	686			
2730 Vehicle Services& Maintenance Services				
100 Salaries				
120 NonCertified	688			
200 Employee Benefits				
210 Insurance	690			
220 Social Security	692			
290 Other	694			
300 Purchased Professional and Tech Services	696			
400 Purchased Property Services	698			
500 Other Purchased Services	700			
600 Supplies	702			
730 Equipment	704			
800 Other	706			
2790 Other Student Transportation Services				
100 Salaries				
120 NonCertified	708			
200 Employee Benefits				
210 Insurance	710			
220 Social Security	712			
290 Other	714			
300 Purchased Professional and Tech Services	716			
400 Purchased Property Services	718			
500 Other Purchased Services	720			
600 Supplies	722			
730 Equipment	724			
800 Other	726			

FIGURE 4.2 (*Continued*)

GENERAL EXPENDITURES	Code 06 Line	12 mo. 2016-2017 Actual (1)	12 mo. 2017-2018 Actual (2)	12 mo. 2018-2019 Budget (3)
2900 Other Support Services				
100 Salaries				
110 Certified	895			
120 NonCertified	900			
200 Employee Benefits				
210 Insurance	905			
220 Social Security	910			
290 Other	915			
300 Purchased Professional and Technical Services	920			
400 Purchased Property Services	925			
500 Other Purchased Services	930			
600 Supplies	935			
700 Property (Equipment & Furnishings)	940			
800 Other	945			
3300 Community Services Operations	785			
4300 Architectural & Engineering Services	790			
5200 TRANSFER TO:				
980 Supplemental General	792		XXXXXXXXX	XXXXXXXXXX
932 Adult Education	795	0	0	0
934 Adult Suppl Education	800	0	0	0
936 Bilingual Education	805	0	0	0
937 Virtual Education	807	0	0	0
938 Capital Outlay	810	0	0	0
940 Driver Training	815	0	0	0
943 Extraordinary School Prog	823	0	0	0
944 Food Service	825	0	0	0
946 Professional Development	830	0	0	0
948 Parent Education Program	835	0	0	0
949 Summer School	837	0	0	0
950 Special Education	840	0	0	0
954 Career and Postsecondary Education	850	0	0	0
960 Special Reserve Fund	853	0	0	0
963 Special Liability Expense Fund	855	0	0	0
965 KPERS	856	#N/A	XXXXXXXXX	XXXXXXXXXX
972 Contingency Reserve	885	0	0	0
974 Textbook & Student Materials Revolving Fund	889	0	0	0
976 At Risk (4yr Old)	891	0	0	0
978 At Risk (K-12)	893	0	0	0
TOTAL EXPENDITURES & TRANSFERS	xxxx	#N/A	0	0

FIGURE 4.2 (*Continued*)

include instruction (Code 1000), support services (Code 2000), school administration (Code 2400), operations and maintenance (Code 2600), and so on up to architectural and engineering services (Code 4300). These expenditure codes are broken down further by *object*, for example, teacher salaries (Code 1000–110), teacher benefits (Code 1000–200) and general administration salaries (Code 2300–100).

The benefits of such coding are multiple. First, federal and state data tracking are satisfied by uniform reporting methods because the system in Figure 4.2 both derives from and conforms to Generally Accepted Accounting Principles (GAAP) and the Governmental Accounting Standards Board (GASB) as promulgated by the U.S. Department of Education in its controlling guidance.[11] Second, the school district may choose to further analyze the minimum required data by expanding it to include codes that report at progressively more detailed levels, wherein the purchase of teaching materials could be tracked to each school and classroom. To underscore again, accounting is not just an assurance against ineptitude, carelessness, or fraud; rather, it is the *other* key dimension of accountability in that costs of programs can be calculated, and those costs can be linked to pupil performance data if the accounting system is properly structured. For example, if low performance and underfunding simultaneously appear at an identifiable grade level, appropriate interventions can be made: Perhaps new instructional materials should be bought; teachers may need targeted professional development; or teacher aides or reduction in class size might be warranted because large class sizes may be leading to inadequate individualized attention. In other words, a host of options can be explored using data available through accounting in combination with educational information.

The Accounting Transaction

The overhead view of the accounting function next leads to a brief description of the accounting transaction in order to have a complete grasp of how money is tracked in schools. Administrators and school board members need such understanding because they are ultimately the responsible agents for both money and educational programs. Teachers need to understand too because they are instantly affected if anyone in the system engages in bad fiscal management.

Earlier discussion in this chapter showed how the various funds provide a structure for grouping the financial activities of a school district by revenue and expenditure dimensions. This is an important first step in the accounting transaction because it segregates money according to its use. The next step is to create individual *accounts* within each fund wherein the actual money transactions occur. These accounts make up the record of assets, liabilities, revenues, and expenditures that occur under the broader fund umbrella.

Generally, five classifications of accounts are established within any given fund (e.g., the general fund). The five accounts are *expense, income, asset, liability,* and *net worth* or *fund balance* accounts. The purpose of each account is singular: All transactions involving revenue or expenditure or increases or decreases in the value of assets are entered (posted) to these accounts. Schools use the *double entry* method of posting transactions to the various accounts in a fund. Double entry means entering both a *debit* (an entry on the left-hand side of the account ledger) to one account and a *credit* (an entry on the right-hand side) to another account for each transaction. Asset and expenditure accounts (left-hand side accounts) are increased by debiting and decreased by crediting. Conversely, an income account (a right-hand side account) is decreased by a debit and increased by a credit.

The double entry posting of an account transaction can be illustrated using a school district that has just received a general fund tax distribution of $1,000,000. Using a double entry system, this payment involves two general fund account groups: The income account and the asset account (the cash account). The income account increases as the transaction is entered as a credit. The cash account also increases as the transaction is entered as a debit to its side of the ledger. If the district then hires a new teacher at a salary of $40,000, a new transaction in the general fund immediately occurs. Categories affected are the cash account and the appropriate expenditure account containing teacher salaries. As a result, cash balance in the asset account is credited (decreased), and the expenditure account for salaries is debited (increased). The purpose of this two-sided process is important: Double entry is a tool that creates *a self-balancing set of books*, so that the assets of the district are not falsely inflated. If this were not done, assets and liabilities would not balance, falsifying the actual cash position of the fund because appropriate additions and subtractions would not cross-balance revenue and expenditure activity—an error in financial position that would worsen if subsequent decisions were made on the basis of bad information.

The individual accounts in each fund are listed in the *general ledger*, a set of *books* that keeps all records in a single location. Each transaction is recorded in the general ledger by a complicated process. Before being entered in the general ledger, revenue and expenditure transactions are first recorded in a *general journal*, which is a chronological listing of transactions as they were initiated. Transactions are transferred from the general journal and posted to the appropriate accounts on the general ledger, always using double entry. This process brings together (summarizes) all similar accounts. Figure 4.3 is a sample journal entry for a given day showing the unpaid bills and charges to the appropriate expense and asset accounts. Figure 4.3 also shows how double entry creates a self-balancing set of books; that is, expenses are debited in the amount of $3,238.84, thus increasing the expense account, while assets are credited $3,238.84, thereby decreasing the district's assets. From this transaction, the district knows exactly how much it owes compared to its assets—a reflection of true cash position.

This process is repeated for each fund and transaction during the accounting cycle. Each accounting transaction is one of ten steps:

1. Journalizing transactions;
2. Posting transactions;
3. Preparing a trial balance;
4. Preparing a work sheet;
5. Preparing financial statements;
6. Journalizing closing entries;
7. Posting closing entries;
8. Balancing, ruling, and bringing forward balances of balance sheet accounts;
9. Ruling temporary accounts;
10. Preparing post-closing trial balance.[12]

Expense Accounts			
Debit No.	1	Supplies	$3,175.63
	18	Miscellaneous	63.21
			$3,238.84
Asset Account			
Credit No.	20	Accts. Payable	$3,238.84

FIGURE 4.3 Typical Journal Entry for the Journal Period Ending June 1

The meticulous nature of the accounting cycle underscores the need to account for all fiscal activity in a tax-supported organization. To that end, it is important that school districts hire qualified professionals with the expertise to carry out these tasks, such as a chief financial officer (CFO) or school business administrator, along with accountants, fiscal analysts, and accounting clerks as needed, depending upon the size of the school district and its budget. In addition, it is important to remember that these employees need regular professional development just like other school district employees in order to remain current on best practices and changes in state statutes. In small school districts, it may be more cost-effective to secure qualified outside assistance for some of these activities. Importantly, these professionals provide school leaders with financial data that in conjunction with other types of data allows schools to make sound educational program decisions.

Auditing

Finally, the accounting cycle requires school leaders to grasp the concept of auditing. Auditing is critical to understanding schools and money because accounting and reporting would have no authority without the checks and balances of auditing. Auditing is the independent examination of accounting systems to ensure the accuracy of the accounting records of a district.

It is a key concept to internalize that auditing is the best protection for anyone in a fiduciary role in a school district because auditing assures the public, employees, and the school board that the financial affairs of the district meet state statutory and accounting guidelines. The purposes of audits are several. First, audits are designed to detect errors in accounting. Given the enormous amount of financial data in a school district, errors can easily occur. Importantly, errors can be accidental or intentional. Auditing serves a second purpose of recommending changes to accounting procedures in order to improve operations. Finally, auditing demonstrates to the state, the federal government, and local taxpayers that revenues are being used lawfully and appropriately. Thus, audits advance the educational mission of the school district, strengthen stakeholder trust, and protect school officials' professional reputations.

There are several types of audits, each serving a different need. Audits fall into two broad categories of *internal* and *external*. Audits are additionally known as *pre*-audits, *post*-audits, or *continuous* audits based on timing and purpose. Finally, external audits are classified as *general comprehensive* audits, *state* audits, or *special* audits. Each type has a unique purpose based on the data being sought.

Internal Audits

Internal financial auditing within a school organization is meant to provide a system of self-checks. Internal auditing ranges from basic monthly board of education budget reports to a full system of continuous internal monitoring, generally with accountants employed by the district to study and improve accounting systems. All districts, regardless of size, should engage in rigorous internal auditing. Internal auditing is required to produce monthly financial statements because journals and ledgers must be examined to generate income and expense statements. Mandatory state reports also require internal auditing to produce and verify the data on which state aid requests are based. Internal audits are usually either pre-audits or continuous audits. A pre-audit ensures proper accounting procedures in advance of a transaction. A continuous audit implies constant observation of the accounting system. Continuous auditing occurs through the system of checks and balances in place in most school districts whereby multiple approvals must be secured to spend money. The hierarchy from one actual district, shown in Figure 4.4, shows protections in place to guard against error or wrongdoing. Although internal auditing is never sufficient alone, it is an important tool of good management.

External Audits

External auditing is a formal examination of financial records in a school district by a qualified outside entity hired to verify accuracy and compliance. External audits are always conducted by an independent auditing organization such as a certified public accounting firm or, in some instances, by state auditors checking for compliance with state regulations.

External audits yield an audit report with recommendations on the audit findings. External audits are accompanied by a letter of transmittal stating the purpose of the audit, procedures followed, a statement of findings, and a list of recommendations. In most instances, the audit is conducted at the same time as preparation of the school district's comprehensive annual financial report (CAFR). As a general rule, most external audits are *general comprehensive audits* occurring at the close of an accounting period, usually an entire fiscal year. The report generally contains summaries of revenues and expenditures and compares cash balances against encumbrances to determine if statutory requirements were met. Governmental funds are examined separately under statements of budgetary accounts, and other funds such as fiduciary expendable trust funds and proprietary funds are also separately examined. If no problems were noted, the report will yield an *unqualified opinion* because its findings were not qualified by any *audit exceptions*. If concerns are present, the report will yield a *qualified opinion*. Audit reports are presented to the board of education, with the board required to show receipt of the audit in its minutes and to show action to correct audit exceptions.

Accounting and auditing affect everyone connected to schools. Trouble-free audits are the ultimate affirmation of trust, in that school leaders, boards, teachers, staff, children, and the community are well served by good financial management. On the other hand, everyone suffers if bad fiscal management goes undetected. The price paid for accounting and auditing services is money wisely spent, although these tools still do not ensure accountability for wise educational decision-making. Nonetheless, accounting and auditing play an important part in overall accountability by assuring the public of conformity with the law.

State Audits

In addition to internal audits and external audits, a variety of *state* audits may occur in school districts. State audits serve a different purpose and are designed to monitor compliance with statutes and regulations involving state or federal money.

The variety of individual state audit requirements makes it difficult to provide details. Primarily, differences rest in how states choose to control elementary and secondary education. In states where local control is emphasized, state audits may serve mostly to meet minimum compliance standards. In states where control has been placed at the state level, state audits may be interested in a more exhaustive review of finances and programs.

All state audits have a common goal of determining whether the state's financial stake in schools is protected. State audits thus focus particularly on those funds to which the state either supplies direct aid or for which state agencies act as a channel for federal aid to local school districts. In the case of federal funds, state agencies are interested in maintenance of applications, expenditure reports, and transmittal documents. In the case of state funds, state agencies are especially interested in documentation relating to state aid claims. For example, transportation claims are often closely examined because many states invest very large sums in pupil transportation services. Likewise, state agencies closely audit districts to ensure that federal monies are not commingled or improperly spent. State audits are state-specific, although the goal is always to verify that the state's educational obligations and priorities are met.

As indicated earlier, accounting standards are set by the Governmental Accounting Standards Board (GASB).[13] Generally accepted accounting principles (GAAP) require use of the modified accrual basis of accounting for governmental funds. This means that revenues are recognized when they become measurable during the fiscal period.

Special Audits

Finally, school districts may be subject to *special* audits. Although fairly uncommon, the purpose of a special audit may relate to concerns involving error or fraud. One of the logical ways special audits occur is as an offshoot of a normal state audit. For example, a transportation audit might reveal that a school district was claiming more children than were actually being transported. Likewise, internal auditing might lead a district to voluntarily seek a special audit; for example, inability to reconcile expense claims with receipts could result in a special audit. Other events such as inventory loss might result in a special audit. Unfortunately, these examples are not entirely implausible as it is not possible to fully control individual behavior.

Accounting and accountability are constant companions for school leaders, board members, policymakers, teachers, and the general public. The right way to engage in financial transactions requires at least the following:

- Strong internal accounting procedures, including segregation of duties based on checks and balances (see Figure 4.4);
- Competent employees with sufficient time to do the work of accounting in order to avoid making errors;
- Extensive documentation based on a system that includes the following:
  - Proof of board of education approval of expenditures;
  - Statements showing receipts and disbursements;
  - Reconciled bank statements, including all canceled checks;
  - A system of purchase orders;
  - A strict no-cash disbursement policy.

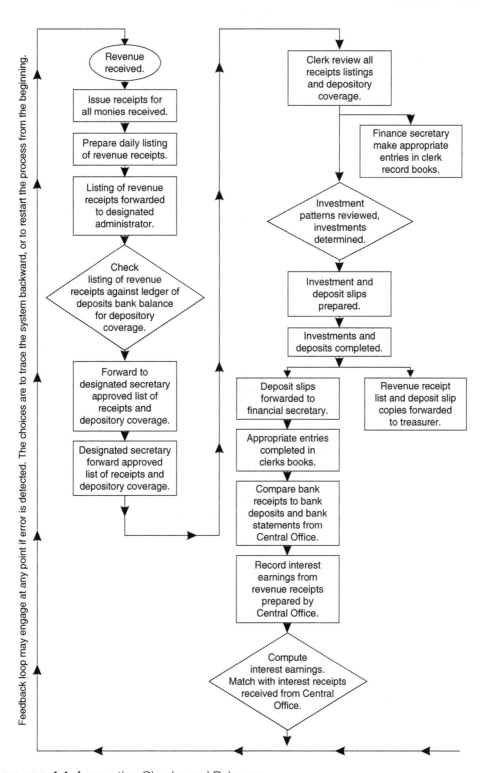

FIGURE 4.4 Accounting Checks and Balances

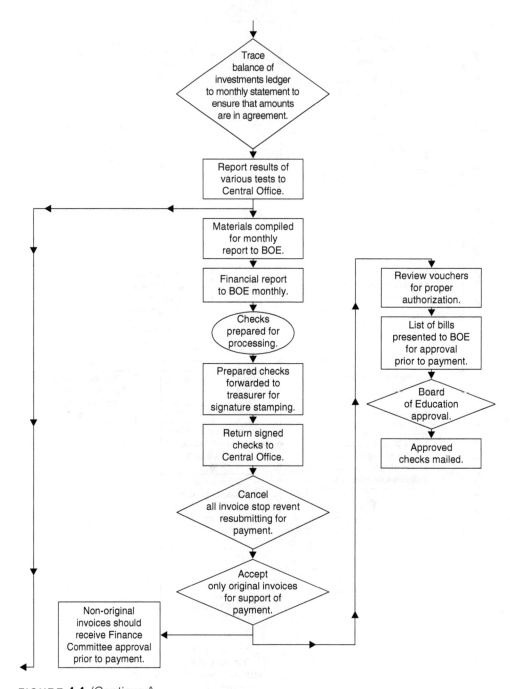

FIGURE 4.4 (Continued)

A FINAL WORD CONCERNING PROFESSIONALISM

This chapter has urged that the gravity of the fiduciary trust cannot be overstated. This is the issue of *professionalism* in handling school money. Although professionalism in the broad context has been addressed here, the published ethical standards of the school finance profession should be followed in every school district in America.

Codes of ethics exist for most professions. School leaders, teachers, and many community members belong to professional or trade organizations that have adopted ethical conduct codes. Standards are key to the integrity of the entire social order, and people with fiduciary capacity for public money have an exceptional duty to ethical conduct. The Association of School Business Officials (ASBO), International has published a code of ethics that is fundamental to school leaders. ASBO's Professional Standards and Code of Ethics[14] states:

> ASBO International considers professional standards for school business officials a key to gaining and maintaining the trust of policymakers and citizens. The Association has been actively developing and disseminating standards for the position of school business official for nearly five decades. Throughout those years, ASBO International has operated under the principle that public trust is built when written standards are in place, professional development supports the standards, and the performance of members of the profession are judged in concrete terms against the standards. Being judged as "professional" is critical to the school business official. The term engenders an image of expertise, trust, and dedication. ASBO International believes all school business officials today must strive for this image.

Even more specifically, ASBO has issued strong guidance in unmistakable terms as it demands of its membership the following knowledge, dispositions, and skills:[15]

Ethical Standards

In all activities, members and associate members in good standing of ASBO International and its accredited affiliates shall

- Make the well-being of all students, staff, and fellow members a fundamental value in all decision-making and actions.
- Fulfill professional responsibilities with honesty and integrity.
- Support the principle of due process and protect the civil and human rights of all individuals.
- Obey all local, state, and national laws.
- Implement the policies and administrative rules and regulations of the employing organization (school district, private school, and/or associated organization).
- Pursue appropriate measures to correct those laws, policies, and regulations that are not consistent with this code of ethics.

- Not tolerate the failure of others to act in an ethical manner and will pursue appropriate measures to correct such failures.
- Never use their positions for personal gain through political, social, religious, economic, or other influence.
- Honor all contracts until fulfillment or release.

Ethical Conduct

In all activities, members and associate members in good standing of ASBO International and its accredited affiliates shall demonstrate their adherence to the standards set forth above by

- Actively supporting the goals and objectives of the educational institution with which they work.
- Interpreting the policies and practices of their employer to the staff and to the community fairly and objectively.
- Implementing, to the best of their ability, the policies and administrative regulations of their employer.
- Assisting fellow members, as appropriate, in fulfilling their obligations.
- Supporting a positive image of the educational institution with which they work.
- Not publicly criticizing board members, superiors, administrators, or other employees.
- Helping subordinates achieve their maximum potential through fair and just treatment.
- Maintaining confidentiality of data and information.
- Accurately and objectively reporting data, in a timely fashion, to authorized agencies.

Expectations of Personal and Professional Integrity

In the conduct of business and the discharge of responsibilities, each member will

- Conduct business honestly, openly, and with integrity.
- Avoid conflict of interest situations by not conducting business with a company or firm in which the official or any member of the official's family has a vested interest.
- Avoid preferential treatment of one outside interest group, company, or individual over another.
- Uphold the dignity and decorum of their office in every way.
- Never use their position for personal gain.
- Never accept or offer illegal payment for services rendered.
- Not accept gifts, free services, or anything of value for or because of any act performed or withheld.
- Support the actions of colleagues whenever possible.
- Actively support appropriate professional associations aimed at improving school business management and encourage colleagues to do likewise.
- Accept leadership roles and responsibilities when appropriate.

POINT–COUNTERPOINT

POINT

Educational leaders operate in a highly complex business environment wherein they must balance the best interest of children with fiscal accountability to local, state, and federal entities. As instructional leaders and business people, they are responsible for the academic and fiscal success of schools, and they should be held strictly accountable for failures in either of these areas. In other words, school people must be business people and not only educators.

COUNTERPOINT

Current and future school formal leaders should be educators, not business executives. Their first and near-sole priority is the education of children. Managing the business and finances of schools should be left to the district's school business manager or chief financial officer, neither of whom need educational expertise.

- Which of these two points of view most closely resembles your own thoughts? Explain.
- Are there budget responsibilities in your school district that fall to school-level leaders? If so, how can these leaders ensure that their school budgeting, accounting, and fiscal management knowledge is adequate to fulfill their responsibilities to students, staff, and the community?
- How can a school leader ensure that those performing the daily work of budgeting and accounting under his or her supervision are carrying out their duties accurately and ethically?

CASE STUDY

As a new high school principal in your relatively large school district, you were surprised at last night's football game to be approached by three school board members who cornered you as the crowd was leaving the stadium. You quickly learn this is not a social call to celebrate either your arrival or your team's having just trounced its cross-town gridiron rival. Rather, you hear from these board members that they have been receiving irate calls from parents of football players that each member of the team is required to sell a certain number of discount cards, with sales proceeds being used to purchase personal gear for the players.

While you knew none of this, you were further surprised and concerned to hear that the parents who are upset are especially incensed that their players (who are not on the varsity squad) are required to sell discount cards but do not receive any rewards. More particularly, the board members told you that angry parents are alleging that the varsity players get fed after games, get new warm-ups, new uniforms, and new team jackets. Additionally, these parents are upset because they have noticed that the coaches wear new team shirts, jackets, and hats every year, and that when these parents inquired about where the money came from, they were told it was from the football budget. Apparently, though, one parent asked a school employee friend who works in bookkeeping at the high school and was told that there had been no school money spent on coaching apparel in recent years and that the money came from an outside account set up and managed by varsity football parents. To conclude this tale, you were told that the complaining parents confronted the coaching staff about the existence of outside money and asked to know more about it, but were denied any information.

Your school board members were confused and upset, and they became more perturbed to learn that you were clueless about the situation. As you drove home, you became convinced that this topic would hit full board awareness probably by the next day and that questions would arise that would even interest the local press—in fact, one board member had said that the angry parents had threatened to go public with the allegations. Your head was swirling with questions as you thought about what tomorrow might bring. Among those questions were: How did all this happen? How did the district not know about this situation, or did it have knowledge? Is it legal for student fundraising proceeds to go into a separate account controlled by parents? What does your coaching staff know about this, and what hand—if any—have they had in decisions involving these monies? How widespread is this practice in your school and in your district? How will you control the negative publicity that is likely to arise? What are your next steps?

- What are the pitfalls to be avoided as you resolve this situation?
- What are your legal and ethical duties in this situation?
- How will you approach this matter with your superintendent?

PORTFOLIO EXERCISES

- Obtain a copy of your school district's budget document and review the fund structure for revenues and expenditures. Identify which funds your district operates. Identify special revenue funds, capital projects funds, and any debt service funds.
- Closely examine the general fund in your school district. Interview your chief fiscal officer to determine what expenses are paid from the general fund. Discuss cash flow and fiscal resource management to determine how the district optimizes its assets. Ask about any problems the school district encounters in this area.

- Obtain a copy of the monthly revenue and expenditure report for your school site. Identify account codes and learn how the district accumulates and reports revenues and expenditures, including any program planning uses. Interview a school site accounting staff member to trace one or more receipts and disbursements through the entire accounting cycle. Ask how the district ensures the safe handling of money and disbursements, and compare these to the safeguards mentioned in this chapter.
- Obtain a copy of your school district's annual audit and review the strengths and weaknesses of your district's accounting system. Interview the district's chief accountant to ask what audits are conducted, how often, and for what purposes. Ask what training activities the district's business office provides for school sites and staff to ensure that they understand sound fiscal management.

NOTES

1 PL 107–110.
2 PL 114–95.
3 Legal Dictionary, http://dictionary.law.com/Default.aspx?selected=744.
4 R. Craig Wood, David C. Thompson, Lawrence O. Picus, and Don I. Tharpe, *Principles of School Business Management*, second ed. (Reston, VA: Association of School Business Officials, 1995).
5 See, for example, the extensive and important revisions to fiscal reporting contained in the U.S. Department of Education's most recent accounting handbook, *Financial Accounting for Local and State School Systems: 2014 Edition*, by Gregory S. Allison and Frank Johnson (Washington, DC: National Center for Education Statistics, March 2015).
6 Today financial data are not recorded in physical books or journals, but rather are recorded using accounting software.
7 The term *funds* is often loosely used to mean money, as in "s/he didn't have the funds to pay bills." From this point forward in the textbook, a *fund* is a formal accounting entity for segregating types of money for receipt and expenditure purposes, and no longer refers to money itself.
8 Gregory S. Allison and Frank Johnson, *Financial Accounting for Local and State School Systems: 2014 Edition* (Washington, DC: U.S. Department of Education, National Center for Education Statistics, March 2015).
9 Describing each state's taxable property scheme is beyond the scope of this text. In Figure 4.1, for school purposes *real* property (real estate) is subject to taxation, as are the improvements on that land (*ad valorum*, or added value tax). The sample state in Figure 4.1 also taxes *personal* property in the form of motor homes and other recreational vehicles, but exempts automobiles as a direct source of school tax revenue. The nuances among states are significant: For example, in Figure 4.1, automobiles are not taxable locally but the state itself collects a motor vehicle tax, some of which finds its way into the state school aid distribution formula as state general fund revenues.
10 Allison et al., *Financial Accounting for Local and State School Systems.*
11 Allison et al., *Financial Accounting for Local and State School Systems.*
12 Ronald E. Everett, Raymond L. Lows, and Donald R. Johnson, *Financial and Managerial Accounting for School Administrators: Superintendents, School Business Administrators and Principals*, fourth ed. (Lanham, MD: Rowman & Littlefield, 2012).

13 The reporting model for school districts is based on GASB Statement 34, Basic Financial Statements—and Management's Discussion and Analysis—for State and Local Governments, and is updated through GASB Statement 70.

14 https://asbointl.org/publications-resources/professional-standards-and-code-of-ethics

15 https://asbointl.org/asbo/media/documents/Resources/ASBO-Professional-Standards.pdf

WEB RESOURCES

American Institute of Certified Public Accountants, www.aicpa.org

Association of School Business Officials International, www.asbointl.org

Financial Accounting Standards Board, www.fasb.org

Government Finance Officers Association, www.gfoa.org

Governmental Accounting Standards Board, www.gasb.org

The Institute of Internal Auditors, www.theiia.org

National Business Officers Association, www.nboa.net

National Center for Education Statistics, www.nces.ed.gov

RECOMMENDED RESOURCES

Allison, Gregory S. and Frank Johnson. *Financial Accounting for Local and State School Systems: 2014 Edition*. Washington, DC: U.S. Department of Education, Institute of Education Sciences, National Center for Education Statistics, March 2015.

Bruck, W. Earl and Lauren Miltenberger. "A School District Financial Condition Assessment System and its Application to Pennsylvania School Districts." *Journal of Education Finance* 39, 2 (Fall 2013): 115–131.

Everett, Ronald E., Donald R. Johnson, and Bernard W. Madden. *Financial and Managerial Accounting for School Administrators: Tools for Schools*, second ed. Lanham, MD: Rowman & Littlefield, 2012.

Government Finance Officers Association. "Fiscal First Aid." www.gfoa.org/index.php?option=com_content&task=view&id=937&Itemid=416.

Granof, Michael H. and Saleha B. Khumawala. *Government and Not-for-Profit Accounting*, fifth ed. Hoboken, NJ: John Wiley, 2011.

Hartman, William T. *School District Budgeting*, second ed. Lanham, MD: Rowman and Littlefield, 2003.

Mead, Dean Michael. "Tips for Schools Districts: GASB's New Fund Balance Standards." *School Business Affairs* 76 (November 2010): 8–11.

Okrzesik, Daryl J. and Bert G. Nuehring. "Reduce Fraud Risk in Your District with Stronger Internal Controls." *School Business Affairs* 77, 5 (May 2011): 20–22. http://files.eric.ed.gov/fulltext/EJ966676.pdf.

Ratcliffe, Thomas A. and Charles E. Landes. *Understanding Internal Control and Internal Control Services*. New York: American Institute of Certified Public Accountants, Inc., 2009. http://media.journalofaccountancy.com/JOA/Issues/2009/09/Understanding_Internal_Control_Services_2.pdf.

Ruppel, Warren. *GAAP for Governments*. United Kingdom: Wiley & Sons, 2017.

CHAPTER 5

Budget Planning

CHAPTER DRIVERS

Please reflect on the following questions as you read this chapter:

- What is the primary purpose of a budget?
- What is a budget at its most basic level?
- What is a sound budget philosophy?
- What are common approaches to budgeting?
- What is the general budget process?
- How are budgets constructed?
- How are individual schools funded?
- What are the roles of stakeholders in budgeting?

BUDGETS AND SCHOOLS

Considering how this book has sequentially linked each topic, the focus next turns to the specific elements of building P–12 budgets. This comes naturally after having gained an understanding of the social context of public schools, including acceptance of an engaged and at times demanding constituent base. Second, budget-building blocks come after having gained a new respect for the weight of handling school money and grasping how revenues and expenditures are accounted for via the fund structure. Third, all these follow after having been introduced to the wide-ranging decisions underlying the construction and operation of state aid formulas. In all, the previous four chapters built a framework for understanding money and schools.

Consequently, it is time to apply these understandings to the actual elements of budgeting for P–12 schools.

It is useful to begin by examining school district budgets from a broad perspective. Later chapters will explore additional aspects of budgeting in greater detail, but this chapter sets a foundation for all that follows. The chapter provides an overview of how budgets are built, with some attention to how money is directed to individual schools. The starting place is to define a budget in conceptual terms. Discussion of common approaches to budgeting follows, including a brief evaluation of those same approaches in terms of sound budget frameworks. The last half of the chapter is devoted to describing the general budget process and the roles of stakeholders. In this manner, a complicated process is made simpler while staying true to the primary goal, i.e., a better understanding of how district and school budgets are operationalized.

BASIC BUDGET CONCEPTS

Earlier chapters argued that public education is facing a paradigm shift in policy; that is, there are increasingly urgent calls for higher pupil achievement as U.S. standardized test scores trail those in other developed countries. These calls come amidst demands from some of the same voices for a new level of fiscal conservatism, based in a burning desire to shrink the role of government to a position of severe fiscal austerity. At the same time, the nation has continued to slowly recover from an economic recession second only to that of the Great Depression of the 1930s, with record levels of child poverty having spillover effects on schools. In light of all the above, public schools have faced increased state and local scrutiny of operations in the name of efficiency, cost-effectiveness, and accountability. As such, how budgets are envisioned, constructed, and implemented are topics of vital importance to school leaders.

In today's political and fiscal environment, outdated assumptions about school budgeting must be set aside. For example, some view education budgeting as a low priority for educators, one that should be the exclusive domain of accountants. Nothing could be further from the truth. "Budget planning is indivisible from educational planning, and program planning is the very foundation of academic achievement." Specifically, the primary purpose of a budget is to translate educational priorities into programmatic and financial terms; as such, the budget is the fiscal expression of the educational philosophy of the school district.

Furthermore, budgets do not just happen. Rather, they require acts of genuine and creative leadership. Such leadership is quite broad and includes the community at large; the school board, which is legally charged with approval of the district's budget; and all school personnel who design and implement educational programs. District and school leaders are hired to build the district's financial plan and to provide philosophical leadership and technical expertise—leadership that must be shared with the instructional staff. Board members bring educational and political views which are often directly influenced by the community. At the same time, it is critical to remember what enables educational programming—it is money, purely and simply—tax dollars taken from a public whose desire to support schools depends in large part on their confidence in local leadership.

Very importantly, budgets are political as well as financial tools in that they reflect the values and attitudes of community-elected school board members. Again, money talks loudly, and the budget process cannot avoid being highly political. Although politics are often negatively viewed by educators, in many instances these realities represent opportunities as well as obstacles. For example, community engagement and advocacy in the budget process has saved important education programs such as music, art, and student activities from the chopping block in more than one school district. Conversely, failure to engage the public in the budget process has proved to be a grave mistake in many communities because ownership and enthusiastic support for schools is vital to their success. It is worth internalizing as a first-order rule of leadership that a disengaged community is often apathetic or even hostile.

Rather than seeing budgets as dry documents engaging only to accountants and clerks, school leaders need to understand budgets as tools that enable schools to function. A budget is a description of a desirable educational program. Likewise, a budget is an estimate of revenues and expenditures needed to carry out programs. The educator's definition of a budget is therefore three-sided. Though different from an accountant's view that sees only revenue and expenditure, the three-dimensional view best expresses a sound budget philosophy, one that acknowledges that programs should drive both revenue and expenditures. Figure 5.1 illustrates this philosophy, with the educational program serving as the base of the budget triangle. Although fiscal problems may threaten to invert the triangle as programs are constrained by resources, it is important for community members, parents, boards, administrators, teachers, and other stakeholders to not lose sight of the goal that budgets should be first and faithfully built on the basis of program needs. As Figure 5.1 illustrates, the definition of a budget first depends on quality programs and only then is supported by revenue and expenditure plans to make envisioned outcomes possible.

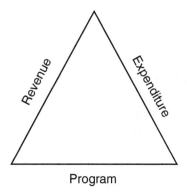

Program

FIGURE 5.1 Ideal Budget Triangle

ORGANIZING FOR BUDGETING

In brief, discussion to this point leads to one conclusion: Budgeting is critical to the success of everything that happens in schools. Needless to say, something so important demands a high degree of organization, attention to detail, and accuracy. Still, school budgets have long been a mostly local matter, with minimal state control relating to a few reporting procedures in order to qualify for state aid. Today, however, with greater calls for fiscal accountability from seemingly every quarter, the budget process must include development of a budget framework consistent with the district's vision and operating philosophy. A brief look at common approaches to budgeting is helpful in understanding the various ways districts can choose to organize their budgeting activities.

What Are the Common Approaches to Budgeting?

Efforts to improve budget practices have led to common approaches, particularly at the district level. These include *line-item* budgeting; *percentage add-on* budgeting; *zero-based* budgeting (ZBB); *planning, program, budgeting, and evaluation systems* (PPBES); *performance-based* budgeting; *site-based* budgeting; *outcome-focused* budgeting; and *student-based* budgeting. For the most part, the order of this list relates to chronological appearance. The main purpose of any approach to budgeting is to detail where resources are targeted in response to students' needs. Each approach has benefits and drawbacks.

Line-Item Budgeting

Line-item budgeting has been widely used for many years to assign differing amounts to each line of the budget. In line-item budgeting, emphasis is placed on the specific objects for which funds are spent. As a result, budgets are planned around each budget line. Typically, line-item budgets have as their base three broad lines: Personnel; maintenance and operations; and supplies and equipment. Personnel costs include salaries, wages, and benefits for all school district employees. Maintenance and operations include day-to-day operational expenses, ranging from utilities to upkeep; and supplies and equipment cover everything from cleaning supplies and textbooks to computers and photocopiers.[1]

Line-item budgeting has several advantages. First, it is simple to understand even for those largely unfamiliar with budgets and who might find a more detailed format intimidating. Second, there are those audiences who do not want to peruse a detailed budget, instead finding a line-item budget provides them with sufficient information. Third, each line item can be expanded to provide more detail if desired. For example, the personnel line can be disaggregated by instructional vs. noninstructional expenditures. Others might want to know what portion of personnel costs are dedicated to benefits, or how much the district is paying for substitute teachers. The other two line items, maintenance and operations, and supplies and equipment, can be disaggregated in a similar way. Because line-item budgeting has been in place for many years and because it is easily understood, it has survived despite the availability of newer and better budgeting approaches.

— lacks detail on specifics

— early criticized

Despite its popularity, line-item budgeting has drawbacks. Although a line-item budget can be used as a building block for program budgeting, alone it does not provide program costs. As such, a line-item budget is an ineffective tool for adequately educating the public regarding expenditures on various programs in the district. Particularly when a district wants to add, cut, or expand programs, it is helpful for both internal and external audiences if district and school leaders are able to clearly present and discuss program costs. In that sense, a line-item budget is open to criticism for lacking transparency, which can make it harder for districts to demonstrate to stakeholders that they are willing to be held accountable for the ways in which school monies are spent.

Percentage Add-on Budgeting

Percentage add-on budgeting is a fairly simplistic model that uses the prior year's expenditures as a base for creating the next year's budget. Sometimes called incremental budgeting, it takes its name from the assumption that each budget line should receive an increment (usually a percent) increase or decrease for the next budget cycle. The process of percentage add-on budgeting can be attractive to school districts as it is easy to understand, even for those unfamiliar with budgets, and it seems on its face to be fair in that each major line of the budget receives a clear (and often equal) percentage increase or decrease. Percentage add-on budgeting's major flaw, however, is the assumption that next year's combined federal, state, and local allocations will always represent an increase over the prior year's funding.[2] In reality, this has never been the case in public education, but now more than ever given today's turbulent economic, political, and social environment, districts cannot count upon ever-rising revenues, even in affluent school districts. Importantly, political discourse today is often dominated by the rhetoric of fiscal restraint and accountability, such that many school leaders feel fortunate if next year's budget does not contain budget reductions necessitating cuts in programs.

Percentage add-on budgeting also lacks sophisticated budget strategies, such as targeting and reallocation of existing funds to maximize educational impact, most likely because it was developed at a time before high stakes testing and value-added evaluations of teachers.[3] Finally, it is obvious that percentage add-on budgeting can result in uncritical equal increases to each budget line, potentially causing overfunding or underfunding of individual areas. Overall, this approach fails to consider strategic allocation or returns on investment in educational programs.

Zero-Based Budgeting

The advent of zero-based budgeting (ZBB) in schools coincided with fiscal problems that began to surface during the high inflation years of the 1970s. ZBB was first instituted in the federal government under former President Jimmy Carter as an effort to control federal spending by enacting sunset laws to zero out unproductive government programs. Popular with anti-tax constituencies, ZBB was also implemented by many local governments in response to taxpayer discontent, and it was only a matter of time until schools experimented with the concept. The basic premise of ZBB is that budgets must be justified (even rebuilt) each year, with the central goal of cutting waste and improving efficiency. Over the years, many school districts adopted a modified ZBB model. A typical procedure is to build new budgets based on a percentage reduction from the prior year, with maintenance of prior year funding requiring justification. The rationale is that greater efficiency can be injected into any district, and reductions as a matter of course help drive that end. Another form of ZBB requires staff to prepare multiple scenarios and to justify each scenario, e.g., decreased, static, and increased expenditure. The first scenario requires extensive description of the educational plan, with the new budget set at a specified percentage below current funding. The second scenario requires maintenance of both the educational plan and the budget at the same level as the current year. The third scenario allows improvement or expansion of services and expects the budget to increase above the current year. In all instances, each scenario must detail differences between the current year and the next budget cycle, with full expenditure justification.

Benefits of ZBB are several. The product of an era of high inflation and perceived government waste, ZBB represents an opportunity to appease hypercritical taxpayers by taking strong and visible action to reduce waste and increase efficiency. Particularly sound is the idea that budget growth should not occur absent questioning about actual contribution to the organization. The idea of multiple spending scenarios is sound, in that planning may improve if expenditures must be justified. Finally, districts may be better braced for reductions if systematic groundwork is laid ahead of the actual need to do so. On the other hand, drawbacks are real because the process of zeroing budgets is complex and time-consuming and at times is proved to be an unnecessary exercise. Additionally, some critics hold that ZBB is a cost-reduction tool that can require more resources for effective strategizing than is saved in the end. Also, the potential for internal conflict exists with ZBB, e.g., core subjects must make the same justification for existence as elective and enrichment courses. In extreme cases, animosity among staff can linger long after the budgeting process has ended and can negatively affect morale. In light of these drawbacks, ZBB is generally not used by schools except in extremely challenging fiscal situations.

Planning, Programming, Budgeting, and Evaluation Systems

Planning, Programming, Budgeting, and Evaluation Systems (PPBES) arose from a realization that the budget should be more clearly tied to the educational program. This approach requires each unit in a district or school to establish goals and measurable educational objectives through systematic planning that reviews programs before determining expenditures. The process requires an educational plan whereby each unit seeks to define and measure its instructional objectives—a plan for spending, initially justified by needs and anticipated outcomes. Money then follows the plan. The benefits of PPBES are real. This model represents a major conceptual shift from line-item budgeting by deliberately linking programs and expenditures to a presumed cause-and-effect of money. PPBES contributes to accountability, both by its focus on program goals and measurable objectives and by its potential to assess cost-effectiveness.

Like other budgeting approaches, PPBES has drawbacks. School districts must invest significant time and expense upfront in professional development to educate staff on how the model works and their related responsibilities. Importantly, the district must provide staff with sufficient out-of-classroom time to develop and implement the model. Clearly, PPBES requires a paradigm shift for many schools and districts, making it a challenging approach to budgeting. Yet schools and districts have been forced to consider PPBES-like structures at increasingly higher levels, as the advent of more stringent accountability has forced this concept on them, ready or not.

Performance-Based Budgeting

Performance-based budgeting is a variant on numerous other models, believing it takes the best from multiple perspectives to yield an outcome tailored to specific situations. Performance-based budgeting begins with the assumption that there are standard costs for inputs that can be multiplied by the number of activities and participants within a defined timeframe. Performance-based budgeting usually relies on narrative descriptions of programs or activities proposed for funding, and the focus turns to measuring and evaluating outcomes. A major benefit to performance-based budgeting is the flexibility it offers in resource allocation and reallocation, meaning that money can be viewed as more fluid across an organization in ways that are responsive to changing needs. Perhaps the key benefit is that the information flow and assessment is more authentic than in more basic or incremental models, and particularly so since the concept of learning outcomes underlies performance-based budget models. Drawbacks, though, are inevitable as the model is most useful for purposes and tasks that are more amenable to routinization and measurement, and failure enters unless the district has very reliable cost information: Like other things, the outputs are only as good as the inputs.

School Site Budgeting

School site budgeting is a school-based management tool following closely after the popularity of decentralized administration, with budget decisions increasingly pushed downward to the individual school level. It can be said that school site budgeting is a variant of program budgeting applied to each individual school within a district. Under this plan, each site is granted resources based on a district-level distribution formula that takes into account the number of pupils at each site in each grade level and program. Typically, the principal and a school site council, often comprised of community members, parents, and staff are given responsibility for developing and managing a budget within limits of the total allocation. Depending on state statutes or local preference, the council may be authorized to make decisions in such areas as staffing, salaries, supplies, and activities—all within the parameters of not violating bargaining agreements, regulations of federally funded programs, and any statutory requirements such as class size limits or district policies such as school calendar or length of school day.

School site budgeting is appealing because it complements the philosophical underpinnings of site-based leadership. In concept, site budgeting supports recent advances in learning theory because it values the impact of resources at the point of utilization—i.e., resources are most meaningful at the individual classroom level under the care of the teacher as applied to student needs. Site budgeting is sound in that it involves key stakeholders, especially parents and teachers, in the education of children. The concept is especially attractive by incentivizing greater parental involvement because it asserts the role of the home and community in each child's progress. The special value, then, is in providing a more holistic view of education, making school site budgeting a viable option.

School site budgeting also has drawbacks. A primary disadvantage is its complexity, wherein school sites are suddenly asked to take on new and unfamiliar roles related to decision-making. Throughout history, schools have been semi-closed social systems, and the addition of staff, community members, and parents to budgeting can create new tensions and stresses. Site-based budgeting requires meaningful training for stakeholders, as administrators, teachers, and parents must learn about organizational and technical aspects of funding and must learn to work together cooperatively. And there are real dangers in the site concept; that is, unless attention is paid, equity among schools within a district may be affected by site-based budgeting in that some schools will enjoy greater expertise, participation, and advocacy. Likewise, there is danger to site decisions in human resource matters, raising many legal and ethical questions. However, given current trends, school site budgeting is a real possibility for the foreseeable future.

Outcome-Focused Budgeting

Outcome-focused budgeting is the practice of connecting the aims of the allocation of resources to measurable outcomes, such as test scores. It has grown in popularity in governmental circles in recent years in response to interest in accountability. Fiscal austerity and political squabbles about resource allocation, along with competition for resources, have only served to increase this approach's presence.

Outcome-focused budgeting holds that linking allocation of resources to learning outcomes is sensible and inescapable. A testy proposition in the model, however, also suggests that resources should be given to those who use them most effectively—perhaps characterizable as a reward for outcome incentivization. Also inherent to the model is intensive program planning, and advocates urge that such joining of *best parts* of other models is destined to be more effective, more innovative, and more flexible as well as more nimble and responsive. Disadvantages are equally clear: Organizations facing threats to survival are likely to become victims of damaging stress, and the unintended consequence of slavish devotion to performance outcomes ignores the broader aim of educating the whole child. Still, outcome-focused budgeting combined with a site-level focus may be a harbinger of the future.

Student-Based Budgeting

Finally, student-based budgeting is a concept that reflects other trends aiming to ensure that the child is the focus of all behaviors. An extreme example that has become commonplace is seen in the school choice movement, where in some states the money and child are allowed to *walk off* in search of market-driven results. Student-based budgeting at its core argues that the money follows the child to the extent that school site budgets are determined by pupil numbers and educational needs. Such autonomy is said to allow schools to provide responsive services. More neutrally, various state aid formulas incorporate a similar line of thinking by engaging the *weighted pupil* concept, whereby any combination of state aid formula factors in the end is supplemented by a weighting scheme tied to educational needs.

Intermediate Observations About the Budgeting Model

Table 5.1 captures why the choice of a budgeting approach must be carefully considered in order to ensure that districts and schools do not naively seize on an idea that later proves unworkable. As a consequence, there are several considerations to adopting a budget framework. Hartman proposed issues to be raised when adopting a financial structure at either district or individual school levels.[4] These issues relate to style, preference, and congruency of stakeholders in the budget process. Consideration must be given to the district's history, in that rapid or abrupt changes in budget policy and operation may be met with indifference or resistance. For example, if the district has a history of stakeholder apathy in budget affairs, dramatically increased community involvement is unlikely unless time is devoted to changing the district's culture. Likewise, budget decisions must be made in light of the historic role of the school board, in that districts with a history of strong board control may experience tensions and conflict when trying to move to decentralized models such as site-based budgeting. Likewise, the fiscal condition of the district must be analyzed, as districts in precarious fiscal health may need to stabilize their financial position before introducing a new approach to budgeting. In all cases, though, the landscape is changing, with the result being more federal/state/local scrutiny and engagement.

Constructing Budgets

Although school district budgets in every state are significantly affected by federal and state requirements, the actual budget construction work occurs at the local level. Locally, budget construction usually consists of four interrelated activities. The first step is *estimating revenue* for the new budget year. *Envisioning the educational program* is typically the second step. The third step is *estimating the expenditures* required to support the program, while the fourth is a set of *decisions designed to balance program needs against revenue and expenditure* realities. Ideally, programs should be determined first as seen earlier in the budget triangle, but too often revenues drive both expenditures and programs. Although this should be resisted to keep focus on the district's goals, leaders know that the budget process first depends on revenue estimation.

Estimating Revenues

Virtually all revenues for school districts derive from federal, state, and local sources. Federal revenues are set at the national level and usually flow through a state agency with a notice of entitlement sent to qualifying districts. State revenues are determined by legislative process, and districts' allocations are calculated through state

TABLE 5.1 Types of District and School Budgets

Budget	What is it?	Pros	Cons
Line-item	• Historical approach, using historical expenditure and revenue data. • Level of expenditure detail is fund, function, or object. • May be augmented with some supplemental program and performance information.	• Simplicity and ease of preparation. • Budgets by organizational unit and object. Consistent with lines of authority and responsibility. • Allows for accumulation of expenditure data by organizational unit for use in trend/historical analysis.	• Presents little useful information to decision-makers on functions and activities of organizational units. • Justifications for expenditures not explicit. • Invites micromanagement by administrators without performance information.
Percentage add-on	• Adding percentage to previous year's funding level.	• Simplicity for governing body and board.	• May be removed from district's real needs, e.g., school may need a greater increase than add-on budget allows.
Zero-based	• Budget starts from zero each year. No reference to previous year's budget, and each budget inclusion must be justified. • Budget prepared by dividing operations into decision units. Individual units then aggregated to decision packages on basis of program activities, goals, organizational units, etc.	• Staff involved in selecting resource allocation. Fosters public confidence in budgeting process. • Elimination of outdated efforts/expenditures and concentration of resources where most effective. • Particularly useful when overall spending must be reduced.	• Most districts do not have the staff/time to adequately address the level of complexity required to administer. • Requires great deal of staff time, planning, and paperwork. • Limited implementation in schools thus far.
Program & planning	• Bases expenditures primarily on programs, and secondarily on objects. • Used for planning, establishing, modifying and improving goals: Determines cost and alternative plan's cost for achieving each goal. • Transitional form between traditional line-item and performance-based budgets.	• Places emphasis on identifying goals of the organization and then relating expenditures to goals. • Places less emphasis on control/evaluation. • Reports summarized in broad terms and not specific line items. • Allows for long-range planning.	• Can be limited by: Changes in long-term goals, lack of consensus on organizational goals; lack of adequate program/cost data; and difficulty administering programs that involve several organizational units.

(Continued)

Type	Description	Advantages	Disadvantages/Considerations
Performance-based	• Based on standard cost of inputs multiplied by number of units of an activity to be provided in a time period. • Narrative descriptions of each program or activity included in the budget.	• Focuses on measuring/ evaluating outcomes. • Provides more useful information for consideration and evaluation by administrators. • Individual schools given flexibility over budgets as long as they meet school and district goals.	• Most useful for routine and measurable activities (e.g., vehicle maintenance and accounts payable processing). • Lack of reliable standard cost information.
Site-based	• Decentralizes budget authority and process. • Resources allocated to individual sites, and budgetary authority granted to school's principal/staff. • Allows for alignment of goals with resources. • Considered most practical for schools.	• Those who best understand needs have the authority to make decisions. • Provides greater control/ reporting of school-level data and greater school-level accountability. • Staff/community given a voice, generating public support.	• Time/skills necessary to manage process. Few school-level officials are trained to plan and administer site-based budgets. • Site-based budgeting may be burdensome to some local managers and increase conflict.
Outcome-focused	• Linking allocation of resources to the production of outcomes. • Budget resources given to those who use them most effectively.	• Linked to planning process. • Some argue these budgets are more effective in producing desired results, more innovative, and more flexible.	• Goals and objectives must be identified and tied to budget allocations. • Clear communication with stakeholders should be established in advance.
Student-based	• Formula that allows the money to follow the student: School site budgets are determined by student need. • School-level autonomy allows schools to provide different levels of resources and services. • Also known as "weighted student funding" or "student-weighted allocation."	• Transparent funding, so it is known to all what resources flow to which student. • Eliminates accounting and spending money in narrowly defined ways. Offers flexibility in programming decisions.	• Focused on inputs and can be problematic if not linked to outcome accountability. • Decision makers may be unable to redirect added resources in productive ways (given restraints from contracts, state regulations, federal laws, etc.).

Source: Rennie Center for Education Research & Policy. (October 2012). *Smart School Budgeting: Resources for Districts.* Cambridge, MA: Rennie Center for Education Research & Policy. By permission. Excerpted from pp. 6–7.

aid formulas with entitlement notice sent to each district. Each district then calcu-lates its local tax requirement, subject to any existing state limits.[5] For example, states with aid formulas based on the classroom unit may permit total instructional costs of $40,500 per unit, with the state providing $25,000 per classroom. If federal aid were equal to $500 per classroom, then $15,000 must be raised locally. A varia-tion achieving the same result might be through a state aid plan requiring a uniform local tax rate of 20 mills, with revenues generated remitted to the state, which in turn redistributes it through a statewide staffing formula and salary schedule paying for 55 professional staff positions per 1,000 pupils. If local option tax leeway is per-mitted, any additional costs would be funded by a local option levy—which might or might not require local voter approval. Likewise, in states funded on a per-pupil basis, the formula might determine the local tax requirement by providing aid in an equalized ratio between 0% and 100% where the unfunded portion must be met by whatever local tax rate is required to raise the necessary funds. The permutations on such statutory funding schemes are limited only by the fact that there are 50 states, so that in the end how resources are raised and distributed is almost entirely each state's prerogative.

An example of revenue estimation for a hypothetical school district's general fund is shown in Figure 5.2, where, for the 2018–19 school year, state aid is estimated at $4,005,159, and local property tax revenues at $433,712. Total general fund revenue is $4,998,854.[6]

In most states, revenues are estimated for each individual fund using state soft-ware and information from other agencies. As seen in Chapter 4, fund accounting sets up multiple separate funds for revenue and expenditure purposes. For example, a state may require that all financial transactions be made from one of the following funds: (1) general; (2) vocational education; (3) special education; (4) capital outlay; (5) bond and interest; (6) food service; (7) transportation; (8) adult education; (9) bilingual edu-cation; and (10) in-service/staff development. Fund-based budgets permit analysis of how money is spent and also permit states and the federal government to ensure that funds are spent for the stated purpose. For example, federal special education aid must be segregated into a district fund dedicated to special education services. At the state level, transportation aid to districts often comes with the requirement that it must be placed in its own fund account to be spent only for transportation. This is especially important, for example, if a state decides to provide additional transportation aid to sparsely populated rural areas with consequent high transportation costs.

In some states, revenue estimation by fund may include the option or requirement to levy different amounts of local tax for each individual fund. For example, a uni-form tax rate requirement usually refers only to the general fund from which the bulk of education's costs are paid. Some states do not aid capital outlay or bond debt and therefore permit or require districts to levy a special tax for those funds. As a result, the series of funds operated by school districts can result in multiple revenue estima-tions and tax levies. However, it must be remembered that other local governmental units levy property taxes for services and operate fund-based budgets that also may require multiple tax levies.

01 GENERAL		12 months 2016-2017 Actual	12 months 2017-2018 Actual	12 months 2018-2019 Budget
Unencumbered cash balance July 1		683,202	4,657	13,893
Unencumbered cash balance from transportation, bilingual education, and vocational education funds		2,368	12,368	0
Revenue:				
1000 Local sources				
1110 Ad valorem tax levied				
2015 $		407,781		
2016 $		435,968	199,680	
2017 $			414,810	262,990
2018 $				433,712
1140 Delinquent tax		14,897	16,648	6,779
1300 Tuition				
1312 Individuals (out-district)				
1320 Other school district in-state				
1330 Other school district out-state				
1700 Student activities (reimbursement)				
1900 Other revenue from local source				
1910 User charges				
1980 Reimbursements				
1985 State aid reimbursement				
2000 County sources				
2400 Motor vehicle tax		276,484	258,224	252,155
2450 Recreational vehicle tax			6,642	14,166
2800 In lieu of taxes IRBs				
3000 State sources				
3110 General state aid		2,298,537	3,620,788	4,005,159
3130 Mineral production tax				
4000 Federal sources				
4590 Other reserve grants–in-aid				
4591 Title I (formerly Chapter I)				
4592 Title (math/science)				
4599 Other		14,365	15,864	
4820 PL 382 (Exclude Extra Aid for Children on Indian Land and Low Rent Housing) (formerly PL 874)		39,642	42,888	10,000
5000 Other				
5208 Transfer from local option tax		0	0	0
Resources available		4,173,244	4,592,569	4,998,854
Total expenditures and transfers		4,168,587	4,578,676	4,998,854
Excess revenue to state				0
Unencumbered cash balance June 30		4,657	13,893	

FIGURE 5.2 Sample General Fund Revenue Structure

Envisioning Educational Programs

The second activity in the budget process calls for review and establishment of the educational program. This process generally seeks to maintain or improve the present academic program, as well as undertaking new initiatives such as mandates or elective improvements. At times, fiscal issues may force program reductions or eliminations, but districts should try to maintain or improve services consistent with their mission statement and educational philosophy.

Envisioning programs takes many forms. One method assumes the present program is adequate and that the budget should be built around the price of program maintenance. A second method proposes improvements or new initiatives based on consultation with constituencies. This latter method has gained popularity with the advent of school reform, with districts having school improvement plans linked to federal and state mandates, e.g., those aimed at increasing academic achievement among at-risk pupils. Such plans may include curriculum committees, task forces, site councils, community–school partnerships, and business and industry partners. As a rule, envisioning programs is undertaken to better align curriculum and to specify outcomes in exchange for resources invested.

Regardless of how schools assess their programs, the overriding point is that every program costs real dollars. The purpose of program description in budgeting is to identify program needs in order to translate them into fiscal terms in the budget document. If program maintenance is the goal, the district can use prior year data as the basis, with allowance for increased costs in the new year, e.g., salaries, supplies, equipment. If improvements are being considered, the district generally turns to its proposed program description, which should include action statements about resources. A budget development calendar may be used to gather input and build the budget. Importantly, the district's fiscal philosophy, such as site budgeting, will have a powerful impact on educational programs' conceptualization and operation.

Envisioning the educational program is a complex process that requires commitment of time and resources, but it should be the very heart of budgeting because unless it is thoughtfully carried out, nothing more than maintenance of the status quo can occur. In sum, envisioning the program is *the* critical link between estimating revenues and estimating expenditures.

Estimating Expenditures

Estimation of expenditures needed to support the educational program is the third activity in preparing a budget. Like revenue estimation, expenditure plans must follow state requirements for form and content. The process generally calls for placing revenue on the various proposed expenditure lines of each fund in the budget. Although it is difficult to say that any one step is most important, expenditure estimation is one of the most critical because underestimation of costs is disastrous. For example, failure to accurately calculate the costs of a new teacher salary schedule could result in unmet payroll, suit for breach of employment contract, and force school closures because revenues must equal or exceed expenditures.

Expenditure estimation identifies the major cost determinants and makes best estimates of all changes for the new budget year. Estimating general fund expenditures involves costing out employee salaries, wages, and benefits; the number of positions required; movement of each staff member on the applicable salary/wage schedule; maintenance and day-to-day operations costs; quantities and costs of supplies and equipment; and costs of services such as professional development, legal fees, auditing, insurance, printing, security, and information technology. The exhaustive nature of these activities is seen in Figure 5.3, which shows the expenditure side of a sample district's general fund budget. Importantly, these steps repeat for each separate fund.

01 GENERAL EXPENDITURES	12 months 2016–2017 Actual	12 months 2017–2018 Actual	12 months 2018–2019 Budget
1000 Instruction			
100 Salaries			
110 Certified	1,688,504	1,799,864	1,872,000
120 Noncertified	25,682	28,243	29,000
200 Employee benefits			
210 Insurance (employee)	28,949	33,640	34,000
220 Social Security	131,083	138,764	140,000
290 Other	3,039	3,642	3,800
300 Purchased professional and technical services			
500 Other purchased services			
560 Tuition			
561 Tuition/other state LEAs			
562 Tuition/other LEAs outside the state			
563 Tuition/private sources			
590 Other	9,241	10,953	9,000
600 Supplies			
610 General supplemental (teaching)	85,984	102,760	104,000
644 Textbooks	52,486	62,384	65,000
680 Miscellaneous supplies	4,685		3,960
700 Property (equipment & furnishings)	51,863	5,543	6,000
800 Other			62,000
2000 Support services			
2100 Student support services			
100 Salaries			
110 Certified	60,504	64,164	65,500
120 Noncertified			
200 Employee benefits			
210 Insurance (employee)	562	699	750
220 Social Security	4,630	4,984	5,200
290 Other	59	100	100
300 Purchased professional and technical services	7,982	9,641	10,000
500 Other purchased services			
600 Supplies			5,000
700 Property (equipment & furnishings)	4,291	5,007	
800 Other			
2200 Instructional support staff			
100 Salaries			
110 Certified	91,860	96,541	98,000
120 Noncertified			
200 Employee benefits			
210 Insurance (employee)	1,072	1,286	1,400
220 Social Security	7,070	7,509	8,500
290 Other	112	148	200
3300 Community services operations	3,064	3,704	4,000
3400 Student activities	28,564	34,296	35,000
4300 Architectural & engineering services			
300 Purchased professional and technical services			

FIGURE 5.3 Sample General Fund Expenditure Structure

500 Other purchased services			
600 Supplies			
640 Books (not textbooks) and periodicals	14,389	16,841	18,000
650 Audiovisual and instructional software	12,684	15,092	17,000
680 Miscellaneous supplies			
700 Property (equipment & furnishings)	4,066	4,905	5,000
800 Other			
2300 General administration			
100 Salaries			
110 Certified	38,184	40,448	41,500
120 Noncertified	49,860	53,624	54,600
200 Employee benefits			
210 Insurance (employee)	984	1,206	1,300
220 Social Security	7,115	8,492	9,000
290 Other	103	200	200
300 Purchased professional and technical services	17,054	20,384	21,000
400 Purchased property services			
500 Other purchased services 520 Insurance			
530 Communications (telephone, postage, etc.)	4,643	5,605	5,900
590 Other			
600 Supplies	8,106	9,653	10,000
700 Property (equipment & furnishings)	7,964	9,582	10,000
800 Other	13,165	16,769	16,000
2400 School administration			
100 Salaries			
110 Certified	211,864	220,843	227,000
120 Noncertified	84,286	89,300	91,000
200 Employee benefits			
210 Insurance (employee)	4,995	6,001	6,500
220 Social Security	2,505	26,984	28,000
290 Other	324	411	500
300 Purchased professional and technical services			
400 Purchased property services			
500 Other purchased services 530 Communications (telephone, postage, etc.)	1,793	2,174	2,200

FIGURE 5.3 (Continued)

The line item entries in Figure 5.3 are never established in a vacuum. Rather, in most states every item in the local school district budget is driven by enrollment. Staff, supplies and equipment, as well as the size and number of buildings are a direct function of the number of pupils.[7] Estimating enrollment is a critical, but challenging, task because no single method is ever perfectly accurate. Even with powerful population mapping tools, sudden in- and out-migrations and economic shifts can affect accuracy. Enrollment projection techniques are remarkably useful, however, because they are all based on two important features. The first feature is the expectation that conditions characterizing the past will continue. The second feature softens the error of that assumption by requiring constant reevaluation and updating of the model's underlying assumptions. In essence, continually tracking shifts in population over time provides

590 Other			
600 Supplies			
700 Property (equipment & furnishings)	4,001	4,624	5,000
800 Other			
2600 Operations and maintenance			
100 Salaries			
120 Noncertified	192,386	200,784	205,000
200 Employee benefits			
210 Insurance (employee)	1,995	2,396	2,500
220 Social Security	15,750	16,863	18,000
290 Other	209	255	500
300 Purchased professional and technical services	1,248	1,498	1,500
400 Purchased property services			
411 Water/sewer	8,150	9,750	10,000
420 Cleaning			
430 Repairs and maintenance	161,745	188,640	264,860
440 Rentals		61,980	42,840
460 Repair of buildings	218,714	251,574	388,431
490 Other	37,984	45,472	55,000
500 Other purchased services			
520 Insurance	32,345	36,542	37,000
590 Other		13,052	
600 Supplies			
610 General supplies	42,387	50,845	51,000
620 Energy			
621 Heating	45,190	46,842	48,000
622 Electricity	67,810	69,742	71,000
626 Motor fuel (not school bus)			
629 Other	22,196	32,482	26,000
680 Miscellaneous supplies		12,052	4,000
700 Property (equipment & furnishings)	4,284	8,244	6,000
800 Other	2,361	2,876	3,000
2500, 2800, 2900 Other supplemental services			
100 Salaries			
110 Certified			
120 Noncertified			
200 Employee benefits			
210 Insurance			
220 Social Security			
290 Other			
300 Purchased professional and technical services			
400 Purchased property services			

FIGURE 5.3 *(Continued)*

500 Other purchased services			
600 Supplies			
700 Property (equipment &furnishings)			
800 Other			
5200 Transfer to:			
932 Adult education			3,000
934 Adult supplemental education			
936 Bilingual education			
938 Capital outlay	75,246	94,400	97,315
940 Driver training	5,000	5,000	5,000
942 Education excellence grant program		10,000	5,000
943 Extraordinary school program			
944 Food service			
946 In-service education	5,136	4,533	11,798
948 Parent education program			
949 Summer school		10,000	10,000
950 Special education	130,000	100,000	125,000
951 Technology education			
952 Transportation	313,080	323,070	360,000
954 Vocational education	6,000	12,864	15,000
955 Area vocational school			
956 Disability income benefits reserve			
958 Health care services reserve			
959 Group life insurance reserve			
960 Risk management reserve			
962 School workers' compensation reserve			
968 Cooperative elementary guidance			
972 Contingency reserve			
Total expenditures and transfers	4,168,587	4,578,766	4,998,854

FIGURE 5.3 *(Continued)*

a smoothing effect to the data by increasing the experience factor and the number of data points in the model. Such adjustments are foundational to the two most common methods of enrollment estimation: *Trend analysis* and *cohort survival.*

Trend analysis is the application of regression modeling to predict enrollment based on historical years of enrollment data. In its simplest form, trend analysis predicts future enrollments based on the manner in which previous enrollments deviate from a straight line. The formula for the regression line (fitted line) is $Y = Mx + b$ where Y is the future enrollment, M is a coefficient used in the model, x is a future year, and b is a constant showing the relationship between enrollment and year. Using multiyear historical data, a future year is entered, and the result is a predicted enrollment. Figure 5.4 depicts a sample trend analysis. The regression formula casts a line of best fit, yielding projected enrollment for next year (Year 6). In the sample district's case, historical data indicate a steadily increasing enrollment trend, with Year 1 enrollment beginning at 1,990 students and increasing to 2,710 by Year 5. Figure 5.4 projects ahead one year, in this case, an enrollment of 2,900 students.

Trend analysis is more useful for the largest districts because the averages in a regression line do not affect the district to the extent that could be true for smaller districts where the loss of each student represents a greater proportion of the total budget. As a result, medium and small size districts often prefer tools that are more arithmetically straightforward, more intuitive, and more sensitive to small changes in headcount.

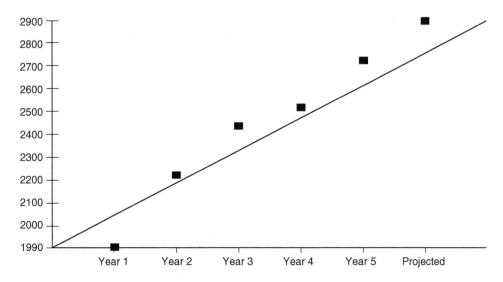

FIGURE 5.4 Trend Line Analysis of Enrollments

Cohort survival is a much more common method for projecting enrollments in U.S. schools. Cohort survival is an enrollment projection tool that groups students by grade level at entry to school and tracks them through each year they remain in the district. In concept, cohort survival looks at entering kindergarten students in Year 1 and calculates how many enter first grade in Year 2, second grade in Year 3 and so on until graduation. Such a system more closely accounts for grade failures, dropouts, and migratory trends impacting student population.

Cohort survival requires enrollment data from previous years as well as the current year for each grade. It calculates enrollment change and survival as a percentage of the previous year's grade-level cohort. For example, Part 2 of Figure 5.5 shows that historically enrollments from first to second grade averaged 94% of the prior year's grade-level population. This means that out-migrations or grade failure resulted in a 6% average loss between first and second grades. This allows entry of the multiyear average into Part 3 of the analysis, where current first grade enrollment can be multiplied by 94% to project 376 students in second grade next year compared to 400 students in first grade in the present year. This process is repeated for each grade for several years into the future, whereupon enrollments are totaled by grade level. Figure 5.6 then graphs the school district's total enrollment trends from 2019 to 2024. One additional point should be made. Kindergarten estimation tends to be less reliable and constitutes a special case in most school districts, requiring use of multiple indicators like birth records, kindergarten roundups, and local preschool attendance data. Except for kindergarten, these numbers are used with relative confidence to assign staff, purchase supplies, plan facility use, and derive other aspects of revenue and expenditure estimation. Since virtually all budgeting is based on enrollment, cohort survival is a good tool due to its instant sensitivity to changes in population.[8]

Part 1: Historic Enrollments

Grade	2013-2014	2014-15	2015-16	2016-17	2017-18	2018-19	Average
PreK	500.0	500.0	499.0	502.0	500.0	503.0	500.7
One	490.0	501.0	498.0	499.0	501.0	400.0	481.5
Two	627.0	499.0	478.0	466.0	489.0	410.0	494.8
Three	590.0	611.0	497.0	477.0	477.0	488.0	523.3
Four	491.0	593.0	601.0	488.0	482.0	469.0	520.7
Five	399.0	478.0	578.0	615.0	479.0	489.0	506.3
Six	617.0	389.0	502.0	477.0	610.0	477.0	512.0
Seven	591.0	616.0	399.0	499.0	470.0	600.0	529.2
Eight	499.0	588.0	618.0	381.0	489.0	479.0	509.0
Nine	650.0	482.0	549.0	729.0	377.0	488.0	545.8
Ten	533.0	623.0	492.0	532.0	716.0	369.0	544.2
Eleven	811.0	540.0	622.0	499.0	415.0	616.0	583.8
Twelve	710.0	815.0	539.0	627.0	481.0	421.0	598.8
TOTAL	7508.0	7235.0	6872.0	6791.0	6486.0	6209.0	6850.2

Part 2: Survival Ratio

Grade	2013-2014	2014-15	2015-16	2016-17	2017-18	2018-19	Average
PreK		100%	100%	101%	100%	101%	100%
One		100%	100%	100%	100%	80%	96%
Two		102%	95%	94%	98%	82%	94%
Three		97%	100%	100%	102%	100%	100%
Four		101%	98%	98%	101%	98%	99%
Five		97%	97%	102%	98%	101%	99%
Six		97%	105%	83%	99%	100%	97%
Seven		100%	103%	99%	99%	98%	100%
Eight		99%	100%	95%	98%	102%	99%
Nine		97%	93%	118%	99%	100%	101%
Ten		96%	102%	97%	98%	98%	98%
Eleven		101%	100%	101%	78%	86%	93%
Twelve		100%	100%	101%	96%	101%	100%

Part 3: Enrollment Projection through 2024

Grade	Multiyear average	2018-19 (actual)	2019-20	2020-21	2021-22	2022-23	2023-24
PreK	100%	503.0	503.6	504.2	504.8	505.8	506.4
One	96%	400.0	482.5	483.1	483.6	484.2	485.2
Two	94%	410.0	376.5	454.7	455.3	455.3	455.8
Three	100%	488.0	409.2	375.8	453.2	453.8	454.3
Four	99%	469.0	484.5	406.3	373.1	450.0	450.6
Five	99%	489.0	466.0	481.4	403.6	370.7	447.1
Six	97%	477.0	473.2	450.9	465.8	390.6	358.7
Seven	100%	600.0	475.8	471.9	449.7	464.6	389.5
Eight	99%	479.0	594.3	471.2	467.4	445.4	460.1
Nine	101%	488.0	485.4	602.2	477.5	473.7	451.3
Ten	98%	369.0	479.1	476.6	591.2	468.8	465.1
Eleven	93%	616.0	344.4	447.1	444.8	551.8	437.5
Twelve	100%	421.0	614.7	343.6	446.2	443.8	550.6
TOTAL		6209.0	6189.0	5968.4	6015.7	5958.4	5912.3

FIGURE 5.5 Cohort Survival Technique

The sheer volume of steps involved in estimating expenditures precludes their explanation in a single chapter. For example, the next major activity after enrollment projection is projecting staffing needs. This involves a complex set of activities engaging labor negotiations, salary/wage schedules, and fringe benefits. Student enrollment and staff numbers also drive the purchase of teaching supplies and equipment, as well as facilities. These topics are covered in later chapters, e.g., budgeting for human resources in Chapter 6 and budgeting for school infrastructure in Chapter 9.

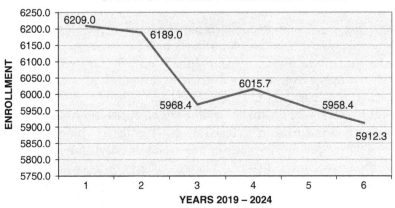

FIGURE 5.6 District Enrollment Trend: 2019–24

Balancing the Budget

The fourth step in the budget process aligns estimated costs for each fund with anticipated revenues. This process is straightforward in states that tightly control revenues by mechanisms such as allocating the number of classroom units to each district. For instance, it takes little time to find salary costs if the state grants 55 professional positions per 1,000 pupils—in such states, school districts will spend the bulk of their time deciding how to meet their instructional needs (given a set staff size) because no options exist for increased staffing except increasing local property taxes if permitted. In states with more staffing flexibility, districts may spend more time determining the allocation of money to various lines in the budget to achieve the best balance for their particular situation. In states where tax rates can vary through local option leeway, districts may also consider raising taxes to pay for additional staff. The process in all states, though, calls for balancing the revenue and expenditure sides of the budget because most states forbid deficit spending by schools.

Efforts to balance revenues and expenditures always result in cause-and-effect scenarios, with real instructional impacts. For example, revenues may need careful review if program needs markedly exceed available funding. Alternatively, program expenditures may have to be reduced if it is clear that revenues will continue to be inadequate. Although state-specific conditions sometimes limit options, these activities—called budget adjustments—usually involve one of three common scenarios. The first scenario happens when school districts receive increased revenues through federal, state, or local sources. The second scenario occurs when revenues are static, and the third appears when revenue declines. Each of these situations has been faced at some time by every school district, and the process for dealing with each can be difficult and complex.

Chapter 1 recommended that school districts plan for the scenarios described above through budgeting approaches that build in program priorities as they relate to the district's mission, vision, and educational goals. This chapter adds a new criterion that focuses on strategies to increase efficiency and reduce costs. These are particularly helpful when a district faces static or declining revenues. However, even when districts enjoy new revenues, implementation of these strategies is helpful because it frees up additional funding for instructional programs.

Examples of strategies actually used by districts include the following:

- *Energy efficiency:* Chapter 9 considers physical infrastructure funding and contains short- and long-term strategies for schools to reduce energy consumption. These tools benefit both the environment and the budget. When faced with the need to immediately reduce expenditures, districts typically look for low or no-cost strategies. The U.S. Department of Energy offers cost-reduction techniques through its *EnergySmart Schools* initiative, providing easy to implement suggestions, e.g., shutting down boilers during unoccupied times when there is no danger of freezing; lowering the temperature on water heaters; and using daylighting in classrooms.[9]

- *More efficient purchasing:* In times of limited budgets, districts must choose between *wants* and *needs* with regard to purchasing supplies and equipment. This may require more central oversight of purchasing, including greater use of written justifications by those making requests. Other approaches to lowering costs include bulk discount buying and *just-in-time* purchasing. Smaller school districts may realize cost savings through cooperative purchasing with neighboring districts or municipalities.

- *Deferral of equipment purchases and maintenance:* Deferring new equipment carries potential benefits and costs. For example, delaying bus purchases may result in older units with higher operating and maintenance costs. At some point buses may become unsafe or lack newer safety features, posing a liability risk for the district that is far greater than the price of a new bus. In addition, purchasing a new *green* bus that uses less fuel or less costly fuel may actually reduce transportation costs. Similarly, deferral of facilities maintenance may result in higher costs at a later time. These issues are covered in more detail in Chapters 9–10.

- *Improved cash management:* Districts are well-advised to hire an experienced school business manager who understands the importance of investing every dollar of idle funds. Although it may be tempting to turn to measures like drawing down cash reserves, districts are advised to reconsider such false wisdom. Reserves exist for emergencies like a boiler breaking down in the middle of winter. In such times, if reserves are insufficient to replace it immediately, the district may be forced to engage in short term borrowing with unfavorable interest rates—a situation that recalls the saying "penny wise and pound foolish."

- *Improved risk management:* Raising insurance deductibles, assessing potential benefits and risks of self-insuring, and competitive bidding of insurance coverages are strategies to reduce risk management costs. However, each of these deserves serious cost–benefit analysis.

- *Refinancing long-term debt:* Here too wise business managers more than earn their salaries given their expertise in fiscal matters. Refunding bonds to take advantage of lower interest rates can save districts thousands of dollars annually in lower interest costs. However, it is unwise to extend bond payments over a longer period of time because, although this can reduce the annual payment, it likely will result in added interest costs.

- *Incentives for employee retirement:* Providing incentives for eligible employees to retire might be another strategy to consider. Experienced employees typically are more costly, so their retirement coupled with replacement by less experienced employees can show substantial savings to the district. However, caution is warranted. First, legal counsel is needed because there are state and federal laws that may affect the crafting of such incentives, including but not limited to discrimination against older employees. Second, the educational cost–benefit of such programs should be considered: That is, losing the expertise and leadership of experienced staff can be harmful to educational programs and staff morale. Finally, the incentives must not only be attractive enough to result in actual retirements—they also must be small enough to result in expenditure reductions.

- *Reduction of employee costs:* When all of the above measures prove insufficient, districts may be forced to reduce employee costs. A district that has undertaken long-range planning using a program-based budgeting system is better situated to make informed decisions that minimize potential damage to instructional programs. Temporary measures like increasing class sizes and reducing electives and extracurricular programs are sometimes seen as first steps. Additionally, retirements and resignations may make reduction in force (RIF) unnecessary. Salary and wage freezes may also be possibilities if labor agreements permit. If not, unions might be asked to make concessions in order to avoid lay-offs. Some districts have used furloughs to make temporary reductions in salary and wage costs. Others have asked employees to shoulder a greater share of fringe benefit costs like insurance and retirement contributions. Outsourcing some services might be considered as well. However as noted in other chapters, outsourcing requires careful cost–benefit analysis to determine if savings are actually realized, as well as giving close consideration to potential community reaction to the change.

In some situations, even these measures may not be sufficient to balance a budget. In that case, the one remaining alternative is to cut programs. Care must be exercised, though, to not violate contracts or state laws. For example, in many states, length of school day, hours of work, and class schedules are part of negotiated agreements, and many states have mandated preschool and extended day programs. Although cuts are never easy, reductions in staff and programs are the most painful and destructive. Such measures should be used only as a last resort.

Completing the Budget Process

Budget construction is nearly complete when programs are envisioned, revenues and expenditures are estimated, and a balanced budget is achieved. However, the budget still must be approved. Approval steps differ among states, but the end result is always legal adoption of the budget under state statutory requirements. For example, in states where school districts are fiscally dependent on some other unit of government, the budget is forwarded to a higher authority, such as a city council or county board, for final approval. In states where districts are fiscally independent, approval is more complex in that several events usually occur in specific order. Although highly state-specific, a general procedure calls for official publication of a budget summary, usually in a newspaper of general local circulation, followed by a waiting period, public hearing, formal adoption of the budget, and certification of the proposed or amended budget to some other governmental unit such as a county taxing authority. Print publications are meant to give notice to the public of the budget hearing, with a waiting period to allow citizens the opportunity to prepare comments and to attend the hearing. State statutes usually call for the school board to vote in open session. The budget, if adopted, must be certified according to state statute. These laws are meant to guard against secrecy and impropriety, and they must be strictly observed.

HOW ARE INDIVIDUAL SCHOOLS FUNDED?

The process discussed so far has examined budgeting at the district level, but nothing has been said about funding individual schools. This is a challenging topic because states generally have not enacted statewide school-level funding laws, leaving most of the nation's roughly 14,000 districts free to adopt their own school site budget philosophy. That is exactly the point of the earlier focus on adopting a local budget philosophy, i.e., districts have great freedom to create internal budget structures, and those choices have a tremendous impact on individual schools. As a result, how individual school sites are funded is as different as the number of school districts that exist. Nonetheless, some common ways that districts fund schools can be reviewed.

Most school districts operate by a budget calendar like the one shown in Figure 5.7. Budget calendars range from very simple to highly complex. Figure 5.7 is

Budget Area	Staff Responsible
General fund	Board/central administration
Administration	Superintendent
School budgets	Principals
Travel: administration/teachers	Director of Human Resources
Special programs	Director of Special Services
Adult education	Coordinator of Adult Education
Bilingual programs	ELL Coordinator
Capital outlay	Director of Maintenance
Driver education	Business Manager
Food service	Director of Food Service
Transportation	Transportation Director
Special education	Director of Special Education
Bond and interest budgets	Business Manager
In-service budget	Director of Curriculum
Vocational school budget	Director of Curriculum
Special projects and grants	Business Manager
Other budgets	As assigned

Calendar		
Date	**Description of Task or Activity**	**Responsible Person(s)**
January	Distribute planning guide Meet with principals and program directors	Business Manager
March	Requests for new programs and personnel due	Superintendent, Business Manager, and Director of Human Resources
April	Seek board input on programs and new personnel	Superintendent, Curriculum Director, and Director of Human Resources
April	Building, program, and capital repair and improvements due	Directors and principals
May	Bid capital outlay, instructional items, and advise of bids	Principals and Business Manager
June	First draft of total budget	Superintendent and Business Manager
July	Board budget workshop	All administrators
July	Budget publication and hearings	Administrators, board, public
August	Adoption and certification	Board, Business Manager

FIGURE 5.7 Sample Budget Calendar with Staff Responsibilities

uncomplicated and is taken from an actual district of about 7,000 students. The calendar identifies all areas of the budget, assigns responsibility to an administrator, and lays out the budget process with deadlines. An important feature is that budgeting is a multi-month process that includes a flow chart of responsibility and (in this case) involves many people, including principals and other staff. The processes of estimating revenues, envisioning school programs, estimating expenditures, and balancing the budget are all evident in the sample budget calendar, as is the overall coordination of the budget process at the district level—all of which are required in order to bring these separate activities into a completed total budget prior to a new school year.

The budget calendar in Figure 5.7 also notes another aspect of school budgeting in that building principals are assigned an active role. Although again dependent on local preference, this budget calendar shows principals involved at most stages including the initial planning stage, program planning, preliminary budget review, requisition and purchase order preparation, and the daily administration of school budgets. Figure 5.7 might be used in a relatively centralized district, but it could easily apply to a district using site-based budgeting. In the first case, school principals would be asked about program needs, supplies, equipment, and facilities. In the latter case, principals would have control over daily resource utilization; the individual school would operate independently with ultimate accountability for productivity. These ideas will come up again in Chapter 7 when looking at budgeting for instruction.

The process of budgeting can be imagined as a pyramid, mostly flowing down from state to local levels. It begins with federal and state policies that make revenue available to school districts. Each district determines its program requirements, matches revenues and needs, and adjusts local revenue and programs to fill the deficit. Districts then allocate revenue to individual schools based on a preferred budget philosophy, using such concepts as fairness, horizontal and vertical equity, and preferences about decentralization and accountability. For example, a district may decide to assign block grants to each elementary school in exchange for the promise to increase pupil achievement on test scores by a certain amount next year. Principals and staffs may then consult with site councils and opt, for example, for more teacher aides and larger class sizes instead of hiring a new teacher. Another school might take a different path by hiring a grant writer to seek external funding to purchase extra supplies, equipment, and staff to meet some other set of learning goals. The range of possibilities depends on state laws and available revenues, in combination with local ingenuity.

WHAT IS THE ROLE OF STAKEHOLDERS?

Every chapter in this book has implied that school money is a rightful place for stakeholders to make their voices heard. This chapter has underscored that there is a place in school budgeting for everyone—school leaders, boards, teachers, policymakers, parents, and community members. If the purpose of a budget is to identify the needs of schools, to prioritize those needs, to match resources with needs, and to operationalize educational goals, then there is much to be gained by broad constituent engagement.

In reality, everyone must take initiative and responsibility for school budgeting. Educational leaders should use budgets to structure the educational plan, to assess progress toward outcomes, to evaluate accomplishment of the plan, and to make adjustments when needed. And budgeting is not solely a central office function; increasingly, principals must account for program decisions and should take greater responsibility for money as instructional leaders. School boards are legally charged with responsibility for expending funds and must take responsibility for progressive fiscal stewardship. The expertise of teachers and other professional staff must be fully utilized in building the educational plan expressed by the budget. Policymakers must be knowledgeable about educational programming, and feedback loops are needed to help them reach the decisions about funding schools that they are constitutionally required to make. Finally, no audience is more crucial than parents and community members whose taxes pay for schools and whose approval every district must have in order to fulfill its educational aims. The interaction of all these constituent roles is clear in Figure 5.8—it is not by accident that the link between strategic planning and school budget *performance* outcomes involves all stakeholders who ultimately decide

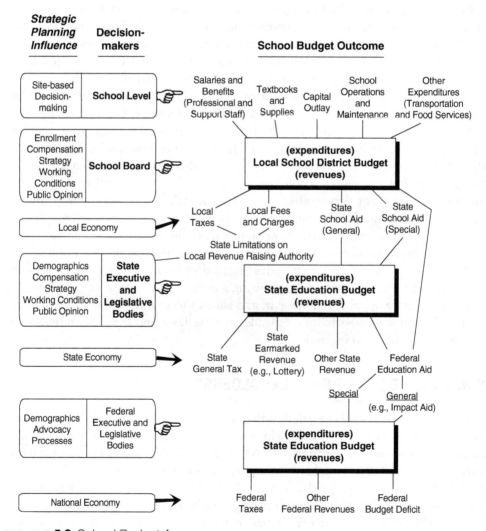

FIGURE 5.8 School Budget Arena

how schools are funded. As Ward urged long ago, education finance is not a "technical and sterile area of study employing complex mathematics, arcane algebraic formulas [nor] a refuge for the methodologically minded to be avoided by those humanists in education who see their emphasis as being on children, instruction, and qualitative aspects of schooling."[10] Instead, a budget truly is the fiscal expression of the educational philosophy of a school district.

POINT–COUNTERPOINT

POINT
School leaders today, especially principals, are charged with the success of high stakes educational programs and must be given responsibility for designing and executing site-level budgets if they are to meet their increased accountability expectations.

COUNTERPOINT
School leaders today, especially principals, are so engulfed by instructional leadership duties, high stakes accountability, and day-to-day operations that school districts should not seek budget involvement by school site administrators—instead, districts should increase central support services to fulfill this management responsibility.

- Which view best represents your own philosophy of budgeting? Explain why.
- How are principals, central office staff, teachers, and others involved in budget construction and daily budget administration in your school district?
- If you were an administrator in your school district, how would you wish budgeting to be structured? Explain why.

CASE STUDY

As a long-time principal in your school district, you were surprised at last week's administrative cabinet meeting when the superintendent announced his desire to redesign the district's budgeting practices. As you listened, you learned he hoped to move many resource decisions back to the central office level. The proposal was particularly concerning because about a decade ago your district had developed an extensive site-level leadership model that included significant resource control by building principals and school site councils. While at times you tired of the constant responsibility and privately thought it took time away from your instructional leader role, you knew that money was power to effectuate change. You knew too that your level of involvement in budgeting would be difficult to relinquish, and you also knew your site council and staff likely would have the same reaction to such bold reordering.

Inasmuch as all district and site-level administrators were in attendance at the weekly cabinet meeting, you were proved correct when a spirited discussion ensued. Several administrators, notably some of your fellow principals, seemed eager to argue that this was a regressive move that would hurt the district's community image and risk the district's enviable academic achievement profile. Others seemed more open, suggesting that such a move would "let principals lead and let teachers teach again." As the dialogue escalated, it became clear that while the superintendent's proposal would be explored in depth, there would be a long hard path involving a lot of debate.

To move to the next level, the superintendent indicated that he would form a study group to consider the merits and propose a redesign. He indicated that a proposal was due on his desk by the end of the school year—about eight months from now. To your surprise, the superintendent indicated that he was appointing you, as the most experienced principal in the district, to co-chair the study group along with the equally veteran assistant superintendent for finance. As the meeting broke up, your co-chair asked you to step into her office, whereupon she requested that you take the lead in organizing the work to be undertaken at the committee's first meeting. Although you mentally pondered that her job title might be better suited to the task at hand, you recognized that her motivation included the fact that you would have an insider's grasp of concerns likely to be held by the district's numerous school site administrators and that your insights might help avoid some pitfalls. In that you hope to move to a central office role shortly, you agreed to accept the task and determined to yourself that you would be both careful and exhaustive in your approach.

Below is a set of questions. As you respond, consider your learning in this chapter and apply your knowledge and emerging beliefs/preferences to the situation:

- Do you believe the proposal this district is pursuing is wise? Why or why not? What benefits do you see? What problems might follow?
- What steps should you take to begin this planning process? What factors need to be taken into account? What do you believe are the critical elements for such organizational changes to succeed?
- How are your own school district's budgeting practices organized? What would happen if such a proposal were raised in your district? If such a design is already in place in your district, assess how effective it is.
- If you had been the superintendent in this case study, would you have embarked on this course? If so, explain why. If not, what would you have done differently?

PORTFOLIO EXERCISES

- Interview the appropriate central office leader(s) in your school district about the relationship between budgeting and strategic planning. Explore how the district conceptualizes its budget and the processes by which budgeting occurs. Discuss the overall process of estimating revenues and expenditures, including how the district involves stakeholders in the process. Discuss the act of balancing the budget and the district's efforts to maintain and improve instructional programs.

- Obtain a copy of your school district's most recent enrollment projections and interview the author as to how the projections were developed, e.g., methodology and data sources. Discuss the assumptions used in the projections. Consider how different assumptions or methodologies might affect the projections. Explore how the projections affect budget planning in the district.

- Talk to one or more school site administrators in your district to determine how they are involved in the budget process. Ask how they involve their staffs and stakeholders, and how they prioritize requests when expenditures exceed budget allocations. Ask how they would improve the budget planning process.

- If your state, district, or school has site councils, explore the extent to which councils are involved in budget planning. Review state or school district policy documents and analyze the strengths and weaknesses of the decision-making roles these bodies play.

- Obtain a copy of your district's budget calendar. Determine how and when your district obtains public input into the budget process at formative and final stages. Interview your district's business manager or chief financial officer to determine how the district tries to ensure smooth passage of the final budget.

- Obtain a copy of your school and district budgets. Which budgeting approach described in this chapter is used by each? In your estimation, is this the optimal approach for your school or district? Explain your answer.

NOTES

1 Budgets for capital expenditures are generally developed separately.
2 In all fairness to school districts, it should be noted that governors, legislatures, and state education agencies themselves often couch budget discussions in terms of overall percentage changes from year to year.
3 Value-added models evaluate teachers based upon gains in standardized test scores by students in an individual teacher's classroom over the course of an academic year. For a more detailed description and analysis, see Daniel F. McCaffrey, J. R. Lockwood, Daniel M. Koretz, and Laura S. Hamilton, "Evaluating Value-Added Models for Teacher

Accountability" (Santa Monica, CA: Rand Corporation, 2003), www.rand.org/content/dam/rand/pubs/monographs/2004/RAND_MG158.pdf.

4 William T. Hartman, *School District Budgeting* (ScarecrowEducation, 2003).

5 As introduced earlier in Chapter 3, local tax effort is calculated in most states using mill rates. A mill is 1/1000 of a dollar or $1 of tax yield for every $1,000 assessed valuation. A property valued at $100,000 market value and fractionally assessed at 12% for tax purposes and to which a 20 mill tax rate is applied would result in a tax bill of $240 (i.e., $100,000 × 12% = $12,000 × 0.020 = $240). A district's tax rate is found by dividing the local tax requirement by the sum of the district's total assessed valuation (e.g., $5,000,000 local share ÷ $250,000,000 assessed valuation = 0.020 mills).

6 Note that this school district estimates additional revenues for the general fund budget from the local, state, and federal levels. It estimates $6,779 in delinquent tax collections. This particular district also estimates a little over $252,000 from county sources related to motor vehicle taxes. Finally, the district estimates receipt of $10,000 in federal revenues. Note that the district will likely receive more than that amount in federal revenues, but because of the targeted nature of much federal education aid, these revenues will likely be placed in segregated fund accounts.

7 States use various methods of pupil counts, e.g., headcount; average daily membership (ADM); average daily attendance (ADA); full-time equivalency (FTE); and more. Variations on these matter too, such as weighted average daily membership (WADM), and so on.

8 See, for example, *Enrollment Projection/Demographic Study for the Marcellus Central School District*. Marcellus, NY (2012). http://www.marcellusschools.org/tfiles/folder1180/marcellus%20enroll%20study%5B2%5D.pdf Retrieved September 22, 2018.

9 U.S. Department of Energy, *EnergySmart Schools Tips: Retrofitting, Operating, and Maintaining Existing Buildings* (Washington, DC: Office of Energy Efficiency and Renewable Energy, Building Technologies Program), https://www.energy.gov/sites/prod/files/2013/11/f5/ess_quick-wins_fs.pdf

10 James G. Ward, "An Inquiry into the Normative Foundations of American Public School Finance." *Journal of Education Finance* 12 (Summer 1987): 463.

WEB RESOURCES

American Association of School Administrators, www.aasa.org

American Federation of Teachers, www.aft.org

Association of School Business Officials International, www.asbointl.org

National Conference of State Legislatures, www.ncsl.org

National Education Association, www.nea.org

National Governors Association, www.nga.org

National School Boards Association, www.nsba.org

U.S. Department of Energy, www.energy.gov

RECOMMENDED RESOURCES

American Association of School Administrators. "School Budgets 101." AASA (2012). https://www.aasa.org/uploadedFiles/Policy_and_Advocacy/files/SchoolBudgetBriefFINAL.pdf

Crampton, Faith E., and Randall S. Vesely. "Resource Allocation Issues for Educational Leaders." In *Handbook for Excellence in School Leadership*, fourth ed., edited by Stuart C. Smith and Philip K. Piele, 401–427. Thousand Oaks, CA: Corwin, 2006.

Foley, Ellen. "Student-Based Budgeting: The Potential for More Equitable Funding for Schools." Providence, RI: Brown University, Annenberg Institute for Education Reform (February 21, 2011). http://annenberginstitute.org/commentary/2011/02/student-based-budgeting-potential -more-equitable-funding-schools.

Government Finance Officers Association. "Best Practices in School Budgeting: 1A – Develop Principles and Policies to Guide the Budget Process." (n.d.). http://www.gfoa.org/sites/ default/files/PK-12_1A.pdf

Government Finance Officers Association. "Making the Budget Document Easier to Understand." (February 2014). www.gfoa.org/making-budget-document-easier-understand.

Kavanagh, Shayne. *Making the Grade: Long-Term Financial Planning for Schools.* Chicago: Government Finance Officers Association, 2007. www.gfoa.org/sites/default/files/GFOA MakingtheGradeLTFPforSchools.pdf.

McCaffrey, Daniel F., J. R. Lockwood, Daniel M. Koretz, and Laura S. Hamilton. "Evaluating Value-Added Models for Teacher Accountability." Santa Monica, CA: Rand Corporation (2003). www.rand.org/content/dam/rand/pubs/monographs/2004/RAND_MG158.pdf.

REL West. "School-Based Budgeting and Management." San Francisco, CA: WestEd (August 2009).

Sorensen, Richard D. and Lloyd M. Goldsmith. *The Principal's Guide to School Budgeting.* Thousand Oaks, CA: Corwin, 2006.

CHAPTER 6

Budgeting for Human Resources

CHAPTER DRIVERS

Please reflect on the following questions as you read this chapter:

- What is the scope of the human resource function in school districts?
- How are staffing needs determined?
- How do school districts successfully recruit and select staff?
- What other human resource budget issues must school districts consider?
- What are the issues in human resource compensation?
- What role do negotiations play in human resource and budget functions?
- What is current thinking about alternative reward systems?
- What are the fiscal and legal ramifications of RIFs and dismissals?
- Why is due process important in RIFs and dismissals?
- What are the roles of various stakeholders in human resource matters?

THE GENERAL LANDSCAPE

The opening questions to this chapter and all the learning in this book thus far point to a highly complex relationship between the aims of schooling and the adults in schools charged with carrying out the educational mission. The introduction to the budget process in the last chapter noted that the single largest proportion of public elementary and secondary education's costs is the human resource function. Today's school budgets are highly stressed, especially given the considerable costs of education reform and other policy wars. States have increased academic requirements for schools without matching increases in funding, and federal reforms such as the *Every Child*

Handwritten note: Unit 3 discussed the formation of di

Handwritten note: 172

Succeeds Act have resulted in new performance demands on schools
have repercussions throughout the entire school district budget.

Because human resources are the single largest item in school
ing the total cost of salaries, wages, and benefits is the next most
in balancing revenues and expenditures." As a consequence, this chapter ex
the act of budgeting for human resources. It begins by considering the scope of
the human resource function, followed by the examination of determining staffing
needs for each school throughout a district. The chapter then examines recruitment
and selection, along with an analysis of issues affecting compensation structures,
including those associated with traditional salary schedules and alternative reward
systems. Finally, the chapter examines the legal context of budgeting for human
resources; that is, the human resource budget cannot be separated from the myriad
risks and obligations that have implications for total district resources. In brief, the
act of budgeting for human resources consumes a major portion of a school district's
finances—an act that in large measure determines the school district's ability to
accomplish its educational mission.

THE HUMAN RESOURCE FUNCTION

That public education in the United States is a labor-intensive industry cannot be
overstated. As such, it is often the focus of taxpayer concern when the annual school
district budget is presented for public comment, debate, and adoption. However, it is
important to remember that expenditures for salaries, wages, and fringe benefits have
positive impacts on the larger economy because school employees are active consumers
who spend large portions of their salaries in the state and local economies for necessities like food, housing, and clothing as well as other expenditures like transportation
and entertainment. School employees are citizens too, and their consumption sustains
or increases employment in myriad community businesses. An additional point often
missed by school critics is that school personnel pay a full range of taxes—property,
sales, income—that in turn contributes to the support of public schools as well as all
other tax-supported services. Education's human resource function thus represents an
investment rather than an expenditure over time. Indeed, the human resource function
is a cost that becomes an economic engine.

Handwritten note: Two reasons why school employees should be an expenditure focus.

The human resource function takes into account everyone who is employed by a
school district. When the general public thinks of school employees, they immediately
think of teachers. Although teachers are the core of what schools do, this view is
incomplete because the human resource function embraces both licensed staff (teachers, administrators, and other professionally licensed employees), noncertificated
professional staff (accountants, technology and data specialists), and classified staff
(secretaries, custodians, bus drivers, teacher aides, cafeteria workers, and more). All
these individuals have indispensable roles in operating a school district. As districts
have become more organizationally complex and inclusive of the many elements that
contribute to equal educational opportunity, the number of licensed and noncertificated employees has greatly increased over time.

The size of the human resource function is exceeded only by its importance to successful school district operation. In fact, regardless of how well the fiscal operations of a district are managed, the true success of a school district ultimately depends on the people who work with children each day. Recruitment, selection, employment, and retention of competent employees are the keys to cost-effective operation of schools. The critical role of the human resource function has led most districts to centralize this operation, with one person having line authority over all aspects of this function. Although administrative titles vary with local custom and even by district size, an assistant superintendent for human resources, a director of human capital, or the superintendent may have direct responsibility for this function. As districts increase in size, responsibility is often further subdivided.

Regardless of how the human resource function is structured within a school district, good administration requires clear written policies that assist in furthering the work of the district and that link operations under one authority. The specific authority and linkages should be specified in the district's policy manual that specifies all aspects of human resource policy. Good policies assure uniform communication and help monitor relationships between the goals of the district and the expectations of personnel. Policies must be clearly stated in order to avoid confusion for either the employer or employee, to promote accurate interpretation and legal evaluation in the event of serious disagreement, and to be clearly based on applicable federal and state law. An added benefit of strong district policies is to provide a blueprint for consistent action that will simultaneously enhance morale and increase productivity. Because educational program quality is a direct result of the skill of all employees working in unison, an effective and efficient school district wisely invests time and money in creating and maintaining sound human resource policies and operations.

When the human resource function is correctly assigned to an individual or office, governed by written policies and procedures, and organized efficiently, the benefit is evident in the form of strong leadership and good management. A school district that merely maintains the status quo cannot consistently improve its programs. Alternatively, reliance on charismatic leadership to the neglect of proper management of the human resource function endangers the district in many ways, including liability for the many problems and conflicts that can arise among employees in a labor-intensive organization. The district's overall goals and objectives cannot be met except by proper management of all instructional and support staffs. Although it is sometimes hard to distinguish between the nuances of leadership vs. management, the organizational and directive functions of the human resource division must be carefully handled if the district is to function effectively because schools rely on competent personnel to fulfill their goals.

The scope of the human resource function is broad, encompassing six major tasks:

1. Determining staffing needs.
2. Recruiting and retaining the most competent staff.
3. Assisting in individual development of competencies.
4. Ensuring that staff are assigned and used efficiently.
5. Increasing and improving staff satisfaction.
6. Establishing clear expectations and ensuring competent performance evaluation.

The human resource function thus *assesses staffing needs* and *recruits, selects, inducts, compensates, evaluates,* and *retains* employees. It also includes *discipline* and *dismissal* of staff. These tasks are explored more fully here due to the close relationship to building a budget.

Determining Staffing Needs

Ability to properly determine staffing needs is a function of organizing and using information about the school district and its current and prospective staff. All districts maintain a database of employee information, if for no other reason than to calculate payroll. A basic database contains information on each employee's salary or wages; fringe benefits and the cost to employer and employee; and record of leave days. Human resource files generally include projected retirement information, as well as records of employees' additional coursework, professional development, and training that may qualify them for raises and other types of rewards pursuant to state statutes, local collective bargaining agreements, and district policies. All district employees, including part-time and temporary, should be included in the database although they may not have the same level of fringe benefits as permanent, full-time staff.

Information about the school district and staffing is interrelated and should be designed to permit electronic linking because, in every instance, the district's profile drives staffing patterns.[1] The database should contain other information, such as population of the community, population of each school, percentage of households with school-age children, ages of children in preschool through twelfth grade, in/out migration patterns, commercial and industrial characteristics of the district, major sources and types of employment, income and age of residents, and, of course, fiscal data on the district itself. This information is useful as a general backdrop to a district's annual enrollment projections. In most states, enrollment is the basis for state fiscal aid to the district, and the population of a community drives enrollment. It should not be missed that demographic data can be useful in predicting community attitudes toward schools and budgets.

While many school districts keep extensive employee information on file, it is often not effectively organized for projecting staffing needs. For example, small districts may still rely to some extent on paper files while larger school districts are more likely to use extensive electronic databases. Specialized software for management of human resources can be quite costly, and the smallest school districts may find it cost-prohibitive. However, cash-strapped or minimally staffed districts should not overlook database management software that now comes with many desktop computers as a resource for organizing human resource systems.

As a school district grows in size, the human resource system is likely to contain information on prospective employees and projections of staff attrition by area and level. However, regardless of district size, the creation of databases with community profiles and employee information is essential because these can be used to project whether staffing needs can be met internally, whether it will be necessary to hire new employees, or if it will be necessary to reduce staff. Thus, the employee database should be broader than simple retrieval of basic information; it should also permit other projections such as calculating the cost of existing or proposed early retirement incentives.[2] Such information intersects with the budget function, in that the cost of early retirement plans (compared to other scenarios such as savings accrued through hiring less experienced staff) must be available when making long-term policy and staffing decisions. Likewise, projections indicating a need for new staff also require budget office input. The use of extensive databases makes it possible to descriptively assess present reality and to forecast future scenarios—an obviously critical function for the budget side of planning and organization. In most instances, the basic database is built and maintained by the human resource office and electronically linked to the budget office.

Although each school district must develop databases to meet its unique needs, the goal is always the same. The human resource and budget functions must share information, but the most frequent interaction comes when staffing needs are reviewed. The human resource side annually considers whether the employment of current staff will continue, and those decisions must coordinate with the budget side which must find money for projected salaries. Sometimes the scenario is reversed: If the budget office finds that personnel costs are too high, then the human resource side must find ways to deal with economic reality. Although these functions are interdependent, the realities of the modern comprehensive school district cause the human resource function to most often drive the fiscal side by communicating to the business office staffing projections for the next school year.

Although a comprehensive community and staff database is essential, the technical side of determining staffing needs differs across states and school districts. For example, some state education finance formulas calculate the number of pupils at each grade level and allocate staff positions to each district on a per-classroom basis. In this case, the district has little meaningful control over the most basic human resource function of determining how many teachers it will hire because it can afford to hire only those teachers reimbursed through the aid formula. In other states, local boards of education are free to decide how many staff members to hire by choosing among competing expenditure categories within overall budgetary constraints; for example, a choice to reduce overall class size may be at the expense of expanding extracurricular or academic enrichment programs. An example of a centralized system would be where a state aid formula converts full-time equivalency (FTE) students into staff units, which are then multiplied by a statewide salary and benefits schedule, with additional allocations for non-personnel-related costs. Such a formula has the effect of leveling expenditures (with staffing implications) downward in some districts in order to bring greater fiscal parity across all districts in the state. At the opposite extreme are states that have tried to reduce class size, where state-initiated reform mandated lower pupil/teacher ratios with the practical effect of driving up staffing requirements for nearly all school districts at significantly higher cost to local taxpayers. A middle-ground example of local decisions driving staffing is found in districts with board of education policies limiting class size, with resultant staffing increases. A more complicated but common situation occurs when local boards of education have either been required by state law to negotiate class size or have voluntarily negotiated such agreements only to find it difficult to later renegotiate such contracts. In all these examples, it is clear that the human resource and budget functions are tightly linked.

Regardless of local circumstance, once a policy or law governing staffing is set for a school district, it is time to apply the appropriate staffing formula to enrollments. After projecting enrollment, the process calls for applying a staffing formula, usually by dividing the number of pupils at each grade level by the approved ratio, yielding the required number of staff members. The process is typically carried out at the district level, with input from individual schools. A simple illustration using a single high school could result in the following staffing pattern:

Formula: *Enrollment + Approved Ratio = Staffing Needs**

421 ninth graders + 20:1 ratio	=	21 ninth-grade teaching positions
373 tenth graders + 20:1	=	18.6 tenth-grade teaching positions
297 eleventh graders + 20:1	=	14.8 eleventh-grade teaching positions
312 twelfth graders + 20:1	=	15.6 twelfth-grade teaching positions
1,403 pupil FTE	=	70.0 teaching staff FTE

---

*This example considers only teaching staff—separate discussions about other staffing needs also apply.

Of course, funding positions is much harder than simply calculating staffing needs, at times requiring adjustment to the staffing formula if funding is inadequate. This is especially true when enrollment fluctuates across years, grades, or school sites. If the database reveals, for example, that other schools in the district are gaining enrollment and if in the same example a high school presently has 78 existing faculty (instead of the calculated 70 needed for next year), the school district could reassign surplus teachers to other schools if their professional licensure matches vacancies. Obviously this solution becomes more feasible as district size increases because many small districts have only one teacher per grade or only one high school. If reassignment is not feasible, reduction of full-time to part-time positions or layoffs may have to be considered.

Determining staffing is at once simple and complex. It is mathematically easy, but it is complex because decisions affect real people and because governmental policy may limit the options. Regardless, sound decisions cannot be made without a comprehensive database that takes into account both community and employee profiles. For example, the school district in the scenario just described might be able to lessen the impact of staff reductions if the database holds information on attrition, retirements, or early contract buyouts. In a more positive vein, data can be used for targeted information-sharing such as in-house electronic notices to employees when employment opportunities arise. For many reasons, an orderly plan for determining staffing needs is the next step after projecting enrollment.

Recruitment and Selection

When openings occur, the next major task is recruitment, followed by selection of personnel. Regardless of the type of position, every employee classification needs a formal recruitment plan. The school district needs to make decisions regarding number and type of positions, as well as minimum and preferred qualifications for each employee classification. The budget and human resource functions again intersect at this point, particularly regarding pay for current staff and whether the district must hire entry-level or can afford more experienced or educated staff. The goal is always to attract and retain the most highly qualified talent. This goal may be hard to achieve because it is often at odds with competing goals to minimize taxpayer cost. Although there are no easy solutions, there are procedures in the recruiting and selection process to help soften the harshness of these realities.

At the outset of the recruiting process, the budget and human resource offices should jointly produce a manual for the school district containing a clear description of the hiring process, starting with application procedures and continuing through description of screening committees, interviews, contract offers, and pay periods and amounts. Every current and prospective employee should be informed of training requirements and opportunities, and this information should be consistent within each employee classification. These procedures should be closely tied to position advertising by the district and standardized with regard to internal and external search procedures consistent with equal opportunity selection of the best candidate for each vacancy.

After recruitment policies and procedures have been set, the school district is ready to recruit. For large districts, this may mean hiring on the basis of anticipated vacancies. In many instances, these districts are taking little risk because they know that they will not be able to hire staff for all openings. In smaller districts, the process is simpler; for example, small districts might advertise via university placement offices and wait for applications to arrive. Even here, though, the human resource and budget functions continue to intersect, as success in recruiting is related to how well the salary schedule is designed and funded. Because most states do not have uniform or statewide teacher salary schedules (or if local districts are permitted to exceed the statewide salary schedule), recruitment is the joint responsibility of prudent human resource and budget coordination.

When the school district has successfully determined its staffing needs and has recruited as effectively as possible, the selection process begins. Because success in meeting district goals depends on the quality of human capital, selection is a critical task. Even though the depth of the candidate pool and the marketplace affect who is hired, it must be recognized that the district's first obligation is to select employees on the basis of skills. Skills must be judged on the basis of documented training, experience, and satisfactory performance. Additionally, many positions in a school district require specific licensure from the appropriate state agency. Every position should be filled only after the appropriate person, often the superintendent, has made a final recommendation to the board of education. As will be seen in a later chapter regarding legal liability, a valid employment offer usually cannot be made unless the school board has approved the offer in a public meeting pursuant to state law.

The intersecting and sometimes conflicting goals of the human resource and budget offices are most apparent at the time of selection. The goal of the human resource function is to select the most qualified person to perform the duties of a specific position. This applies across all vacancies, regardless of whether the person is being interviewed for a teaching position or a custodial position. The goal of the budget office is to hire that same person within the constraints of a realistic cost. The budgeted amount for a position clearly affects the stated qualifications in the position announcement as well as the recruitment plan. Selection thus involves many steps, all aimed at hiring the best candidate within the financial means of the district. From the beginning of the hiring process to its end, the relationship between the human resource and budget functions is close in that whatever candidate is hired, the position must be funded.

Other Human Resource Budget Matters

Although it is beyond the scope of this textbook to deeply examine the human resource side of school district operations, it is important to note that there are other issues in budgeting for human capital that go beyond recruitment and selection. The most obvious issue is compensation policies and procedures, a topic developed in detail in the last half of this chapter. Other human resource tasks including induction, orientation, assignment, mentoring and ongoing support, evaluation, and staff development also intersect with the district's budget because these activities require financial support and are even more costly if poorly done because the result can be sub-optimal job performance. These issues are so important that they actually consume most of the time of the human resource office and require large sums of money.

In brief, the human resource function can be described as working closely with the budget office to determine staffing needs based on enrollment projections in the context of salaries or wages and operating costs across the entire school district. More specifically, the human resource function in tandem with the budget function is responsible for:

- Recruitment and selection:
  - Describing role expectations for positions;
  - Assessing qualifications needed to fit the role;
  - Compiling appropriate information on candidates;
  - Evaluating candidates on role and personal expectations;
  - Rating eligible candidates on the criteria;
  - Making the employment decision from among choices.
- Compensation policies and procedures:
  - Placing the employee in the most appropriate position;
  - Determining appropriate pay structures.
- Staff development:
  - Inducting new staff into the district;
  - Assigning staff to positions based on program needs;
  - Orienting staff to the position and role;
  - Providing mentoring and ongoing support;
  - Evaluating staff on objective performance criteria;
  - Developing staff through additional training.

HUMAN RESOURCE COMPENSATION POLICIES AND PROCEDURES

To emphasize again, enrollment drives revenue, which in turn drives budget and expenditures. For better or worse, these realities may drive program decisions. As a result, the next section examines compensation policies and procedures because inability to fund a sound staffing plan invariably impacts the quality and quantity of services available to children.

What is the Role of Compensation?

The role of employee compensation is clear in the bulleted list above. Compensation is the reason most people work—it provides their livelihoods, rewards their professional achievements, and allows them to support their families. Compensation forms the basis for purchased human services in schools and covers a range of work including leadership; instruction and instructional support; transportation; food service; maintenance and repair, and much more. As noted earlier, compensation is comprised of not only salaries and wages, but also fringe benefits offered by and paid (partly or totally) by the district.[3] These usually include health insurance, pension, and paid leave. In sum, the strength of the total compensation package can be the primary basis for employees' willingness to enter into an employment contract.[4]

General Issues

When the topic of public school compensation is raised, most people think of salaried employees like administrators and classroom teachers. This section, though, focuses on teacher salaries not only because they represent the greatest portion of a school district's human capital investment but also because they attract the most scrutiny in the community, the state, and the media. Historically, single-salary schedules for teachers were developed as a means to correct pay inequities that unfairly discriminated by race, gender, and grade-level across the nation. Also, in many districts teachers were paid based on political party affiliation or other non-meritorious bases. Although opponents today argue that the single-salary schedule discourages individual merit, proponents have long held that it is far superior to other choices because it fosters better working relationships, is less expensive to administer, and avoids problems such as favoritism, discrimination, and retaliation.[5] The concept of a single-salary schedule is not unique to school districts since many local, state, and federal governmental units use a similar approach.

Administering employee compensation begins with determination and formulation of a job description for each position in a school district. Complete, detailed, written job descriptions should be developed for every employee job classification. If done properly, job descriptions are based on surveys, interviews, and assessments of what every position is expected to contribute to organizational goals. Job descriptions should be very clear so that all parties can agree on the nature, duties, and expectations. Each position should have a performance-based job explanation that includes statements about the method and amount of remuneration. Evaluation of performance based on objective goals can then follow, i.e., performance should form the basis for an employee's location on the salary schedule. Obviously, descriptions vary by position. For example, the job description for a school principal is very different and far more complex than the job description for a school clerical staff position, although both positions are indispensable to organizational effectiveness. Examples of job descriptions for these two positions are shown in Figures 6.1 and 6.2.

POSITION:	**High School Principal**
REPORTS TO:	**Associate Superintendent for Administrative Services**
	Secondary
CONTRACT:	**230 Days**

I   General Responsibilities

Supervises all professional and support staff in the school building. As the educational and administrative leader of the school building, the building Principal is responsible for implementing school system policies and achieving educational objectives.

II   Examples of Duties

A.   Administrative Services

1. The building principal administers the school in conformity with the policies and procedures of the Board of Education, federal, state and local laws, regulations, and mandates
2. The building principal communicates District goals, objectives, policies, and procedures to staff members, students, parents, and the community
3. The building principal develops school goals with staff, students, and the community
4. The building principal follows the district employment process when selecting and assigning candidates to building positions
5. The building principal evaluates personnel in compliance with district policy and procedures
6. The building principal submits reports and apprises District personnel of special needs and/or concerns
7. The building principal attends, participates and/or coordinates, when appropriate, building, area, and district meetings
8. The building principal supervises student events both on and off campus ensuring safety as well as sportsmanship
9. The building principal maintains effective student discipline in all activities
10. The building principal explores available community/business resources to meet school goals
11. The building principal develops a staffing plan and a master schedule
12. The building principal demonstrates commitment for professional development including organizing and participating in professional development activities
13. The building principal completes other duties as assigned

B.   Educational Services

1. The building principal diagnoses and prescribes curricular/program needs and develops and implements programs to promote academic excellence
2. The building principal implements plans to improve instruction
3. The building principal articulates and coordinates the curriculum within and between the school levels (elementary, middle, and high school)
4. The building principal creates and maintains a safe and positive learning environment
5. The building principal ensures an academic environment that meets individual student needs
6. The building principal is the Local Education Authority for all Individual Education Plans and is accountable for delivery of the services prescribed therein
7. The building principal develops, implements, articulates, and evaluates student activity programs

FIGURE 6.1   Sample Job Description for High School Principal

Source: Shawnee Mission Public Schools USD 512, by permission (2018).

8. The building principal provides for a variety of opportunities for student recognition
9. The building principal uses data to determine the needs of individual learners and creates ways to meet needs
10. The building principal promotes and supports collaboration amongst content or grade level teachers
11. The building principal monitors the instructional program of the school to ensure quality delivery of the district curriculum

C. **Personnel Services**
1. The building principal establishes high expectations for staff performance
2. The building principal supports the attainment of school goals
3. The building principal supports the professional development of all staff members
4. The building principal provides for staff recognition

D. **Business and Operations Services**
1. The building principal implements a systematic process for budget development and monitors expenditure of funds
2. The building principal ensures clean and safe conditions of building and grounds
3. The building principal maintains proper inventories and ensures equipment is in proper and safe working condition
4. The building principal encourages and monitors optimal community facility use

III **Desirable Qualifications**
A. Graduation from an accredited college or university with at least a Master's Degree in public school administration or related field
B. Possess or be eligible for administrative licensure in the State of Kansas
C. Five years of successful experience as a teacher, administrator, or supervisor at the appropriate school level
D. Knowledge of principles and practices of public school education and ability to apply them to the needs of the school
E. Knowledge of curriculum and instructional methods, school organization, and administration
F. Ability to supervise others and develop effective working relationships with the staff, students, and community
G. Knowledge and ability to utilize appropriate technology including but not limited to office software and presentation devices
H. Ability to collaborate and communicate effectively both verbally and in written language

LANGUAGE SKILLS
Ability to read and interpret documents including the analysis of district assessment data. Ability to effectively write detailed reports and correspondence. Ability to communicate well, verbally and in writing, with parents, patrons, staff, and students. Ability to speak in front of large and/or small groups. In addition, as an organization/community that reflects and appreciates diversity, bilingual communication skills are noted and valued.

FIGURE 6.1 (Continued)

Although job descriptions should lead to objective salary decisions based on placement of employees according to school district salary schedule policies, the actual salary structure is often a function of two realities. In some states, collective bargaining applies to both licensed and classified employee groups. In other states, teachers bargain under collective negotiations, while classified employees and administrators are

CLASSIFIED EMPLOYEES
POSITION DESCRIPTION

POSITION TITLE	Secretary IV
DIVISION:	Administrative Services
DEPARTMENT:	Elementary Education
DAYS SCHEDULED:	215 Days
SALARY SCHEDULE:	General, Grade 9
REPORTS TO:	Elementary Principal

I. **GENERAL DESCRIPTION**

Prepares and maintains files, reports, and records of administrative and confidential nature. Assists in collecting and assembling data for special reports requiring minor research and initiative. Performs many clerical tasks requiring broad knowledge of office practices and procedures. Has many and varied public contacts.

II. **EXAMPLES OF DUTIES AND RESPONSIBILITIES**
   A. Acts as receptionist for building and operates phone and intercom system
   B. Assists substitute personnel when they report to building
   C. Assists teachers with correspondence and reports as approved by the principal
   D. Maintains bookkeeping system using an online accounting system
   E. Keeps accurate enrollment and withdrawal records. Requests records from pupil's former school and sends records to district office or receiving schools of students who move
   F. Assists cashier with daily deposit and accounting
   G. Requisitions all supplies and materials; maintains adequate supply of expendable materials
   H. Completes daily, weekly, monthly and yearly reports
   I. Maintains records and collection of book fees and medical cards
   J. Fills in for nurse when he/she is not available

III. **TRAINING, SKILLS, AND EXPERIENCE REQUIREMENTS**
   A. Training and experience should be equivalent of that normally received by graduation from high school
   B. Good knowledge of modern office practices, current office software, procedures and of business English, spelling, and related subjects
   C. Skill in keyboarding, maintaining office files and records, and compiling reports from standardized information
   D. Maintain effective working relationships with district personnel at all levels, ability to meet the public and other visitors to the district and/or schools, ability to exercise sound judgment in making administrative decisions
   E. Must be able to operate photocopying machinery, fax machine, computer keyboard, printer, calculator, telephone equipment, and other office machinery, and perform alphabetizing and filing tasks

FIGURE 6.2 Sample Job Description for School Secretary

Source: Shawnee Mission Public Schools USD 512, by permission (2018).

outside the negotiations law. In such instances, nonteaching staff salaries and wages are often a function of prevailing rates obtained by informal or formal comparisons with comparable school districts. Once salaries are in place, annual adjustments across employee groups are often a function of similar percentage increases. For example, it is unlikely that administrators will receive a much higher percentage salary increase than teachers simply due to the resultant negative publicity, although headlines sometimes report otherwise in the name of market adjustments. In states where nonteaching staff have no legal bargaining status, it is likely that salaries and wages will be decided after collective negotiations with teachers are complete, often with percentage increases closely conforming for the same public relations reasons.

Negotiations

The fiscal aspect of collective bargaining can be time-intensive and complex. Because so much is at stake, both financially and in terms of future working relationships, it is important for all parties to develop trust and respect for each side's information and philosophical position. Many school districts hold informal contract discussions during the school year about employment concerns, including compensation. Discussions should always be with appropriate employee association or union leaders to avoid allegations of unfair labor practice under applicable state statutes. Throughout the school year, and in multiyear contracts as well, dialogue with all groups can ease the negotiations process by preventing tensions from silently festering.

The negotiation process is unique to each state due to different bargaining laws. The National Labor Relations Act of 1935[6] dictates that for employees of state, county, and municipal governments, including public school districts, collective bargaining rights are governed by state statutes rather than by federal law. Thus, collective bargaining rights and subjects are totally controlled by state laws and state courts. In principle, however, the steps are similar depending on the extent to which outside arbitration is required in state law. At whatever time of year salary and contract discussions begin, the budget office is called on by the human resource division to provide salary data for use in making fiscal projections and to provide cost analyses of all salary proposals. The reason is that short- and long-range costs must be known for all salary and contractual proposals before agreement can be reached regarding a new compensation plan. The budget office must consider not only all direct costs of salary and fringe benefits, but also cash flow, cost of employee time, and any other items placed on the negotiations table by either side. Each of these issues must be analyzed for present and future costs and for the long-range impact on school district fiscal health. The essence of all these activities is to conduct negotiations in good faith and to accurately anticipate all costs of compensation in order to balance revenues and expenditures in the final budget.

Basic Components of Collective Negotiations

Again, collective negotiations are governed by state statute. State law, as well as administrative rules and regulations, varies greatly from state to state, ranging from states with highly favorable employee leanings to a total inability of employees to negotiate in any manner. Thus, this section is an overview that must be carefully applied within state-specific statutes, administrative rules, and regulations.

The process begins once all relevant salary and contract data are collected and verified by both sides. Agreement on the facts makes bargaining easier because the school district's position at the table, the potential for favorable review if negotiations go to impasse or arbitration, and the union's receptiveness are all enhanced. Items on which initial agreement should be sought include cash projections, the impact of these data on the district, historical data related to the issues at hand, and data showing how the district compares to other districts of similar profile in the region and state. Careful preparation and presentation always increase the potential for agreement at the bargaining table, along with aiding favorable treatment if fact-finding and arbitration should eventually be required.

The goal of both sides in contract negotiations should be to have rational discussions regarding the facts in order to agree on a fair salary and benefits package.

Once an agreement is struck, any changes are applied to the appropriate salary and benefit schedules. For example, for certificated teaching staff the first and most direct impact is often an adjustment to the salary schedule, both in terms of new dollars and any changes to the structure of the salary schedule itself. For noncertificated staff, the impact occurs either in the similar application to relevant salary or wage schedules or by the adjustment to each individual's contracted salary or wage. The goal of fairness must be extended to the fringe benefit package as well. Thus, data reflecting the need to attract and retain high quality staff, as well as to promote employee professional development, must be balanced with the district's ability to fund all contractual obligations.

During the negotiations process, management and labor come to the bargaining table with items they expressly want to negotiate. Preparation on the part of the school district focuses on collecting and examining financial data and any other current concerns of the district. The employee organization has an interest in these same items, although for mostly different reasons. Items brought to the table by both sides are fairly common and often include the following:

- *Strengths and weaknesses* of the entire contract;
- *Salary schedule*, including number and costs of each cell of the salary matrix over the life of the contract and a projection into the near future;
- *Basic data* on minimum, maximum, and average cost per employee over the life of the contract;
- *Comparative salaries* in competing school districts and industries;
- *Living standards* of the local community;
- *Staff turnover*, including pending retirements;
- *Movement on the salary schedule* due to advanced education/training, experience, and other criteria;
- *New program needs and curtailments*;
- *Future revenues and expenditures*, including tax levies and state aid projections.

In addition, the school district and employee groups will need to bring other nonfinancial data to the table. Generally this consists of such issues as the following:

- Are there parts of the contract that have not worked well?
- Is there a pattern of grievances over parts of the contract?
- Should parts of the contract be modified or dropped?
- What new issues may prove problematic?

These data are critical to the negotiations process and to compensation policies because, without good data, accurate costs cannot be known and the ability to fund a future contract is unclear. Indeed, the school district's fiscal integrity is at the mercy of accurate data.

Costing-Out Salary Proposals

Although terms and conditions of employment make up a large part of the total negotiations process, the most elemental aspect comes when salary is discussed. It is at salary negotiation time when the human resource and budget functions are most closely related because, if contract agreement is not reached, the district is likely to suffer lowered staff morale or even work interruptions.

For certificated staff, discussion of salary is likely to center on improving the basic structure of the salary schedule and on increasing the dollar amount of the base salary while taking into consideration any increase in the cost of fringe benefits. Table 6.1 contains several steps related to a single-salary schedule for a sample school district and offers an illustration of how contract negotiations occur. The first part shows an indexed salary schedule[7] where the base salary is set at $35,000 with every cell in the matrix a multiplier against the base. The next part converts those percentages of the base into salary dollars. The next part applies these salaries plus benefits to individual teaching staff for this budget year and the next, indicating the additional cost for next year would be $4,200. The next part proposes a new base of $36,000 (i.e., the act of negotiating salaries). Using the same percentages (index) as the first part, the next part presents the new proposed salary schedule. The part applies these new salary amounts to representative teaching staff and adds $300 to fringe benefits to come up with a total $6,420 increased cost to the district over the previous year. Table 6.1 therefore provides concrete information to negotiators as to the impact of a $1,000 increase to the base salary and a 10% increase in the cost of fringe benefits.

In addition to increasing the base salary in Table 6.1, other enhancements to the salary schedule might be proposed during negotiations. It is also possible that adding *columns* to reward additional units of college credit may be proposed. Another proposal might be to add steps to the bottom of some or all columns as a reward for years of teaching experience in the school district (unfreezing staff). Naturally, all these proposals will increase the district's salary costs. On the other hand, to reduce costs the district's negotiating team might seek more restrictive language on non-salary items, such as limiting or refining discretionary leaves. Realistically, negotiating a salary decrease to save money is unlikely except under conditions of fiscal exigency. Then, at best, the district might obtain an agreement on a salary freeze.

All changes to compensation must be reviewed carefully. The effect of increasing the base by $1,000 is seen in Table 6.1. Importantly, increasing the base by even a modest amount affects the entire schedule because (in this example) each step is indexed to the base. In addition, current teachers will receive a step increase in the next school year. Also, given the relative maturity of many teaching staffs throughout the nation, care must be taken in salary negotiations because, as salary schedules load on experience, district costs rise, although at least in the short run the higher cost of experienced staff may be offset due to turnover.[8] Hence, a modest $1,000 base increase raises salary costs by several thousand dollars (note that $300 was added to fringe benefits to reflect increased health insurance costs). The cost of increasing the number of columns cannot be ascertained from Table 6.1 although the general impact can be seen. Needless to say, salaries for teachers with advanced degrees are more expensive, so that despite the benefits of well-qualified staff, the district must be alert to the increased human resource costs involved.

Proposals to add steps to columns are also costly. The purpose, of course, is to reward and retain experienced teachers. Adding steps, for example, beyond the 18 years of experience in Table 6.1 may be much higher than it first seems. Before a

TABLE 6.1 Sample Salary Schedule

BASE – $35,000

YEAR	BA + 0	BA + 15	BA + 30	Masters	MS + 15	MS + 30	Doctorate
1	100%	102%	104%	106%	108%	110%	112%
2	102%	104%	106%	108%	110%	112%	114%
3	104%	106%	108%	110%	112%	114%	116%
4	106%	108%	110%	112%	114%	116%	118%
5	108%	108%	112%	114%	116%	118%	120%
6	110%	112%	114%	116%	118%	120%	122%
7	112%	114%	116%	118%	120%	122%	124%
8	114%	116%	118%	120%	122%	124%	126%
9		118%	120%	122%	124%	126%	128%
10		120%	122%	124%	126%	128%	130%
11			124%	126%	128%	130%	132%
12			126%	128%	130%	132%	134%
13				130%	132%	134%	136%
14				132%	134%	136%	138%
15					136%	138%	140%
16					138%	140%	142%
17						142%	144%
18							146%

YEAR	BA + 0	BA + 15	BA + 30	Masters	MS + 15	MS + 30	Doctorate
1	$ 35,000	$ 35,700	$ 36,400	$ 37,100	$ 37,800	$ 38,500	$ 39,200
2	$ 35,700	$ 36,400	$ 37,100	$ 37,800	$ 38,500	$ 39,200	$ 39,900
3	$ 36,400	$ 37,100	$ 37,800	$ 38,500	$ 39,200	$ 39,900	$ 40,600
4	$ 37,100	$ 37,800	$ 38,500	$ 39,200	$ 39,900	$ 40,600	$ 41,300
5	$ 37,800	$ 37,800	$ 39,200	$ 39,900	$ 40,600	$ 41,300	$ 42,000

(Continued)

TABLE 6.1 Continued

6	$ 38,500	$ 39,200	$ 39,900	$ 40,600	$ 41,300	$ 42,000	$ 42,700
7	$ 39,200	$ 39,900	$ 40,600	$ 41,300	$ 42,000	$ 42,700	$ 43,400
8		$ 40,600	$ 41,300	$ 42,000	$ 42,700	$ 43,400	$ 44,100
9		$ 41,300	$ 42,000	$ 42,700	$ 43,400	$ 44,100	$ 44,800
10		$ 42,000	$ 42,700	$ 43,400	$ 44,100	$ 44,800	$ 45,500
11			$ 43,400	$ 44,100	$ 44,800	$ 45,500	$ 46,200
12			$ 44,100	$ 44,800	$ 45,500	$ 46,200	$ 46,900
13				$ 45,500	$ 46,200	$ 46,900	$ 47,600
14				$ 46,200	$ 46,900	$ 47,600	$ 48,300
15					$ 47,600	$ 48,300	$ 49,000
16					$ 48,300	$ 49,000	$ 49,700
17						$ 49,000	$ 50,400
18						$ 49,700	$ 51,100

Projections based on **zero** dollar increase on base (see asterisk note below).

Name	Current salary	Current benefits	Current pkg.	New salary	New benefits	Proposed pkg.	% increase
Mary A.	$ 35,000	$ 3,000	$ 38,000	$ 35,700	$ 3,000	$ 38,700	1.8%
Bob B.	$ 41,300	$ 3,000	$ 44,300	$ 42,000	$ 3,000	$ 45,000	1.6%
Julie C. (frozen)	$ 44,100	$ 3,000	$ 47,100	$ 44,100	$ 3,000	$ 47,100	0.0%
James D.	$ 37,100	$ 3,000	$ 40,100	$ 37,800	$ 3,000	$ 40,800	1.7%
Janet E.	$ 46,900	$ 3,000	$ 49,900	$ 47,600	$ 3,000	$ 50,600	1.4%
Bill F. (frozen)	$ 51,100	$ 3,000	$ 54,100	$ 51,100	$ 3,000	$ 54,100	0.0%
Paula G.*** and so on…	$ 49,700	$ 3,000	$ 52,700	$ 51,100	$ 3,000	$ 54,100	2.7%
TOTALS	$ 305,200	$ 21,000	$ 326,200	$ 309,400	$ 21,000	$ 330,400	1.32%

	COST TO FUND
	$ 4,200

***will obtain doctorate by end of current school year.

BASE - $36,000

YEAR	BA + 0	BA + 15	BA + 30	Masters	MS + 15	MS + 30	Doctorate
1	100%	102%	104%	106%	108%	110%	112%
2	102%	104%	106%	108%	110%	112%	114%
3	104%	106%	108%	110%	112%	114%	116%
4	106%	108%	110%	112%	114%	116%	118%
5	108%	108%	112%	114%	116%	118%	120%
6	110%	112%	114%	116%	118%	120%	122%
7	112%	114%	116%	118%	120%	122%	124%
8	114%	116%	118%	120%	122%	124%	126%
9		118%	120%	122%	124%	126%	128%
10		120%	122%	124%	126%	128%	130%
11			124%	126%	128%	130%	132%
12			126%	128%	130%	132%	134%
13				130%	132%	134%	136%
14				132%	134%	136%	138%
15					136%	138%	140%
16					138%	140%	142%
17						142%	144%
18							146%

YEAR	BA + 0	BA + 15	BA + 30	Masters	MS + 15	MS + 30	Doctorate
1	$ 36,000	$ 36,720	$ 37,440	$ 38,160	$ 38,880	$ 39,600	$ 40,320
2	$ 36,720	$ 37,440	$ 38,160	$ 38,880	$ 39,600	$ 40,320	$ 41,040
3	$ 37,440	$ 38,160	$ 38,880	$ 39,600	$ 40,320	$ 41,040	$ 41,760
4	$ 38,160	$ 38,880	$ 39,600	$ 40,320	$ 41,040	$ 41,760	$ 42,480

(Continued)

TABLE 6.1 Continued

Step						
5	$38,880	$40,320	$41,040	$41,760	$42,480	$43,200
6	$39,600	$41,040	$41,760	$42,480	$43,200	$43,920
7	$40,320	$41,760	$42,480	$43,200	$43,920	$44,640
8	$41,760	$42,480	$43,200	$43,920	$44,640	$45,360
9	$42,480	$43,200	$43,920	$44,640	$45,360	$46,080
10	$43,200	$43,920	$44,640	$45,360	$46,080	$46,800
11		$44,640	$45,360	$46,080	$46,800	$47,520
12		$45,360	$46,080	$46,800	$47,520	$48,240
13			$46,800	$47,520	$48,240	$48,960
14			$47,520	$48,240	$48,960	$49,680
15				$48,960	$49,680	$50,400
16				$49,680	$50,400	$51,120
17					$51,120	$51,840
18					$51,840	$52,560

Projections based on **$1,000** increase on base (see asterisk note below).

Name	Current salary	Current benefits	Current pkg.	New salary	New benefits	Proposed pkg.	% increase
Mary A.	$36,000	$3,000	$39,000	$36,720	$3,300	$40,020	2.6%
Bob B.	$42,480	$3,000	$45,480	$43,200	$3,300	$46,500	2.2%
Julie C. (frozen)	$45,360	$3,000	$48,360	$45,360	$3,300	$48,660	0.6%
James D.	$38,160	$3,000	$41,160	$38,880	$3,300	$42,180	2.5%
Janet E.	$48,240	$3,000	$51,240	$48,960	$3,300	$52,260	2.0%
Bill F. (frozen)	$52,560	$3,000	$55,560	$52,560	$3,300	$55,860	0.5%
Paula G.*** and so on...	$51,120	$3,000	$54,120	$52,560	$3,300	$55,860	3.2%
TOTALS	$313,920	$21,000	$334,920	$318,240	$23,100	$341,340	1.96%

COST TO FUND

$6,420

***will obtain doctorate by end of current school year.

school district enters into such an agreement, it should determine how many teachers would qualify for this vertical movement. Additionally, the district should try to determine how many individuals might qualify to move horizontally due to additional coursework or attainment of advanced degrees. In other words, both horizontal and vertical movement on a salary schedule cumulatively add to the total cost.

This brief illustration has many applications. One of the most important benefits is the ability to automate salary schedules for instant *what-if* scenarios. Salary schedules such as Table 6.1 can be placed in a spreadsheet so that all cells update if the base is changed. Also, both sides can immediately see the effect. Both sides also profit from the entire negotiations process in that, although the board of education will have to increase salaries next year at the budget's expense, the board does so in exchange for the least dollar amount possible at which it can hire and retain highly qualified employees. It is important for board members, administrators, teachers, and the public to understand that collective bargaining is a series of compromises and that one side rarely has total success. In brief, if the district anticipates staffing needs, recruits and selects highly qualified staff, and prepares and uses budget data for sound compensation policies, both sides have a better chance of reaching an acceptable compromise.

Whatever proposals come to the table, several features must be understood. Negotiations can be confrontational, but the risk of bad relationships can be lessened through transparency and trust. Second, a decision to meaningfully improve a salary schedule may come at a cost to other operations. However, failing to offer competitive salaries and benefits is destructive to long-term district health at many levels. Third, it is important to understand that an average 3% increase in teacher salaries, for example, will likely result in a 3% increase for all nonteaching staff, including administrators. In sum, a single decision to increase teacher salaries can have broad implications for all human resource costs that spread throughout the district. Furthermore, annual state aid increases may not be sufficient to cover the new costs, requiring either new taxes if statutorily permissible or reductions in other operating expenditures.

The human resource and budget functions work with both sides during negotiations to produce data and to determine costs of proposals. In many instances, the board's chief negotiator may be a central office administrator such as an assistant superintendent for human resources and/or finance, or the chief negotiator may be an attorney selected for his/her experience in collective bargaining agreements in the public sector. Regardless of who serves as the board's spokesperson, the human resource and finance functions must be aware of all developments and must be constantly consulted to determine the viability of proposed actions.

Whoever serves in the lead role must possess certain skills if the outcome is to be successful. The chief negotiator must be very familiar with state bargaining statutes and knowledgeable about unfair labor practices, as well as experienced in these complex matters. Additionally, the negotiator should be emotionally mature, articulate, flexible, and able to reject ideas without needlessly alienating the other side.

In addition to a spokesperson, the board's team often consists of the district's chief fiscal officer, a recorder, a board subcommittee, and others as appropriate. Team composition varies by local custom. Teachers are often represented by an attorney, a professional association or union, or a local faculty member; that is, each school district differs in its culture. Most negotiating sessions follow customs—for example, only spokespersons may speak, written initial nonexpandable proposals must be exchanged in advance, and caucuses are generally unlimited unless agreed otherwise. Again, it must be stressed that each state varies in statute and custom; for example, in some states bargaining sessions may be closed to the public. The scope of a sample state negotiations law is illustrated in Figure 6.3.

Impasse Resolution

Despite best efforts, negotiations may reach an impasse. In most states, school districts are required to recognize impasses and to engage in fact-finding, followed either by binding arbitration or by a unilateral board of education contracts. Generally, an impasse and

Mandatorily Negotiable

1. Salary	14. Jury duty
2. Wages	15. Grievance procedure
3. Pay under supplemental contracts	16. Binding arbitration
4. Hours of work	17. Discipline procedure
5. Amounts of work	18. Resignations
6. Vacation allowance	19. Contract termination
7. Holiday leave	20. Contract nonrenewal
8. Sick leave	21. Reemployment
9. Extended leave	22. Contract terms
10. Sabbatical leaves	23. Contract form
11. "Other" leaves	24. Probationary period
12. Number of holidays	25. Evaluation
13. Retirement	26. Insurance benefits
	27. Overtime pay

Permissibly Negotiable

1. Academic and personal freedom (except constitutional)	7. Teacher copyrights
2. Assignment and transfer of personnel	8. Facilities, equipment, materials, supplies
3. Association rights	9. Grading frequency
4. Class size	10. Security
5. Classroom management	11. Substitutes
6. School library hours	12. Teacher aides

Nonnegotiable

1. Number of days or total hours of school	5. First Amendment issues
2. Nondiscrimination	6. Affirmative action
3. Special education placement procedures	7. Student discipline if constitutional issue
4. Teacher discipline if constitutional issue	8. Federal programs

FIGURE 6.3 Sample Negotiations Law

TABLE 6.2 Sample Negotiations Timeline

February 1	Exchange of notices and proposals. A petition to the state to declare impasse may be filed.
June 1	Notice of impasse must be filed if applicable.
June 5	Five days set aside for consultation with state on impasse.
June 15	State issues findings. Arbitration process begun if needed.
June 20	Fact-finding board appointed with 5 days.
July 10	Fact-finding report issued within 20 days.
Immediate	Parties must meet to discuss fact-finding results.
July 20	Report made public after 10 days.
July 30	Board may issue unilateral contracts if no agreement has been reached.

fact-finding occur when parties cannot reach an agreement on terms and conditions of a new employment contract by some date specified in state statute. For the human resource and budget functions, failure to negotiate a new contract leads to uncertainty and tension in employer–employee relations—a stress that is hard to heal even over extended time.

When negotiations fail, most states invoke a timeline calling for a third party to review the last best offers from both sides and issue a report. Depending on state statute, this person may be a representative of the state's employment relations board or someone approved by some other state agency. Fact-finding in many states is not binding, but it is often persuasive to the parties. In contrast, some states require mediation and/or binding arbitration if fact-finding does not produce a settlement. Mediation usually precedes arbitration, although in practice each state's statutes are unique. In several states, binding arbitration is immediately invoked: An impartial panel issues a report and both sides must obey. Such a ruling cannot be challenged unless it can be successfully argued that the arbitrator exceeded legal authority. In other states, the process only calls for impasse, fact-finding, mediation, and unilateral contracts if an agreement has still not been reached. In all instances, a statutory timeline like the one in Table 6.2 must be followed.

In states where binding arbitration exists, the budget and human resource functions typically cannot issue contracts, set budgets, or engage in most employment activities until negotiations are settled. This can be uncomfortable for both sides since often they must continue to work together, especially in states where public employee strikes are prohibited. Even more complex in such cases is the total subjugation of the school district to the will of an outside arbitrator who may make a decision that is financially difficult to fulfill. In states without binding arbitration, issues are tense too, but the budget and human resource functions can resume operation much sooner. At the opposite end of the spectrum, the issue of salary costs in unilateral contract states is obviously under far greater control although the interpersonal issues remain.

Pursuant to state law, a similar set of negotiations may repeat with each employee group. When contracts are finally settled, a major task of the budget and human resource functions is complete and these divisions can resume employer–employee relationships wherein the new contract is administered on a daily basis.

OTHER ISSUES IN HUMAN RESOURCE BUDGETING

Although labor negotiations are the most critical part of school district budgeting once projecting enrollment and staffing needs is complete, there are other important issues for human capital services. For legislators, school boards, administrators, staffs, and communities, three particular areas are important because they impact compensation structures and financial liability. These areas are proposals for *alternative reward systems*, *reductions-in-force and other dismissals*, and *due process* concerns.

Alternative Reward Systems

A recurring theme related to compensation in public schools is the concept of alternative reward systems for teachers. Most common and longstanding among these is the push for merit pay. More recently, individuals calling for total redesign of compensation systems have offered up plans that include salary incentives for knowledge- and skills-based performance, differentiated duty pay, differentiated staffing, extra pay for national board certification, and cash incentives such as signing bonuses and supplemental pay to attract teachers to fields where supply is low or to attract high-performing teachers to low-achieving schools. In all cases, the purpose is plain—to aggressively attract the most competent teachers to the field and to reward them along some discriminating performance dimension. In fact, there is relatively little difference between the aims of traditional merit pay and the aims of these other alternative reward systems; both aim not merely to provide additional compensation for extra duties, but to reward superior performance on school or district goals by identifying performance differences between people with similar jobs.

Although any differential reward system for teachers has long been subject to strenuous criticism, there is new evidence that school budgets increasingly will be expected to financially support some type of merit pay. Despite opponents' claims that merit systems are often based on unproven evaluation methods, induce discord on goals, and generally fail to accurately measure performance over time in any consistent fashion, merit systems continue making headlines. Recent examples are found in various states where the concept of merit pay by value-added measures or otherwise linking pupil achievement with individual teacher performance awards is being actively explored.[9] Broadly, these performance plans include differentiated pay that rewards additional responsibilities or offers titles and duties involving mentoring, peer coaching, and serving as lead teachers; staffing plans that recognize advanced achievement and offer more responsibilities and longer contracts along with titles such as career teacher or master teacher; knowledge- and skill-based pay to reward persons who demonstrate named competencies at apprentice or mastery levels; and other state and local school-based performance plans tied to achieving established performance goals.[10] Whether strictly defined merit pay or some other performance-based plan is inevitable seems not to be the question; that is, school districts will continue to budget for single-salary schedules, but public interest in alternative reward systems will increasingly define the compensation picture in a meaningful fashion.

However, as school districts build budgets, two key concerns regarding alternative pay should predominate. First, for the school- or district-level leader there is a concern for how redesigned compensation systems will affect internal working relationships. It is noteworthy that the vast majority of those advocating for merit pay plans are outside the public education system.

Second, district leaders should be very concerned regarding how alternative pay systems will augment or supplant traditional pay structures and the resultant fiscal impact on the school district. While single-salary schedules are costly even with only modest changes rippling nearly exponentially throughout the entire schedule, it is nearly inviolate that alternative compensation plans cost more, either by supplementing existing salary schedules or by supplanting them. In either case, the costs of politically driven reforms will be at least additive to current costs, and it is rare when the political entities driving reforms also fully fund those same reforms. In brief, school districts have reason to celebrate when compensation systems offer increased rewards, but the consequence and cost of systems need to be uppermost—at the legislative lobbying level, at contract negotiation time, and at budget management time.

RIF and Other Dismissals

Another area of concern for the budget process involves reduction-in-force (RIF) and other dismissals. RIFs occur when school districts have more staff than they need, while other dismissals occur for reasons like unsatisfactory performance. Although dismissals are carried out through the human resource office, the budget is impacted because salary and benefits will be terminated, a new hire may be contemplated, and dismissal always involves risks related to wrongful acts on the part of the district. In sum, the budget and human resource functions must minimize the damage and estimate the impact of these actions.[11]

In contrast to merit pay which offers more money for desired behaviors, RIF reduces a school district's cash outlay. In some instances, merit pay and RIF might be joined purposely, but the primary concept behind RIF is to reduce the budget, often in response to enrollment decline or another fiscal stress. RIF dismisses untenured or tenured staff for reasons unrelated to performance. Conversely, though, if an employee's performance should lead to enrollment decline, dismissal or nonrenewal may still be treated as RIF. The usual reason for RIF, however, is fiscal exigency. It must be understood that when fiscal exigency is claimed by a school board, counterclaims by the teachers' union will center on validity of the board's data. Consequently, the district must be able to substantiate its actions based on evidence. In this arena, the need for clear and precise data is paramount. When data are clear, dismissals for the right reasons will be supported by the courts.

When RIF is invoked, a series of complicated events is put in motion. Generally state law is very detailed regarding this discussion, although federal employment law is important too. For example, care must be taken to observe any federal protections such as free speech; to follow all state statutes and local negotiated contract provisions such as employee rights to seniority (e.g., *bumping*); and to make certain that no allegations of preferential treatment can be made during the dismissal process. Extreme care must be taken to avoid liability because some courts have granted broad rights to both tenured and untenured staff. Other courts have ruled that as long as constitutionally protected rights are respected, untenured teachers have no expectation for employment and have none of the rights of tenured staff. The concept of bumping is common in such situations, placing an extra burden on districts to be certain that both laws and negotiated agreements are correctly followed; that is, in such situations teachers may bump other teachers with less seniority so long as other requirements such as professional licensure in teaching fields are met. Public school leaders must be aware that when legally challenged under state law and applicable collective bargaining agreements, courts may watch to ensure that RIF is not a ruse for voluntary budget reduction or a diversionary scheme to avoid a difficult dismissal fight. As a consequence, school leaders must be informed about all aspects of statutory and employment contract law.

Other dismissals also happen. Although it is often thought that tenure is a life appointment, in reality both untenured and tenured staff may be dismissed. There should be no mistaking the local board of education's power in human resource matters. Boards and supervisors have the authority to evaluate and dismiss, powers that come by virtue of states granting both implied and delegated authority to operate the public schools.

Although boards of education can dismiss staff, termination by RIF or other reason must not be lightly undertaken. This is true because in the majority of states significant differences exist between dismissal procedures for untenured vs. tenured staff. Tenure carries expectation for a continuing contract and entitles the staff member to due process of law. In contrast, untenured teachers may expect only a term contract under whatever employment and dismissal rights are granted by constitutional and federal or state employment law. This does not mean untenured staff have no protections because no one can be denied constitutional rights; untenured staff may demand full due process if alleging that fundamental rights such as freedom of speech have been violated. In addition, state statutes govern other rights of untenured staff, making it mandatory to understand state statutes, the termination process, and the terms of the employment contract.

Tenured teachers may be dismissed too, but the task may be harder because state statutes usually require specific reasons for termination of tenured employees, i.e., for cause. Under state statutes, cause generally includes issues like incompetence, immorality, insubordination, felony conviction, unprofessional conduct, incapacity, and neglect of duty. Within limits of seniority and bumping, fiscal exigency is also a defensible cause for tenured dismissal. When any of these reasons is invoked, however, the right of termination falls to employers only if employer claims can be substantiated. If challenged, failure to substantiate will likely result in a lawsuit along with liability for various types of restitution and/or reinstatement. As a result, great care should be taken when contemplating the dismissal of any employee.

The most challenging dismissal cases typically involve tenured staff. Courts have allowed a broad definition in matters of incompetence, requiring only reasonable evidence relating to lack of ability, lack of legal qualification, or failure to discharge duties. Proof of incompetence is measured against others having similar duties. Incompetence may be shown by any one of the following criteria or some combination thereof:

- Lack of a proper teaching license;
- Lack of knowledge of subject matter;
- Lack of ability to establish reasonable discipline in class;
- Deficiency in teaching methods;
- Emotional instability demonstrating inability to teach effectively.

Both untenured and tenured staff may be dismissed for these reasons. In dismissing tenured staff, however, great care must be taken to document the charges in case litigation ensues. Additionally, in some states there is a duty to remediate before moving to dismissal. Remediation must be documented and should include a variety of activities designed to bring the employee up to an adequate level of performance. Remediation should help employees become successful in the specific job, should define activities and duties of all parties, and should demonstrate good faith by the district to salvage the contractual interest of the employee. Documentation of failure by the employee to respond to remediation must be thorough because the first defense will be to say that the employee is not the worst case and that the district did not perform in good faith. Serious liability, including award of monetary damages, can accompany improper dismissals, along with reinstatement of the staff member to his or her original position.

As noted, staff may be dismissed for immorality. In today's context, immorality is not solely limited to sexual misconduct. In a court, immorality can be based on prevailing community standards in which the test is whether the act was detrimental to public welfare. Actions such as corruption or indecency constitute immorality, in that the standard may be defined as conduct offensive to the morals of a community and which sets a bad example for youth whose ideals a teacher is supposed to foster. Although immorality is broadly defined, care must be taken not to expose the district to liability for misapplication of the standard. For instance, in a conservative community a sensitive area might be an unwed pregnant teacher. However, courts generally have not supported claims of immorality in such cases due to lack of proof. This simply means that it is difficult to prove in the majority of communities that pregnancy results in harm to students in the learning environment, or that the teacher's respect in the community has been diminished. And to complicate matters, even though the teacher's pregnancy may offend the sensibilities of some in the community, in 1978 Congress passed the Pregnancy Discrimination Act,[12] amending Title VII to include pregnancy under equal benefits coverage.

Similarly, dismissals involving insubordination are guided by state statutes and controlling case law. Willful disregard or repeated refusal to obey reasonable professional directives related to the safety, health, and welfare as well as the educational functions of the school, nearly always constitutes insubordination. Courts place the burden of proof on the school district, however, particularly with tenured staff given the property rights inherent to a continued employment expectation. The following represent guidelines regarding insubordination in which the school district generally will prevail:

- The employee should be given clear directives and, if possible, these directives should be in writing with written acknowledgement by the employee copied to the appropriate files;
- There is evidence that the employee understood the directive by signature or other acknowledgement;
- The directive was reasonable and related to the safety, health, and welfare of students as well as the educational mission of the school;
- The directive did not place the employee in danger of his or her safety or health or was not beyond the scope of their knowledge or expertise;
- The order did not violate public policy such that it would violate the rights of students, fellow employees, or the purpose of schools;
- The employee was informed of the consequences of disobeying the directive and the employee acknowledged the consequences, including possible termination;
- Insubordination and willful neglect must be proved and not merely assumed.

Finally, employees may be discharged without liability for neglect of duty. In practice, neglect of duty may be part of a claim of incompetence. For example, neglect of duty might include failure to follow curriculum standards, failure to maintain discipline, failure to follow teaching lessons, and other similar actions or inactions. Neglect is distinct from insubordination, wherein an employee blatantly disregards directives. To withstand judicial challenge, charges of neglect of duty or insubordination must reflect prior notice and evidence of established policy or directives. Finally, other dismissals for acts such as felony conviction likely will be upheld because such offenses may have an impact on the performance and standing of the employee in the community. In many states, statutes provide that felony conviction is automatic evidence of unfitness. But as always, carelessness in substantiating dismissals may lead to harm to the school district.

Due Process

The seriousness of budgeting for human resource issues is clear when it is realized that school districts are financially liable for wrongful acts. Liability is broad and includes risk for improper dismissal given the near-certainty of attendant claims for reinstatement, back pay, and actual and punitive damages for violating the rights and reputation of the accused. These modern realities place a grave duty on school districts to properly discharge all legal and professional obligations and to follow both procedural and substantive due process. Procedural due process ensures that parties are entitled to notice and hearing. Substantive due process is a constitutional guarantee that no one may be deprived of rights and must be protected from unreasonable action.

Although the human resource function has primary responsibility for developing due process guidelines conforming to the requirements of law, the financial implications of liability mean that the budget office is greatly affected and should be involved in such policy development. All policies should be approved by the board of education and made known to staff. Assuming a tenured employee does not commit an act that is defined by state statute warranting immediate termination, the process of hearings and appeals is found in controlling state statutes. Generally, due process, as defined by state statute, consists of four elements that also apply to dismissal and should be invoked any time there is reason to suspect that a financial risk might arise. In the case of contract termination, the tenured employee first must receive written notice giving specific reason(s) for nonrenewal, and notification must conform to state law on timing and method of delivery. Second, an impartial hearing is required so that the employee can hear, examine, and refute evidence. Third, the employee must be given the opportunity to challenge these statements and to call witnesses. Fourth, hearings must occur at several levels in the school district so as to demonstrate that all administrative procedures and remedies were afforded. The process begins with the immediate supervisor and administratively ends with the board of education. This ensures that the employee has the opportunity to be heard and to challenge actions at each level. Failure to provide these proceedings will almost certainly result in severe consequences.

Determining whether due process has been provided is a function of the external mechanics of proceedings and closer scrutiny of the process. District leadership and the board of education must be careful to deal objectively with the facts and to procedurally follow each due process step. This is especially critical for tenured employees because they may have property rights to continued employment, and procedural and substantive due process must be observed in that property rights may not be arbitrarily removed. The duty of the school district is grave, as the U.S. Supreme Court long ago ruled that such interests of employees are broad and majestic.[13] At the same time, appropriate dismissals should be carried out because—notwithstanding the seriousness of violating rights and due process—failure to reverse poor employment decisions causes genuine harm to children over time. As noted earlier, dismissals must be reasonable, must not be arbitrary or capricious, must be supported by documentation, and due process must be properly observed throughout the entire process. In such cases, justice prevails.

WHAT IS THE ROLE OF STAKEHOLDERS?

Human resource costs typically drive over 80% of school district expenditures. Public education is a truly labor-intensive industry, and as such human capital is the single largest annual investment a district makes with its finite resources. Indeed, a district's ability to reach its educational goals depends entirely on a highly qualified staff.

When viewed as a total process, the topics presented in this chapter (projecting enrollments, determining staffing needs, recruiting, selecting, compensating, and retaining a highly qualified workforce) constitute the most critical elements of budgeting. When these elements are properly addressed, the probability of success in providing a sound education for all children is greatly enhanced. If done poorly, the outcome is predictably unsatisfactory. For boards of education, a state constitutional duty to deliver a free and appropriate education rests in large part on the relationship between the budget and human resources. For school leaders, the success of creating and balancing a sound budget is at stake. For teachers, professional success, employment stability, and personal happiness are at stake via the act of budgeting for human resources. And for the general public, the climate of the community and the economic and personal wellbeing of everyone, including children, is dependent upon offering the next generation a quality education. In brief, budgeting for human resources drives revenue, expenditures, and programs at the most fundamental level.

POINT–COUNTERPOINT

POINT

Traditional single-salary schedules based on college credits and years of teaching experience do actual harm to individual teachers' initiative by denying them the opportunity to be rewarded for real improvements to teacher quality and pupil performance. Pay-for-performance plans that are independent of years of experience and which link teacher pay directly to pupil achievement offer the best opportunity to recruit and retain top talent and to address staff shortages. Public schools should embrace these plans because traditional single-salary schedules are obsolete.

COUNTERPOINT

Traditional single-salary schedules were developed in response to repeated failures of merit pay. The history of discriminatory salary practices in public schools was overcome only through the adoption of the single-salary schedule. It is hypocritical to suggest that advanced education is an invalid basis for rewards in schools, and it is nonsensical to argue that skills don't increase with experience. If tired merit pay systems are forced on schools under misleading names like "pay for performance" or "value-added," the culture and productivity of public education will be changed for the worse by pitting teacher against teacher and school against school for limited superficial financial rewards. Students and learning alike will suffer.

- Which of these starkly opposite views best represents your beliefs and experience? Explain.
- Would you be willing to accept new employment in a school district that had adopted an alternative compensation system like pay for performance? Why or why not?
- If your current school district announced it was considering a move to a new pay plan designed to improve achievement scores, would you be willing to participate in its development? Why or why not?

CASE STUDY

Until last year, you were an experienced and highly successful middle school principal in one of the largest school districts in your state. In fact, you had won a couple of prestigious state awards for your school's academic performance, and your staff had been visibly distraught when you decided to begin looking for new professional horizons. Indeed, upon completion of your doctoral degree this past spring, you were immediately hired by a similarly sized school district in a neighboring state, with a large salary increase to sweeten the deal. Your new position as Assistant Superintendent for Human Resources has put you in charge of nearly 4,300 faculty and staff. Your reason for taking this new position was that you had always wanted to work in a school district that seemed to have almost unlimited fiscal resources, and your new district fit that description, along with enviable achievement scores in most of its schools. And of course a major motivation was your success as a principal—as you told your spouse, you could take your success to a new level to effectuate a wider scope of systemic excellence.

A couple of months into your new position, you began to think that your new school district might look better from the outside than from within—not so much regarding either plentiful resources or high learning outcomes, but rather from some of the personnel issues you seem to increasingly encounter. Just last week you attended a national conference and deliberately sat in on sessions relating to professional collaboration among staff. As Assistant Superintendent for Human Resources, everything from hiring classified staff to hiring central office administrators is now your responsibility, and you have become quite concerned about relationships between numerous teachers and their building principals. More particularly, while you were at the conference you thought back on your own hiring experience and recalled that you were given only positive information about the district and how there had been no trace of discord in anything you heard. Your own sleuthing, though, was now indicating that several elementary principals were not adhering to the negotiated agreement and have been assigning teachers in their buildings to extra duties during their plan/duty-free lunchtime. You have learned that at six schools the teachers are not upset about it because they admire their principals, and you learned that they are compensated at the approved hourly rate when they lose their planning times. It seems to be working very well in those schools, as these attendance centers have recently won awards for improvement and innovation, and they are vigorously supported with plentiful resources from the Parent Teacher Organizations (PTOs) at their school sites. But you also have learned the same thing has happened at five other schools, and in those cases the teachers are extremely unhappy with their principals and their increased workloads. Indeed, just yesterday you heard that several teachers at those school sites are planning to file grievances against their principals for the forced work during their planning/duty-free lunch times. You have further heard that those same teachers have since refused to stay after school for any meetings and have refused any committee work until there is a hearing about the alleged violations of the negotiated agreement.

This morning the superintendent called you to his office and quizzed you at length about the situation. You learned even more from him, as he knew additional details of which you were unaware. You promised to get to the bottom of the situation, and after leaving his office you spoke with several principals in the unhappy schools. You were stunned by what you learned: In a nutshell, you learned that not only is it a negotiated agreement issue, but there are tensions between faculties at the various school sites regarding supposed systemic haves and have nots. More specifically, you learned that the PTOs in the six happy buildings are very active and have the financial means to support teachers with treats and gift cards, while the other five buildings have parents who volunteer but do not have the funds to provide perks. You were also told that several principals themselves have feuded behind the scene about the inequalities, but that these wounds are festering because principals have the authority to manage their individual budgets without much central office oversight. As you reflected that night on your predicament, you realized that you may have a real problem on your hands, i.e., there are principals who are not following the negotiated agreement; there are PTO disparities that affect district harmony and performance; and you sense that the slow simmer is likely to turn into a public relations nightmare if it comes to full boil.

Earlier in the day the superintendent had told you that he expects a quick solution. You know he expects a favorable progress report within a week. The question is where to begin and how to not make matters worse.

- Identify and describe the major problems confronting you in this situation.
- As you contemplate the need for action, where should you begin? What needs to be done? Who should be involved? What can you do right away that will be positively perceived? What pitfalls should you anticipate? Develop an action plan to address these questions.
- Could this situation occur in your own school district? Have there been instances in which similar tense moments have occurred? If so, what were the circumstances, and how were the problems resolved?

PORTFOLIO EXERCISES

- Talk to your school district's human resource director and outline the functions of the office. Make a list of duties, prioritized from highest to lowest, including estimates of time spent on each function. Explore coordination between the human resource and budget offices.

- Obtain a copy of your school district's salary schedule(s) for employee groups and analyze the structure of each. Experiment with changes to the salary schedule, noting the impact of changes that would be popular in your district—for example, you might analyze changes proposed during recent negotiations.
- Talk to your local teachers' union representative and a school district official to obtain a balanced view of human resource-related budget issues.
- Obtain a copy of your school district's human resource policy manual. Discuss its contents with a range of district employees such as the human resource director, a school principal, a teacher, a classified staff member, and a union representative. Ask them to assess whether the manual is clear and comprehensive. Ask for suggestions for improvement. Summarize these and discuss whether you agree or disagree and explain why.

NOTES

1   Much information in human resource files is confidential and protected by federal and state privacy laws. When a school district builds linkages between databases (e.g., personnel and community demographics), it must take care to build in appropriate security measures so only those authorized to view confidential personnel information have access to that data. See, e.g., "Public Sector Employee Privacy," in *Employment Law for Business*, seventh ed., by Dawn D. Bennett-Alexander and Laura P. Hartman (Boston: McGraw-Hill, 2011), 661–671.

2   It has long been known that early retirement plans, dependent upon the specifics, may not save public school districts money over lengthy periods of time. See, R. Craig Wood, "The Early Retirement Concept and a Fiscal Assessment Model for Public School Districts," *Journal of Education Finance* 7, 3 (1982): 262–276.

3   Some employee benefits are required under federal law. These include workers' compensation insurance, unemployment insurance, FICA (Federal Insurance Contributions Act), and Medicare Hospital Insurance. Employers pay for the first two in full, while employers and employees both make contributions to FICA (Social Security) and Medicare.

4   It should be noted that our discussion refers to full-time employees. Fringe benefits for part-time employees may differ significantly.

5   Some economists attempt to classify all single schedule salary plans as inefficient in that certain teachers are perhaps paid more than they are actually worth, while others are paid less than their level of productivity.

6   29 U.S.C. §151–169.

7   Indexing is only one type of salary schedule construction. Other types could include a flat dollar increase to each cell in the salary matrix. Indexing makes each successive cell a percent increase above the base salary. An index may also be constructed so that each successive cell is a percent increase above the immediately preceding cell. Such choices are important because the total cost of a design depends on construction.

8   Edwyna Synar and Jeffrey Maiden, "A Comprehensive Model for Estimating the Financial Impact of Teacher Turnover," *Journal of Education Finance* 38, 2 (Fall, 2012): 130–144; Abigail J. Levy, Lois Joy, Pamela Ellis Erica Jablonski, and Tzur M. Karelitz, "Estimating Teacher Turnover Costs: A Case Study," *Journal of Education Finance* 38, 2 (Fall, 2012): 102–129.

9 Stuart S. Yeh, "The Reliability, Impact, and Cost-Effectiveness of Value Added Teacher Assessment Methods," *Journal of Education Finance* 37, 4 (Spring, 2012): 374–399.

10 Katharine O. Strunk and Dara Zeehandelaar, "Differentiated Compensation: How California School Districts Use Economic Incentives to Target Teachers," *Journal of Education Finance* 36, 3 (Winter, 2011): 268–293.

11 See, R. C. Wood, "Reduction In Force," in *Principles of School Business Management*, edited by R. C. Wood (Reston, VA: Association of School Business Officials, 1987), 537–557.

12 See, 29 C.F.R. §1604.10.

13 *Board of Regents v. Roth*, 408 U.S. 564 (1972).

WEB RESOURCES

American Association of School Administrators, www.aasa.org

American Association of School Personnel Administrators, www.aaspa.org

American Federation of Teachers, www.aft.org

Association of School Business Officials International, asbointl.org

National Center on Performance Incentives, www.performanceincentives.org

National Education Association, www.nea.org

National School Boards Association, www.nsba.org

National School Public Relations Association, www.nspra.org

North American Association of Educational Negotiators, www.naen.org

U.S. Department of Labor, www.dol.gov

RECOMMENDED RESOURCES

American Association of School Personnel Administrators. "Best Practices in School Personnel." (May/June/July 2015). http://aaspa.org/wp-content/uploads/2015/04/2015-Best-Practices-Digital.pdf

Aragon, Stephanie. "Teacher Development and Advancement: A Series." Denver, CO: Education Commission of the States (2018). https://www.ecs.org/teacher-development-and-advancement/

Bennett-Alexander, Dawn D., and Laura P. Hartman. "Public Sector Employee Privacy." In *Employment Law for Business*, seventh ed., 661–671. Boston: McGraw-Hill, 2011.

Cowen, Joshua M. "Teacher Unions and Teacher Compensation: New Evidence for the Impact of Bargaining." *Journal of Education Finance* 35, 2 (Fall 2009): 172–193.

DeMitchell, Todd A. *Labor Relations in Education: Policies, Politics, and Practices*. Lanham, MD: Rowman & Littlefield, 2009.

Foster, John M., Eugenia F. Toma, and SuZanne P. Troske. "Does Teacher Professional Development Improve Math and Science Outcomes and Is It Cost Effective?" *Journal of Education Finance* 38, 3 (Winter 2013): 255–275.

Geier, Brett A. "Michigan's Public Educator Retirement System – On the Road to Bankruptcy: A Legal Analysis of Michigan." *Journal of Education Finance* 41, 4 (Spring 2016): 451–472.

Goff, Peter, Ellen Goldring, and Melissa Canney. "The Best Laid Plans: Pay for Performance Incentive Programs for School Leaders." *Journal of Education Finance* 42, 2 (Fall 2016): 127–152.

Jurist Levy, Abigail, Lois Joy, Pamela Ellis, Erica Jablonski, and Tzur M. Karelitz. "Estimating Teacher Turnover Costs: A Case Study." *Journal of Education Finance* 38, 2 (Fall 2012): 102–129.

Knight, David S. "Assessing the Cost of Instructional Coaching." *Journal of Education Finance* 38, 1 (Summer 2012): 52–80.

Konoske-Graf, Annette, Lisette Partelow, and Meg Benner. "To Attract Great Teachers, School Districts Must Improve Their Human Capital Systems." Center for American Progress (2016). https://www.americanprogress.org/issues/education-k-12/reports/2016/12/22/295574/ to-attract-great-teachers-school-districts-must-improve-their-human-capital-systems/

Pantuosco, Louis J. and Laura D. Ullrich. "The Impact of Teachers Unions on State-Level Productivity." *Journal of Education Finance* 35, 3 (Winter 2010): 276–294.

Pham, Lam, Tuan Nguyen, and Matthew Springer. "Teacher Pay and Student Test Scores: A Meta-Analysis." Nashville, TN: Vanderbilt University (2017). https://s3.amazonaws.com/ vu-my/wp-content/uploads/sites/868/2013/02/05145950/Pham-Nguyen-Springer-2017.pdf

Ravitch, Diane. *The Death and Life of the Great American School System: How Testing and Choice Are Undermining Education*. New York: Basic Books, 2010.

Rice, Jennifer King. "The Impact of Teacher Experience: Examining the Evidence and Policy Implications." Brief no. 11. Washington, DC: Urban Institute, August 2010.

Shuls, James V. "Examining Inequities in Teacher Pension Benefits." *Journal of Education Finance* 42, 4 (Spring 2017): 435–447.

Southern Regional Education Board. "Fact Book & Ed Data: K-12 Data." Atlanta, GA: SREB (2018) https://www.sreb.org/k-12-data

Springer, Matthew G. and Lori L. Taylor. "Designing Incentives for Public School Teachers: Evidence from a Texas Incentive Pay Program." *Journal of Education Finance* 41, 3 (Winter 2016): 344–381.

Strunk, Katharine O. and Dara Zeehandelaar. "Differentiated Compensation: How California School Districts Use Economic Incentives to Target Teachers." *Journal of Education Finance* 36, 3 (Winter 2011): 268–293.

Synar, Edwyna and Jeffrey Maiden. "A Comprehensive Model for Estimating the Financial Impact of Teacher Turnover." *Journal of Education Finance* 38, 2 (Fall 2012): 130–144.

Toutkoushian, Robert K., Justin M. Bathon, and Martha M. McCarthy. "A National Study of the Net Benefits of State Pension Plans for Educators." *Journal of Education Finance* 37, 1 (Summer 2011): 24–51.

Tran, Henry. "Does the Pay Stance of South Carolina Public School Districts Influence their Math and Science Achievement Scores?" *Journal of Education Finance* 43, 2 (Fall 2017): 105–122.

Watlington, Eliah, Robert Shockley, Paul Guglielmino, and Rivka Felsher. "The High Cost of Leaving: An Analysis of the Cost of Teacher Turnover." *Journal of Education Finance* 36, 1 (Summer 2010): 22–37.

Winters, John V. "Variation in Teacher Salaries in Georgia: Does the Property Tax Base Matter?" *Journal of Education Finance* 35, 2 (Fall 2009): 157–171.

Yeh, Stuart S. "The Reliability, Impact, and Cost-Effectiveness of Value-Added Teacher Assessment Methods." *Journal of Education Finance* 37, 4 (Spring 2012): 374–399.

CHAPTER 7

Budgeting for Instruction

CHAPTER DRIVERS

Please reflect on the following questions as you read this chapter:

- What is instructional planning?
- What are the sources of revenue for instructional budgets?
- What is the role of districts and schools in instructional planning?
- How do schools organize for instructional budgeting?
- What is the role and size of instructional budgets?
- What are the elements of budgeting for instruction?
- What does an instructional budget look like?

THE OVERALL PICTURE

This textbook has provided an introductory overview of broad school funding concepts, with the ultimate goal of more closely examining the individual tasks of budgeting. The text has synopsized the modern context of schools, the complex social milieu in which school funding policy is made, the sources of school funding, the seriousness of handling school money, the general process of budgeting, and the costs associated with human resources. This helicopter view has steadily narrowed as the text has introduced each specific element of budgeting. *Budgeting for instruction* is next examined because it is logical to understand the application and operationalization of money as it arrives at the classroom level—a topic of intense interest to education's many stakeholders.

The chapter begins by moving from a general framework to increasingly specific elements. If school budgets and instruction are to be wed, the starting point is defining instructional planning and the role of districts and individual schools in the process. Underlying are issues of organizational structure: i.e., how schools in a particular district are organized has great influence on many other structures, including the roles and responsibilities in budget decision-making. Once these structures have been set, instructional budgets can be built and put in motion. As a consequence, this chapter moves still deeper into the world of school money.

THE PLANNING FUNCTION

While the complete range of instructional planning is not the focus of this text, the emphasis on strategizing for effective learning organizations makes it absolutely clear that building a budget based on the instructional goals of a school district is critical. In fact, the whole purpose of budgeting is to build a revenue and expenditure plan to carry out the district's instructional mission.

What Is Instructional Planning?

Research and practice hold many lessons about organizing and operating schools, with three overriding realities. The first reality is that successful instructional planning requires the use of experts who grandly and specifically envision and direct the teaching and learning process. The second reality is that a sound instructional plan requires the support of a strong fiscal plan. The third reality is that effective instruction requires something inseparable from the first two; i.e., a deliberate plan based on a formal mission with a set of measurable goal statements. In sum, while the budget is the fiscal expression of the educational philosophy of a school district, it is ineffective until the instructional plan brings together revenue sources in support of expenditures in order to articulate and enact the district's mission and goals.

District Mission and Goals

Mission and goal statements are cornerstones in today's education world, as much positive benefit has come from deliberately focusing on formal guiding documents. The primary value has been that once mission and goal statements are set and known by the community, the weight of performance accountability is set in motion. Although critics may question the wide sweep of mission and goal statements, there is an increased duty to the school district when it makes public statements such as "all children can learn to high standards." Sadly, history reveals that schools and society have not always believed that all children can learn, and the proof lies in the heated debates concerning the value and costs of special education and compensatory programs. Those debates are beyond the scope of this textbook, but it is sufficient to say that a mission statement serves to *define and drive the organizational culture* of the district such that it has the effect of focusing attitudes and performance on a promise made publicly.

The same is true of goal statements. In contrast to a mission statement which is meant to be broadly exhortative, goal statements are *specific* and may be *performance-based*.

For example, school districts may adopt goal statements like "all children will reach at least the 60th percentile on grade-level standardized tests before promotion to the next grade," or "all high school seniors will pass a criterion-referenced test with a state-approved minimum score permitting entry into the state's higher education system without remediation." The range of possibilities for goal statements is endless, but the purpose is simple—to focus the district on pupil performance outcomes in the larger context of the stated mission and to operationalize the mission in objective, specific, and measurable terms. Both mission and goal statements have strong budget ramifications, so much so that budgeting for instruction is central to all planning.

School Mission and Goals

Mission and goal statements also apply to individual schools within a school district. Although it may seem redundant for school sites to restate district goals, it is symbolic for schools to spend time and energy building loyalty to larger organizational aims. A simultaneous requirement, however, is that each school should create its own mission and goals specific to its unique culture, needs, and demographics. Although school mission and goal statements should assist those of the district, a school's mission and goal statements must reflect its programs' strengths and target the particular needs of its population.

If it is financially meaningful for a school district to tie mission and goals to the budget, there are equally significant fiscal implications for school mission and goal statements. As discussed later, districts often provide some degree of latitude for school sites to pursue specific goals, and it is unquestioned that needs vary from school to school. Consequently, budget philosophy and fiscal operations at the school site level may differ based on needs and preference. In other words, mission and goals are not only district-level activities—they are essential budget-building blocks that focus each school's planning on learning outcomes, which in turn drives instructional spending.

For budgetary purposes, the planning function is the act of determining district and school mission and goals, coupled with an explicit expenditure plan to achieve those outcomes. As discussed in Chapter 6, human resources are a major cost, but there remains a significant portion of every school district's budget that goes to non-salary instructional expenses. Those investment opportunities are the focus of this chapter, together with how instructional budget decisions are made—decisions affected in significant ways by how school systems are organized.

ORGANIZATIONAL OPTIONS

Instructional planning raises issues of how schools are structured. Chapter 6 introduced organizational options and budgeting strategies, using the example that budgeting for schools adopting site-based leadership will be structured differently from schools operating under a more centralized hierarchy. Because instructional decisions are strongly influenced by organizational design, it is important to examine some options before considering how instructional budgeting actually occurs.

How Are School Districts Organized?

Instructional budgeting is greatly dependent on district organizational design. Although there are many variations, school districts are almost always driven first by central administration's leadership style. As a result, the most common organizational designs include varying degrees of centralization, management teams, and site-based leadership. The impact of such a design is pervasive through many system layers, and it drives most planning and decision-making processes.

Centralized Structure

Most decisions in centralized school districts are made in a tightly controlled central office environment, with budgets closely held at that same level. Highly centralized organizations are typically committed to line-item or program budgeting, and there are usually efforts to make uniform allocations to schools as an expression of evenhandedness. However, centralization usually is not absolute in that it is often characterized by degrees of delegated responsibility. Ultimately, though, delegation of decision-making is still accompanied by strict central reporting and accountability— i.e., a high degree of central control.

Centralized control has benefits and drawbacks. Among the benefits is the idea that the central office is ultimately responsible for everything that happens in the district and that top leaders are expected to have the expertise to make every important decision. An additional benefit is organizational efficiency, as indecisiveness has no place when leaders are strong individuals. On the negative side is the obvious fact that decision-making and ownership are tightly held, so that unquestioning endorsement of mission and goals and actions by subordinates is a rule of daily life. In such organizations, there is typically little staff involvement at any level in budgeting and only marginal involvement in instructional planning.

Management Teams

While highly centralized school districts actually still exist, the use of management teams has grown rapidly. Known by various names, management teams are a middle ground between complete centralization and its opposite—decentralization. The management team concept holds that more heads are better than one, although many hallmarks of centralization remain. The basic structure finds most major decisions made by central office staff who advise the superintendent from within a closely held cabinet. Central office staff, though, may offer advice after having listened to various groups within the district and community.

Management teams also offer benefits and drawbacks. One benefit comes from advice more widely gathered, often via trial balloons by senior officials before controversial decisions are made known. Benefits also include checks and balances of constituent input, and the efficiency inherent to central decision-making is preserved. On the downside, individuals or groups may complain that their input is not taken seriously or that input is structured to elicit preferred answers. In such organizations, centralization is still evident, but budgets and instructional decisions are likely to be delegated, albeit to varying degrees.

Site-Based Management

Although no good data exist regarding how many of the nation's roughly 14,000 school districts are still highly centralized, many districts have sought to shed that image. Indeed, it is difficult to imagine that such a design could exist today given demands by employees and communities to have a voice in decision-making. Such expectations have given rise to site-based management (SBM) on at least an informal scale, and there are instances where SBM has been written into statutory guidelines.

The impetus for SBM in schools is often regarded as beginning with the sweeping education reform in *Rose v. Council for Better Education*[1] in Kentucky, as the legislature responded to a state supreme court order to fix a constitutionally flawed education system. In answer to the court, the state ordered a total restructure of public elementary and secondary education. The Kentucky Education Reform Act[2] of 1990 was a monumental piece of legislation that required local school boards to implement school-based decision-making vested in site councils composed of parents, teachers, and principals. Site councils were given vast and unprecedented responsibility, including management of schools on a daily basis. For example, the Kentucky law charged site councils with the following:

- Setting school policy to provide an environment to enhance pupil achievement;
- Dividing staff into committees by areas of interest for the purpose of making recommendations to the council;
- Determining the number of persons employed in each job and making personnel decisions on vacancies;
- Determining instructional materials and support services;
- Determining curriculum, including needs assessment, curriculum development, alignment with state standards, technology utilization, and program appraisal;
- Assigning use of staff time;
- Assigning students to classes and programs;
- Determining the schedule of the school day and week;
- Determining use of school space during the day;
- Planning and resolving issues of instructional practice;
- Implementing discipline and classroom management;
- Selecting extracurricular programs and determining policies relating to participation;
- Administering the school budget, including discretionary funds, activity funds and other school funds, as well as maintenance, supplies, and equipment funds;
- Assessing student progress, including testing and reporting to parents, students, the board, the community, and the state;
- Creating school improvement and professional development plans;
- Coordinating parent, citizen, and community participation.

The demands of the Kentucky law left no question about its intent. The rules had changed, and the purpose of putting stakeholders in charge of a decentralized system was clear. While by no means universal, other states adopted the basic design in subsequent years so that today SBM's ideals remain pervasive in visible and subtle ways. The underlying rationale was always the same: Stakeholders want a strong voice in schools; expertise exists among educators and non-educators alike; and many decisions are believed to be best made closer to the school site.[3]

Predictably, site-based leadership designs have had benefits and drawbacks. One benefit is that SBM stands as the epitome of shared decision-making in which all stakeholders are engaged. As such, parents and communities have little ground to stand on if they try to complain that schools are unresponsive. On the downside, efficiency of professional decision-making can quickly decrease when laypeople become involved in complex decisions. Additionally, the many sensitive areas in SBM such as human resource decisions made by site councils can be a source of legal and ethical jeopardy. Further, the potential for fiscal and program inequality may increase as some schools perform better and more effectively strategize financial and parental support structures.

The budgetary impacts of SBM are real. Although implementation of the SBM model varies according to local preference or state statutes, schools engaged in SBM are required to accept far more responsibility for budget decisions—tasks formerly reserved for the district's central office. For example, individual school sites may have to choose between buying supplies and hiring more personnel, or between maintaining facilities and funding student activities. As a result, latitude in decision-making is gained, but difficult decisions must be made by individual schools which are then obligated to consult an array of stakeholders (boards, central office staff, principals, teachers, parents, and other site council members) who must agree on mission and goals, available resources, and measurable outcomes. The shift is fundamental at every level; that is, under SBM the central office fades to a role of oversight, while the school site becomes the nucleus of authority, power, and direction.

In brief, many individual schools are taking on new powers, even under more centralized organizational designs, because statutes and the general public are seeking control of education's goals and outcomes. Accordingly, it behooves all leaders to understand issues of organizational design in order to identify the parameters of appropriate and effective leadership, including answers to the following questions:

- *Who has primary responsibility* for establishing the overall level of expenditure in a district and school?
- *Who has primary responsibility* for establishing expenditures for each major program or organizational unit?
- *Who has primary responsibility* for selecting specific resources within the allotted dollar amounts for each program?
- *Who has primary responsibility* for curriculum selection?
- *Who has primary responsibility* for new programs or for eliminating or reducing the scope of current programs?
- *Who has primary responsibility* for establishing salaries and benefits?
- *Who has primary responsibility* for hiring human resources?
- *Who has primary responsibility* for establishing capital budgets and infrastructure?

INSTRUCTIONAL BUDGET CONCEPTS

As noted, all parts of a budget are serially linked so that the number of pupils drives revenues, which in turn drives staffing, thereby driving a huge proportion of total expenditures. But the instructional budget picture is not yet complete because the next step is to consider non-salary portions of instructional costs.

Instructional Budgets

The instructional budget is the portion of a school district's budget remaining after excluding all noninstructional costs. More particularly, costs for food service, capital outlay, transportation, debt service, and most other separate funds are excluded. Under these limitations, the definition of an instructional budget defaults to the entire general fund as the best description of instructional expense. Although not entirely accurate, it is useful to picture instructional costs in this way because direct instructional expense is what people really mean in this instance. Using that logic, it is accurate to think of the general fund in this manner because the general fund truly does pay for the vast majority of certificated and classified staff salaries, instructional supplies, and other annual operating expenses associated with school sites and instructional programs. By this definition, 85–87% of a typical district's general fund budget is allocated to instruction (excluding business operations and maintenance—see Figure 7.1). Since everyone working at a school site or in the central office either has a direct instructional role or an instructional support role, nearly all current expenditures can be viewed as instructional dollars.

The instructional budget can also be viewed as that portion of a total budget after subtracting all salary and nonteaching supply expense. By this definition, instructional budgets are not as large, but it underscores the truth that the vast majority of education's costs is in human capital and further illustrates that all other operations are funded by very low percentages of the budget.

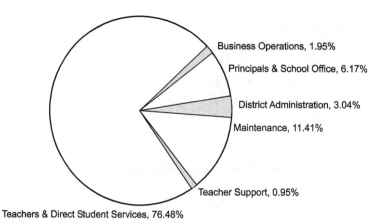

Business Operations, 1.95%

Principals & School Office, 6.17%

District Administration, 3.04%

Maintenance, 11.41%

Teacher Support, 0.95%

Teachers & Direct Student Services, 76.48%

FIGURE 7.1 How Does a District Spend Its Money? Sample School District.

The instructional budget also may be defined as all costs attributed directly to pupils. This would include teachers, supplies, equipment, special education services, and other support services such as librarians, counselors, and nurses, as well as transportation—all of which make up about 76% of the budget (see Figure 7.2). Including professional and physical environments changes the mix but has merit (see Figure 7.3), in that children in fact receive benefits far beyond direct instruction, i.e., the cost of education is more complex than teacher salaries alone. In fact, the strongest argument for including all such costs is that all parts of the budget go together to create an educational plan; that is, instruction would be much less effective if it were not for the contributions of climate-controlled classrooms, safe and clean buildings and grounds, nutrition and health services, and other system costs (see Figure 7.4).

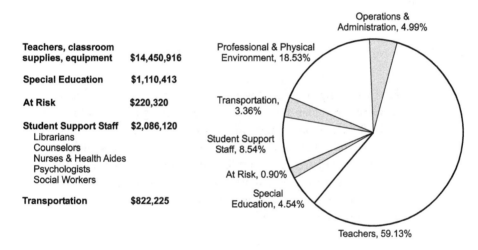

FIGURE 7.2 Direct Student Costs: Sample School District

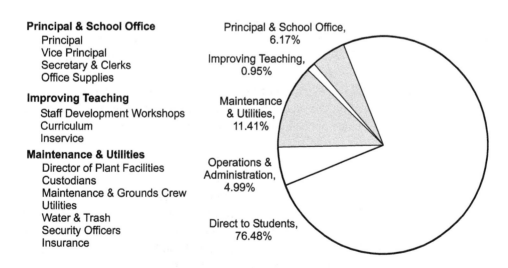

FIGURE 7.3 Professional and Physical Environment: Sample School District

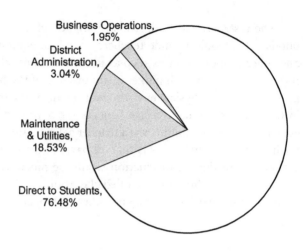

District Administration
   Board of Education
   Superintendent's Office
   Assoc. Supt., Site Support
   Assoc Supt., Central Support
   Research & Evaluation
   Election Expense
   Legal & Audit Services
   Special Education Director
   Transportation Director
   Human Resources
   Information Services

Business Operations
   Director of Accounting
   Director of Business Services
   Payroll
   Accounts Payable
   Data Processing
   Warehousing
   Purchasing

Business Operations, 1.95%
District Administration, 3.04%
Maintenance & Utilities, 18.53%
Direct to Students, 76.48%

FIGURE 7.4 Running the System: Sample School District

Although there are many additional ways to slice instructional budgets, the most important features have been identified. Perhaps the best way to think of instructional budgets is to use the 80% personnel method, remembering that all remaining general fund monies must cover all other general fund costs. This view is also helpful because it shows the role and size of instructional budgets in relationship to the current operating budget which also contains segregated funds that carry out the other business of schools. The view in this chapter is narrower because the central concern is with that portion after human resource costs and selected other general fund operating costs are known.

Sources of Revenue

The discussion in earlier chapters about revenue sources for public schools deserves expansion. Discussion to this point has laid out a revenue scheme made up of federal, state, and local monies. However, these sources only represent funds coming into a school district from external sources in the macro-perspective, and the impact of such monies on individual schools has not been developed. These traditional revenue streams, along with other sources, actually make up a range of revenues that districts receive and allocate using one of the budgeting philosophies discussed earlier.

External Sources

External revenue to school districts comes from three principal sources. Federal aid is mostly targeted to federal priorities such as compensatory and special education. Most federal money is flow-through funding, meaning that state agencies are intermediary recipients and are required to pass revenue on to districts under applicable federal regulations. Additionally, school districts must be able to show that the funds reached individual schools and were not commingled with money from other sources.

The most distinguishing feature of federal aid is its relatively minor status in the total revenue scheme, approximately 8.5% in recent years.

State revenue is distributed to qualifying school districts through state aid finance formulas. Chapter 3 explained that state aid formulas generally are designed to grant aid inversely to local ability to pay; that is, poor districts should receive greater state aid than wealthier districts. It also described variations on state aid formulas, noting that most states rely predominantly on sales (general sales and gross receipts) and personal income tax revenues to fund state aid. The distinguishing feature of state aid is that in some cases it now plays the largest role in funding school districts. This was not always so, as until 1980 the percentage was much lower. But despite a markedly increased role, even today state aid varies considerably across states, ranging from 24.9% to 90.1% of districts' operating budgets, with an average 46.6% across all states (see Table 2.4 earlier).

Local revenue comes to school districts primarily through the local property tax.[4] As seen earlier, local revenue is frequently contentious because citizens may regard local taxes as the only opportunity to cut the cost of government. Increases in tax levies have become increasingly difficult to pass in the last few decades, with little sign of weakening voter resistance. In a few states, school districts have the authority to levy income, sales, or sumptuary taxes without voter approval—such authority, however, is rare and only modestly productive due to statutory tax limitations and tax base overload. Obviously, the distinguishing feature of local revenue is its visibility to local voters. Nationally, about 45% of school district revenue is raised locally, although the percentage varies widely within and across states.

School District Revenue Structures

In a centralized school district, revenues from all sources are gathered in the central office and distributed using a local budget process such as line-item or program budgeting as described in Chapter 5. In more decentralized districts, variants on site-based budgeting may be used. But in all cases, care must be taken to provide an overarching structure to guard against inequitable distribution, to ensure that all programs are adequately funded, and to guarantee that all child-based needs are served.

To meet this goal, school districts exercise available options. Highly centralized budgeting makes initial sense, as this structure allows the district to efficiently meet its neutrality and control objectives. Under this plan, principals gather staff input and forward purchase requests or work orders to the central office, where senior leaders prioritize requests, making sure that each school receives approximately the same budget treatment. The process continues, spending down available resources according to the prioritized master plan. The benefits are clear: Control is present, efficiency is maximized, staff are not burdened by noninstructional financial duties, and schools are treated equally. The drawbacks are equally clear: Control at individual sites is absent, decisions are made far from the point of need, neutrality actually may not be equitable, and staff are uninvolved.

Another option is for central administration to establish allocations to schools for selected purposes, while keeping some items funded centrally. This plan seeks middle ground between centralization and site-based budgeting by arguing that some tasks are best handled at the school site level, while other costs are of no interest to individual schools; for example, maintenance of buildings and grounds, utility costs, transportation, insurance, and salaries are typical candidates for centralization. By this plan, individual school allocations tend to be solely for instructional budget purposes, as is also true of any other discretionary money sent to individual schools. The benefits are clear: Schools are not saddled with tasks that can be handled more efficiently at the district level; a degree of uniformity across the district is achieved; and schools have latitude within their allocations to fund school site priorities. The one drawback is significant: Because salaries consume most of a school district's budget, instructional allocations may entail relatively small amounts of money, and schools still must queue up for capital projects and other large purchases such as textbooks and major equipment. And the scenario can worsen when dissecting salary and staffing patterns, e.g., in many school districts the highest salaries are found in higher socioeconomically advantaged schools—such cases could require very careful analysis to ensure that overfunding or underfunding in all expense categories does not follow.

A third option is site-based budgeting. In its purest form, the school district largely acts as a funnel, channeling available dollars to school sites. Under this plan, the board of education gives a formal charge to each school site based on the district's mission and goals, and each school creates its own financial plan to achieve both district and school objectives. The benefit is clear: Moving money and freedom to the school site confers power on the people who have firsthand knowledge of needs and who have the instructional skills to address local problems. The drawbacks are clear as well: Staff may resent noninstructional duties; poor decision-making is possible; and there is a danger that unequal resources and unequal outcomes will follow.

Regardless of which instructional budgeting option districts choose, the flow of money is transparent. Federal and state monies flow to local districts through distribution formulas, whereupon (within limits of federal and state laws and regulations) each district decides whether to centralize or decentralize fiscal decision-making. Resources at the district level are basically limited to tax dollars, although districts may benefit from private gifts, grants, foundations, business partnerships, and fundraising efforts. On the whole, these *other* sources contribute a very small percentage of school district revenues.

School Revenue Structures

The great majority of school site revenue comes from the district level. However, other revenue may be available. In such cases, school site revenue originates from two sources: The school district, and the individual school site itself.

District revenues have been addressed in this chapter—the only issue is how much revenue is allocated by the district to individual schools and restrictions on how revenue can be used. As already discussed, district-level revenue often takes the form of a uniform amount (e.g., a per-pupil dollar amount) upon which some restrictions are placed by the central office. Figure 7.6 at the end of this chapter more fully develops this idea. In contrast, school site revenue refers to money generated at the individual school level beyond what is normally distributed by the district. Most schools generate some site revenue, but almost always must adhere to board policy regarding revenue generation—and in some cases, must seek board permission. For example, individual schools may be able to apply for small grants from the state's department of education, and state agencies often participate in federal grant programs that may result in school site awards. School districts receiving large grants might hold internal subgrant competitions, with school sites competing for awards. Depending on board policy, schools might also apply directly to corporations, many of which have a record of funding innovative school site projects. Numerous other grants, such as those advertised in the *Federal Register*, are available to either school districts or school sites. In addition, private and charitable foundations are a potential source of school site revenue. Site revenue can also come from local businesses that agree to set up partnerships with selected schools, donating money, time, or materials. Schools sometimes raise money through booster clubs and parent organizations. Although school site revenue can be a benefit, it holds the potential to be a significant concern at the district and community levels if it results in uneven resources among schools in a district. School-generated revenues, while important, still represent a very small percentage of total revenues.[5]

THE ELEMENTS OF BUDGETING FOR INSTRUCTION

Regardless of whether a school district centralizes or decentralizes instructional budgets, certain elements are common to the budget process. In fact, these elements are repeated to some extent at all levels, as discussed later in this chapter when an instructional budget for a hypothetical school district is considered. To illustrate, assume that the hypothetical district has chosen to engage in some decentralization and while retaining some activities at the central office level. Thus, a fourfold interest occurs. First, a needs assessment is required to create the educational plan for both the district and each school. Second, the district must determine its total revenues and make decisions concerning allocations to each school based on the needs assessment. Third, school sites must use the needs assessment and school-level allocations to create educational and expenditure plans. And finally, the district must provide overall coordination—all in the context of pupil performance accountability.

Needs Assessment

Figure 7.5 identifies many important data elements required to build an instructional budget. It shows the environmental scan that should be prepared for both the school district and each school. The scan targets data on many of the conditions discussed in Chapter 1 so that available resources can be prioritized based on the scan's results. The scan paints a distinct portrait of the community, the school district, and each school so that those in leadership positions can see and understand the unique and shared needs of pupils. Assuming that the sample district has set a goal of raising performance on standardized tests and increasing entry rates into postsecondary education, the environmental scan helps identify weaknesses that should become prime targets for increased spending. The political viability of the educational plan also can

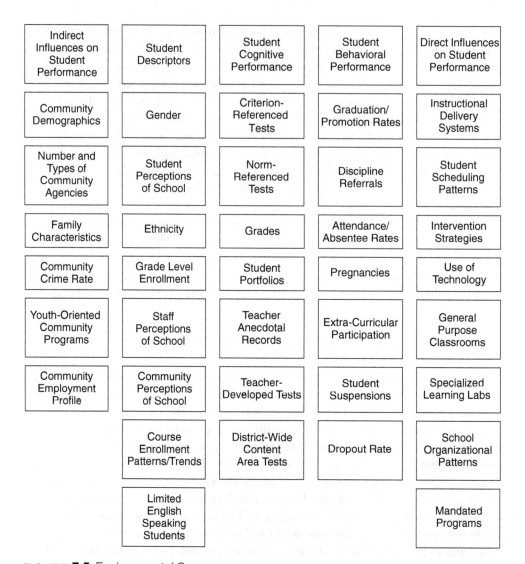

Indirect Influences on Student Performance	Student Descriptors	Student Cognitive Performance	Student Behavioral Performance	Direct Influences on Student Performance
Community Demographics	Gender	Criterion-Referenced Tests	Graduation/ Promotion Rates	Instructional Delivery Systems
Number and Types of Community Agencies	Student Perceptions of School	Norm-Referenced Tests	Discipline Referrals	Student Scheduling Patterns
Family Characteristics	Ethnicity	Grades	Attendance/ Absentee Rates	Intervention Strategies
Community Crime Rate	Grade Level Enrollment	Student Portfolios	Pregnancies	Use of Technology
Youth-Oriented Community Programs	Staff Perceptions of School	Teacher Anecdotal Records	Extra-Curricular Participation	General Purpose Classrooms
Community Employment Profile	Community Perceptions of School	Teacher-Developed Tests	Student Suspensions	Specialized Learning Labs
	Course Enrollment Patterns/Trends	District-Wide Content Area Tests	Dropout Rate	School Organizational Patterns
	Limited English Speaking Students			Mandated Programs

FIGURE 7.5 Environmental Scan

be tested through the demographic data in the scan. Results of all these activities will be used by the hypothetical district at the central office level to establish the district's overall financial support for programs and by the school sites in deciding how to spend site-level allocations to meet these goals.

Determining Revenues and Educational Plans

As noted, revenues flow from federal, state, district, and school site sources. Chapter 5 identified the steps in creating school district budgets, and the present chapter identifies additional revenue sources for individual school sites. In the hypothetical school district, it is assumed that the district has set uniform per-pupil allocations and that all school sites have taken the initiative to secure some external funding for program enhancement purposes. At this point, the educational plan can be built and should address the priorities of the district and each school site, as well as any concerns identified by the environmental scan. In effect, the process calls for setting short-term, intermediate, and long-range priorities for the district, each school and grade level, programs, departments, and classrooms in such a way that resources are matched to students' needs through program-driven budgeting.

District Coordination

Regardless of the extent of decentralization, school districts must coordinate every aspect of the budget. By law only boards of education may spend money, and state statutes typically assign responsibility for educational programs to the local board. Additionally, efficiencies are gained by central coordination and management, and budgets are ultimately the district's responsibility. The budget calendar in Chapter 5 illustrated the district's role in coordination. In this chapter's hypothetical school district, the board has centralized some district-wide activities but has chosen to grant substantial sums of instructional money to individual school sites (see Figure 7.6).

The Instructional Budget

As indicated at the outset of this chapter, instructional budgeting cannot be done in isolation. The various elements are highly interdependent—demographics and pupil needs are revealed through scanning environments and other data collection mechanisms; fund accounting tracks and reveals how money is budgeted and spent; state education finance formulas cause educational programs to grow or starve; liability costs reduce discretionary funds; human resource costs and enrollment drive available resources; and district budgeting philosophies determine how much money is available, how it can be spent, and who makes spending and program decisions. Truly, every aspect of the entire budget of a school district can be viewed as *the* instructional budget, although fund accounting conventions do not see the program side of budgets.

Figure 7.6 presents data for a hypothetical school district and joins concepts from earlier chapters' study of accounting with instructional budgeting. Figure 7.6 is exhaustive, covering all issues in all chapters thus far—it also anticipates future chapters by introducing capital outlay and transportation. Figure 7.6 focuses attention on the budgeting consequences of the chosen organizational structure in the hypothetical district, in that the district has decided to do the following:

- *Track* instructional budgets by accounting codes to permit accumulation of data by individual program;
- *Decentralize* many budget aspects while retaining central office oversight through the board of education and central office directorships;
- *Allocate* uniform amounts per pupil for instructional program purposes;
- *Retain* overall transportation services at the central office level, while also allocating discretionary transportation budgets to schools;
- *Decentralize* some aspects of capital outlay and equipment purchases;
- *Link* expenditures to performance outcomes in a program-driven budgeting model.

General Fund: School Program Codes

Line-items can be refined or expanded in monitoring activities in your school or program
Contact the Director of Business for information.

ELEMENTARY	Year	Fund	Function	Object	Building	Program
Kindergarten	1	−00	−1000	−610	−xx	−01
Reading						−02
Math						−03
Language Arts						−04
Social Studies						−05
Science						−06
Textbooks						−07
Teaching supplies						−08
School office						−09
Postage						−10
Site council						−11
Grants (list)						−31
MIDDLE SCHOOL						
Physical Education	1	00	1000	610	xx	−01
Vocational Arts						−02
Home Economics						−03
Art						−04
Science						−05
Band						06
Vocal music						−07
Languages						−08
Math						−09
Social Studies						−10
Publications						−11
Teaching supplies						−12
School office						−13
Postage						−14
Site council						−15
Grants (list)						−31
HIGH SCHOOL						
Physical Education	1	00	1000	610	xx	−01
Vocational Arts						−02
Home Economics						−03
Art						−04
Science						−05
Band						−06
Vocal music						−07
Languages						−08
Math						−09
Social Studies						−10
Publications						−11
Teaching supplies						−12
School office						−13
Postage						−14
Site council						−15
Grants (list)						−31

FIGURE 7.6 Hypothetical Instructional Budget

INSTRUCTIONS TO PRINCIPALS

You are responsible for all instructional money assigned to your school as outlined in this document. You should gather input from staff members and your site council All budget requests and expenditures should be tied to the site plan for your school. These instructions provide: (a) account codes used by central office to track cost of programs in schools—any purchase request needs to show the right codes; (b) general notes to guide you on how the district expects you to code your purchases; (c) a list of instructional programs that have separate budgets; (d) a listing of all general fund budget allocations—it is here that you know how much you have for your school for all accounts; and (e) sample budget request forms.

GENERAL NOTES

1. Teaching supplies includes general supplies, paper, folders, printer cartridges, etc.
2. School office includes general office expenditures, professional materials, printing, student assemblies, and reserve funds.
3. Materials should be purchased from program budgets: Examples include magazine subscriptions, and other direct program expenses. Do not include textbook or equipment purchases here.
4. Remember to include shipping and handling when preparing purchase orders.
5. Transportation costs for program use will be charged to your school. This does not include transportation on regular routes before/after school.
6. Advance payment purchases are not allowed. Staff may not be reimbursed for out-of-pocket purchases.
7. No purchase will be approved without a purchase order in advance.
8. Repair of district-owned equipment will not be charged to schools. Routine expenses like reeds, pads, printer cartridges, etc. will be charged to programs.
9. Major purchases such as textbooks, curriculum adoptions, achievement tests and so forth are budgeted separately—see OTHER PROGRAMS below.

OTHER INSTRUCTIONAL PROGRAMS

CURRICULUM AND INSTRUCTION

Major purchases district-wide are budgeted separately, rather than charged to school budgets. The following categories are developed and administered by the Director of Curriculum and the Directors of Elementary and Secondary Education:

TEXTBOOKS	STAFF DEVELOPMENT	SPECIAL EDUCATION
CURRICULUM	GUIDANCE	TESTING

INSTRUCTIONAL MEDIA

The Director of Media Services coordinates all media services through school principal and librarians.

STUDENT ACTIVITIES

Athletics, debate, forensics, music contests, dramatics, and related equipment purchases will be subsidized by the district. Separate line items will be set up for each activity. Submit all purchase requests according to the budget calendar.

FIGURE 7.6 *(Continued)*

GENERAL FUND INSTRUCTIONAL BUDGETS BY SCHOOL

The board of education annually sets the per-pupil allocation based on revenue availability and the recommendations of principals, staff, and site councils. It must be understood that the board pays many other expenses centrally—amounts shown here should be considered discretionary in terms of how schools expend.

ELEMENTARY INSTRUCTIONAL PROGRAMS ($27.50 per pupil)

Washington School	(230 pupils)	$6,325
Adams School	(326 pupils)	$8,965
Jefferson School	(270 pupils)	$7,425
Madison School	(189 pupils)	$5,198
Monroe School	(276 pupils)	$7,590
J. Q. Adams School	(250 pupils)	$6,875
Jackson School	(479 pupils)	$13,172
Van Buren School	(159 pupils)	$4,372
Harrison School	(233 pupils)	$6,408
Tyler School	(362 pupils)	$9,955
Polk School	(198 pupils)	$5,445
Taylor School	(289 pupils)	$7,948
Fillmore School	(432 pupils)	$11,880
Pierce School	(459 pupils)	$12,622
Buchanan School	(316 pupils)	$8,690
Instruction-Elementary Totals:		$122,870

MIDDLE SCHOOL INSTRUCTIONAL PROGRAMS ($58 per pupil)

Lincoln School	(601 pupils)	$34,858
Johnson School	(598 pupils)	$34,684
Instruction-Middle School Totals:		$69,542

HIGH SCHOOL INSTRUCTIONAL PROGRAMS ($75.18 per pupil)

Hayes High	(1076 pupils)	$80,894
Garfield High	(986 pupils)	$74,127
Instruction-High School Totals:		$155,021
INSTRUCTION TOTAL	7,729 pupils	$347,433

INSTRUCTIONAL MEDIA ($19.25 per pupil)

Books, periodicals, AV supplies, teacher center, staff $148,783

HIGH SCHOOL ACTIVITY PROGRAMS (each school)

Debate and forensics	$10,500
Dramatics	$1,000
Music contests	$3,250
Band uniform rotation (carries over budget years)	$5,000
ACTIVITY TOTAL 2 HIGH SCHOOLS (×2) =	$39,500

TECHNOLOGY REQUESTS

Instructional technology and computer services will be coordinated through the Instructional Media Center coordinator, in cooperation with the District Technology Committee.

FURNITURE AND OTHER EQUIPMENT

Direct all requests to central office for district-wide purchasing.

FIGURE 7.6 (Continued)

TRANSPORTATION BUDGETS BY SCHOOL

EDUCATIONAL FIELD TRIPS ($3.20 per pupil)

Washington School	(230 pupils)	$736
Adams School	(326 pupils)	$1,043
Jefferson School	(270 pupils)	$864
Madison School	(189 pupils)	$605
Monroe School	(276 pupils)	$883
J. Q. Adams School	(250 pupils)	$800
Jackson School	(479 pupils)	$1,533
Van Buren School	(159 pupils)	$509
Harrison School	(233 pupils)	$746
Tyler School	(362 pupils)	$1,158
Polk School	(198 pupils)	$634
Taylor School	(289 pupils)	$925
Fillmore School	(432 pupils)	$1,382
Pierce School	(459 pupils)	$1,469
Buchanan School	(316 pupils)	$1,011
	Field Trips-Elementary Total:	$14,298

MIDDLE SCHOOL FIELD TRIPS ($3.85 per pupil)

Lincoln School	(601 pupils)	$2,314
Johnson School	(598 pupils)	$2,302
	Field Trips-Middle School Total:	$4,616

HIGH SCHOOL FIELD TRIPS ($3.85 per pupil)

Hayes High	(1076 pupils)	$4,143
Garfield High	(986 pupils)	$3,796
	Field Trips-High School Total:	$7,939
FIELD TRIP TOTALS		$26,852

ATHLETICS

Lincoln School	$9,000
Johnson School	$9,000
Hayes High	$27,500
Garfield High	$27,500
ATHLETIC TOTALS	$73,000

ACTIVITIES ($1.90 mid-high, $5.65 sr. high)

Lincoln School	$1,142
Johnson School	$1,136
Hayes High	$6,079
Garfield High	$5,571
ACTIVITY TOTALS	$13,928

DEBATE and FORENSICS

Hayes High	$7,000
Garfield High	$7,000
DEBATE/FORENSIC TOTALS	$14,000

FIGURE 7.6 (*Continued*)

CAPITAL OUTLAY BUDGETS BY SCHOOL

Major capital projects are the district's responsibility. Schools have a small amount available for minor equipment needs. Money for copiers is available as shown here. Direct all items to central office that are not covered below.

MINOR EQUIPMENT ($4.50 per pupil)

Washington School	(230 pupils)	$1,035
Adams School	(326 pupils)	$1,467
Jefferson School	(270 pupils)	$1,215
Madison School	(189 pupils)	$850
Monroe School	(276 pupils)	$1,242
J. Q. Adams School	(250 pupils)	$1,125
Jackson School	(479 pupils)	$2,156
Van Buren School	(159 pupils)	$716
Harrison School	(233 pupils)	$1,048
Tyler School	(362 pupils)	$1,629
Polk School	(198 pupils)	$891
Taylor School	(289 pupils)	$1,301
Fillmore School	(432 pupils)	$1,944
Pierce School	(459 pupils)	$2,066
Buchanan School	(316 pupils)	$1,422
Lincoln School	(601 pupils)	$2,704
Johnson School	(598 pupils)	$2,691
Hayes High	(1076 pupils)	$4,842
Garfield High	(986 pupils)	$4,437
MINOR EQUIPMENT TOTALS		$34,780

SCHOOL EQUIPMENT BUDGETS

Elementary total	$10,000
Lincoln Mid-High	$13,000
Johnson Mid-High	$13,000
Hayes High	$25,000
Garfield High	$25,000
Instructional Media Center	$16,000
SCHOOL EQUIPMENT TOTALS	$102,000

COPIER BUDGETS

Elementary total	$16,000
Lincoln Mid-High	$15,000
Johnson Mid-High	$15,000
Hayes High	$15,000
Garfield High	$15,000
Central office	$16,000
COPIER TOTALS	$92,000

GRAND TOTALS

Total Instructional Budgets	$535,716
Total Transportation Budgets	$26,852
Total Athletics, Activities, and Debate	$100,928
Total Capital Outlay Budgets	$228,780
TOTAL SCHOOL BUDGETS	**$892,278**

FIGURE 7.6 (Continued)

WASHINGTON ELEMENTARY

Program Area: Reading
Code: 4-00-1000-610-80-01
Outcomes: Replaces 2010 copyright collection of storybooks. Children will increase
reading time by 20 minutes per pupil.
Supplier: ABC Publishers, Inc.
12345 State Street
Uptown, NY 00000-0000

(See requisition for titles, grade levels, and numbers of books per grade.)

Cost per book:	$9.65
Quantity:	230
Freight:	$267.00
TOTAL:	$2,486.50

FIGURE 7.6 (*Continued*)

The result of this hypothetical district's budget philosophy is illustrated by Figure 7.6, where it is clear that the district has transferred considerable budget and program authority to the individual school sites. Efficiency is gained by district oversight of noninstructional functions such as maintenance, repair, and construction of buildings while leaving school sites free to determine how learning programs are executed. The design results in school sites accepting responsibility for large sums of money, along with the accompanying expectation for program accountability. In this hypothetical district of about 7,700 pupils, total money assigned to all sites is $892,278—a sum to be spent on strategically targeted school site needs. The fund accounting structure permits program and expenditure analysis, and proposed expenditures are justified by specifying expected outcomes. School staffs, administrators, and site councils have genuine authority to move money among funds.

Figure 7.6 is additionally complex in that it carries out the central task of creating the educational plan for the school district *and* multiple school sites. The plan must be viewed first in terms of the overarching district plan and then in terms of what it means to each school site. A school principal receiving this document should understand it as a comprehensive planning tool to direct the educational process for the entire district and each school. On the assumption that principals will work closely with their staffs and site councils to create thoughtful instructional budgets for their schools, the following series of questions makes a complex task and a lengthy planning document both purposeful and manageable:

- *General Background Questions*
  - What is the school district's overall mission?
  - What are the district's goal statements?
  - What is my school's overall mission?
  - What are my school's goal statements?
  - What were the results of the district's environmental scan?
  - What were the results of my school's environmental scan?
  - Does my school's educational plan address these needs?
  - How can I spend my school's budget to meet these needs?

- *General Budget Questions (and Answers)*
  - Where are the account codes I need to make purchases? (*See the beginning of* Figure 7.6.)
  - Can I accumulate program costs? (*Use the account codes.*)
  - What does my budget have to cover? (*See instructions in* Figure 7.6.)
  - How much money do I have for instructional programs? (*See portions of* Figure 7.6.)
  - What if I need more money? (*Generate site revenue or seek more district funds.*)
  - How will I be accountable for outcomes? (*Provide program outcomes for each purchase. Account codes will accumulate costs over time. The district will determine if outcomes are being met.*)
  - What do I do when I have a question? (*Contact the central office.*)

The budget structure in Figure 7.6 is general in scope, but it clearly illustrates the underlying budgeting philosophy and operational elements that drive this hypothetical school district. From Figure 7.6, the school principal, staff, and site council know to turn to the central office to learn more about the district's mission and goals. They also know they must be intimately familiar with the school's environmental scan, and they know to link the scan to student needs and to use these elements to construct the school site educational plan. They also know that many resource needs, such as textbook adoptions, will be handled by the district and that each school has been allotted money on a per-pupil basis—in fact, principals will find their schools listed by name; see the exact amount of available funds for instructional programs, transportation, and capital outlay; and understand that uniform per-pupil allocation is the basis for funding in the district. Principals also know that program budgeting is in their hands and that performance accountability—tied to mission, goals, and school profile—will follow for resource decisions they make at the school site level. While no model is perfect and countless permutations are possible, this hypothetical district's budget philosophy goes to the heart of balancing efficiency with distributed leadership and includes money as the engine that enables true accountability and productivity.

WRAP-UP

Many school districts resemble the model in Figure 7.6, taking the best parts to join with local tradition and preference. No matter the model, district structure drives all resource decisions and revenue availability alters those decisions. Note that the instructional budget consumes most available resources, leaving only the details of how to divide the remaining pieces.

Regardless of whether school districts volunteer to become more performance-accountable or whether they are forced to do so by state-mandated constituent involvement in site councils or other structures, school and district budgets will remain the focus of intense public interest and accountability. In the case of budgeting for instruction, it should not be otherwise—*money pays for schools, and schools provide opportunities for children.* Instructional budgeting truly is the heart of public education.

POINT–COUNTERPOINT

POINT

State-mandated site-based management plans, while well-meant, have had the unwanted effect of forcing uninformed and perhaps disinterested people to make decisions about school operations. While some genuine level of community involvement is important, this fundamentally political movement has gone too far and has resulted in meddling that—under some circumstances—can be highly inappropriate.

COUNTERPOINT

For far too long, school boards and district leaders have operated closed educational systems that made a monopoly of society's most important tax-funded enterprise. Site-based models ought to serve as a welcome wake-up call to educators, but in true bureaucratic fashion the actual implementation has only managed to trivialize citizen participation by assigning site councils to mostly unimportant business while school districts conveniently claim legal proscription against citizen involvement in the truly important operations— namely, hiring, evaluating, and firing teachers and administrators. Bluntly said, site-based systems are a significant first step toward school reform, but more is needed to truly accomplish the initial purpose.

- How are principals, central office staff, teachers, and others involved in budgets in your school and district?
- What limits, if any, are imposed on site councils in your school district?
- Based on your readings so far, what do you consider the strengths and weaknesses of your school's and district's instructional budget practices? What recommendations would you make for improvements, if needed, and why?

CASE STUDY

Until recently you thought you would be content to spend your career as a classroom teacher in your current school district. After taking a doctoral degree in curriculum and instruction from your local university, you began to wonder whether there might be opportunities to have a wider influence since you had thoroughly enjoyed the systems perspective you gained through your advanced studies. You were fairly certain you did not really want a formal administrative career, although aspects of the role interested you because you instinctively knew that broader responsibilities also accompanied more opportunity to affect larger systems. So you decided to seek a position as executive director of curriculum in a medium-size public school district in your state.

Happily, you were offered an interview which turned out to be a two-day marathon. The superintendent spent considerable time describing the landscape and the roles and responsibilities of the position. She informed you that several schools in the district were on a state-mandated plan of improvement due to academic performance, and she revealed that these schools receive additional funding from the state for targeted improvement and professional development. She also told you that several other schools in the district are in danger of being identified for targeted improvement but that they do not currently qualify for extra funding. Finally, she indicated that the principals in the latter group of schools are pushing for in-district funding to help them reverse the achievement decline. She seemed open to that possibility, particularly since the board of education was openly worried about even more schools coming under state sanction.

In your exit interview, the superintendent told you that she was most impressed and that, if hired, your paramount responsibility would be to provide leadership to reverse this pattern. More specifically, she said you would be tasked to work with her and other central office leaders to devise a plan to continue the support of those schools already on improvement notice, and to additionally develop a plan to distribute additional district resources to the other low performing schools. Importantly, she added that you would be the key person who would work with the district as a whole to bridge a simmering schism that has developed as several high-performing schools are openly resentful that their staffs do not have the same professional development monies. Just as you thought the interview had ended, she concluded by saying that you would need to handle the whole situation with great aplomb because the achievement gap is following socioeconomic boundaries within the school district and parent groups from various viewpoints are watching closely.

A week later you received the job offer from this school district. Although you privately thought to yourself that this sounded very much like an administrative role, you accepted the offer, knowing that you would face a tough challenge. The problem, you mused, is the typical one leaders always face—where to begin, how to get others involved, how to build support, what tasks to engage and in what order, and—of course—how to manage high stakes with too little time.

- What do you think should be your first action when you arrive in this school district?
- How will you go about resourcing the problem? Who should be involved in the initial stages? Who are the most critical players? How will you garner their support? What barriers do you anticipate?
- What are the most pressing priorities in beginning this process?
- How will you approach the complaints by principals in the high-achieving schools, and what do you think will be their rationales and defenses? Will you support additional resources for their staffs too?

PORTFOLIO EXERCISES

- Make an appointment with your school district's curriculum director to discuss instructional budgeting. Prior to your meeting, request a copy of the school district's instructional budget. Discuss the curriculum director's perceptions as to how this budget interfaces with district mission and goal statements. Ask how the district develops curriculum-based instructional budgeting.

- In your interview with the curriculum director, use the series of planning questions appearing in this chapter as a discussion guide. For example, ask questions about who has responsibility for establishing the overall level of instructional spending, who sets budgets for each major program or school, who selects the curriculum, and who has responsibility for new programs or for eliminating current programs.

- If your school district incorporates elements of site-based budgeting, obtain a copy of your own school's budget. Interview your principal to determine how resource decisions are made at your school site. If your district does not use site-based budgeting, determine the level of funding available to each school site and discuss the decision-making process with your principal and the district's chief financial officer. Be sure to include discussion of resource and program accountability.

NOTES

1   790 S.W.2d 186, 60 Ed. Law Rep. 1289 (1989).

2   The Kentucky legislature approved House Bill 940 in 1990. It was signed into law as the Kentucky Education Reform Act (Chapter 476 of the Kentucky Acts of 1990).

3   In 2005, 34 states had enacted relevant statutes. Among these were 17 states mandating SBM statewide in some form (Alabama, Arizona, Colorado, Florida, Georgia, Hawaii, Kansas, Kentucky, Massachusetts, Michigan, New Mexico, New York, North Carolina, South Carolina, Texas, Utah, West Virginia). Two states (Illinois and Ohio) had mandated SBM for specified districts—Illinois required SBM in all Chicago schools, and Ohio mandated that a site council be established in at least one building in districts with more than 5,000 students that had not been identified as "effective" or "excellent" through the state accountability system. New York both mandated SBM statewide and also placed additional SBM requirements on the New York City District. See Jennifer Dounay, "Site-Based Decisionmaking: State-level Policies," *ECS State Notes* (Denver, CO: Education Commission of the States, 2005). A mid-2011 update found 63 SBM-related bills passed in state legislatures between 2000 and 2011. Review by the authors of this textbook in late 2018 found ongoing interest, as ECS recorded 94 legislative bills involving SBM in the years 1994–2016 with most having been signed into law. https://b5.caspio.com/dp.a sp?AppKey=b7f93000695b3d0d5abb4b68bd14&id=a0y70000000CbouAAC.

4   It is important to note that while many people associate local property taxes with schools and this perception is often reinforced by local media, the local property tax generally finances a wide range of local services, such as fire, police, and sanitation, and it is frequently an important source of revenue for local municipalities and counties.

5   See, for example, Faith E. Crampton and Paul Bauman, "A New Challenge to Fiscal Equity: Educational Entrepreneurship and Its Implications for Schools, Districts, and States," *Educational Considerations* 28 (Fall, 2000): 53–61.

WEB RESOURCES

American Association of School Administrators, www.aasa.org

American Federation of Teachers, www.aft.org

Association for Supervision and Curriculum Development, www.ascd.org

Association of School Business Officials International, asbointl.org

Education Commission of the States, www.ecs.org

National Conference of State Legislatures, www.ncsl.org

National Education Association, www.nea.org

National Governors Association, www.nga.org

National School Boards Association, www.nsba.org

U.S. Department of Education, www.ed.gov

RECOMMENDED RESOURCES

Bird, James J., Chuang Wang, and Louise M. Murray. "Building Budgets and Trust through Superintendent Leadership." *Journal of Education Finance* 35, 2 (Fall 2009): 140–156.

Dounay, Jennifer. "Site-Based Decisionmaking: State-Level Policies." *ECS State Notes*. Denver, CO: Education Commission of the States, 2005. www.ecs.org/clearinghouse/61/13/6113. htm.

Dynarski, Mark. "It's Not Nothing: The Role of Money in Improving Education." Washington, DC: The Brookings Institution (2017). https://www.brookings.edu/research/ its-not-nothing-the-role-of-money-in-improving-education/

Eckert, Jonathan, Ed. *Local Labor Management Relationships as a Vehicle to Advance Reform: Findings from the U.S. Department of Education's Labor Management Conference.* Washington, DC: US Department of Education, 2011.

Education Commission of the States. "State Legislation: Governance—Site-Based Management." Denver, CO (Database accessed October 18, 2018). https://b5.caspio.com/dp.asp?AppKey=b 7f93000695b3d0d5abb4b68bd14&id=a0y70000000CbouAAC

Leithwood, Kenneth, Karen Seashore Louis, Stephen Anderson, and Kyla Wahlstrom. *Review of Research: How Leadership Influences Student Learning.* Minneapolis, MN: Center for Applied Research and Educational Improvement, University of Minnesota, 2004.

Ouchi, William G. "Power to the Principals: Decentralization in Three Large School Districts." *Organization Science* 17 (March/April 2006): 298–307.

REL West. *School-Based Budgeting and Management.* San Francisco: WestEd, August 2009.

Trussel, John M. and Patricia A. Patrick. "Predicting Significant Reductions in Instructional Expenditures by School Districts." *Journal of Education Finance* 37, 3 (Winter 2012): 205–233.

Wallace Foundation. "Optimize the Use of Resources to Improve Student Learning – The Three Essentials: Improving Schools." New York: Wallace Foundation (n.d.). https://www. wallacefoundation.org/knowledge-center/pages/strategy-6-three-essentials-improving- schools.aspx

CHAPTER 8

Budgeting for Student Activities

CHAPTER DRIVERS

Please reflect on the following questions as you read this chapter:

- What is the role of student activities in schools?
- What are district and student activity funds?
- What are the controls and lines of authority on activity funds?
- What policies are needed regarding segregation of duties, internal controls on handling cash, and disbursement procedures?
- What policies are needed for nonactivity funds such as fee receipts, sales tax, and petty cash?
- What cautions apply to the whole process of budgeting for student activities?

ACTIVITIES AND SCHOOLS

The opening questions to this chapter propose yet another key aspect to funding equal and high-quality educational opportunity in public schools in that educating the whole child includes learning experiences beyond the formal classroom setting. A major aspect of the act of budgeting thus involves providing a sound fiscal base for the many student activities found in comprehensive school districts today.

There should be no doubt that student activities require large amounts of time and money. In fact, activities are so central to the life of schools that many public attitudes about education are based almost entirely on the countless activities found in today's school districts. Although it is unusual for books about school funding to contain much discussion of activity programs, the topic is so important to an accurate view of school money that this textbook devotes an entire chapter to ensuring that student activities are regarded as an essential element of educational opportunity.

Like previous chapters, the journey begins with general concepts before moving to the more specific elements of budgeting—in this case, budgeting for student activities. The chapter first establishes the role of activities in schools and then delves more deeply into the operational aspects of activity funding. More specifically, the chapter first defines activity funds and distinguishes between student activity funds and district activity funds, followed by the examination of controls on activity funds and relevant lines of authority for receiving and expending those same monies. The chapter next provides an examination of best practices relating to segregation of duties, internal controls on handling cash, and disbursement procedures, as well as best practices related to treatment of nonactivity funds like fee receipts, sales tax, and petty cash. The chapter ends with a stern warning because misuse or lax oversight of activity funds can have serious consequences for those tasked with their administration.

What is the Role of Student Activities?

The importance of student activities in the life of schools today cannot be overemphasized. An immediate sense of their importance is captured by simply glancing at the long list of activity programs supported by nearly every school district today. For example, a typical high school may support art clubs, chess clubs, journalism clubs, language clubs, pep clubs, photography clubs, science clubs, chorus, marching band, orchestra, drama, debate teams, drill teams, math teams, and student government. The list is nearly endless and includes organized intramural and varsity sports like baseball, basketball, cross-country, football, golf, hockey, soccer, swimming, tennis, track, volleyball, and wrestling. All these activities require one or more resource outlays like stipends for faculty sponsors, coaching salaries, transportation, equipment, and facilities, some of which can be costly. For example, building a new 400 meter track exceeds $1 million, and resurfacing an existing track can cost in excess of $300,000 in addition to maintenance costs; and it must be recognized that track is a sport that usually generates little in the way of offsetting revenues. The point here is not to imply that school activities should be self-funded, but rather that student activities represent significant direct and indirect costs for schools and districts. As a result, investment of time and money, along with issues like liability, firmly establish activities as a major school funding concern.

There is an additional reason why the role of student activities cannot be overemphasized: i.e., their importance to the lives of children and young people. Starting in the early elementary grades, children enthusiastically present vocal and instrumental concerts as well as dramatic performances for proud family and appreciative community audiences. Progressing into the high school years, young people form character, develop self-discipline, and persevere in school as a result of activity programs. In many cases, these activities encompass programs related to academics, so in essence they represent an extension of the school day. Whether or not school leaders actually enjoy attending every student activity, they quickly learn to support them because they come to understand that activities are not extracurricular—rather, wise school leaders accurately view activities as part of the curriculum[1] which are deserving of strong support.

Finally, beyond the noble reasons for supporting student activity programs is a practical justification: The valuable role they play with regard to public perception and public relations. School leaders sometimes joke that the quality of academic programs is judged by the shine on the floor of the school and the success in student athletic competitions. But savvy school leaders quickly grasp that popular activities and shiny floors boost local pride in all school programs by broadcasting the school's achievements to the community in priceless ways. Because a large percentage of people in a typical district do not have school-age children, it follows that many taxpayers and voters see schools only from a spectator's view, e.g., sports fans and consumers of local media. In brief, a district's student activity programs play a critical role in generating community support, fiscal and otherwise, for local schools.

BUDGETING FOR ACTIVITIES

The sheer scope of cocurricular and extracurricular programs today underscores the fact that a very large amount of money is allocated to and generated by student activities. Budgeting for activities is at once similar and different compared to other budget issues explored in this text. Similarities lie in how many of the general accounting principles discussed earlier also apply to activity funds; as such, revenue and expenditure dimensions and various account structures are already familiar. However, differences arise because activity funds typically are more loosely structured in the sense that fewer controls may exist, and revenue and expenditure operations frequently are housed at multiple sites. Similarly, statutes controlling activity funds may be less stringent in some states, so some aspects of activity fund accounting might not be as strictly prescribed. In brief, the potential for error and fraud is highest in activity funding, making it critical to establish local accounting structures that not only enhance the contribution of activities to student learning, but also guard against error, mismanagement, and abuse.

What are Activity Funds?

Activity funds are legal entities created by state statute for the purpose of segregating money in support of student activities. The unique nature of activity funds is evident in that statutes often define activities as *extra*curricular (see note 3) events, which may be further defined as student activities outside the classroom that complement the formal curriculum. Making such distinction has two key advantages. First, it creates a basis for expending district funds in support of activities by linking nonclassroom learning with the academic curriculum. Second, it sets up a mechanism for districts to separately support student activities and to account for money spent on activities. The first distinction is important because it is reasonable to believe that districts are not authorized to spend resources on programs not measured by the formal curriculum.

The second distinction sets up controls and permits the existence of student-owned organizations—a unique situation as will be seen later.

Activity funds are therefore accounting entities analogous to the general and special revenue funds and account structures found in a school district's regular budget. Each activity fund is an independent entity created to segregate its financial activities from all other funds, usually due to special restrictions on how money can be spent. Activity funds may only be spent for statutorily approved purposes, which are usually quite broad and limited only by the intent to spend activity funds for such purposes as athletics, music, and special projects—i.e., activity funds may not be appropriated or redirected to any other use. Operation of activity funds, though, is very different from the district's regular budget. As will be seen later, the collection, disbursement, and accounting for activity fund monies usually is housed at the school site level, with building principals designated as the activity fund supervisor. Further, activity funds are distinguished by ownership; that is, whether monies are owned by the school district or by student organizations. In addition, the activity fund supervisor typically is responsible for accounting for all nonactivity fund monies, including student fee collections, sales tax, and petty cash accounts. To make matters more complex, the ownership distinction creates special collection and disbursement issues. Complicating the mix is a vague and sometimes incorrect perception among school organization sponsors and students regarding allowable uses of activity funds. Thus, the school principal faces challenges by virtue of being simultaneously responsible for funds belonging to students, funds belonging to the district, administration of nonactivity funds belonging to the district, collecting and disbursing funds from a school site, and transferring certain funds to the district for deposit and disbursement. The potential for error, misunderstanding, and deliberate wrongdoing is evident.

Student Activity Funds

One of the unique features of activity funds is the distinction of ownership. There is no similar question regarding who owns the district's regular budget because the school board has complete legal authority and control subject only to applicable statutes. In contrast, activity funds are of two types. One type is student activity funds that are owned by students, i.e., students are the legal owners of certain activity fund monies and have the right to control how the money is spent, pursuant only to statutes, accounting guidelines, and board policy.

Student activity funds consist of those monies involving a student-owned organization. Operationally, students in such organizations not only participate in the organization's activities but also are involved in the management of the organization. Examples include many of the clubs listed earlier. The definition is important for two reasons. Most obvious is that no one in the school district (other than students) can legally expend money from a student-owned activity fund account. In other words, money on deposit in a district-maintained activity fund is not automatically owned by the district. The other critical reason is subtler, in that districts must be careful in subsidizing activities because district money could come under student ownership and control if not carefully directed.

District Activity Funds

In contrast, district activity funds belong to the school district. District activity funds support cocurricular activities in which students participate but which are administered by the school district. Examples of district activities include district-sponsored organizations such as choir, band, orchestra, debate teams, and sports. The definition is important in that the distinguishing feature is that ownership and approval to expend these monies belongs to the school board, rather than students. The accounting process is different too in that district activity funds are centralized in the district's accounting books, rather than at individual schools as is the case with student activity funds. District activity fund structures avoid the potential problems cited earlier, in that activities supported by the district are accounted for at the district level, and all money is deposited through the district treasurer to the district's bank account.

The distinction of district ownership is not trivial. School boards are responsible for maintaining control of district resources used to support student activities, and control would be lost by moving district funds into school-level student activity fund accounts.[2] Although parallel activity fund structures may seem redundant, ownership determines who controls how money is spent.

Additionally, distinction of ownership may have legal ramifications. For example, school districts have experienced legal problems when trying to control organizations like booster clubs and religious groups that may organize around school-based activities, often with a request to be included in the district's chart of activity fund accounts. Because conflicts involving ownership and apparent sponsorship may arise, it is best to require groups not directly sponsored by the school district to maintain separate bank accounts and records.

What are the Controls on Activity Funds?

The topics raised here recognize that significant amounts of money are involved in student activity budgets and that a complicated process governs what happens at both the district and individual school site levels. This raises questions of controls on activity funds, which logically lead to further examination of issues such as lines of authority and prudent policy development designed to make budgeting and administration transparent. Almost nowhere in school budgeting is the word *control* more welcome than in activity funding, i.e., controls are for the wellbeing of everyone. Indeed, far too many school leaders are dismissed for mismanagement of activity funds.

Lines of Authority

The need for clear lines of authority in handling activity budgets is underscored by the discussion up to this point. Segregating activity funds from all other funds in the school district, along with the complications brought on by numerous school sites handling activity fund monies, indicate a real need to maintain strict control, e.g., gate receipts at an athletic event on a given night may easily exceed $10,000, assuring that activity budgeting and accounting is no small matter. In fact, it is not unusual for the activity fund chart of accounts at a typical high school to have a fund balance well in excess of $100,000. Large balances aside, even the first penny is important because there is almost no stain on a professional reputation as damaging as violating a fiduciary trust, and mismanagement of an activity fund account has the real potential to invoke a cloud of suspicion.

The general guidance for lines of authority for activity funds calls for the district's board of education to adopt clear policies governing establishment and operation of all activity funds. The board treasurer, as the district's fiscal officer, is generally appointed to implement and enforce a system of internal controls. These individuals have first-line responsibility for all activity funds in the district because both district and student activity funds are held on deposit by the district and must be reported in the district's financial statements. In brief, student-owned funds are agency (fiduciary) funds wherein the district acts as agent, while district-owned funds are classified as special revenue funds earmarked for support of student activities.

At the school level, the principal is generally designated as the activity fund supervisor. Supervisory designation means the principal is responsible for overall operation of activity funds housed in that school, including collection and deposit of activity fund monies, approval of disbursements from the activity fund, and all bookkeeping responsibilities. The burden is a weighty one because, although custodial duties may be delegated, final responsibility cannot. It is precisely this point that gives rise to many of the policies that will be seen shortly regarding handling of money and multiple safeguards against misuse, embezzlement, and fraud. In short, a school principal may delegate duties, but responsibility may never be delegated.

Multiple levels of activity fund ownership, responsibility, and sponsorship give rise to one more set of players in the line of authority. Organizational sponsors, often teachers or coaches with little or no financial background, often initiate an activity fund transaction. Without proper training it is unlikely that they will fully understand either the process or reasons for controls on activity funds. Here, the principal serves an important role in ensuring compliance with district policies and procedures for safe handling of activity funds by arranging orientation and training for sponsors of school-level student activities at the beginning of each school year so that they understand the process of approved purchases, purchase orders, handling of cash, and issuance of receipts. Generally, someone from the district's business office is happy to provide this training. In sum, sponsors serve as a critical first line in ensuring that funds are used appropriately for the particular student activity they oversee.

Recommended Activity Fund Policies

The responsibilities and risks involved in activity funds demand strong local policies because the scope and size of activity fund budgets require the same professional accounting and auditing standards that apply to all other school money. Further, in order to gain control over an arena that finds multiple people at multiple sites handling money, a set of clear policies and procedures must be established and followed by everyone. Although it is not feasible for a textbook of this nature to go into deep detail, best practices can be summarized: More particularly, those relating to general policies on activity fund operation, segregation of duties, internal controls on handling cash, and disbursement of money.

General Policies

Establishment and operation of activity funds requires clear controls to ensure safe and effective management of district and student monies. Several of the following bulleted items have already been discussed, with others added here to call attention to additional potential problems:

- The district should use the services of a certified public accountant to set up the activity fund accounting system for the entire school district;
- The district should provide all staff and organization sponsors with training on activity fund management on an annual basis;
- The district should task the district treasurer with establishment of standardized forms and procedures. Because the district accumulates and reports all student and district activity fund transactions, the district is responsible for ensuring that standardized controls are in place;
- The district should require that all activity funds must be approved by the board. Requests to create a student organization should include a statement of purpose and potential fundraising activity. To avoid confusion and to aid organizational goals, the name of the organization should be descriptive of its purpose;
- The district should require that organizations not directly sponsored by the district must be excluded from its financial activities;
- The district should formally designate activity fund supervisors. Usually only one supervisor per school or attendance center should be appointed;
- The district should require that all fundraising be approved in advance. All groups included in the district's activity fund chart of accounts should receive district approval for their activities, including fundraising. Unauthorized fundraising can create significant community relations problems;
- The district should make clear that activity funds are spent only on students. Although this seems obvious, problems frequently arise when organizations expire with unspent funds on deposit (e.g., senior class). Insofar as possible, money should be spent on those students who raised it;
- The district should make clear that cash basis is strictly applied to student activity funds. Cash basis requires that no money be spent or encumbered unless an equal or greater amount is already on deposit. Strict adherence to advance purchase orders, as well as a prohibition against loans or deficit spending, resolves this problem;
- The district should require that all activity funds be regularly audited along with other funds in the district. Full audits should be done annually;
- The district should make clear that activity funds are never to be used for any purpose that results in a benefit, loan, or credit to anyone.

Segregation of Duties

The importance of clear policies on handling activity funds is underscored by sound business practices relating to the segregation of financial duties. Bookkeeping errors can occur inadvertently, and the potential for intentional mishandling is always a possibility. Risk of error, theft, and fraud can be minimized by the segregation of duties that reinforce general policies, tighten cash controls, and regulate all receipt and disbursement procedures.

Segregation of duties speaks to both intentional and unintentional error through the rule that no one person should be responsible for handling money. Daily cash handling occurs in all schools, and segregation of duties reduces risks. At the school level, the activity fund bookkeeper, appointed by the principal, should take the lead on most operations, including collecting the activity fund money, preparing and making deposits, preparing fund accounting reports, and preparing activity fund disbursements. These activities will be subject to audit and should be reviewed internally. Four additional duties need close attention from the school leader:

- Although a bookkeeper should prepare checks, a separate signatory should be required;
- The principal, as activity fund supervisor, should be the primary signatory on checks—in some states, it is required by law that the principal sign all checks;
- All checks should bear two signatures;
- Bank statements must be reconciled regularly with the fund accounting records, and someone other than the bookkeeper should prepare this reconciliation.

These procedures, among others, protect against error and other malfeasance on the accounting side and serve to back up internal controls on cash.

Internal Controls on Cash

The quantity and scope of student activities in today's schools guarantee frequent handling of large cash amounts. Yearbook sales, event receipts, fundraisers, student photos, and student class projects such as vocational arts result in many thousands of dollars in cash transactions at the school site. Naturally, cash represents the greatest risk of loss, requiring strong internal controls.

The most important aspects of internal cash controls are well-trained employees and careful establishment of an audit trail to provide physical evidence for each step in cash transactions. In fact, the audit trail gives more insight to what might be missing rather than showing something was incorrectly done. Although professional accounting advice is required to properly handle cash, at least the following cash controls must be in place:

- Fund supervisors and sponsors must be trained and provided with written guidelines on handling cash;
- All forms, receipts, and tickets should be prenumbered;
- Prenumbered items should be safeguarded;
- Prenumbered items should not be printed in-house;
- Persons collecting cash should be rotated regularly;
- More than one person should be present when cash is collected;

- No cash collections should be given to another person without a receipt;
- Bookkeepers must use prenumbered, bound receipts for all currency and checks received;
- Cash receipts should be kept intact and may not be used to make change or to make any kind of disbursement;
- Bookkeepers should make daily deposits. Undeposited cash should be kept locked away;
- Everyone handling cash should be bonded.

It may come as a surprise to learn how often these procedures fail to be followed even though the consequences for not doing so can be devastating. For example, a harried principal or club sponsor sticks school cash into their wallet, purse, or even an unlocked desk drawer for later deposit; volunteer ticket-takers at school events naively tear off extra tickets to make the cash and tickets balance; blank prenumbered cash receipts lie in plain view on a busy secretary's desk; an office clerk leaves cash unattended, even if for only a short time. Especially appalling is the fairly common practice of tossing a bank bag stuffed with athletic gate receipts into a car trunk to be delivered to the school office the following Monday morning. Any one of these examples represents a disaster-in-waiting, not only for the school employee involved, but also for the students who were to benefit from the cocurricular activity that the lost money was meant to support.

Disbursement Procedures

The final activity fund area needing explanation is disbursement procedures. Disbursement refers to any financial transaction in which money leaves an account. This discussion can be short because other chapter discussion already involved disbursement as part of the total process. As a result, a bulleted list of guidelines makes these points quickly.

As noted earlier, activity funds are either district-owned or student-owned. Also noted was that student funds typically are handled at the school level, meaning most activity on these accounts occurs at various school sites. District funds are considerably more complicated in that there can be an extra transaction involved because district funds are accounted for at the district level but may have flowed through a school first. An example makes this clearer. Assume the school board has agreed to partially subsidize students' woodworking projects.[3] Materials are ordered, and the supplies bill arrives. The district pays the entire bill and calculates how much each student owes. Students then reimburse the school office, which in turn makes a deposit to the revolving woodworking account within the school's activity fund. The school site activity fund must then transfer these *district-owned* amounts to the district treasurer for deposit back to the district. It is not as difficult as it seems, but this relatively simple example underscores the meticulous nature of activity fund budgeting and accounting.

A more frequent daily activity fund transaction involves a student club purchase. In that case, advance approval is obtained, a purchase order is issued, goods are received, and the bookkeeper makes payment. Accordingly, disbursement procedures for student activity funds are:

- Disbursement requires approval of the student group's sponsor and the activity fund supervisor (usually the school principal);
- Disbursements should be backed up by a voucher signed by the sponsor and principal;
- Disbursements should be made by prenumbered check with multiple signatures;
- Documentation must show who requested the purchase, what was purchased, which activity fund account should be charged, the amount, and the check number.

In sum, there are three overarching rules with regard to activity funds:

- Be very careful when handling money;
- Spend money only for what it is intended;
- Use fund accounting (the tool for segregating money) so that the first two rules can be efficiently met.

It is prudent to always remember that activity funds have the potential to be a major source of financial problems for school leaders if the practices outlined here are not followed.

What about Nonactivity Funds?

In addition to activity funds, school districts and individual school sites collect other kinds of money that must be handled just as securely. This task falls to the same people who are in charge of activity funds although, in a strict sense, these are nonactivity fund monies. The money in question here often relates to curricular programs and does not definitionally belong in the activity fund structure. Examples of this type of money include fees related to various programs such as class materials, laboratories, and physical education. Still other kinds of nonactivity fund monies are handled at district and school levels, such as sales tax and petty cash. The interest here has less to do with the intricacies of these monies and more to do with ensuring that school leaders know that these monies exist and must be handled carefully because—once again—this is an area fraught with pitfalls.

The following descriptions introduce different kinds of nonactivity fund monies that are typically received by schools. The most important thing to focus on is that these are generally monies that will be transferred to the district because they are almost always district-owned or received on behalf of a fiduciary account. A more detailed examination is not appropriate for this textbook because these monies are merely tools to satisfy certain accounting principles and do not represent educational planning devices—although they do represent opportunity for mishandling.

Fee Funds

As noted earlier, schools usually have several fee fund accounts. For example, schools collect fees for specialized instructional supplies and materials, such as those associated with art classes; advanced placement courses; food service; laboratory usage associated with science classes; and musical instrument rental. These fees represent user charges and are owned by the district, which will in turn replenish the appropriate district fund when the school site activity fund bookkeeper remits collections to the district treasurer. The district then uses fee receipts to continue providing services. Fee funds do not represent usable revenue at the school level. Rather, they are *receipt-only* funds, and no disbursements can be made from fee funds. The school merely acts to collect fees on behalf of the district for later central transfer.

Sales Tax

Another type of nonactivity fund money often collected at the school site is sales tax. The concept requires little explanation, although at times it can be confusing as to when schools must charge sales tax. The universal rule is that when schools do collect sales tax, the school is merely the collection point and acts as the remitter to a higher level. School districts usually have the freedom to choose whether to let individual school sites directly remit sales tax collections or whether to centralize tax collection for a single remittance to the state or locality. The confusing aspect is usually related to individual states' laws because it is not always clear whether sales tax should be charged. That issue is answerable only in the context of each state, with the general guiding principle that items for resale are usually subject to sales tax collection in most states.

Petty Cash

The last area of nonactivity funds common to individual school sites is petty cash. Every school site in the nation likely has a petty cash account, although its appropriate use and accounting requirements are often poorly understood. Petty cash is a source of cash used for making small disbursements without writing checks or, alternatively, making payment more quickly than could be done when going through the district's normal bill-paying channels. Petty cash accounts do not involve much money as a general rule, although again even the smallest sum of money must be handled properly. Examples of uses for petty cash might include paying game referees with a check drawn on the petty cash fund on game night, buying postage stamps, and other small cash purchases.[4]

Because petty cash accounts represent more exposure than may be the case for other kinds of school money, petty cash is often statutorily limited in amount. In addition, districts need to establish clear policies on uses of petty cash due to the ease with which these accounts can be defrauded because it is possible (unlike other district funds) to make actual cash payments from petty cash. Board policy should include at least the following:

- The board should set a maximum amount for petty cash accounts and clearly state the intended uses. A maximum disbursement should be set, above which board approval is required;
- The activity fund bookkeeper should act as the petty cash custodian. Access to petty cash should be strictly regulated;
- The petty cash custodian should require signed receipts from all persons receiving cash to create an audit trail. Receipts should document the purpose of the disbursement and which fund should be charged when petty cash is replenished at month's end.

What Does an Activity Fund Report Look Like?

Although the different requirements of state laws and wide range of student groups recognized by school districts prevent a universal format for activity fund reporting, the complex picture and set of responsibilities involved in activity funding is best conceptualized visually. Figure 8.1 presents a month-end activity fund balance report for a hypothetical high school in a district of about 4,000 students. Numbers tell great stories, and Figure 8.1 speaks in telling fashion. First, it easily can be seen that this high school has a wide range of student activities—almost every conceivable

ACCOUNT NUMBER/TITLE		BEGINNING CASH BALANCE	CURRENT MONTH TRANSACTIONS		ENDING CASH BALANCE
109 .XXXXX.XXX.XX.XXX.X	SEASON TICKETS	$ 1,362.03	$ –		$ 1,362.03
110 .XXXXX.XXX.XX.XXX.X	ACTIVITY TICKETS	$ 11,235.09	$ –		$ 11,235.09
111 .XXXXX.XXX.XX.XXX.X	CONCESSIONS	$ –	$ –		$ –
112 .XXXXX.XXX.XX.XXX.X	PARKING PERMITS	$ 8,739.84	$ 565.00		$ 9,304.84
114 .XXXXX.XXX.XX.XXX.X	FOOTBALL	$ 4,114.05	$ 1,871.20	–	$ 2,242.85
116 .XXXXX.XXX.XX.XXX.X	BOYS BASKETBALL	$ 10,131.35	$ 3,182.17	–	$ 6,949.18
117 .XXXXX.XXX.XX.XXX.X	BASEBALL	$ 161.84	$ 187.10		$ 348.94
118 .XXXXX.XXX.XX.XXX.X	BOYS TRACK	$ 140.00	$ 490.00		$ 630.00
119 .XXXXX.XXX.XX.XXX.X	SOCCER	$ –	$ –		$ –
120 .XXXXX.XXX.XX.XXX.X	WRESTLING	$ 8.42	$ –		$ 8.42
122 .XXXXX.XXX.XX.XXX.X	CROSS COUNTRY	$ –	$ –		$ –
124 .XXXXX.XXX.XX.XXX.X	BOYS TENNIS	$ 308.86	$ 120.00		$ 428.86
126 .XXXXX.XXX.XX.XXX.X	GOLF	$ 17.50	$ –		$ 17.50
128 .XXXXX.XXX.XX.XXX.X	BOYS SWIMMING	$ 2,788.38	$ 109.03		$ 2,897.41
130 .XXXXX.XXX.XX.XXX.X	GIRLS TENNIS	$ 469.02	$ –		$ 469.02
131 .XXXXX.XXX.XX.XXX.X	GIRLS SOCCER	$ 33.68	$ 426.10		$ 459.78
132 .XXXXX.XXX.XX.XXX.X	GIRLS VOLLEYBALL	$ –	$ –		$ –
134 .XXXXX.XXX.XX.XXX.X	GIRLS BASKETBALL	$ 6,745.51	$ 1,282.03	–	$ 5,463.48
135 .XXXXX.XXX.XX.XXX.X	SOFTBALL	$ 32.97	$ 111.32		$ 144.29
136 .XXXXX.XXX.XX.XXX.X	GIRLS SWIMMING	$ 1,603.06	$ 129.45		$ 1,732.51
138 .XXXXX.XXX.XX.XXX.X	GIRLS GYMNASTICS	$ –	$ –		$ –
140 .XXXXX.XXX.XX.XXX.X	GIRLS GOLF	$ –	$ –		$ –
141 .XXXXX.XXX.XX.XXX.X	WEIGHT TRAINING	$ 7,035.23	$ 4,076.40	–	$ 2,958.83
142 .XXXXX.XXX.XX.XXX.X	TOURNAMENT ACCOUNT	$ 925.26	$ 1,008.58		$ 1,933.84
143 .XXXXX.XXX.XX.XXX.X	WRITERS CLUB	$ 1.64	$ –		$ 1.64
144 .XXXXX.XXX.XX.XXX.X	STUDENT SUPPORT GROUP	$ 16,602.31	$ 11,040.44	–	$ 5,561.87
145 .XXXXX.XXX.XX.XXX.X	CITY BASKETBALL	$ 3,551.84	$ 110.00	–	$ 3,441.84
146 .XXXXX.XXX.XX.XXX.X	DRAMATICS	$ 1,834.92	$ 41.00		$ 1,875.92
147 .XXXXX.XXX.XX.XXX.X	DRAMA TRIP	$ 19,998.54	$ 14,780.01	–	$ 5,218.53
148 .XXXXX.XXX.XX.XXX.X	THESPIANS	$ 656.88	$ 16,008.06	–	$ (15,351.18)
150 .XXXXX.XXX.XX.XXX.X	DEBATE	$ 920.35	$ –		$ 920.35
151 .XXXXX.XXX.XX.XXX.X	SCHOLARSHIP BOWL	$ 825.00	$ –		$ 825.00
152 .XXXXX.XXX.XX.XXX.X	CAP AND GOWN	$ –	$ –		$ –
154 .XXXXX.XXX.XX.XXX.X	NEEDY STUDENT	$ 355.42	$ 5.00		$ 360.42
156 .XXXXX.XXX.XX.XXX.X	NEWSPAPER	$ 1,400.00	$ 848.00	–	$ 552.00
158 .XXXXX.XXX.XX.XXX.X	MUSIC CONTEST ACCOUNT	$ 216.12	$ 195.19	–	$ 20.93
160 .XXXXX.XXX.XX.XXX.X	MUSIC SUPPORT GROUP	$ 1,517.89	$ –		$ 1,517.89
161 .XXXXX.XXX.XX.XXX.X	VARIETY SHOWS	$ –	$ 1,347.05		$ 1,347.05
162 .XXXXX.XXX.XX.XXX.X	SPECIAL MUSIC	$ 1,916.19	$ 100.00		$ 2,016.19
164 .XXXXX.XXX.XX.XXX.X	CHORALE	$ 4,817.36	$ 4,817.36	–	$ –
166 .XXXXX.XXX.XX.XXX.X	SCHOOLWIDE TALENT	$ 134.92	$ –		$ 134.92
168 .XXXXX.XXX.XX.XXX.X	JAZZ GROUP	$ –	$ –		$ –
170 .XXXXX.XXX.XX.XXX.X	ORCHESTRA	$ 263.00	$ 50.00		$ 313.00
172 .XXXXX.XXX.XX.XXX.X	CHOIR FUNDRAISING	$ 9,679.28	$ 10,530.00	–	$ (850.72)
173 .XXXXX.XXX.XX.XXX.X	PEP CLUB	$ 1,924.66	$ 192.24		$ 2,116.90
174 .XXXXX.XXX.XX.XXX.X	CHEERLEADERS	$ 598.73	$ –		$ 598.73
178 .XXXXX.XXX.XX.XXX.X	STUDENT COUNCIL	$ 12,338.69	$ 2,104.76	–	$ 10,233.93
			FUND BALANCE =		$ 69,442.08

FIGURE 8.1 Sample Cash Balance Report for Activity Fund Accounts

organization has a place in this school's programs. Second, it can be seen that some accounts are district-owned, e.g., athletics, while others are student-owned, e.g., choir fund-raising. Third, it can be seen that fee funds are reported in the school's activity fund, e.g., parking permits, although the revenue will be transferred to the district at a later time. And fourth, the reality of handling significant sums of money is highlighted here, as this one high school in a medium-size district has a month-end cash balance of $69,442.08—not an insignificant amount of money for which the school's leader must take responsibility.

A FINAL WORD OF CAUTION

School activity programs have long been applauded for making critical contributions to equal educational opportunity. Fiscal outlays for support of student activities are much larger than most people realize in that district cash subsidies, student-owned deposits, and the value of facilities and staff required to carry out a successful activity program are significant. But as underscored at the outset of this chapter, there is a worthwhile payoff for everyone involved.

The high profile of student activity programs raises the stakes of budgeting in many ways, and—if such monies are mishandled—outcomes can be unpleasant. Two such cases illustrate this point. The first case involved a respected school principal who lost his job and his professional licensure as a result of cash receipts that were stolen from his unlocked car. The second case underscores the political power that can be unleashed when activity programs are threatened. In that case, a district facing a $5 million shortfall because of state aid reductions decided to cut several athletic programs—a decision that cost several school board members their elected positions and school leaders their professional employment. Nearly everyone has heard similar stories, but the central point is that the prominence of student activity programs makes them a dangerous place to engage in lax fiscal practices or short-sighted decision-making. The critical feature always loops back to wise leadership in the context of fiduciary trust. Finally, and importantly, in the case of activity funds, it is often school-level leaders who find themselves on the firing line.

POINT–COUNTERPOINT

POINT
School leaders today, hard-pressed to find funding for both academic and cocurricular programs, have been dealt a blow through federal and state action to ban or severely restrict vending machine sales of candy, soda, and chips in schools. These vending contracts, some of which have generated tens of thousands of dollars per year in revenue for individual schools, are critically important because those funds are typically used to support a wide range of student activities.

COUNTERPOINT

Given the heightened concern about child and adolescent nutrition in this nation, school leaders' first responsibility is to ensure that the school environment is one where healthy eating choices are reinforced. School leaders should welcome initiatives that discourage if not bar the sale of junk food in schools. Furthermore, funding student programs and activities with such money is highly unethical, analogous to using taxes on tobacco sales to fund smoking cessation programs.

- Which of these views best represents your beliefs and experiences? Explain.
- How are student activities funded in your school and district?
- In your estimation, would your school or district offer more extracurricular or cocurricular activities if there were more funding available? If yes, what types of activities do you think are most needed and why?

CASE STUDY

Upon assuming your new position as principal of a large high school, you decided to undertake a review of your building's activity fund operations.

As you educated yourself about local activity fund practices, you became concerned about lax financial procedures. Among your list of anxieties was the fact that last year's comprehensive audit had noted problems in activity fund cash receipts and disbursements. For example, auditors had noted 42 instances of cash entries to the student yearbook account for which no prenumbered receipts could be found. Nearly $90,000 in athletic equipment purchases were made for which corresponding requisitions/purchase orders were signed and dated after the vendor's invoice had already been paid. Several activity fund accounts showed negative balances. Monies received were not always deposited in a timely fashion because on multiple occasions cash deposits were not made for several days after receipt. Your business clerk was apologetic but indicated that the district had reduced office staff to such an extent that student office aides were now used to carry out tasks such as selling yearbooks. The clerk also indicated that it had been the prior principal's longstanding practice to allow the athletic director to order equipment on the spot from sales calls and to complete the purchasing paperwork later. And the clerk added, as if it somehow alleviated your concerns, that other high-ranking school leaders engaged in similar activities, pointing out that several assistant principals working under you frequently took cash boxes home or left them in their personal vehicles until the next day because athletic events were almost always off-site and the assistant principals did not want to have to travel back to the school vault after a long night.

As if these discoveries were not troubling enough, your review has led to still more disturbing data. From your own observations over the last several days, you have seen that office staff often keep the petty cash box in an unlocked desk drawer, and you watched an office worker make a quick run to the supply closet at the back of the office complex while leaving uncounted cash lying on top of a desk. Recently, you also saw cash register drawers at athletic concessions stands left open while the attendant was distracted while serving multiple customers. So far there have been no reports of missing cash, but on the other hand you have only been on the job for a few short months. With nearly a half-million dollars in the activity fund budget in your care, you wonder what else you don't know. But you do know something has to change—very quickly.

Below is a set of questions. As you respond, consider what you have learned in this chapter and apply your knowledge and experience to the situation.

- What elements of this case study most concern you? Why? What steps should you as principal take immediately to address the most pressing concerns? *Accounting procedures + lax fund handling*
- Since these issues seem to have developed over time, what barriers do you anticipate in correcting the situation? How will you go about overcoming these? *This is the way we've always done it + new procedures require more work.*
- What can and should a school leader do to protect against lax activity fund practices? *Set clear protocols & follow-through*
- Using your experience as an educator, have you encountered any examples of lax activity fund management accounting? If so, how could these have been avoided?

PORTFOLIO EXERCISES

- Obtain a list of student activities in your school district from your central office and determine how each is funded. Identify which activities are student-owned and which are district-owned.
- Make an appointment with your district's chief financial officer or representative to discuss handling of student activity funding. Obtain a copy of school board policies and guidelines on activity funding. Determine the district's procedures for receipting and disbursing activity fund monies.
- Obtain a copy of an activity fund report from your school. Determine total revenues and expenditures for activities associated with the school site; the number of student groups; and revenues and expenditures by group. Talk to the principal about how the activity fund is supervised and the lines of authority and control that are in place. Identify strengths and weaknesses in the system and develop recommendations on how any weaknesses might be remedied.

NOTES

1   Strictly parsed, *extracurricular* means outside or in addition to the formal curriculum, while this textbook prefers *cocurricular* meaning in support of all learning in the school.
2   The importance of ownership is apparent in the consequences of inattention. If, for example, a school board wished to subsidize a single student event, it should do so by direct expenditure from its own funds. In contrast, if the board were to transfer district monies directly into a student-owned activity fund account (e.g., senior class), the transferred monies would immediately become the property of the senior class and the board could no longer require that the money be used for the targeted event.
3   Discussion in the next section will reveal that this transaction actually involves a nonactivity fund account, although it is carried in the activity fund chart of accounts at the school site level. The activity described here is a student fee type transaction. However, it is a common transaction easily recognized by the reader and serves the purpose of demonstrating a disbursement activity.
4   As an alternative to petty cash, an increasing number of districts are likely no longer using petty cash as coinage, moving instead to internal procurement cards or some equivalent non-cash system.

WEB RESOURCES

American Association of School Administrators, www.aasa.org

Association of Certified Fraud Examiners, www.acfe.com

Association of School Business Officials International, www.asbointl.org

Institute of Internal Auditors, www.theiia.org

National Association for Elementary School Principals, www.naesp.org

National Association for Secondary School Principals, www.nassp.org

National Business Officers Association, www.nboa.net

RECOMMENDED RESOURCES

Allison, Gregory S. and Frank Johnson. *Financial Accounting for Local and State School Systems: 2014 Edition.* Washington, DC: U.S. Department of Education, Institute of Education Sciences, National Center for Education Statistics, March 2015.

Cuzzetto, Charles E. *Student Activity Funds: Procedures & Controls.* Lanham, MD: R&L Education, 2005.

Dessoff, Alan. "Fighting Fraud in Schools." *District Administration* (August 2009). www.districtadministration.com/viewarticle.aspx?articleid=2088.

Dycuss, Dennis. "The Fraud Examiner: The 'Lost Deposit Bag' and Other Frauds in Schools, Government Organizations." Association of Certified Fraud Examiners. Austin, TX. http://www.acfe.com/fraud-examiner.aspx?id=4294978536.

Everett, Ronald E., Donald R. Johnson, and Bernard W. Madden. *Financial and Managerial Accounting for School Administrators: Tools for Schools*, third ed. Lanham, MD: Rowman & Littlefield, 2012.

Granof, Michael H., and Saleha B. Khumawala. *Government and Not-for-Profit Accounting*, fifth ed. Hoboken, NJ: John Wiley & Sons, 2011.

Hassenpflug, Ann. "Missing Funds." *Journal of Cases in Educational Leadership* 15, 2 (2012): 3–9.

Ray, John R., Walter G. Hack, and Carl I. Candoli. *School Business Administration: A Planning Approach*, eighth ed. Boston: Allyn & Bacon, 2005.

CHAPTER 9

Budgeting for School Infrastructure

CHAPTER DRIVERS

Please reflect on the following questions as you read this chapter:

- How is school infrastructure defined?
- What is included in a comprehensive definition of school infrastructure?
- What is the role of infrastructure in public schools?
- What is the current condition of school infrastructure?
- How much money do schools need for infrastructure?
- How is school infrastructure currently funded at state and local levels?
- What are the goals of and activities involved in infrastructure planning?
- What is the role and nature of maintenance and operations?
- How do schools organize for maintenance and operations?
- What is the role of the school site leader in maintenance and operations?

SCHOOL INFRASTRUCTURE NEEDS IN PERSPECTIVE

phys. env. suitable places for students to learn.

No study of school funding is complete without an examination of the role of the physical environment of schools. The staggering costs of school construction, modernization, debt service, maintenance and operations, and associated capital outlays such as those for technology have quietly lurked behind the scenes as this textbook has worked its way through the maze of school funding topics. In the case of school infrastructure, some costs go unnoticed in the rush to adequately fund instruction, but these less visible costs are just as important as the more obvious ones. In other words,

includes classrooms, labs, hallways, facilities, equipment and more.

while the role of funding school facilities is critically important, it is other costs that actually consume the vast majority of education's resources. As a consequence, this chapter reveals school infrastructure needs and considers how the budgeting process addresses this aspect of equal educational opportunity.

The journey begins by exploring the role of school infrastructure, including its nature and size. Attention next turns to the condition of school facilities in the United States, along with estimates of costs to redress deficiencies. An extended discussion follows regarding how school infrastructure needs are funded, with the observation that capital funding lags far behind progress that has been made in funding other areas of school and district needs. With a general framework in place, different but related issues arise: How are school infrastructure planning, maintenance, and operations carried out? More specifically, attention must be given to how infrastructure planning occurs; the effect of demographics and academic programs on school facility planning; the role of maintenance and operations; and how schools organize their maintenance activities. In sum, although school infrastructure has never held the high profile of topics like school reform, budgeting for the physical environment of schools plays a crucial role in funding education given the substantial cost of facilities and the relationship between infrastructure quality and student success.

NATURE AND SIZE OF SCHOOL INFRASTRUCTURE

Stated bluntly, public education's infrastructure needs in the United States are shocking and pose a serious—even dire—problem for the foreseeable future. This assessment derives from the many stressors on school budgets described in this textbook, combined with the fact that while much effort has been exerted in recent years to reform schools, far less attention has been given to the need for physical environments conducive to teaching and learning. Unfortunately, this is not a new problem. Nearly 30 years ago, the American Association of School Administrators (AASA) noted:

> [F]rom every corner have come reports, articles, speeches and goal statements about student achievement, unmet needs and education reform ... but all these pronouncements have been strangely silent about one essential ingredient ... that affects every child's health, safety and ability to learn: *the classroom*.[1] [emphasis in original].

Pronouncements of this nature have continued nearly unceasingly in the ensuing years. The problem is pervasive, as even the World Bank in 2017 weighed in, saying "Buildings, classrooms, laboratories, and equipment – education infrastructure – are crucial elements of learning environments in schools and universities. There is strong evidence that high-quality infrastructure facilitates better instruction, improves student outcomes, and reduces dropout rates, among other benefits."[2] And while infrastructure problems are specific at each level ranging from global to local, there are too few places where needs are fully redressed.

The school infrastructure problem in the United States has been widely critiqued, and the deficits and backlogs in construction and maintenance are enormous. Problems are worsening, as the American Society of Civil Engineers (ASCE) reported in 2017 that just two years prior at least 31 states were providing *less* funding per pupil for infrastructure than was true in 2008,[3] all in the face of vast evidence as scholars have warned about unaddressed concerns.[4] Though deficit estimates have run into hundreds of billions of dollars, school districts have had little choice except to fund other current needs to the detriment of infrastructure, primarily by delaying facility maintenance, repair, and modernization. Stated bluntly, districts have had to choose between spending for instruction and spending for facilities in which to house essential learning programs. None of that, however, has diminished the critical role of planning and budgeting for capital needs because infrastructure remains the single largest investment a school district makes at any one time.

What is the Role of Infrastructure in Public Schools?

Various terminology has been used over time to describe the physical environment of education. *School plant* and *school facilities* have traditionally been used to describe school buildings while *capital outlay* usually has referred to other aspects of paying for the permanent facility and major equipment needs of schools. More recently, the term *infrastructure* has dominated because it captures a fuller range of capital needs in a single word. All these terms have been useful in describing the role of the physical environment of schools and the critical role it plays in the education of children. The role of infrastructure is captured in the following statement by AASA:

> The most exciting curriculum innovations in the world have trouble succeeding in cold, dank, deteriorating classrooms. If the work environment is unattractive, uncomfortable, or unsafe, school districts have difficulty competing with other sectors of the economy to woo talented teachers ... Students know the difference too![5]

Obviously, not all schools in the United States are in deplorable condition. More accurately, it is the case that needs far outstrip resources, and the data point to little progress in reversing the trend. And it must be recognized that the goal posts are constantly moving, as over time the fiscal crisis has broadened beyond just deferred maintenance issues because pressure has been placed on school facilities through the expanding scope of education mandates and reforms, as well as exacerbated by the complex and sometimes arcane ways in which schools are financed and maintained. Yet it is clear that the best advances in teaching and learning will fail if the physical environment fails to support or—worse—impedes instruction. In sum, deferring maintenance, construction, and modernization has long been used as a short-term solution to tight school district budgets, but such decisions ultimately represent false economy.

The Condition of Schools

Recent headlines heralding school infrastructure decay make it easy to think that the poor condition of schools in the nation is a new reality. But as early as 1831, William A. Alcott was graphically describing problems involving school facilities:

> Few, indeed, of the numerous schoolhouses in this country are well lighted. Fewer still are painted, even on the outside. Playgrounds for the common schools are scarcely known. There is much suffering from the alternation of heat and cold and from smoke. The feet of children have even sometimes been frozen. Too many pupils are confined to a single desk or bench where they jostle or otherwise disturb each other ... Hundreds of rooms are so small that the pupils have not on average more than five or six square feet each; here they are obliged to sit, breathing impure air, on benches often not more than six or eight inches wide, and without backs.[6]

Fortunately, few schools today suffer such extreme conditions, although some evidence suggests that parallels are not entirely gone.[7] Federal, state, and local health standards have been enacted, and most schools provide more tolerable light and thermal environments than was the case in Alcott's day. Standards for new construction and retrofitting of buildings, including schools, have been set by a wide range of U.S. construction-related professional associations, although many are voluntary.[8] Today, all school facilities are subject to local and state building and safety codes, but it must be noted that these vary with regard to rigor and enforcement. At the federal level, school facilities are subject to Environmental Protection Agency (EPA) regulations for hazards such as asbestos, radon, and lead; standards of the Occupational Safety and Health Administration (OSHA); and accessibility requirements under the Individuals with Disabilities Education Act (IDEA)[9] and the Americans with Disabilities Act (ADA).[10]

Although enforcement of laws and regulations results in safer, healthier, and more physically accessible schools, it does not necessarily lead to modern, educationally appropriate facilities. Furthermore, although many aspects of the physical environment in new schools are legislated and regulated, not all standards are consistently enforced across states and locales. The result has been that existing schools remain the object of concern because numerous national reports have concluded that school infrastructure still is in a state of emergency. Although many safe, modern schools exist, reports have found others that are badly deteriorated, with many too old to safely function or too outdated to meet the demands of a modern education and equality of opportunity.

Other evidence resembling Alcott's time lingers today. Research on the quality of school environments has exposed shamefully substandard school facilities in the United States where unsafe and unhealthy classrooms resemble those in poverty-ridden nations.[11] In addition, research describes health hazards associated with air quality in portable classrooms which are often used as an alternative to new construction.[12] These conditions, not entirely unlike what Alcott described, are juxtaposed with new research linking pupil achievement to the physical environment.

As awareness and research on school infrastructure have grown, new understanding indicates that the depth of needs is much larger than previously believed—and is still growing.[13] Previous estimates of deferred maintenance in U.S. schools were estimated at $112 billion in 1995 by the U.S. Government Accountability Office (GAO) and $127 billion in 1999 by the U.S. Department of Education.[14] More recent research has shown these needs remain unfunded; and the newest data argue that if unmet needs are vast in only the context of general upkeep and repair, they are staggering in context of a fuller definition of school infrastructure and educational opportunity. More specifically, a comprehensive definition of school infrastructure is bigger than deferred maintenance in that it includes new construction, renovation, retrofitting, additions to existing facilities, and major improvements to grounds:

- *Deferred maintenance*: Refers to maintenance necessary to bring a school facility up to good condition, i.e., a condition where only routine maintenance is needed. An essential question in deferred maintenance is whether such costs approach the price of total demolition and new construction;
- *New construction*: This might be a response to pupil overcrowding; to federal, state, or local mandates requiring additional facilities such as class size reduction; or to enrollment growth. Construction of new facilities includes buildings; grounds (purchase, paving, and landscaping); and fixtures, major equipment, and furniture needed to furnish it;
- *Renovation*: Includes improvements to existing facilities for health, safety or accessibility. Renovation may include work needed to accommodate mandated learning programs;
- *Retrofitting*: Applies to areas such as energy conservation (e.g., installation of insulation or energy-efficient windows) and technology readiness (e.g., electrical wiring, phone lines, and fiber optic cables);
- *Additions to existing facilities*: May be required to relieve overcrowding or to meet federal, state, or local mandates such as class size reduction; or to accommodate enrollment growth. Cost of additions includes fixtures, major equipment, and furniture necessary to furnish them;
- *Major improvements*: Refers to grounds, such as landscaping and paving.[15]

Again, the costs are staggering. Results from a recent comprehensive national study of school infrastructure found that states' underfunding annually exceeded $29 billion (see Table 9.1).[16] Other studies have decried the shortfall, with one study placing the cost to fully restore school infrastructure at $256 billion.[17] It is unsurprising that the American Society of Civil Engineers, an organization that rates the quality of the nation's infrastructure, gave schools a grade of "D" in its recent 2017 evaluation.

Although it is easy to understand that the eventual impact of failure to address infrastructure funding is deterioration of learning environments, policymakers have found it too challenging to fully redress, partly due to the magnitude of funding need. In response, litigation has emerged as a grassroots solution to force reluctant states to address inadequate and inequitable facilities and funding schemes. Accordingly, Thompson and Crampton noted:

TABLE 9.1 State-by-State Estimates of School Infrastructure Annual Funding Gap: 2017

State	Annual Shortfall	State	Annual Shortfall
Alabama	$299 million	Montana	$191 million
Alaska	$121 million	Nebraska	$292 million
Arizona	$350 million	Nevada	$52 million
Arkansas	$587 million	New Hampshire	$324 million
California	$3.2 billion	New Jersey	$1.58 billion
Colorado	$640 million	New Mexico	$407 million
Connecticut	$689 million	New York	$2.9 billion
Delaware	$102 million	North Carolina	$660 million
Florida	No data	North Dakota	$162 million
Georgia	No data	Ohio	$683 million
Hawaii	$88 million	Oklahoma	$624 million
Idaho	$301 million	Oregon	$457 million
Illinois	$862 million	Pennsylvania	$1.4 billion
Indiana	$518 million	Rhode Island	$241 million
Iowa	$499 million	South Carolina	$90 million
Kansas	$257 million	South Dakota	$125 million
Kentucky	$453 million	Tennessee	$768 million
Louisiana	$553 million	Texas	No data
Maine	$304 million	Utah	$496 million
Maryland	$615 million	Vermont	$198 million
Massachusetts	$1.4 billion	Virginia	$973 million
Michigan	$1.3 billion	Washington	$556 million
Minnesota	$818 million	West Virginia	$265 million
Mississippi	$289 million	Wisconsin	$836 million
Missouri	$685 million	Wyoming	$149 million
Total			$29.4 billion

Source: Calculated from American Society of Civil Engineers 2017 Infrastructure Report Card. Infrastructure Super Map. https://www.infrastructurereportcard.org/infrastructure-super-map/

By most apparent indicators, efforts to blaze a trail of successful state-level school facility litigation have increased, as there has been a noticeable spike since 2001 in state supreme court-level school finance lawsuits containing substantial facility claims. Results have ranged from slowly evolving language in facility equity/adequacy holdings such as New York's gains above a basic constitutional requirement to provide enough light, space, heat, and air to permit children to learn, to relatively aggressive requirements for equitable access to adequate facilities such as Arkansas' constitutional requirement for substantially equal facilities, New Jersey's requirement of adequate facilities including 100% state financing in plaintiff districts,

Ohio's requirement that the state's educational system cannot result in indefensible facility deficiencies, Texas' requirement that facilities cannot be judged apart from a system-wide context, and Wyoming's requirement to measure adequate school facilities that must be provided at state expense.[18]

Plaintiffs in at least 38 states have cited funding for infrastructure in school finance lawsuits, with some finding success.[19] But in most instances the path has been arduous and uncertain. Decades can pass waiting for redress; what does not wait is attorney fees and lost educational opportunity. While real progress has been made through state aid formula inclusion supporting infrastructure, it remains a low priority compared to funding for instructional programs and other competition for scarce tax dollars. And in the end, politics weigh heavily on outcomes despite intervention in some instances by courts. Unsurprisingly, solutions have continued to rest on some combination of legislative persuasion and litigious force.

Unless forced by courts, most states have not embraced aggressive school infrastructure funding. Table 9.2 reveals the fractured approach states have taken, with slightly less than half of all states providing no infrastructure funding. Care must be taken with Table 9.2 however, as it is easy to overestimate true state participation: For example, some states in Table 9.2 showing some level of state aid may do so only indirectly (e.g., such as favorable loan repayment terms) rather than through a true grant-in-aid plan, while other states' aid ratios may range from minimal aid to nearly 100% funding for school infrastructure. In many ways, equity is not only elusive—it is open to interpretation.

In the end analysis and despite how health, safety, and construction standards have improved school environments, many situations are grim due to the magnitude of infrastructure funding needs; spiraling growth in deferred maintenance; reluctance of many state legislatures, the U.S. Congress, and certain federal administrations to include school infrastructure as important to equal educational opportunity; and vast inequities in local fiscal tax capacity—all of which have contributed to the seriously deficient condition of school infrastructure in the U.S: i.e., an abysmal failure to uniformly offer every child a physical environment conducive to learning. As a result, many school districts lurch from one infrastructure-related crisis to another by diverting instructional funds to pay for emergency repairs, and only when no deferral option remains.

How Is School Infrastructure Funded?

The condition of public education's physical infrastructure is a cumulative portrait of how states have chosen to aid (or not aid) funding of school facilities.[20] As will be seen, there is a sharp difference in how general education is aided compared to how facilities and related capital needs are funded. In contrast to the complex formulas developed to provide school districts with state funding for operating costs through basic aid, categorical aid, and weighting factors, funding for infrastructure in those states where it does exist is nearly primitive by comparison.

TABLE 9.2 State School Infrastructure Funding Programs 2018

State	Aid Provision	State	Aid Provision
Alabama	Yes	Montana	Yes
Alaska	Yes	Nebraska	No
Arizona	No data	Nevada	No
Arkansas	Yes	New Hampshire	No data
California	Yes	New Jersey	Yes
Colorado	No	New Mexico	Yes
Connecticut	Yes	New York	Yes
Delaware	Yes	North Carolina	No
Florida	No	North Dakota	No
Georgia	Yes	Ohio	Yes
Hawaii	Yes	Oklahoma	No
Idaho	No	Oregon	Yes
Illinois	No	Pennsylvania	Yes
Indiana	No	Rhode Island	Yes
Iowa	No	South Carolina	No
Kansas	Yes	South Dakota	No
Kentucky	Yes	Tennessee	Yes
Louisiana	No	Texas	Yes
Maine	Yes	Utah	Yes
Maryland	Yes	Vermont	No
Massachusetts	Yes	Virginia	No
Michigan	No	Washington	Yes
Minnesota	No	West Virginia	No
Mississippi	No	Wisconsin	No
Missouri	No	Wyoming	Yes

Interpreted from Verstegen, Deborah. A Quick Glance at School Finance: A 50 State Survey of School Finance Policies and Programs 2018. "Capital Outlay and/or Debt Service." Word Press: https://schoolfinancesdav.files.wordpress.com/2018/09/capital-outlay.pdf

One explanation for the lack of state aid to school infrastructure may be reluctance of states to abandon the tradition of local control. From the inception of state aid to local school districts dating from the Common Schools Movement in the nineteenth century, states have regularly delegated the building and maintenance of facilities to local communities. Within such delegation, states have permitted districts to use local property taxes for infrastructure expenditures, although local voter approval was—and is—usually required. The dawn of the twentieth century, however, brought many economic, educational, demographic, legal, and societal changes that increased pressure on local tax bases. As the United States moved from an agrarian to an industrial society, there was rapid growth in the size and number of cities with their own infrastructure needs—e.g., roads and sanitation systems—that placed new demands on local tax bases. At the same time, a public education system that largely had been confined to elementary grades had expanded to include high schools, requiring increased expenditures for operations and infrastructure. Successive waves of immigration further swelled school enrollments and costs. Additionally, numerous states passed laws restricting child labor in factories, making it more likely they would attend public schools.[21] Lastly, as education's value to society grew, more states passed compulsory education laws or expanded laws already in existence, further increasing enrollments.

Although schooling's growth in the early twentieth century was accompanied by economic growth that helped to accommodate increasing enrollments, the stock market crash in 1929 plunged the nation into the Great Depression, and education spending plummeted. In contrast, the baby boom years after World War II necessitated the rapid construction of new schools, but the resulting buildings were often of poor quality. Their deficiencies added to a backlog of maintenance costs while the emergence of new education technologies made them, as well as more solidly built older schools, obsolete.

All these problems were worsened by the reluctance of states to become involved in funding school facilities. There were a few exceptions, but these were generally narrowly targeted to a specific goal. For example, in 1901 Alabama began to aid capital outlay—the purpose, though, was to help rural schools and did not imply a broader state duty to education. In 1903, Delaware and South Carolina began offering capital aid to schools for African-American children; and between 1898 and 1927 aid plans incentivizing school district consolidation were enacted in Arkansas, Delaware, Maine, Minnesota, Missouri, New York, Oklahoma, Pennsylvania, Rhode Island, Tennessee, and Wisconsin. The result of selective aid schemes was that, as late as World War II, only 12 states provided any type of aid to capital outlay and debt service for schools.

Over time, states became more aware of school infrastructure concerns, especially as some courts began to link infrastructure to school finance fairness. Table 9.2 illustrated that a bare majority of states now provides some type of financial support, be it direct or indirect, to school infrastructure—although not necessarily adequate, equitable, or uniform. And as seen earlier, the level of contribution still varies widely today: Only a few states provide large supports through grants-in-aid resembling general fund finance plans, while others provide project-specific grants that may or may not be truly equalized. States making less aggressive efforts sometimes turn to indirect aid mechanisms like loans or bond guarantees, and of course nearly half of all states provide no aid at all. The differences and options are great and worthy of additional exploration in order to understand how states approach their single largest one-time investment in the form of bricks and mortar.

Full State Funding

As the name implies, full state funding plans assign total responsibility to the state for the cost of building programs. Under these conditions, the state pays for school facility construction, and in return may expect to control much of the planning and construction. Under a full state funding scheme, a school district may need to develop specifications promulgated by a state building authority and receive formal agency approval before commencing construction, renovations, or additions to existing facilities. In addition, the district may be placed on a wait list that reflects the authority's assessment of the urgency of the request in relation to all other districts in the state. Most states have never even considered full state funding for infrastructure—and in historical context states may waver in and out of any funding design based on politics of the time and available resources. Those states having approached full state funding have done so either through unique situations or external pressures—for example, the state of Hawaii has only one school district and consequently its school infrastructure aid is de facto full state funding. Arizona approached full state funding by way of school finance litigation, but the struggles still continue as a new action is currently contemplated on a set of broader issues that includes capital concerns.[22]

Full state funding for school infrastructure has the same advantages found in fully funded general aid formulas (see Chapter 3). Full state support conceptually represents the most equitable system, in that facilities are funded based on the wealth of the entire state rather than the individual district. The scope of identifying the full extent of needs in all districts often results in the creation of a state department or agency whose sole or primary responsibility is school infrastructure funding. However, as attractive as full state funding of school infrastructure may be to districts, local communities are often wary of the perceived loss of local autonomy in exchange for state aid.

Project-Based Aid

Project-based aid for school infrastructure is used in various forms by some states. It may or may not be equalized, and it rarely covers the full cost of an infrastructure project, e.g., the cost of constructing a new school or renovating an existing facility. If it is not equalized, it resembles a flat grant.

When equalized, the amount of aid the school district receives is generally inversely related to its fiscal capacity, usually defined as property wealth per pupil. However, the state may cap aid per project based on state assessment of what a particular project should cost—or it may be based on limited state funds. In some cases, the state may allow the district to raise additional funding to exceed the state cap, although this distorts the equity impact of state aid. Equalization aid for school infrastructure bears some similarity to equalized general aid formulas because the funding amount is meant to be relative to the local district's ability to pay. However, equalization aid for infrastructure is particular to a defined building project and so, unlike general aid, is time-limited to the project's duration. Project-based aid also bears some similarity to categorical aid in that it can be used only for a specific building project. However, as seen earlier, some states do not equalize categorical aid.

Equalized project-based aid can also be compared to matching grants if the match set by the state is reflective of the district's ability to pay. On the other hand, if the state sets an arbitrary ratio (e.g., 50/50) based on political belief that all districts should be treated the same, a matching grant ends up being helpful but still disequalizing because it advantages property-wealthy districts. In addition, the state will likely need to cap total aid since its revenues are not limitless, and so the state would be well advised to develop sensitive criteria in determining eligibility and priority.

A variation on project-based aid is debt service aid, where debt service is defined as the annual payment of principal and interest a school district makes on its long-term debt for school infrastructure. Only a handful of states have ever used debt service aid as either the only form of financial support for school infrastructure or in addition to other types of aid. Debt service aid resembles categorical aid in that it too is targeted for a specific purpose. While school districts generally welcome any state aid for infrastructure, debt service aid generally requires the district to first make its annual debt payment from existing funds and only afterward seek whatever percentage reimbursement the state offers.

General Aid Support

A few states have built infrastructure aid into their general or basic aid programs. Separate from maintenance and operations (which are often considered current operating expenses and thereby already included in general aid formulas), general aid to infrastructure has only recently been included as a component. The logic for inclusion of infrastructure funding as an integral part of general aid lies in the belief that facilities are key to the total educational program of the district and therefore deserving of identical levels of support.

State Loans and State Bond Guarantees

State loan programs and state bond guarantees represent a manner of indirect aid to school infrastructure. Several states have enacted loan programs, and some of those same states may combine loans with other capital supports. State loan programs may be more helpful to districts with a less than optimal credit rating; here, the state's stronger credit rating may lower the district's cost of borrowing. However, it should be realized that some localities may have better credit ratings than the state; as such, a state loan could actually increase interest costs. However, if the state loan program does not require local voter approval, the district may find it preferable compared to risking voter rejection in a local bond referendum. But importantly, a state loan must be repaid, and local property tax revenues are usually the only revenue source available.

A state bond guarantee can also lower a school district's borrowing costs for infrastructure. Because the state guarantees to repay the local bond if the district defaults, the district may be able to borrow funds at a lower cost (i.e., interest rate). Over the course of paying back a 20-year bond, for example, this can amount to a substantial savings in interest costs to the district. Unlike state loans, the state makes no upfront investment of its own money with a bond guarantee. However, states are exposed to risk with both loan and bond guarantee programs if a district defaults.

State School Building Authorities

A state school building authority (SBA) is not a type of actual aid, but rather a mechanism for distributing aid. It is worth mentioning here because it is a variation on the more traditional method of distributing infrastructure aid through a state department of education. Hence, an SBA is the exception rather than the rule with regard to state administration of school infrastructure funding.

Historically, an SBA has offered the advantage not only of distributing aid or making loans but also providing experts like architects and engineers on whom school districts can call at low or no cost during the planning stages of an infrastructure project. Depending on state law, an SBA may draw on private investors, issue state bonds, or receive legislative appropriations to provide school infrastructure funding. In all cases, SBAs are subject to state law and regulation. More recently, SBAs have been used in the wake of court decisions demanding equitable and adequate funding for school infrastructure. In states like Arizona and Ohio, SBAs have assessed school infrastructure needs and associated costs; prioritized school infrastructure projects across the state; set criteria for new school buildings, e.g., square footage; and allocated funding based upon those criteria. Often school districts have little or no leeway to supplement the state's funding. As such, SBAs have both advantages and disadvantages. On the positive side, they can offer expertise in planning and designing a school facility at little or no local cost. This is helpful particularly for smaller districts that usually do not have expert facilities staff. Second, SBAs may offer aid or loans to districts without the requirement of local voter approval. On the other hand, SBAs may control the type of facility a district can build, leading to criticisms of cookie cutter designs that are not responsive to local needs or preferences.

Intermediate Summary

Although some state courts have mandated state aid to school infrastructure to remedy physical and fiscal inequities, too many states still provide no aid to school facilities, and many others offer only limited aid. Among those states aiding school infrastructure costs, classification of aid schemes is challenging because states do not use comparable language, and the numerous hybrid funding plans are difficult to categorize. Taken conjointly, several types of aid programs exist, although it must be emphasized that almost no state supports school infrastructure at the same level seen for general operating aid. As will be seen in the next section, school districts remain heavily impacted by infrastructure costs.

How is the Local Cost Share Funded?

By every measure, the cost of school facilities is enormous. Recent data indicate that since the 1995 alarm sounded by the U.S. Government Accounting Office (GAO),[23] the ensuing years 1995–2016 saw new investment of nearly $2 trillion in school infrastructure across the nation—yet the same report indicated that $145 billion more is needed annually.[24] In this large sum was a call for $58 billion for maintenance and operations, $77 billion for capital construction, and $10 billion for new facilities. While the same report indicated that historic spending for these categories totaled $99 billion, a $46 billion annual gap remained which was contributing to a growing infrastructure deficit equal to a 32% annual shortfall. Such numbers are enormous and in the minds of many citizens seem impossible to repay.

These figures, however, did not take into account existing school district debt on construction projects, which the U.S. Department of Education estimated at

$17.9 billion in 2014 for interest alone.[25] Although state aid undoubtedly pays some portion of these long-term costs, the vast majority of school districts across the nation have had to finance a large share of infrastructure projects using only revenue derived from local property taxes. Generally, the local share plus debt service is paid from some combination of three funding sources: *Current revenues, sinking funds,* and *bonded indebtedness.*

Current Revenues

In most states, school districts must locally supplement any available infrastructure aid, and in no-aid states the full responsibility for infrastructure costs rests entirely with the local district. Although several methods for raising local monies exist, financing capital needs through current revenues is the oldest. As implied by its name, local revenue is derived from property taxes levied during the current year. For example, if a district has a taxable assessed valuation of $500 million and a statutorily permissible tax rate for capital outlay of four mills, the district can generate $2 million in current revenues for infrastructure purposes. Similarly, if a district has a valuation of only $10 million and the same maximum tax rate, current revenues for capital projects will raise only $40,000. If, in the same example, the state were to have no limit on tax rates in local districts, the poorer district would have to levy 200 mills to generate the same revenue available to the wealthy district at four mills (see Chapter 3 notes for a refresher on millage/tax rate calculations).

The benefits and limitations of local financing via current revenues are evident in the previous illustration. The major advantage is that current revenue is a cash or *pay as you go* method that avoids interest costs. Additionally, districts are likely to be more cost-conscious if revenue must be in hand prior to expenditure. At the same time, serious drawbacks exist. The most important drawback results from disparate property wealth across school districts in a state, in that high property-wealth districts can better afford state-of-the-art school facilities while low-wealth districts will struggle to provide even minimally adequate ones.

Very few school districts use the current revenue method because many local tax bases are woefully insufficient. In addition, most states limit the maximum millage that can be levied for school infrastructure. However, even if states allowed unlimited local tax leeway, it would be impossible to raise adequate funds in property-poor districts. As a result, the usefulness of the current revenue approach is mostly confined to smaller annual projects.

Sinking Funds

A sinking fund is similar to a savings account where the school district accumulates funds until they are sufficient to pay cash for an infrastructure project. In this scenario, states allow districts to levy general or special taxes to be placed in a reserve fund for a specified project or for undesignated purposes.[26] Assuming an adequate tax base, sinking funds also have the ability to grow if the money is invested in interest-bearing accounts. For example, a tax levy of $1 million per year invested at 5% interest would amount to $1.28 million at the end of a five-year period.

A sinking fund has advantages for both school districts and taxpayers. A major benefit is that it encourages long-term planning for school infrastructure. Additionally, a sinking fund saves the district money because no interest costs are incurred since no money is borrowed. However, sinking funds still depend on the property wealth of the district. As a result, only wealthier districts generally have sufficient resources to set aside. Second, inflation will reduce the future value of a sinking fund; even a low inflation rate of 2% reduces the value of $1 to only 67¢ after 20 years. Third, accumulating large sums is often not advisable unless they are earmarked for specific projects because voters who originally approved a tax levy might disfavor eventual uses of the sinking fund.

Bonded Indebtedness

Because neither current revenues nor sinking funds are feasible solutions for larger infrastructure projects, school districts frequently turn to bonded indebtedness. Bonding is a device by which districts are statutorily permitted to incur long-term debt for the purpose of acquiring high-cost fixed assets such as facilities. Although debt is generally prohibited under state law for school districts' current operations, it is generally allowed for infrastructure projects. Methods by which districts may incur bond debt depend on the laws of each state.[27] In most states, districts are authorized to bond for infrastructure subject to statutes on referenda and debt limitations. In other states, differences relate primarily to whether districts are fiscally independent or dependent, and on whether the state controls bonding through a central state authority.

Although bonding is a form of borrowing, it is different from traditional private mortgages in several ways. When individuals or businesses want to borrow money for construction, they usually approach a lending institution to request a mortgage or its commercial equivalent—i.e., a debt instrument that uses the purchased property as collateral in case of default. In contrast, governmental units do not operate in this manner. Although bonds still create a legal debt, the private paper is replaced by the bond mechanism, which has two key features. The first feature is that bonds are sold at open market and purchased by investors instead of by a traditional mortgage lender. The second feature is that public properties purchased through bond sales cannot be foreclosed. Thus a bond sale for school facility purposes creates neither a mortgage nor collateral. Rather, the school district as a unit of local government pledges its full faith to secure the debt.

Bonding has many benefits. Investors see government bonds as attractive investments because the likelihood of default is low, and the interest is usually tax-exempt for investors. Although government bond interest rates are generally lower than private market rates, bonds are attractive investments because the untaxed earnings may net the investor more income than higher yield investments after taxes—a win/win situation as schools pay lower interest rates and investors profit under favorable tax conditions. The only drawback to bonding is the added cost of interest the district pays over the life of each bond, which for a new school facility is usually 20 years.

Bonding follows similar steps in all states. Most states require a local referendum (bond election) whenever a school district wants to pursue an infrastructure project that exceeds current revenues or cash reserves. A referendum is a request for voter approval of infrastructure debt by placing the question on the ballot at a general or special election. When voters approve a bond issue, they are agreeing to pay higher property taxes over the life of the bond to retire the debt, or more specifically, to repay the bond buyers. To amortize the bond, the district levies taxes that are deposited to a special bond fund from which it makes structured payments.

When a district decides to initiate a bond sale, a series of steps is involved. Determination of the infrastructure project and an estimate of cost is usually the first step. Next, the district determines if it can afford to undertake the project. This step is critical because every state places debt limits on local units of government, including school districts. Generally, the debt limitation is expressed as a percentage of the assessed valuation of the district. For example, if a district were to have an assessed valuation of $500 million with a 10% debt ceiling, total debt in terms of borrowed principal could not exceed $50 million.[28] The third step is to schedule a bond election. State statutes are specific in these matters. While the local district usually has little involvement in actually conducting an election, the district typically makes all decisions about election timing and carries sole responsibility for any campaigning to enhance the likelihood of voter approval. If the referendum fails, the district must regroup to determine cause and decide whether to resubmit the question to voters. Generally, any new election is accompanied by escalated public relations and may include a scaled-down project at lesser cost. If the referendum is successful, the district can proceed to the fourth step of preparing the bond sale. Specialized legal counsel is required due to the complexity of bond laws, and financial counsel is required because the bond market is complex and competitive. After counsel has prepared for the bond issue, an official advertisement is issued to investors, usually through widely read financial publications and by bond prospectus.

Although the bonding process is normally completed by following these four steps, the infrastructure project is only beginning. The planned work must be performed, and the project actually extends beyond construction completion and initial occupancy because the district has committed to long-term debt repayment. This requires revisiting the financial plan on an annual basis, levying taxes and depositing proceeds into special debt service funds in preparation for disbursement, and maintaining and protecting the new physical assets. As seen in earlier chapters on budgeting, accounting, and taxation, all of these processes are important to the successful operation of a school district. Facilities and bonding are areas of special care not only because so much money is at stake, but also because a district's infrastructure makes it possible to carry out the instructional mission of schools.

INFRASTRUCTURE PLANNING AND FACILITY MAINTENANCE

Until now the chapter's discussion has centered on how schools raise money for infrastructure projects, primarily from the viewpoint of building new facilities, remodeling and renovation, or acquisition and integration of technology—projects requiring large sums of money, or in some limited cases, carried out through current revenues. However, there are two other facets to budgeting for infrastructure that need to be discussed: *Facility planning* and *maintenance and operations*.

What Is the Role of Infrastructure Planning?

Although school districts engage in long-range planning in many areas, in some ways planning for infrastructure predicts the success or failure of all other plans. An excellent curriculum built on the latest technology will be weaker if facilities are poorly designed or maintained. Likewise, the most highly skilled teachers will be frustrated if classrooms are cramped or unsuited to the curriculum. For example, older buildings with inadequate infrastructure often cannot support the technology expected in today's classrooms and media centers. Similarly, older buildings with inadequate ventilation systems are unsafe for chemistry labs. Even new buildings may be unworkable if overcrowded or built with inadequate attention to the learning environment. Although modern, safe facilities will not overcome poor teaching, planning for infrastructure is more than just architectural design—it is the integration of space with the instructional and support functions of a modern school system.

The value of infrastructure planning has long been known. Poor planning is costly through wasted money, lack of long-range flexibility, and underutilization of facilities. As a result, planning requires organization to oversee all aspects of facility design and operation. Larger school districts often have an assistant superintendent who oversees all facility-related tasks. Usually this person has staff who perform more specialized functions. In smaller districts, these duties may fall to the superintendent or business manager, with greater reliance on outsourcing for special services. Although district size may drive how the school system organizes its planning activities, all districts need at least one staff person who is knowledgeable about both education and infrastructure management.

Alternatively, large districts may have an office of facility planning. This office has as its major task the ongoing study and analysis of facility needs according to five goals. The first goal is to prepare and maintain a comprehensive analysis of all facilities in the district. The second is to assure a well-designed physical environment to enhance teaching and learning. The third goal is to assure that all facilities remain useful over the life of each building because outmoded facilities hinder teaching and learning and are costly to maintain. The fourth goal is to evaluate facilities for future educational programs in ways that assist decisions to reconstruct or retire buildings. The fifth goal is to preserve maximum flexibility in all buildings so that future generations are well served. Facilities planning should thus reflect careful thought about the following:

- School-age population to be served;
- Location and transportation of school-age population;
- Programmatic offerings of the district and each school;
- Long-range capital needs of the district;
- Fiscal capacity of taxpayers in the district;
- Organizational structure of the school system;
- Economic and demographic future of the district.

The following areas make up planning for infrastructure: *Demographic planning, capital program planning, facility planning and programming, architectural planning,* and *construction planning.* Because they are the elements school districts use to justify many decisions about the total educational program, each deserves a brief discussion.

Demographic Planning

Demographic planning is the study of a school district's profile including social, economic, and population issues. Demographics drive school infrastructure planning because the goal is to serve the complete needs of the school community.

Demographic planning varies greatly based on the unique characteristics of each school district. For example, districts with growing populations must anticipate housing patterns so that school sites (vacant land) can be bought ahead of rising market trends. Other districts engage in demographic planning to predict future facility needs relating to stable or declining enrollments. A major task of demographic planning is to conduct accurate facility surveys that research the district's profile, analyze findings and propose alternative solutions, and recommend a plan of action. A comprehensive educational survey describes the community's characteristics and educational needs, determines pupil population characteristics, describes the educational program, appraises existing facilities in relation to needs, develops a master plan, assesses resources, and makes recommendations. Because it is truly comprehensive, the survey forms the basis for careful long-range infrastructure planning.

Description of community characteristics and educational needs is the starting point. The survey should analyze population characteristics, density, and changes over time. It should examine changes in land use, including zoning and changes that have occurred because of population patterns. Analysis should examine traffic and assess development and land use under growth conditions to predict likely locations for new schools, as well as continued viability of existing facilities. Other community characteristics such as vocational opportunities, parental expectations, and public attitudes toward schools and taxes should be studied as well. Finally, one of the most important elements in demographic planning is enrollment projection, which was discussed in Chapter 5.

Capital Program Planning

Capital program planning is the anticipation of a school district's capital needs in relation to its demographic profile. Its purpose is to analyze the district's financial characteristics and status to estimate the ability of the district to pay for current and future infrastructure needs.

The normal result of capital program planning is the creation of a capital improvement plan (CIP) that projects all school district capital needs for the future, usually over a period of five to 20 years. The CIP prioritizes projects, primarily because resources are seldom sufficient to address all needs at one time, especially if current revenues are expected to provide a significant part of the money. For example, roof replacement on all buildings more than ten years old might be the highest priority. Another example might find the district trying to replace computers in all classrooms according to a priority schedule. More aggressive implementation of CIPs can occur if bonding is used. For example, a district might replace all roofs and HVAC (heating, ventilation, air-conditioning) systems in a single bond issue, or it might retrofit all buildings with technology upgrades to support new high-speed school-based technology centers. When renovation, retrofitting, or new construction is contemplated, the CIP must provide an analysis of revenues over the full period of debt retirement. Finally, the CIP should be reviewed and updated as projects are completed and as needs and financial conditions change.

Facility Planning and Programming

The purpose of facility planning and programming is to identify the desires and constraints under which any learning facility will have to function. Generally, this activity involves consideration of the educational goals and objectives of the district and each individual school, and it also usually defines instructional and organizational plans. Stakeholders should be involved in facility planning and programming, including community and staff along with professional planners, such as architects. Overall goals should focus on the following areas and, if not, the district should undertake modifications:

- Is the facility structurally sound?
- Is it healthy and safe?
- Is it efficient to operate?
- Does it support the educational program?
- Is it attractive and comfortable?
- Is its location convenient for the users?
- Is its space optimally used?
- Is it the right size?
- Can it be modified?

In addition, school districts are increasingly taking into consideration environmental issues in facility planning and programming, commonly referred to as *green* building and construction.[29] The U.S. Green Building Council offers a LEED (Leadership in Energy and Environmental Design) certification that provides frameworks for identifying and implementing practical and measurable green building design, construction, operations, and maintenance solutions.[30] Even with a strong commitment to green construction, school districts still need to do a careful cost–benefit analysis of options.

Architectural Planning

Major facility projects require professional architectural planning. This has become especially true with regard to statutory and regulatory requirements for health, safety, and accessibility. Additional considerations are energy efficiency and sensitivity to environmental concerns and green practices. Consequently, architectural planning represents a fourth activity in school infrastructure planning.

Although architects or engineers are generally engaged to design new or reconstructed schools, some states now require school districts to use architectural services any time a learning facility is modified. For example, the addition of an elevator to improve the accessibility of an existing school building may be subject to state and local building and safety codes that might require the entire facility to be brought up to current code, thereby dramatically increasing the cost of the project. Similarly, removal of an interior wall in an older school to create a larger space may expose asbestos, requiring costly removal or containment in addition to possible closure of parts or all of the facility.

Selection of an architect is a critical aspect of facility planning. Most districts use the services of one architect for smaller projects, but engage in design competition if larger projects like new construction are involved. Retrofitting and remodeling projects like the installation of new HVAC systems or divider walls to reshape interior spaces are sometimes noncompetitive. Large projects such as renovation, expansion, or new construction usually require competition. Because competition is complex and costly, the process is usually reduced to asking architects to submit portfolios containing a description of their experience and qualifications, examples of their work, and rough cost estimates. The board, administrative staff, and consultants make a judgment based on such items as experience of the firm, budget, and overall reputation. As emphasized in earlier chapters, care must be taken to follow all statutory requirements in awarding competitive contracts, including contracts for professional services.

Construction Planning

The value of architectural services is evident in two critical aspects of facility planning. The first aspect involves planning the project and working to develop project specifications. The role of the architect is to work within the physical and fiscal realities of the district and to work with staff to be sure the facility will function well. The second aspect involves actual oversight of the project to completion. These two features are part of the architect's overall responsibility in construction planning. The legal liability and technical competence involved in these tasks make architectural services an absolute necessity.

Construction planning represents the fifth task of infrastructure planning by joining architects, educational consultants, and school staff in designing a facility. Because architects are not educators, school districts generally need the services of an educational consultant to create educational specifications that communicate the district's vision to the architect. Educational specifications are first stated in general terms by school and district staff and communicated to the consultant. The consultant reviews these statements and examines existing facilities. Depending on the nature and size of the project, the consultant may work with a committee to define needs and expectations. The goal is for the consultant to use the district's broad vision to create a specific document that leads the architect to develop the most appropriate design. For example, educational specifications define the school program by classroom and by instructional facility, including requirements for special areas, e.g., media center/library, cafeteria, auditorium, and areas for physical education, art, music, and vocational programs. The importance of these activities is underscored by the Association for Learning Environments (A4LE) which has described educational specifications as the blueprint for the future.

If new construction is required, activities may lead to preliminary design drawings being presented to the school board. Once preliminary plans are approved, actual working drawings and specifications are developed. Plans must be reviewed to ensure the design is integrated with curricular and instructional goals. Input from school site and instructional leaders is essential during the design phase to avoid inefficiency and waste.

When the design is complete, actual physical improvements begin. The major task of school and district officials during the work phase is to maintain close contact with the project. Lack of oversight could result in legal problems if it is later found that the district should have kept itself better informed. A second reason is that the district must state in writing any concerns about or changes to the project. A third reason is that payments for work will be made periodically during the construction phase, and the district must be satisfied before money is released.

The work phase requires scheduled payments from the school district's cash reserves or from bond proceeds.[31] These payments satisfy material and labor claims. Architectural fees are usually a percentage of the project; in contrast, contractor fees are set by competitive bidding. When the project is finished, a percentage is typically held back pending final acceptance and proof that bills, payrolls, and mechanics' liens by all contractors, subcontractors, and vendors have been satisfied. Additionally, the board's attorney must assure that the district has clear title.

The role of planning for infrastructure is broad and includes demographic plans, capital program plans, educational program plans, and architectural and construction plans, all of which apply to both alteration and expansion of facilities and to new construction. All infrastructure projects must be financed by legally permissible methods using cash or debt, and expert counsel ranging from legal and financial services to architectural and construction services must be used. The role of the school district is to acquire and coordinate these services—a role that demands sound educational and fiscal planning.

What is the Role and Nature of Maintenance and Operations?

ed. programs depend on school facilities

The value of planning has been repeatedly stressed because the cost of physical infrastructure and the dependence of educational programs on school facilities are enormous. As noted earlier, a sound educational program is always hindered by poor school facilities. As a result, an effective program of maintenance and operations (M&O) is critical in order to keep buildings and grounds in good condition and ready for use.

Organizing for Maintenance and Operations

The maintenance and operations function is often organized under a central office administrator with line authority over all physical plant activities and related staff. Organizational structure depends on school district size, with large districts employing dozens of skilled workers. A medium-size school district might resemble the organizational chart in Figure 9.1, where both diversification of work and efficiency of scale are evident. As Figure 9.1 shows, final responsibility rests with the school board, which should delegate to the superintendent, who in turn may delegate to a general director. Facilities planning and operations and maintenance are thus joined, with a key person coordinating performance.

Figure 9.1 develops a central maintenance division that provides services to all schools in the district. These services may be provided on an in-house basis if the district has decided it is more cost-efficient to employ permanent staff with specific skills, rather than outsourcing some or all of these functions to private firms.

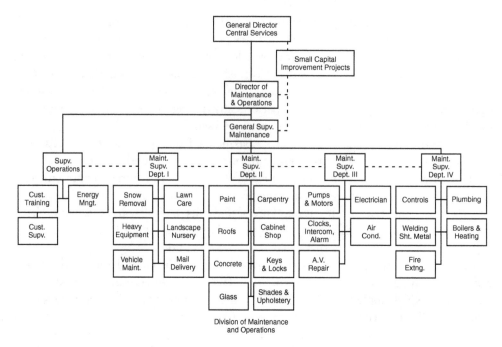

FIGURE 9.1 Sample Facilities Organizational Chart

Figure 9.1 illustrates a school district of approximately 16,000 students and provides an example wherein the district has decided that it has enough work to justify the cost of operating its own maintenance division. An assistant superintendent for facility planning might oversee a general director, who in turn might oversee a director of maintenance and operations. In this example, the director of maintenance and operations oversees a supervisor of maintenance and a supervisor of operations. As district size decreases, the organizational chart becomes simpler, although the same tasks still need to be performed.

Organizing for M&O demands assessing facility needs on the basis of cleaning, repairing, and replacing the district's capital assets. The overarching organizational tasks therefore include determining maintenance and conducting facility operations.

Determining Maintenance Needs

As a rule, maintenance of buildings requires skilled evaluation of all component systems. Component systems include footings, foundations, and basements; interior and exterior walls; roofs and flashings; doors, windows, and frames; floors and ceilings; mechanical systems; electrical systems; aesthetics, equipment, and furniture; grounds; and energy conservation. This list points out the need for skilled employees and specially contracted maintenance. Foundations, footings, and basements should be regularly inspected by staff for visible problems, and routine evaluation by engineers or architects should be scheduled. Walls and roofs should be inspected regularly, with repairs like sealing cosmetic cracks and light masonry repointing done in-house. Mechanical and electrical systems must be inspected, with problems reported promptly. Painting, refastening trim, cleaning traps, replacing washers in valves, adjusting doors and windows, and replacing shades and lighting can be done in-house. A maintenance plan should also address energy conservation, including a formal energy audit and energy-saving steps.

The goal of determining maintenance needs is to identify concerns and to prevent new problems. Once needs are known, the district must schedule and fund repair or replacement. As a general rule, districts should spend a minimum 4% to 6% of the general operating budget for maintenance. Much of the problem of poor facility conditions today stems from failure to follow a program of routine and preventive maintenance. In difficult financial times, schools and districts often cut back on routine maintenance or postpone preventive maintenance in order to protect educational programs and staffing levels. As discussed earlier, this only results in a backlog of deferred maintenance that will cost the district more in the long run and could negatively affect the learning environment for students and staff.

Conducting Facility Operations

Although maintenance is key to the financial and instructional health of schools, smooth day-to-day operation of facilities is equally important to the safety and welfare of everyone at school. There is no doubt that the physical condition of facilities has an impact on learning: Dirty or poorly maintained schools send a message to staff, students, parents, and the community that education is not valued. Students attending well-maintained schools feel pride, staff morale is higher, and parental and community support for learning is enhanced. Routine maintenance is essential, and its contribution to academic success should not be undervalued.

The maintenance function comprises the tasks of keeping a school open for use. As a rule, the most important skill is organization. Maintenance staff must be organized for efficiency within the limits of cost, labor, and time. Every aspect of maintenance must be organized by task and timetable so that staff know what needs to be done and when it must be accomplished. Generally, tasks can be broken down into routines of vacuuming, sweeping, mopping, dusting, cleaning glass, and emptying trash; steam-cleaning, buffing, or waxing floors; cleaning whiteboards or chalkboards; cleaning halls including walls, water fountains, and waste bins; and noting damage needing repair. Daily activities include both routine tasks and minor repairs, although component system evaluation by staff can occur on a monthly or quarterly basis. Minor repairs like fixing trim or changing lightbulbs can be scheduled on an as-needed basis, while other tasks like painting can be done during non-school times. Daily tasks should be performed on staggered schedules using a square-foot formula or by enrollment size of the school.

Although many additional activities not described here are needed to ensure a clean, safe, and healthy school, no aspect is more important than initial and ongoing training and development for custodial and maintenance staff. Training may result in overall improvements including higher standards of service, lower employee costs stemming from greater efficiencies, less waste, fewer hazards, less deterioration of school plant and equipment, more flexibility in shifting employees among buildings, and greater respect for custodial and maintenance workers on the part of the public.

Facility operations and maintenance are critical to the good work of schools and depend on highly competent staff to create the best possible conditions for equal educational opportunity.

The Role of the School Leader in Maintenance and Operations

Site-level school leaders are ultimately responsible for the appearance and condition of their schools—consequently, they must become familiar with district M&O policies and procedures because it is their duty to ensure that the total school environment is conducive to learning.

Depending on school district size and the presence or absence of collective bargaining agreements, the responsibilities of school site leaders for M&O can vary greatly. In smaller districts, they may be directly involved in hiring, supervising, and evaluating maintenance staffs. In larger districts where custodial staffs are more likely to be covered by a collective bargaining agreement, hiring, supervision, and evaluation may be centralized. Alternatively, in large school systems custodial and maintenance operations may be outsourced to one or more private contractors. In such cases, site leaders must be familiar with the content of collectively bargained agreements or outsourced contracts. By doing so, they will avoid many problems and will be better prepared to engage all staff—both instructional and noninstructional—proactively in maintenance, repair, and operational issues. The overall goal is to create a school culture that values schools' physical condition and appearance as important factors in the learning environment.

Although the size, cost, and complexity of M&O—indeed, the entirety of infrastructure—causes primary responsibility to be located in the school district's central office, the opportunity to enhance the safety and security of school facilities and grounds through sound maintenance and operations occurs first at each school site, and the school leader plays a key role. Some measures are straightforward—e.g., requesting and maintaining sufficient exterior lighting of buildings, parking lots, and other areas including athletic fields is an effective low-cost safety measure. Other maintenance issues fall to school site leaders such as ensuring that exterior and interior door locks are in good working order and cannot be easily bypassed. Likewise, if the school's grounds have shrubbery near doors and windows, the school leader should request that they be pruned in order to prevent their use as cover by vandals and criminals. Likewise, school leaders should request prompt repair of cracked or uneven sidewalks and parking lot potholes that place students and adults at risk of injury. Similarly, prompt removal of graffiti discourages gang activity and vandalism. In other words, risk management and maintenance/operations are district-wide and school-wide obligations, and close attention to these issues can greatly reduce barriers to effectiveness and likewise increase enjoyment of the learning environment.[32]

Schools and districts are increasingly interested in creating and maintaining environmentally friendly or sustainable facilities that are inclusive of both indoor and outdoor spaces. Although many of these concerns are addressed at the district level, (e.g., projects to retrofit schools with energy efficient doors and windows), there is much that school site leaders and their staffs can do regarding green initiatives. By doing so, leaders not only set a good example for students: They can also include them in these efforts, particularly because many students today have an intense interest in preserving and improving the environment.[33]

Energy efficiency is also attractive to school and district leaders not only because it addresses environmental sustainability, but also because it reduces costs. On average, 53% of a school's energy cost is attributable to heating and cooling, with an additional 30% for lighting and 10% for hot water (see Figure 9.2). Focusing on environmental impact and energy efficiency, the U.S. Department of Energy (DOE) has undertaken the EnergySmart[34] initiative to provide schools with suggestions on how to reduce energy use without compromising the quality of teaching and learning environments.[35] Some tips are low or no-cost and can be initiated by school leaders with the assistance of staff and students. Simple steps like turning out lights in classrooms when not in use or turning off computers and peripherals at the end of the day not only reduce energy use but also make staff and students more energy aware.

A similar approach can be used at the site level with regard to 'green cleaning.' For example, the overuse of some cleaning chemicals contributes to poor air quality in schools. The Healthy Schools Campaign offers inexpensive suggestions that can be implemented at the school level such as recycling paper and plastic; conserving water; maintaining uncluttered classrooms and work spaces; and proper handling of food and potential contaminants.[36] More comprehensive approaches that involve custodial practices are subject to the cautions mentioned earlier; that is, before initiating changes school site leaders must consider whether custodial services and staff supervision are centralized or outsourced. Overall, however, school leaders with assistance from site councils, staffs, and students can have a significant impact on environmental issues at the site level.

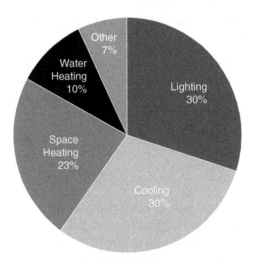

FIGURE 9.2 Typical School Energy Use Distribution

Source: U.S. Department of Energy. "EnergySmart School Tips." http://files.eric.ed.gov/fulltext/ED511654.pdf.

WRAP-UP

Budgeting for school infrastructure is highly complex, but as noted at the outset of this chapter, it is false economy to underspend for facilities. The physical environment of schools is important for academic learning and staff morale, and key to parental and community support for local schools. Although this chapter has presented many broad issues that are often thought to be the domain of central administration, school site leaders play a critical role in the maintenance and operations of their respective schools. Importantly, site leaders set the tone that the built environment of the school, along with school grounds, is an essential component of academic success.

POINT–COUNTERPOINT

POINT

With research urging that school infrastructure plays a critical role in academic success, states have a responsibility to ensure that all children attend safe, clean, and modern schools. As such, states must take the lead role in funding school infrastructure to compensate for inequities in local fiscal capacity.

COUNTERPOINT

Since the beginning of the Common Schools Movement, construction and maintenance of school facilities have been a local responsibility. The tradition of local control was intended to allow school districts to decide for themselves the kinds of facilities they want. Because greater state funding always leads to more state control, states should not take a lead funding role in order to respect local autonomy.

- With which of these viewpoints are you most in agreement? Why?
- In your estimation, would your school district benefit from a larger or smaller state role in funding school infrastructure than is currently state law? How so, and why?

CASE STUDY

As the newly hired assistant principal at a relatively large high school of about 1,600 students, you were brimming with enthusiasm at the thought of working closely with colleagues, parents, and students. You were especially eager to impress the principal, who had already earned your esteem by informing you that she saw you as an equal partner in leading the school, even though this was your first formal administrative position. She had indicated she wanted you to become involved immediately and that one of your many responsibilities was oversight of the day-to-day operations of the school, including maintenance of the building and grounds. You knew this was an important role because you had already noticed the cleanliness and attractiveness of the school and because the principal had repeatedly emphasized that the appearance and condition of the building were symbolically important to staff, students, and community. She had also noted that this was accomplished on a very limited budget. The principal had then introduced you to the head custodian, who had been with the school 20 years. When the principal left the two of you to get acquainted, the head custodian's pleasant demeanor vanished. Wasting no time, he curtly told you that he obviously knew his job well and that he would not welcome any interference in his maintenance of the building and grounds. He also told you that your predecessor had been horribly disorganized and misguided and that under no circumstance were you to ever approve facility usage requests without first consulting him because he knows his job and he will not allow you to overburden his staff. You had thanked him for his candor and assured him that you wanted to work cooperatively, but inwardly you had an uneasy feeling.

At the initial all-school meeting, the principal introduced you to the faculty and mentioned that one of your responsibilities was ensuring the smooth daily operation of the school. She encouraged faculty and staff to come to you with any maintenance or repair issues. Literally minutes after the faculty meeting ended, you were deluged with an onslaught of requests. Your first complaint was from the head volleyball coach who stated that the gym floor was not properly refinished over the summer, resulting in slippery spots that create a hazard for players. As you finished that conversation, the head football coach was waiting to see you, complaining that maintenance staff had caused tire ruts by mowing a wet practice field. That conversation had barely ended when the athletic trainer demanded to see you, saying that a roof leak in her office had not been fixed over the summer and that papers on her desk were soaked. As you emerged from your office to physically check on these complaints, your administrative assistant whispered that a community member representing a local church group was waiting to see you in order to reserve the school cafeteria for a fall prayer banquet.

Below is a set of questions to consider as you try to resolve this dilemma:

- What are the issues confronting you, ranked by priority?
- What are the powers and possible restrictions on your authority?
- How will you address the head custodian's attitude and demands?
- What are the pitfalls facing you, and what are possible solutions—again ranked by priority?
- As you look toward the rest of the school year, how will you ensure the smooth day-to-day operations of the school?

PORTFOLIO EXERCISES

- Research how school infrastructure is financed in your state. This may include obtaining state department of education documents or examining relevant statutes. If your state uses an aid formula to assist debt service, determine the type of aid, the size of allocation, how districts qualify for aid, and the impact of the formula on your district. If your state does not provide aid to facilities, determine whether any surrounding states do.

- Interview your director of facility planning (or the central office administrator having this responsibility) to determine how current infrastructure projects are funded in your school district. Identify how much debt your district currently carries for school infrastructure, the nature of the debt, and the amortization schedule.

- Obtain a copy of your district's capital improvement plan. Interview your director of facility planning to determine how planning for school infrastructure occurs in your district. Ask how your district assesses its short, intermediate, and long-term needs. Determine the total cost of the CIP and its impact on local taxes.

- Interview the appropriate central office person regarding daily and scheduled maintenance and operations. Learn how these functions are organized at the district level and the amount and percentage of the school district's annual operating budget devoted to M&O. Ask about the role of site leaders, like principals, in school maintenance and operations.

- Does your school use green cleaning methods? If so, how do these compare to the recommendations in this chapter? If not, how could your school start to incorporate them?

NOTES

1 American Association of School Administrators (AASA), *Schoolhouse in the Red. A National Study of School Facilities and Energy Use* (Arlington, VA: AASA, 1991), 1.

2 World Bank. "Why Education Infrastructure Matters for Learning." Education for Global Development. Washington, DC, October 3, 2017. http://blogs.worldbank.org/education/why-education-infrastructure-matters-learning

3 American Society of Civil Engineers. "2017 Infrastructure Report Card." Reston, VA: ASCE (2017).

4 See, for example, Faith E. Crampton and David C. Thompson, "The Condition of America's Schools: A National Disgrace," *School Business Affairs* 68 (December 2002): 15–19. See also, Faith E. Crampton, David C. Thompson, and Janis M. Hagey, "Creating and Sustaining School Capacity in the Twenty-First Century: Funding a Physical Environment Conducive to Student Learning," *Journal of Education Finance* 27 (Fall 2001): 633–652; see also Faith E. Crampton and David C. Thompson, *School Infrastructure Funding Need: A State-by-State Assessment and an Analysis of Recent Court Cases* (Washington, DC:

American Federation of Teachers, 2008); and see also U.S. Government Accountability Office, *School Facilities: Condition of America's Schools* (Washington, DC, 1995).

5 AASA, *Schoolhouse in the Red,* 11.

6 William A. Alcott, "Essay on the Construction of School-Houses," August 1831, cited in David C. Thompson, Educational Facility Equity and Adequacy: A Report on Behalf of the Plaintiffs in *Roosevelt v. Bishop* (Manhattan, KS: Wood, Thompson & Associates, 1991), 1.

7 David C. Thompson, Educational Facility Equity and Adequacy: A Report on Behalf of the Plaintiffs in *Roosevelt v. Bishop* (Manhattan, KS: Wood, Thompson & Associates, 1991), 1. New action was being filed in late 2018, finding some same issues and expanding to next litigation phases as understandings mature and support systems change.

8 A partial listing of such organizations that publish standards includes the American Concrete Institute (ACI), American Institute of Architects (AIA), American Institute of Steel Construction (AISC), Architectural Woodwork Industry (AWI), American Welding Society Code (AWSC), National Building Code (NBC), National Electric Code (NEC), National Fire Protection Association (NFPA), National Illuminating Engineering Society (NIES), National Plumbing Code (NPC), Uniform Building Code (UBC), Underwriters Laboratories, Inc. (UL), American Association for Health, Physical Education, and Recreation (AAHPER), American Association of School Administrators (AASA), American Institute of Electrical Engineers (AIEE), Association of Physical Plant Administrators (APPA), Association of School Business Officials (ASBO), American Society of Mechanical Engineers (ASME), American Society for Testing and Materials (ASTM), Association for Learning Environments, (A4LE), National Board of Fire Underwriters (NBFU), and the National Bureau of Standards (NBS). In addition are state and local building and safety codes.

9 P.L. 94–142.

10 See, "Americans with Disabilities Act of 1990, as Amended," for the full text of the current law, U.S. Department of Justice, Civil Rights Division, www.ada.gov/pubs/adastatute08.htm.

11 See, for example, Jonathan Kozol, *Savage Inequalities: Children in America's Schools* (New York: Harper Perennial, 1992); Jonathan Kozol, *Shame of the Nation* (New York: Crown Publishers, 2005).

12 See, e.g., California Environmental Protection Agency, *Environmental Health Conditions in California's Portable Classrooms* (Sacramento: California Air Resources Board and California Department of Health Services, 2004), www.arb.ca.gov/research/indoor/pcs/leg_rpt/leg_rpt.htm; and, U.S. Environmental Protection Agency, "Portable Classrooms" (Washington, DC: IAQ Design Tools for Schools), www.epa.gov/iaq/schooldesign/portables.html.

13 See generally, Faith E. Crampton and David C. Thompson, Eds., *Saving America's School Infrastructure* (Greenwich, CT: Information Age Publishing, 2003). See, also, a special issue of the *Journal of Educational Administration* (Spring 2009) titled "Building High Quality Schools."

14 U.S. Government Accountability Office, *School Facilities: Condition of America's Schools*; and Laurie Lewis, Kyle Snow, Elizabeth Faris, Becky Smerdon, Stephanie Cronen, and Jessica Kaplan, *Condition of America's Public School Facilities: 1999* (Washington, DC: U.S. Department of Education, National Center for Education Statistics, June 2000).

15 Faith E. Crampton, David C. Thompson, and Janice M. Hagey, "Creating and Sustaining School Capacity in the Twenty-First Century: Funding a Physical Environment Conducive to Student Learning," *Journal of Education Finance* 27 (Fall 2001): 633–652.

16 American Society of Civil Engineers. "2017 Infrastructure Report Card." Reston, VA: ASCE (2017). See interactive map at https://www.infrastructurereportcard.org/infrastructure-super-map/

17 Faith E. Crampton and David C. Thompson (eds). *Saving America's School Infrastructure.* Volume Two in series, *Research in Education Fiscal Policy and Practice* (Greenwich, CT: IAP, 2003). See also Faith E. Crampton and David C. Thompson, *School Infrastructure Funding Need: A State-by-State Assessment and an Analysis of Recent Court Cases* (Washington, DC: American Federation of Teachers, 2008).

18 David C. Thompson and Faith E. Crampton, "An Overview and Analysis of Selected School Finance and School Facilities Litigation," *West's Education Law Reporter* 243, 2 (June 11, 2009): 507–545.

19 See, Crampton and Thompson, *School Infrastructure Funding Need*; Faith E. Crampton and David C. Thompson, "When the Legislative Process Fails: The Politics of Litigation in School Infrastructure Funding Equity," in *Money, Politics, and Law: Effects on Education Finance: Intersections and Conflicts in the Provision of Educational Opportunity*, Yearbook of the American Education Finance Association, edited by Karen DeMoss and Kenneth K. Wong (Larchmont, NY: New York: Eye On Education, 2004), 69–88. See also, David C. Thompson and Faith E. Crampton, "School Finance Litigation: A Strategy to Address Inequities in School Infrastructure Funding," in *Saving America's School Infrastructure*, edited by Faith E. Crampton and David C. Thompson (Greenwich, CT: Information Age Publishing, 2003), 163–190.

20 This section does not specifically address federal funding of school infrastructure, given its extremely limited role. The only recent federal support was through "tax credit bonds" which do not provide school districts with direct funding, but rather reduce the cost of borrowing. See, "Stimulus Funding and Tax Credit Bonds for School Construction" (Washington, DC: National Clearinghouse for Educational Facilities, 2011), www.ncef. org/school-modernization/chart.pdf. See, also, Cassandria Dortch, "School Construction and Renovation: A Review of Federal Programs" (Washington, DC: Congressional Research Service, December 2013), www.fas.org/sgp/crs/misc/R41142.pdf. The current administration failed to include any provision in the most recent State of the Union address for school facilities despite a presidential call for substantial funds to pay for "gleaming new roads, bridges, highways, railways, and waterways" (see Klein, Alyson, "Advocates Build Case for Federal School Construction Aid," *Education Week* (February 13, 2018), https://www.edweek.org/ew/articles/2018/02/14/advocates-build-case-for-federal-school-construction.html.

21 U.S. Department of Labor, "Child Labor Laws and Enforcement," *Report on the Youth Labor Force* (Washington, DC: Bureau of Labor Statistics, 2004), www.bls.gov/opub/rylf/rylfhome.htm.

22 *Roosevelt Elementary School District No. 66 v. Bishop*, 877 P.2d 806 (Ariz. 1994). New litigation pending in 2018.

23 U.S. Government Accounting Office, *School Facilities: Condition of America's Schools* (Washington, DC, 1995).

24 Center for Green Schools. *State of Our School*. (Washington, DC, 2016).

25 U.S. Department of Education, *Digest of Education Statistics*, "Summary of Expenditures for Public Elementary and Secondary Education and other Related Programs, by Purpose: Selected Years, 1919–20 through 2014–15," Table 236.10, https://nces.ed.gov/programs/digest/d17/tables/dt17_236.10.asp?current=yes

26 Many states do not permit the existence of sinking funds. Others statutorily enable such funds.

27 The discussion here is generalized, but practice is state-specific. The discussion accurately describes many states, but in others situations like the following may occur. For example, in some states, school districts are allowed to sell private instruments of debt, generically referred to as Holding Corporations, that are exempt from assessed valuation limitations of general obligation bonds. The private company advances the money to the school district, the building is completed, and the school district pays the private firm in a series of one-year payments so as to eliminate the long term bonded indebtedness

requirement (essentially lease-purchase). Dependent upon controlling statutes, these arrangements may be permitted along with a lengthy set of rules and regulations controlling such arrangements. State statutes also regulate which tax levies are utilized to pay for such arrangements.

28 State laws are highly specific: e.g., in this example, the allowable debt ceiling [ratio] for a district may be cumulative to $50 million (i.e., a district might be allowed only $50 million total for all projects at one time).

29 *Green* refers to methods and practices that reduce or avoid adverse environmental impacts. See, National Research Council, *Green Schools: Attributes for Health and Learning* (Washington, DC: Committee to Review and Assess the Health and Productivity Benefits of Green Schools, The National Academies Press, 2007).

30 U.S. Green Building Council, "The Next Step for LEED is LEED v4.1. (2018). https://new.usgbc.org/leed-v41.

31 Schedule payments must be made in accordance with federal rules and regulations governing tax exempt bonds.

32 Some school districts have proactive policies in place for use by school site leaders. Additional assessment tools are available—see, e.g., Tod Schneider, Hill Walker, and Jeffrey Sprague, *Safe School Design: A Handbook for Educational Leaders* (Eugene, OR: ERIC Clearinghouse on Educational Management, College of Education, University of Oregon, 2000), 40–41; and Jessie Shields Strickland and T. C. Chan, "Curbside Critique: A Technique to Maintain a Positive School Yard Image," *School Business Affairs* 68 (May 2002): 24–27.

33 Organizations, such as the Healthy Schools Campaign (www.healthyschoolscampaign.org) and Association for Learning Environments (https://www.a4le.org) offer suggestions to engage students in activities.
See, for example, U.S. Department of Energy, *EnergySmart Schools Tips: Retrofitting, Operating, and Maintaining Existing Buildings* (Washington, DC: Office of Energy Efficiency and Renewable Energy, Building Technologies Program), http://apps1.eere.energy.gov/buildings/publications/pdfs/energysmartschools/ess_quick-wins_fs.pdf.

34 Office of Energy Efficiency. "Renewable Energy." energy.gov. ◆https://www.energy.gov/eere/office-energy-efficiency-renewable-energy

35 See, for example, U.S. Department of Energy, *EnergySmart Schools Tips: Retrofitting, Operating, and Maintaining Existing Buildings* (Washington, DC: Office of Energy Efficiency and Renewable Energy, Building Technologies Program), http://apps1.eere.energy.gov/buildings/publications/pdfs/energysmartschools/ess_quick-wins_fs.pdf.

36 Healthy Schools Campaign, "The Quick + Easy Guide to Green Cleaning in Schools," http://greencleanschools.org/#num1.

WEB RESOURCES

Association for Learning Environments, https://www.a4le.org

Healthy Schools Campaign, www.healthyschoolscampaign.org

National Center for the Twenty-First Century Schoolhouse, edweb.sdsu.edu/schoolhouse

National Clearinghouse for Educational Facilities, www.ncef.org

The Center for Green Schools, www.centerforgreenschools.org

U.S. Department of Education, "Green Ribbon Schools," www2.ed.gov/programs/green-ribbon-schools/index.html

U.S. Environmental Protection Agency, "Creating Healthy Indoor Environments in Schools," www.epa.gov/iaq/schools

U.S. Environmental Protection Agency, "Healthy School Environments," www.epa.gov/schools

INTERACTIVE WEB RESOURCE

American Society of Civil Engineers, "School Infrastructure Funding Needs by State," https:// www.infrastructurereportcard.org/state-by-state-infrastructure/

RECOMMENDED RESOURCES

Bello, Mustapha A. and Vivian Loftness. "Addressing Inadequate Investment in School Facility Maintenance." School of Architecture Paper 50. Pittsburgh, PA: Carnegie Mellon University Research Showcase (2010).

Bowers, Alex J. and Angela Urick. "Does High School Facility Quality Affect Student Achievement?: A Two-Level Hierarchical Linear Model." *Journal of Education Finance* 37, 1 (Summer 2011): 72–94.

Bowers, Alex J. and Jingjing Chen. "Ask and Ye Shall Receive?: Automated Text Mining of Michigan Capital Facility Finance Bond Election Proposals to Identify which Topics are Associated with Bond Passage and Voter Turnout." *Journal of Education Finance* 41, 2 (Fall 2015): 164–196.

Bowers, Alex J., Scott Alan Metzger, and Matthew Militello. "Knowing What Matters: An Expanded Study of School Bond Elections in Michigan, 1998–2006." *Journal of Education Finance* 35, 4 (Spring 2010): 374–396.

Core, Brandon H. and Mario S. Torres Jr. "The Uncertainty of Policy Ambition: An Analysis of Key State Actor Perspectives on Seeking Equity Through Facilities Funding." *Journal of Education Finance* 41, 4 (Spring 2016): 419–437.

Council of Educational Planners International. *Safe Schools: A Best Practices Guide.* Washington, DC: Spring 2013. http://media.cefpi.org/SafeSchoolsGuide.pdf.

Crampton, Faith E. and David C. Thompson, Eds. *Saving America's School Infrastructure.* Volume II in the series "Research in Education Fiscal Policy and Practice: Local, National, and Global Perspectives." Greenwich, CT: Information Age Publishing, 2003.

DeAngelis, Karen J., Brian O. Brent, and Danielle Ianni. "The Hidden Cost of School Security." *Journal of School Finance* 36, 3 (Winter 2011): 312–337.

Earthman, Glen L. *Planning Educational Facilities: What Educators Need to Know,* third ed. Lanham, MD: Rowman & Littlefield, 2009.

Healthy Schools Campaign. "The Quick + Easy Guide to Green Cleaning in Schools." http:// greencleanschools.org/#num1.

Ingle, W. Kyle, Alex J. Bowers, and Thomas E. Davis. "Which School Districts Qualified for Federal School Facility Funding under the American Recovery and Reinvestment Act of 2009?: Evidence from Ohio." *Journal of Education Finance* 40, 1 (Summer 2014): 17–37.

Kozol, Jonathan. *Savage Inequalities: Children in America's Schools.* New York: Harper Perennial, 1992.

National Clearinghouse for Educational Facilities. "Mitigating Hazards in School Facilities." Washington, DC (2008). www.ncef.org/pubs/mitigating_hazards.pdf.

National Research Council. *Green Schools: Attributes for Health and Learning.* Committee to Review and Assess the Health and Productivity Benefits of Green Schools. Washington, DC: National Academies Press, 2007.

Thompson, David C. and Faith E. Crampton. "An Overview and Analysis of Selected School Finance and School Facilities Litigation." *Education Law Reporter* 243, 2 (June 11, 2009): 507–545.

U.S. Department of Education. *Planning Guide for Maintaining School Facilities* (Washington, DC: School Facilities Maintenance Task Force, National Center for Education Statistics, 2003), http://nces.ed.gov/pubs2003/2003347.pdf.

U.S. Department of Energy. *EnergySmart Schools Tips: Retrofitting, Operating, and Maintaining Existing Buildings*. Washington, DC: Office of Energy Efficiency and Renewable Energy, Building Technologies Program, http://apps1.eere.energy.gov/buildings/publications/pdfs/energysmartschools/ess_quick-wins_fs.pdf.

Vincent, Jeffrey M. and Paavo Monkkonen. "The Impact of State Regulations on the Costs of Public School Construction." *Journal of Education Finance* 35, 4 (Spring 2010): 313–330.

CHAPTER 10

Budgeting for Transportation and Food Service

CHAPTER DRIVERS

Please reflect on the following questions as you read this chapter:

- What is the definition, role, and scope of auxiliary services?
- What are the origins, purposes, and scope of school transportation systems?
- How is school transportation funded?
- How does the law relate to school transportation funding?
- What other school transportation issues are relevant to budgeting?
- What are the origins and purposes of food service systems?
- How is food service funded?
- What other food service issues are relevant to budgeting?

SETTING THE STAGE

No study of how public schools are funded is complete without examining the area of auxiliary or support services. The goal is twofold. First, there is a tendency by society to see the work of schools as almost exclusively instructional, which can lead to other areas of school district operations being undervalued when, in fact, they should be prized for their role in serving equal educational opportunity. Second, a book examining the many aspects of schools and money would be flawed if it ignored transportation and food service because schools would be badly damaged absent these key operations. In sum, every child has an equal right to a full educational opportunity and should be able to get to and from school without hardship and attend classes free from hunger. Equal opportunity is mocked when schools are physically inaccessible or when children are underfed.

The discussion opens by defining the role and scope of auxiliary services. Interest then turns to the origins and purposes of pupil transportation systems, along with review of the intersection of law with the transportation function. The section ends with an overview of how transportation is funded in the 50 states, along with consideration of other issues such as bus purchasing, bus maintenance, and bus safety.

Discussion next turns to food service systems, examining the issues and funding methods used throughout the nation. Of importance to the discussion is consideration for the organization and fiscal management of food services, inasmuch as food service (unlike most district operations) is typically designed as a revenue-neutral enterprise, i.e., self-supporting and subject to federal regulation. In brief, this chapter considers a key element of children's educational experience through exploration and appreciation for the contribution of auxiliary services to the teaching and learning mission.

The Role of Auxiliary Services

Although auxiliary services can be more broadly defined,[1] the term here refers to selected noninstructional support services, usually funded under segregated fund accounting systems. This definition typically limits auxiliary services to the areas of pupil transportation and school food services. These two auxiliary operations are complex regardless of school district size. For example, urban districts may use a large fleet of buses to transport thousands of pupils over relatively short distances, while rural districts with much smaller enrollments often operate many buses to transport much longer distances in sparsely populated areas. Regardless of enrollment or geography, school districts face similar types of operating costs: Staffing, bus safety, vehicle maintenance and replacement, and liability insurance. Similarly, food services often must employ a range of staff to plan and operate a program that includes breakfast, lunch, afterschool snacks, and summer meal programs; free and reduced-price meals for low income children; commodity support programs that lower the cost of meals and bolster agricultural markets; federal and state subsidies; and extensive federal oversight and regulation. Given the scope and cost of pupil transportation and food services, with annual expenditures of $24.3 billion and $23.0 billion respectively in 2015,[2] it is clear that each of these represents a major cost center for schools. Thus, the role of auxiliary services is substantial and demands efficient organization and close management because these essential noninstructional support services contribute greatly to the educational mission of schools.

THE TRANSPORTATION FUNCTION

Pupil transportation is one of the most visible services provided by school systems. Bright yellow school buses arrive in front of the homes of more than 25 million schoolchildren in the United States each morning, and the bus is often the last school contact of the day. The transportation function is even larger, however, ferrying students on field trips and to athletic and academic events, so that transportation is a huge cost factor in most district budgets. In addition, schools as a whole are viewed more favorably by parents and the public when the transportation function operates smoothly. When buses are late or a child is dropped off at the wrong location, everything about schools can become suspect in the community's eyes. As a consequence, transportation is one of the most critical noninstructional activities of any school system.

What are the Origins, Purpose, and Scope?

Widespread transporting of pupils to and from school largely developed as a result of school district consolidation dating from the early twentieth century. Although assumed to have arisen solely as a result of the invention of motor vehicles, school transportation and state financial support actually have been in existence since 1869 when Massachusetts became the first state to expend public funds for pupil transportation. While the Massachusetts law was the first of its kind, pupil transportation grew rapidly with the enactment of compulsory attendance laws and school and district consolidation, as well as through the advent of automobiles. School district consolidation alone led to major changes in the role of transportation, with the number of districts decreasing dramatically from 117,108 in 1940 to 13,584 in 2016.[3]

Unlike some aspects of fiscal support for schools, from the earliest days U.S. taxpayers have been willing to spend for transporting children. Support was likely due to a common recognition that what individuals could do only poorly could be done far more efficiently by an entire community. Early on, a spurring factor was geographic isolation in a largely agricultural nation, a demographic that has greatly changed over time. The size and scope of pupil transportation has also been affected by federal laws, such as the 1975 enactment of P.L. 94–142, *The Education of All Handicapped Children Act*, a landmark law that mandated equal opportunity for special education pupils, including not only instructional programs but also transportation. Additional court rulings following after *Brown v. Board of Education*, and the passage of the Civil Rights Act of 1964 mandated busing to achieve racial integration.[4] More recently, year-round schools, charter schools, private schools, and intradistrict and interdistrict school choice have enlarged the scope and cost of pupil transportation services. As a result of the sheer magnitude of transportation systems along with regulation for safety, dramatic fluctuations in fuel prices, environmental concerns and alternative *green* fuels,[5] and rising insurance costs for operation and liability, the transportation function has experienced enormous changes in size, complexity, and importance since its humble origins.

While the purpose of pupil transportation is simple, its application is complex. No child has equal educational opportunity if schooling is inaccessible due to lack of transportation, and states and local districts have long worked to make schools available to those who live beyond reasonable walking distance. Providing such service has evolved into a multibillion-dollar industry ranging from employment of bus drivers to purchasing insurance against a set of myriad risks. These costs are affected by issues of efficiency and accountability—concepts that are themselves made more complicated by competing public goals. For example, parents often have one set of expectations for a transportation system, while the state and school district might operate from a different perspective. Similarly, pupil transportation may require new facilities, and shifts of populations in a community may create new transportation demands. Additionally, each state, as well as each school district, has unique needs that may impact transportation system designs. For instance, no two states or school districts are identical on variables such as population density, number of pupils to be transported, topography, climate, road conditions, and length of routes—factors which affect the number and size of buses placed on routes. To make such matters even more challenging, there are many other decisions that fall to the local level, such as whether a district should operate its own bus system or outsource the transportation function to a for-profit company. Local decisions are also affected by the design and funding of state aid formulas.

Because the design, operation, and implementation of a transportation system is so complex, districts often devote a salary line to a transportation director who is charged with setting and implementing bus management policies; developing and administering the transportation budget; recruiting, screening, and hiring staff; providing staff training programs; and coordinating maintenance services. Also, the transportation director has responsibility for planning bus routes for regular and special education students as well as cocurricular activities and field trips.

The director of transportation services must have a range of talents and skills. The relevant knowledge base includes the ability to efficiently organize a transportation fleet, effective human relations skills in working through human resource problems, and the ability to maintain positive relations with parents and the community. Additionally, the transportation director must be skilled in decision-making in order to lead people and manage problems effectively. The director must have expertise in technology-assisted route development, route-planning software, budgeting and labor laws, as well as competence related to legal requirements such as employee drug testing and handling of hazardous materials. Because of potential liability involved in all aspects of the transportation function, the director must demand strict accountability because that office, in cooperation with administrative supervisors, is ultimately responsible for all school vehicle issues.

Although many people are involved in carrying out the total transportation function, the transportation director is the first-line person responsible for overseeing operations and ensuring district transportation goals are met. These goals and accompanying policies, procedures, and responsibilities should be placed into a comprehensive manual that is written in a style accessible to a layperson. All transportation regulations, as well as employee evaluation policies, should be included. Recruitment plans, job descriptions, training information, and requirements for each job should be included, with special emphasis on bus safety, driver training, pupil discipline, energy conservation, accessibility issues, public relations, bus routes, and bus schedules. School districts should also place relevant information on their websites for staff, parents, and the community. While these elaborate procedures and responsibilities seem only distantly akin to the origins of transporting children at taxpayer expense, the basic purpose has not changed; that is, making education available to every child on an equal basis still remains the first goal.

What is Transportation Law?

While all transportation issues are complex, none are more serious than the area of transportation law. Many court cases have focused on liability in transporting students, and a large body of case law has centered on the issue of authorization to provide transportation at public expense.[6] Several cases have addressed the use of public funds to transport private school students,[7] and other cases have addressed who can be transported,[8] as well as whether districts have authority to deny transportation.[9] Of course, transportation for desegregation has been heavily litigated and continues to be of court interest.[10] While it is not the purpose of a school finance textbook to deeply review the law's relationship to school transportation, a brief overview underscores its potential impact on the budget process.

Access to education via transportation services has been the focus of lawsuits at the U.S. Supreme Court level on many occasions. In a case seemingly unrelated to transportation, the U.S. Supreme Court ruled in *Cochran v. Louisiana State Board of Education*[11] in 1930 that public funds could be used to buy textbooks for children attending private schools because it applied a test that became known as the child-benefit theory. According to *Cochran*, courts could relax the church–state entanglement prohibition in the U.S. Constitution by deciding whether the child is the prime beneficiary of a public expenditure involving private schools.[12] If children received the benefit, the Court reasoned, the expenditure would not violate separation of church and state if other care was taken. *Cochran* became the basis for a 1947 ruling affecting transportation in *Everson v. Board of Education*[13] when the Court ruled that reimbursing bus fare to parochial and private school children was permissible in that public and private interests were not crossed with the establishment of religion by applying the child-benefit theory to busing. The Court observed that transportation is like police, fire, and other protections available to churches and other private organizations, saying that to deny a benefit would make the state an adversary of the church. Yet, despite the Court's long-ago rulings in *Cochran* and *Everson*, issues of commingling public funds with private and religious interests have returned many times for further judicial rulings.[14]

The arena of transportation law has continued to be unsettled, as illustrated by an oft-cited case involving questions of violating equal opportunity when children must pay bus fees to get to school. This issue was taken by the U.S. Supreme Court in *Kadrmas v. Dickinson Public Schools*.[15] Underlying the dispute was an attempt by the state of North Dakota to encourage school consolidation, which included financial incentives for districts that chose to participate. A school district chose not to consolidate and simultaneously decided to begin charging fees for bus service. Plaintiff parents brought suit, claiming violation of a constitutional right to a free public education. The Supreme Court ruled for the defendant state, holding that the fee was rational and that equal protection was unharmed. The Court held that the state's financial problems were a rational basis for instituting fees, that transportation services need not be provided, and that purely economic legislation must be upheld unless it is patently arbitrary. The Court left several issues unsettled, however, such as whether education is a Constitutional right, but it settled that schools may charge user fees generally.

In an unfolding world, the right to a free public education presently includes allowing charges for transportation—a practice permitted in some states despite protests by state court litigants who assert that transportation is part of a free system of public schools.[16]

A large body of other transportation litigation also financially impacts schools, particularly since transportation is an activity fraught with potential liability. Although pupil transportation is generally very safe, bus-related accidents and injuries do occur. The risk element is heightened for school districts because they serve as a common carrier and consequently have the utmost duty to ensure child safety. Liability is controlled by various state tort concepts and is further affected by individual states' statutes regarding pupil transportation. As will be discussed later in greater detail in Chapter 11, liability claims often arise when a district or employee is charged with negligence. To establish negligence, someone must have been injured, and it must be shown that a reasonable person similarly situated could have foreseen and prevented the injury. When school employees control and operate the transportation function, opportunity is ripe for an injured party to charge negligence and bring a liability claim against school district resources. For example, the transportation director is usually the person who sets bus stops—if an accident occurs at such a location, liability may arise if hazards were ignored.

Although exhaustive legal analysis is well beyond the scope of this chapter, it is important to emphasize that liability suits raising transportation claims have had varying results. For example, in *Vogt v. Johnson*[17] a seven-year-old child waiting for a school bus at the designated stop tried to cross the highway and was killed. The Minnesota Supreme Court ruled that the bus driver, acting as agent of the district, was not liable at the time of the accident because custodial responsibility for the child had not yet arisen and because no amount of precaution on the part of the district would have prevented the accident. Significantly, while some cases have upheld this logic, there have been other cases to the contrary, as in the Oklahoma decision in *Brooks v. Woods*[18] which stands in sharp contrast. In *Brooks*, the district was held negligent due to the location of a school bus stop and the subsequent resulting injury to a child. The bus stop had been established adjacent to a five-lane highway with a 45-mile-per-hour speed limit, and the scheduled arrival of the bus fell directly within rush hour traffic. While waiting for the bus, a child was hurt. Key to the ruling was that the child was known by the school to have physical and cognitive disabilities. The appeals court ruled that the district's duty to exercise responsible care extends to any activity of bus transportation that rests outside the control of parents.

No exhaustive set of guidelines can be created for every situation a school district and its employees may face. However, in a negligence case the defendant must show that actions were those of a reasonable and prudent person under the circumstances. A few more cases illustrate how such liability may turn. In *Mitchell*,[19] a North Carolina school district was held liable when a child fell on an icy sidewalk and was crushed under the bus wheels. Testimony revealed that the bus was not in its usual loading spot and that adequate supervision was lacking. In the New York case of *Cross*,[20] a bus left the road after failing to negotiate a curve. Testimony revealed that the driver had said he was sleepy and had asked students to talk to him. In addition, he was seen rubbing his eyes and yawning. Other transportation liability cases also exist involving violence, drugs, and unruly activity. Questions of governmental immunity under individual states' laws may apply, as in the Texas case of *King*[21] where a girl was struck by a car as she crossed the road after being dropped at a school bus stop. According to the bus driver, the girl and her friends routinely walked along the drop-point side of the road for some distance after exiting the bus, and consequently the driver regularly left the location rather than waiting several minutes for the girls to eventually cross the road. The court held for the defendant school district, ruling that since several minutes had lapsed between the time of bus stop departure and the time of accident that the state's statutory immunity against tort claims applied; and that any waiver of immunity would have required conditions similar to those in a sister case of *Hitchcock*[22] where the state's immunity was waived given that the child was struck immediately upon exiting the school bus.

Because the specifics of each case, requirements of individual state law, and applicability of standard of care based on the age of the child are controlling, exhaustive discussion is not feasible. What matters is that school districts can be held negligent in the arena of pupil transportation. In such cases, evidence has shown that the potential for injury was foreseeable and that actions by the board or its agent did not meet a minimum standard of care. As will be seen in Chapter 11, failure to protect children may be the causal factor leading to injury, and districts and school staffs may be held liable. Under these conditions, the transportation function and the law are ever-constant companions.

How is Transportation Funded?

Growth in school transportation systems in the United States since the beginning of the twentieth century has led to vast increases in the number of children carried in school vehicles at public expense. Costs are high and made even higher by transportation for cocurricular activities and field trips.

Table 10.1 reveals that most states provide some form of aid to local school districts for pupil transportation purposes. Like other forms of state aid, transportation aid varies widely in amount and distribution method. Many states use some type of reimbursement formula, be it equalized, capped (allowable), or full reimbursement. Likewise, many states include transportation aid as a component of their general aid formula, while other states create categorical funding schemes. Nearly all states base transportation aid on pupil ridership, and rural states tend to take pupil geographic density into consideration. Almost all states require local districts to share in transportation costs—i.e., only two states purport to provide 100% transportation aid, although in some instances the 90% level is either realized or available based on some set of calculated variables. But regardless of transportation formula simplicity or complexity, every state's aid formula and funding are outcomes of the legislative process. Part of every state's legislative determination is driven by the constituent profiles each legislator represents, and other parts are driven by resource availability.

The large sums of money involved in pupil transportation systems invariably result in high levels of state scrutiny. A significant part of watchfulness is carried out through the accounting side of school finance, more particularly through state audits.

TABLE 10.1 State Transportation Aid Formulas: 2018

State	Aid Provision	State	Aid Provision
Alabama	Aid to salaries, fuel, non-salary costs and bus purchases	Montana	State/county share in schedule costs
Alaska	Per-child cost reimbursement grant program	Nebraska	Formula calculating actual costs and route miles
Arizona	Per-mile state aid formula	Nevada	Formula determining per pupil costs compared to state average
Arkansas	Isolated school districts	New Hampshire	Not applicable
California	0% to 60% reimbursement formula	New Jersey	Formula aid based on distance from school
Colorado	Per-mile rate adjusted to maximum 90% reimbursement	New Mexico	100% aid based on diversified factors
Connecticut	Not applicable	New York	6.5% to 90% reimbursement formula
Delaware	90% aid	North Carolina	State funds fuel, mechanics, driver salaries and bus equipment based on efficiency and replacement schedules
Florida	Formula based on pro-rata cost share between state and district	North Dakota	Up to 90% reimbursement of actual expenditures using a rate schedule
Georgia	Aid based on standard costs and variable cost schedule	Ohio	Integral to general aid formula
Hawaii	Legislative appropriation	Oklahoma	General aid formula supplement based on factors
Idaho	85% state aid	Oregon	70% to 90% of approved costs paid through general aid formula
Illinois	80% of reimbursable costs	Pennsylvania	Reimbursement at same aid ratio as general fund
Indiana	Not applicable	Rhode Island	Categorical aid taking into account certain excess costs
Iowa	Integral to general aid formula	South Carolina	State funds and monitors entire transportation system
Kansas	State average transportation cost as determined by a linear density formula.	South Dakota	Integral to general aid formula
Kentucky	State average transportation cost calculation	Tennessee	Integral to general aid formula

(Continued)

TABLE 10.1 Continued

State	Aid Provision	State	Aid Provision
Louisiana	Integral to general aid formula	Texas	Formula aid based in transportation system costs with linear density factor
Maine	Formula accounting for pupil density and miles traveled	Utah	Formula based on allowances per mile and per minute
Maryland	Categorical grant	Vermont	Approximately 44.3% reimbursement of district cost
Massachusetts	Annual appropriation, recently 73.4% of calculated costs	Virginia	Calculation of per-pupil costs tied to geographical density and district size
Michigan	Integral to general aid formula	Washington	Formula regressing expected costs on district characteristics
Minnesota	Integral to general aid formula	West Virginia	Formula tied to pupil density
Mississippi	Determined by average daily attendance and density	Wisconsin	Formula based on miles traveled per pupil
Missouri	Up to 75% reimbursement of allowable costs subject to appropriation and efficiency factor	Wyoming	100% state cost

Interpreted from Verstegen, Deborah. A Quick Glance at School Finance: A 50 State Survey of School Finance Policies and Programs 2018. Word Press. https://schoolfinancesdav.files.wordpress.com/2018/09/transportation.pdf

Typically the amount of state transportation aid a school district receives is based on audited records, making aid qualification an outcome of careful and thorough local recordkeeping. Since most states regularly audit school districts for transportation overpayment, districts do not want to shortchange themselves by lax recordkeeping that undercounts the number of pupils transported or the actual number of miles traveled on bus routes. Such auditable records generally include the following:

- Area maps and bus route information;
- Address and destination of pupils claimed for aid;
- List of pupils using more than one type of service (e.g., vocational or special education);
- List of nonpublic school and school choice children transported, if claimed;
- Evidence of bus seating capacity for each child claimed;
- Evidence of bridge or road condemnation or construction if the most direct route from home to school is inaccessible;
- Evidence of mileage driven on all routes by all buses;
- Basis and work paper showing calculation for pro-rated costs;
- Summary and original documents for all pupil transportation for regular routes, special and vocational education, and other eligible transportation;

- Claims for payments in lieu of pupil transportation showing dates, mileage, rates, and total payments;
- Evidence of insurance costs for vehicles;
- Evidence of price of buses and depreciation history;
- List of leased or lease-purchase buses, and dates of lease.

It is also important to note that state laws differ regarding transportation for private school students as well as for students attending charter and voucher schools, in addition to intradistrict and interdistrict school choice programs, sometimes referred to as open enrollment.

Clearly, without accurate records reimbursement problems will arise. Problems range from denial of state aid to liability for negligence, malfeasance, or even fraud if questions about fiscal impropriety are raised. In addition, the state may withhold aid until sufficient documentation is provided or demand reimbursement for aid improperly paid to the district.

What Other Issues are Relevant?

Several other important transportation considerations must be addressed before leaving the topic. These are: Owning vs. outsourcing; the use of technology in transportation operations; elements of bus purchasing; and planning for maintenance and safety.

Owning vs. Outsourcing

With school district budgets increasingly constrained, outsourcing of transportation services may appear to be an attractive approach to controlling costs. The National School Boards Association in 2018[23] cited data suggesting that 34.7% of school transportation services were contracted out. Still, the benefits and disadvantages of district ownership of the transportation fleet vs. outsourcing deserve careful consideration. First, there may be logic to outsourcing bus services for districts with cash flow problems because outsourcing avoids the substantial upfront investment usually required to purchase a bus fleet, along with costs for ongoing maintenance and periodic equipment replacement. At a base cost around $100,000 for a typical 71-passenger school bus,[24] purchasing an entire bus fleet is a major upfront investment for any school district—as would be the regularly scheduled replacement of several buses. Furthermore, state transportation aid may not cover bus purchases, placing the entire financial burden on local taxpayers. Second, labor is a major cost component of pupil transportation, ranging from bus drivers and mechanics to administrative staff. Here school districts may save money by outsourcing if the contractor pays lower wages and provides fewer benefits to its employees than the district might be required to provide for inhouse staff. Third, and particularly for smaller districts, an outside contractor whose sole business is pupil transportation may, through greater experience and volume, be more efficient and hence offer the same service at a lower cost than the district can provide for itself.

Counterarguments include school district and community concerns about how to maintain ongoing, quality service by a private contractor in order to ensure the safety of children and avoid public relations debacles, e.g., a bus accident caused by an unqualified driver that results in student injury. Second, districts lose the ability to screen potential transportation employees, not only for driving records, but also for prior convictions for crimes against children. Finally, a private contractor may not be as flexible or cost-effective when it comes to one-time or infrequent transportation needs, such as field trips or afterschool activities. At the same time, districts are not entirely relieved of liability issues associated with pupil transportation when they outsource, and so they still need to maintain adequate liability insurance. All of these issues underscore the need for careful legal and financial analysis as part of the decision process when a district is considering outsourcing transportation services.

A final note of caution is in order. If outsourcing is chosen, school districts need to engage professional legal advice on many levels, such as specifying that the contractor is an independent agent and will comply with all relevant federal and state statutes, rules, and regulations along with district transportation policies and procedures. Also, the contractor must provide proof of appropriate insurance for property damage and bodily and personal injury, even though the district is well-advised to continue to carry liability insurance.

Technology and Transportation Services

As technology has advanced and become more affordable, most school districts, even smaller ones, have embraced technology-assisted route development and route-planning software. These time-saving technology tools maximize routing efficiency primarily by finding the shortest bus routes. For most districts, these systems significantly reduce labor, maintenance, and fuel costs.[25] Programs can include vehicle tracking so that individual buses can be monitored in real time, ensuring that drivers follow prescribed routes. When two-way communication is added, a driver in distress can immediately contact a supervisor for assistance, e.g., in the event that a bus breaks down. In turn, school district officials know the location of every bus, aiding in accountability and assistance. Although this feature may not necessarily improve efficiency, it significantly enhances safety for both driver and passengers.

In addition to efficient routing, technology can facilitate the creation of fleet maintenance databases. Software programs incorporate garage operations, vehicle replacement, mechanical repair and maintenance, and fuel consumption records into databases that can be manipulated to analyze cost efficiencies such as costs for preventive maintenance and repairs. Additionally, the number and type of repairs for each vehicle, age and condition, operating cost per mile, and cost per individual vehicle repair can be tracked and analyzed. Item and total costs are accounted for and used to inform decisions about continued maintenance or disposal. For example, a district might find that maintenance costs for a particular bus were $1,500 in the first year compared to $7,000 in its fifth year of operation. This information can be joined with other costs, such as labor and vehicle down-time, to determine the most cost-efficient juncture for replacing vehicles. In addition, these types of databases often facilitate the generation of state-mandated transportation reports. The benefit is sizable, in that records can be quickly gathered, formatted, and analyzed, saving many staff hours compared to manual data gathering and calculation.

Purchasing Buses

The earlier discussion about owning, outsourcing, and using cost–benefit analysis is particularly relevant regarding bus purchases. As noted, the price of a typical full size (71-person capacity) school bus starts at $100,000, making this is very a big ticket purchase for any school district. Costs grow by thousands of dollars for each of the following options: A wheelchair lift, seatbelts, or air-conditioning.[26] The district also may need to purchase smaller customized buses to supplement its fleet. The planning and execution of such large expenditures requires care and attention to detail to avoid even more problems at vehicle delivery time that could arise from failure to write thorough and detailed bid specifications or from failure to follow state-specific purchasing laws.

Choice of fuel also affects the initial purchase price of buses. Although countless school buses continue to use gasoline and diesel fuels, many districts are investing in alternative fuels to save money and the environment.[27] Among these are biodiesel, compressed natural gas, and propane. Significant development is also occurring around hybrid and electric buses as the industry and the economy turns *green*.

Bus purchases in most states are handled at the school district level, using state competitive bidding specifications to detail the desired vehicle features. The central purpose of competitive bidding is to secure the lowest price for a bus that meets a detailed set of specifications, often referred to as the lowest reasonable or responsible bid. Competitive bidding also provides a level playing field in that the purchaser, be it state or school district, cannot give a particular vendor an insider advantage. As a rule, most states' bid laws set a threshold purchase price, e.g., $20,000, above which competitive bids must be sought. These laws are usually very specific in regard to how the notice of bids must be published; how bids will be opened; how the lowest responsible bid will be decided; and how errors in bids will be handled. Such laws build accountability and efficiency safeguards into purchases involving large amounts of taxpayer money. In a few states, bus purchases are centralized so that a state agency prepares the bid specifications, awards the bids, and provides buses to districts. This is atypical, however, meaning that experienced school district personnel, usually in the district's business office, are required.

Finally, a few words are needed about the options of leasing or lease-purchase. Although long-term leasing of school buses is less common than purchasing new or even used units, some districts may find it fiscally advantageous. However, there may be state laws and regulations that pertain to leasing and lease-purchase, and these may again include competitive bidding of the contract. Here too districts need to perform careful cost–benefit analyses before making a final decision and should seek legal counsel related to leasing and lease-purchase contracts.

Safety and Maintenance

The importance of competitive bidding laws, rising bus costs, energy efficiency, concern for the environment, and liability issues has increased the amount of time school districts must devote to issues of safety and maintenance of school vehicles. Parents are concerned that the buses their children ride are safe, even though according to the National Highway Traffic and Safety Administration (NHTSA) school buses are exceptionally safe when compared to other motor vehicles in terms of accident, injury, and fatalities. Federal law, primarily through the NHTSA, aggressively mandates certain safety features for school buses. Based on NHTSA regulations that took effect in 1977, school buses are now designed to protect passengers from injury during a crash by compartmentalization which consists of strong, closely spaced seats with energy-absorbing seatbacks. NHTSA requirements for lap/shoulder belts, also referred to as three-point lap/shoulder occupant restraint systems, are gaining increasing favor along with other newer safety measures going beyond simple seat security and restraint.[28] But while safe equipment is an essential aspect of a good transportation system, it must be underscored that vehicle maintenance and ongoing staff training are critical to any aspect of funding pupil transportation services. Obviously, good drivers cannot offset bad buses, nor can new equipment offset bad drivers. Consequently, it bears repeating that issues of liability underscore the connection between safety, maintenance, and personnel so that maintenance and training become critical to saving lives and prolonging equipment life. Safety requires drivers to ascertain that loading and unloading zones are free from moving traffic and that children have adequate time to cross streets. Bus safety information must be distributed to parents and community members, preferably using several types of media. Maintenance includes drivers' daily vehicle inspections, including walk-arounds to detect fluid leaks, tire problems, and faulty lights, flashers, or stop arms. The transportation director must establish a regular maintenance schedule that includes routine maintenance like oil changes and brake inspections, as well as maintenance to ensure safety and equipment life. Bluntly put, good maintenance saves lives and money by reducing accidents due to faulty equipment and by extending the working life of buses—but obviously, all these precautions come at a cost, making transportation a significant demand on the budget.

THE FOOD SERVICE FUNCTION

Like transportation, food service plays a vital role in effective and efficient operation of schools by providing an enveloping support system for the instructional program. It takes knowledge and skill to successfully plan and operate a system that meets the nutritional needs of children, and—as stated at the outset of this chapter—it is nonsense to argue for equal educational opportunity if children come to school hungry. As a result, a brief review of the food service function is needed in order to understand how it operates, how meal prices are set under federal, state, and local participation, and how revenues and expenditures in food service budgets are balanced.

What are the General Issues?

The importance of school food service cannot be overemphasized because the role of nutrition in academic success is fundamental. Data from earlier sections of this book suggest that schools face tremendous challenges, often beginning in the home, that serve as formidable barriers to effective teaching and learning. Most striking among those barriers is evidence that poverty affects a large percentage of schoolchildren today in highly predictable ways. The data in 2018 indicated that 13 million (one in six) children suffer food insecurity. Hunger among children is universal to all 50 states, with 85% of U.S. rural counties experiencing food insecurity. Fully 800,000 food-insecure children live in Los Angeles and New York City alone.[29] These type of data, along with research linking improved academic performance to nutrition, have long sparked interest at federal, state, and local levels. Indeed, the debate over the appropriate role for government has raged for decades, with the federal government supporting health and nutrition in various ways ranging from cash aid to surplus commodity distributions. The role of food services in schools has increased substantially over time, with many schools now serving both breakfast and lunch, in large part because so many children are undernourished. Today there is little argument that while food service cannot solve all the challenges facing public education, it can be a positive force by making school a better learning environment for children.

How is Food Service Funded?

Food service programs in schools have a long history of federal, state, and local support, with the federal government playing a dominant role.[30] All these sources make up the revenue side of food service operations.

Federal Support

Federal support for school food services grew out of the dire economic straits of the Great Depression in the 1930s when farmers were receiving very low prices for crops, if they could sell them at all. As a result, surplus food commodities grew while masses of the unemployed and their families went unfed. In 1935, the federal government intervened, passing the *Agricultural Adjustment Act*,[31] a law that not only assisted farmers, but also authorized the U.S. Department of Agriculture (USDA) to distribute surplus food to public and nonprofit schools. At the same time, as part of the New Deal federal legislation addressing unemployment, the Works Project Administration (WPA) provided jobs for the unemployed on public works projects, including school lunch programs. By 1941, WPA school lunch programs were operating in every state as well as Washington, DC and Puerto Rico.

In 1946, the *National School Lunch Act*[32] expanded the federal government's role in school food services through the distribution of grants to states for food, as well as facilities and kitchen equipment for nonprofit school lunch programs. A few years later, in 1954 Congress passed the *School Milk Program Act*,[33] providing federal funds to schools to buy milk as part of food services. In 1966, federal support expanded beyond school lunch via the School Breakfast Program which began as a two-year federal pilot project targeted to nutritionally needy pupils as authorized in the *Child Nutrition Act*.[34] The school breakfast program was subsequently written into federal law in 1975 through amendments[35] to the *Child Nutrition Act.* Less well known was the federal Summer Food Service Program which was created in 1968 as a three-year pilot to provide meals to low income students over the summer when school was not in session.[36] It was later expanded and formalized through several pieces of federal legislation to its present format. The *Child Nutrition Reauthorization Act*[37] of 1998 expanded the National School Lunch Program to include snacks to students involved in certain after-school activities.

The twenty-first century has seen a greater focus on healthy, nutritional food choices for children in the nation. As part of that movement, the Fresh Fruits and Vegetable Program was enacted as part of the *Farm Security and Rural Investment Act*[38] of 2002. Although this initially was a pilot program in four states and one Indian reservation, subsequent legislation[39] expanded it to all states, the District of Columbia, Guam, Puerto Rico, and the Virgin Islands. More recent federal legislation, the *Healthy, Hunger-Free Kids Act*[40] of 2010, encompassed most of the school nutrition programs previously mentioned. The Act also contained several provisions designed to improve access and food quality of school meal and afterschool snack programs including:

- Upgraded nutritional standards for school meals by increasing the federal reimbursement rate for school lunches for districts that comply with federal nutrition standards;
- Improved nutritional quality of all food in schools by providing the USDA with the authority to set nutritional standards for all foods sold in schools, including vending machines, à la carte lunch lines, and school stores;
- Increased number of eligible children enrolled in school meals programs by using Medicaid data to directly certify children who meet income requirements without requiring individual applications;
- Enhanced universal meal access for children in high poverty communities by eliminating paper applications and using census data to determine school-wide income eligibility;
- Provided more meals for at-risk children nationwide by allowing Child and Adult Care Food Program (CACFP) providers in all 50 states and the District of Columbia to be reimbursed for providing meals to at-risk children after school;
- Empowered parents by requiring schools to make information more readily available about the nutritional quality of school meals, as well as the results of audits;
- Improved the quality of foods supplied to schools by building on and further advancing the work the USDA had been doing to improve the nutritional quality of the commodities that schools get from USDA for use in their lunch and breakfast programs.

Although the Child Nutrition Reauthorization (CNR) was designed to provide Congress with an opportunity every five years to review and amend school nutrition and food service programs, the *Healthy, Hunger-Free Kids Act* expired in 2015, with Congress failing to reauthorize it. The failure to extend CNR was due to political differences between the House and Senate versions of the bill, although all programs continued to operate despite the political breakdown. The impact of food service should never be underestimated, as in 2016 USDA's Food and Nutrition Service allocated more than $13.6 billion through the National School Lunch Program, serving over 30 million children on a daily basis.

State Support

In contrast to the uncharacteristically large federal role, individual states' contributions to school food service funding are difficult to summarize since each state is free to control its level of involvement or to choose no involvement at all. Though most states have opted to accept federal school food aid, no uniform method of state funding has followed. Review of current state laws reveals a wide range in food service participation, with the major feature being little uniformity in approach or support level. Without doubt, the most meaningful observation about the states' role in school food programs is that state funding is small compared to the federal contribution and especially small when compared to the proportion of total spending for school food services that occurs in the United States. However, states can play an important role in the administration of federal school meal programs, including level of state legislative appropriation.

The Local Role

The goal of a school district's food service program is to be self-supporting in that prices set for meals, in tandem with federal aid, must cover the full cost of the program. However, a USDA study found that, on average, school districts provide 18% of school food service budgets. In part this is because when a district funds a portion of the food service budget, it has only two potential revenue sources. First, it can shift local revenue from other budgeted areas—a decision that may prove controversial if, for example, parents allege that this action shifts money away from instructional programs. Second, the district can increase meal prices for students who do not qualify for free or reduced-price meals and for adults. However, raising prices too much is likely to decrease participation; and as participation drops, per-meal cost rises which in turn can spark more price increases, creating a vicious circle. Options are limited, since labor and food costs consume about 90% of a typical food service budget, meaning that districts are vulnerable to fluctuations in costs. Further, districts must factor in long-term capital costs for facilities and kitchen equipment. And to further complicate matters, all these budget items are subject to substantial geographic cost variations. In brief, the local share is at the mercy of federal and state aid ratios, with a direct line leading to how much the child eventually pays.

What Other Issues are Relevant?

While there are entire books on managing food service operations, three additional topics merit introduction here: Federal compliance, organizing for food service, and fiscal management.

Federal Compliance

Because the federal government supplies a large share of a school district's food service revenue, it is unsurprising that these funds are highly regulated. Nutritional requirements are a key focus of regulation, and politics have played into school nutrition in surprising and exhaustive ways.[41] Standards set out under the recent *Healthy, Hunger-Free Kids Act* particularly incensed many opponents,[42] often along political lines, even though the standards sought to ensure that children are offered both fruits and vegetables every day; to increase offerings of whole grain-rich foods; to offer only fat-free or low-fat milk; to limit calories through portion size based on a child's age; and to reduce amounts of saturated fat, trans fat, added sugar, and sodium.[43] The latest war began in 2012, with nutrition requirements published in the *Federal Register*[44]—a battle showing no signs of slackening and with the latest advisory published on USDA's website introducing new flexibilities in requirements for the school year 2017–18[45]—no doubt a nod to political pressure.

Traditionally, changes to federal food service participation related to annual determination of federal school meal price supports. That scenario still exists, as the federal government remains the major avenue for reducing meal prices in schools. For the 2018–19 school year, federal reimbursement per lunch was $3.52 (free lunch eligible), $3.12 (reduced-price lunch eligible), and $0.60 (paid lunch). For the breakfast program, reimbursement per breakfast was $1.75 (free breakfast eligible), $1.45 (reduced-price eligible), and $0.80 (paid breakfast). For the afterschool snack program, reimbursement per snack was $0.88 (free snack eligible), $0.44 (reduced-price eligible), and $0.08 (paid snack).[46] Eligibility for free or reduced-price meals is determined by the USDA. For 2018–19 children from families with incomes at or below 130% of the poverty level were eligible for free meals, while those with incomes between 130% and 185% of poverty level were eligible for reduced-price meals.[47]

The information in this section makes it clear that school districts must be vigilant and detail-oriented to ensure that all meals meet federal guidelines in order to be reimbursed. However, even after taking into account the availability of federally subsidized commodities, maintaining a self-supporting food service program can be a financial challenge at the local level because costs are constantly changing.

Organizing for Food Service

The complexity of school food services has led to cost analyses of how districts can best manage programs and expenses. Organizing has centered on types of management systems best suited to district needs, along with effective management of food service budgets. This has primarily resulted in carefully choosing between outsourcing services to a for-profit company or using in-house operations which may be either centralized or decentralized.

Outsourcing

Districts may choose to outsource all or part of the food service function. Some districts outsource the entire enterprise, including hiring and training of employees, while others outsource only purchasing. Still others limit outsourcing to a consulting role.

The outsourcing decision generally centers around efficiency or cost-effectiveness, but such decisions are never without benefits and drawbacks. Potential benefits may include:

- Full service outsourcing may yield cost savings because contractors may pay lower wages and provide fewer benefits to employees than a school district might incur;
- Full service outsourcing can relieve districts of the time involved in day-to-day management of food services and can reduce the burden of recordkeeping;
- Greater expertise of for-profit companies specializing in food purchasing can yield cost savings, higher quality, and more food choices;
- For-profit companies may have food professionals with expertise in menu planning that yield more appetizing selections which, in turn, increase program participation and hence lower the cost per meal;
- For-profit companies may have professional marketing expertise that can be used to increase participation, leading to cost savings;
- An expert consultant from a for-profit firm may enable a struggling inhouse food service program to successfully address fiscal and operational challenges while keeping the program district-based.

Critics respond that hiring a well-qualified inhouse professional food service director offers many of the same benefits at a lower cost because school districts do not need to and cannot, by federal law, make a profit from food services. Smaller school districts might also consider sharing a fulltime director. Further, privatization of food service employees can be controversial in a community, particularly if district employees are dismissed and replaced with a for-profit company's employees—even though cost savings would be gained. Also, even when contractors retain some or all district employees, they may convert full-time positions to part-time to reduce costs and maximize profits, leaving district employees ineligible for benefits. In this scenario, school boards and community members may raise concerns about increased turnover and the quality of food service personnel who have daily contact with children. Other concerns include:

- Districts may not have the expertise to draft a specific and detailed request for proposals (RFP) that ensures hiring a for-profit firm will result in the envisioned cost savings;
- Outsourcing does not relieve the district of its responsibility and liability to audit the food service program for compliance with USDA and state reimbursement guidelines;
- School–community relations may be negatively affected when an outside firm is perceived as less caring or committed to the children served by the food service program.

Inhouse Operations

Districts choosing to provide the food service function inhouse generally use one of four meal production systems: (1) onsite kitchens; (2) base or central kitchens; (3) mostly onsite kitchens; and (4) mostly satellite kitchens. Onsite kitchens are based in schools, with district employees preparing and serving food at each respective school site. A central kitchen is usually not located in a school but instead sends meals to multiple school sites. In contrast, a base kitchen is located in a school where it prepares food for other schools in addition to its own clientele. Finally, a satellite (warming) school kitchen receives some or all of the food served in the school from a base kitchen or a central kitchen. Although one might be tempted to assume that the greater economies of scale are achieved with a central or base kitchen, there are numerous studies that report differing outcomes. Individual school districts would do well to conduct their own careful cost analyses to determine which approach is most cost-effective for their particular situation. In addition, even though use of central or base kitchens may offer cost savings over school site kitchens, critics point out that effectiveness may be hurt because site control is lower and because rigidity, over-standardization, and nonresponsiveness may follow in a large centralized operation. As always, districts must be alert to community perceptions and preferences. For example, even in tight budget times, communities might forego cost savings so that each school has its own kitchen to tailor meals to its particular student body.

Financial Management

Finally, no discussion of the food service function in schools is complete without consideration of the complexity of budgeting. Food service budgets can be overwhelming due to the number of school sites, food programs, and federal requirements. Generally, the food service manager, in cooperation with the district's budget director, establishes receipts and disbursements for each school site as part of the budget process and provides key leadership in setting meal prices. This process requires an extensive knowledge base, strong organizational skills, and research capacity that includes the ability to analyze historical data and forecast revenues and expenditures. Complexity also arises in that each school site must be evaluated for the impact of changes in enrollments and participation levels; costs of food, labor, and supplies; capital costs; menus; and meal prices. This is detail-oriented work that may be complicated by daily cash-handling duties at the school site.

The goal of food service management is accuracy of records and reliability of projections. Potential trouble spots can be identified in this manner, and plans can be made for the entire year. As with every budget in the school district, monthly food service projections are assembled into an annual budget wherein revenue and expenditure must balance. The food service budget then becomes an integral part of the overall district budget, exactly like budgets for other support services. Discussion about local choices reenters at this point, since actual program cost minus federal and state aid yields the final cost per meal that must be charged or—alternatively—locally supplemented. Figure 10.1 presents a spreadsheet of food service revenues for Fiscal Year 2019 for a hypothetical school district. For example, this district served 64,000 paid elementary meals, for which it received 60.25¢ federal reimbursement and 4¢ state aid. According to the spreadsheet, the district charged $2.79 per elementary meal for students who did not qualify for free or reduced-price meals and

		TOTAL ANNUAL MEALS	FEDERAL RATE	FEDERAL Reimbursement	STATE RATE	STATE Reimbursement	DISTRICT LOCAL PRICE	DISTRICT LOCAL REVENUE	TOTAL 7-1-2018 to 6-30-2019
LUNCHES									
Paid Elem	1.	64,000	.6025	$38,560	.0400	$2,560	2.79	$178,560	$219,680
Jr. High	2.	35,000	.6025	$21,088	.0400	$1,400	2.95	$103,250	$125,738
Sr. High	3.	33,000	.6025	$19,883	.0400	$1,320	3.15	$103,950	$125,153
Free	4.	20,000	3.5225	$70,450	.0400	$800			$71,250
Reduced	5.	12,000	3.1215	$37,458	.0400	$480	0.40	$4,800	$42,738
Adult	6.	5,000					3.65	$18,250	$18,250
TOTAL	7.	169,000		$187,439		$6,560		$408,810	$602,809
BREAKFAST									
Paid Elem	8.	6,000	.3000	$1,800			1.99	$11,940	$13,740
Jr. High	9.	3,500	.3000	$1,050			2.25	$7,875	$8,925
Sr. High	10.	2,000	.3000	$600			2.50	$5,000	$5,600
Free	11.	1,800	1.7500	$3,150					$3,150
Reduced	12.	900	1.4500	$1,305			0.30	$270	$1,575
Adult	13.							$0	$0
TOTAL	14.	14,200		$7,905				$25,085	$32,990
SNACKS									
Paid Elem	15.	64,000	.0800	$5,120			1.25	$80,000	$85,120
Jr. High	16.		.0800	$0				$0	$0
Sr. High	17.		.0800	$0				$0	$0
Free	18.	20,000	.8800	$17,600					$17,600
Reduced	19.	12,000	.4400	$5,280			0.15	$1,800	$7,080
Adult	20.							$0	$0
TOTAL	21.	96,000		$28,000				$81,800	$109,800
KINDERGARTEN									
MILK									
Paid	22.		.2075	$0				$0	$0
Free-Avg Dealer Cost	23.			$0				$0	$0
TOTAL	24.	0		$0				$0	$0
OTHER CASH									
Sales/Income	25.								$0
12 Months									
Total Income	26.			$223,344		$6,560		$515,695	$745,599

FIGURE 10.1 Sample Food Service Revenue Calculation

$3.65 for adult staff based on actual cost. If, when preparing next year's budget, it is believed that costs will go up, the district will have to decide whether to: (a) raise meal prices; (b) use local tax dollars to supplement the food service fund; or (c) seek new efficiencies such as analyzing outsourced versus inhouse services.

WRAP-UP

Discussion in this chapter underscores the vital contribution of auxiliary services to learning outcomes. Equal opportunity cannot exist if children cannot get to school or if they come hungry. Though seldom in the educational spotlight, transportation and food service represent significant expenditures and significant liability. This reality once again concludes that an educational system is made up of intricately interrelated parts where each piece makes a critical contribution. Slighting any piece of the equation will ultimately harm innocent children. In brief, the decisions made at federal, state, and local levels involving these services are a deeply moral enterprise.

POINT–COUNTERPOINT

POINT

Schools today have been forced to take on many costly responsibilities that formerly and rightly belonged to parents, churches, or charities. Diverting limited instructional funds to subsidize school meals, especially breakfast and afterschool snacks, is a questionable use of finite funds, particularly when so many schools are facing budget reductions, laying off teachers, and increasing class sizes.

COUNTERPOINT

With record numbers of school-aged children living in poverty and with middle-class families struggling to make ends meet, it is unrealistic to think that these families are derelict in their parental duty. The only way to raise test scores in a humane nation is to care for the whole child, starting with adequate nutrition.

- Which of these views best represents your beliefs and experiences? Explain.
- How does your district's school food service program measure up on student nutrition? Could your district and school better promote healthy eating within and outside the school? If so, what suggestions would you offer?
- Examine your school district's budget (and school-level budget if available). Is the food service program fully self-supporting? If not, discuss with your food service director the challenges the program faces and what might be done to make it more self-supporting.

CASE STUDY

As business manager of your geographically large suburban school district, you have seen transportation costs and problems increase sharply over the last four years. Chief among your concerns have been fuel consumption, local pressure to address environmental concerns aimed mostly at the district's large diesel fleet, and safety concerns following a recent bus crash. In fact, the superintendent was quoted recently in the local press, stating that the district intended to make significant investment in these matters and that he was certain long-term benefits and savings would accrue from these new expenditures. While no details were given in the press, you later learned that his goal was to reduce bus route travel time and costs through routing efficiencies, cheaper vehicle operation, and new technologies to help with safety concerns. When you met with him later about these ideas, he indicated that he expected you to prepare an analysis of options and costs that would meet with board and community approval.

Back in your office, you reflected on your efforts over the last four years. You had already worked on these problems, but faced significant challenges, e.g., a lack of fuel storage tanks had prevented bulk purchasing that would help hedge against price fluctuations; budget limitations made replacement of aging, inefficient buses too costly; and other efforts such as installing video cameras on the district's buses had been met with opposition by some school board members and parents as unwarranted. As you pondered the situation, you realized the good news was that the superintendent had indicated openness to sizable expenditure in search of long-term solutions—the problem, though, was that you needed to identify and price solutions that might work in your situation.

As you strategized, a plan began to take form. You had recently attended a national conference on transportation and had visited vendor displays featuring innovations in route management and tracking, safety and security, and fuel cost and operational savings. You recalled that you had seen software designed to optimally match smaller buses to routes in order to use less fuel, the use of global positioning systems (GPS) to track bus real-time locations and stops and to remotely monitor vehicle performance, the use of alternative fuels to save money and reduce emissions, and ways to retrofit existing vehicles for fuel efficiency and reduced emissions. You also recalled advances in safety and security such as heat-sensing devices to improve pedestrian safety around school buses. It might work, you thought—the key was how much would it cost to engage these efficiencies and savings.

Below is a set of questions. As you respond, consider your learning in this chapter and apply your knowledge and experiences to the situation.

- In your estimation, which options being considered by the business manager deserve the highest priority? Why?
- Consider the potential costs and benefits associated with each of the proposed options and classify each along two dimensions: High/medium/low cost, and high/medium/low benefit.
- What cost efficiencies and security measures have been taken in your own school district? How much time and money has been invested in these concerns? How successful have these initiatives been in addressing cost, safety, and security?
- Do you believe most school staff members will agree that money spent in search of these improvements is worthwhile, even if at the expense of instruction? Why or why not?

PORTFOLIO EXERCISES

• Identify how transportation is funded in your state. Analyze the state funding formula to determine how many dollars are available and the relative emphasis on transportation in your state. Determine how much state transportation funding your school district receives annually. Learn how the unaided portion of the transportation budget is met in your local district.

• Discuss with your school district's transportation director how transportation services are structured in your district. Include issues related to decisions about owning vs. outsourcing, purchasing, bid laws, maintenance and safety, and driver training. Learn how transportation routing is carried out in your district.

• Determine whether your school or district has a transportation website. If so (using what you have learned in this chapter), review the website and assess its strengths and weaknesses as a resource for staff, parents, students, and the community. If there are weaknesses, suggest ways that these might be addressed.

• Identify how food service is funded in your state. Determine the mix of federal, state, and local aid to food service in your school district. Learn how meal prices are set and the philosophy that drives your district's contribution to the food service fund.

• Meet with your school district's food service director to learn how the district has structured this operation. Include issues such as compliance with federal and state requirements, local decisions about inhouse vs. outsourced services, and satelliting vs. the use of central kitchens. Discuss the responsibilities of the food service director, the basis for approved menus, and other aspects of financial management.

• Determine whether your school or district has a food services website. If so (using what you have learned in this chapter), review the website and assess its strengths and weaknesses as a resource for staff, parents, students, and the community. If there are any weaknesses, suggest ways that these might be addressed.

NOTES

1 Thompson, David C. "Auxiliary Services." In *Encyclopedia of Education Economics and Finance*. Eds. Dominic Brewer and Lawrence Picus (Sage: Thousand Oaks, CA, 2014).

2 National Center for Education Statistics. *Digest of Education Statistics 2018*. "Table 3: Current Expenditures for Public Elementary and Secondary Education, by Function, Subfunction, and State or Jurisdiction: Fiscal Year 2015" (Washington, DC: NCES, 2018). https://nces.ed.gov/pubs2018/2018301/tables/table_03.asp

3 U.S. Department of Education, *Digest of Education Statistics 2018*, Table 214.10, "Number of Public School Districts and Private Elementary and Secondary Schools: Selected Years 1869–70 through 2015–16," https://nces.ed.gov/programs/digest/d17/tables/dt17_214.10.asp?current=yes

4 For a history of busing used as means to achieve racial integration of schools, see *Integrating Suburban Schools*, by Adai Tefera, Erica Frankenberg, Genevieve Siegel-Hawley, and Gina Chiricigno (Los Angeles, CA: The Civil Rights Project at UCLA, 2011), 7–16.

5 See, for example, "Alt-Fuel School Bus Options Are Growing," by Kelly Aguinaldo, *School Bus Fleet*, May 22, 2014, www.schoolbusfleet.com/Channel/Green-School-Bus/Articles/2014/05/Alt-fuel-school-bus-options-are-growing.aspx.

6 See, e.g., *Raymond v. Paradise Unified School Dist.*, 31 Cal. Rptr. 847 (Cal. 1963); and *Woodland Hills School Dist. v. Pennsylvania Dept. of Educ.*, 516 A.2d 875 (Pa. 1986).

7 See, e.g., *Board of Educ. v. Antone*, 384 P.2d 911 (Okla. 1963); and *Cumberland School Comm. v. Harnois*, 499 A.2d 752 (R.I. 1985).

8 See, e.g., *Madison County Board of Educ. v. Brantham*, 168 So.2d 515 (Miss. 1964); and *People ex rel. Schuldt v. Schimanski*, 266 N.E.2d 409 (Ill. 1971).

9 See, e.g., *Shaffer v. Board of School Dir.*, 522 F. Supp. 1138 (Pa. 1981); *Kansas v. Board of Educ.*, 647 P.2d 329 (Kan. 1982).

10 See, e.g., *U.S. v. Jefferson County Board of Educ.*, 372 F.2d 836 (11th Cir. 1967); *Swann v. Charlotte-Mecklenburg Board of Educ.*, 312 F. Supp. 503 (N.C.1970), aff'd, 402 U.S. 43 (1971); *Monroe v. Jackson-Madison County Sch. Sys. Bd. of Educ.*, No. 72–1327, United States District Court for the Western District of Tennessee, Western Division, 2007 U.S. Dist. Lexis 39789. (Decided May 18, 2007); *Parents Involved in Community Schools v. Seattle School Dist. No. 1*, Nos. 05–908 and 05–915, Supreme Court of The United States, 2007 U.S. Lexis 8670, December 4, 2006, decided together with No. 05–915, *Meredith, Custodial Parent And Next Friend Of McDonald v. Jefferson County Bd. of Ed et al.*, on certiorari to the United States Court of Appeals for the Sixth Circuit (June 28, 2007).

11 281 U.S. 370, 50 S. Ct. 335 (1930).

12 The First Amendment to the U.S. Constitution reads: "Congress shall make no law respecting an establishment of religion, or prohibiting the free exercise thereof; or abridging the freedom of speech, or of the press; or the right of the people peaceably to assemble, and to petition the Government for redress." This has been interpreted to mean that "entanglement" of church and state could follow from involving public funds and private schools, and resulted in the so-called "Lemon test" of *Lemon v. Kurtzman* (403 U.S. 602, 91 S. Ct. 2105 [1971] rehg. denied), which applies a tripartite test to determine if a law has the effect of (a) advancing the cause of religion, (b) resulting in excessive entanglement, or (c) has a secular purpose. Opponents of "parochiaid" object on the grounds of these three prongs of the *Lemon* test.

13 330 U.S. 1, 67 S. Ct. 504 (1947), rehg. denied.

14 The net effect of *Everson* was to allow each state to opt whether to offer transportation services to nonpublic school students. As expected, states have not issued identical rulings, e.g., denying transportation as in *Luetkemeyer v. Kaufmann*, 364 F. Supp. 376 (W.D. Mo. 1973), aff'd, 419 U.S. 888, 95 S.Ct. 167 (1974) and permitting transportation as in *Pequea Valley School Dist. v. Commonwealth of Pennsylvania, Dept. of Educ.* 397 A.2d 1154 (Pa. 1979), appeal dismissed 443 U.S. 901, 99 S.Ct. 3091 (1979).

15 487 U.S. 450, 108 S. Ct. 2481 (1988). See, R. Craig Wood, "*Kadrmas v. Dickinson Public Schools*: A Further Retreat from Equality of Educational Opportunity," *Journal of Education Finance*, 15, 3, (Winter, 1990): 429–436.

16 See, e.g., *Sutton v. Cadillac Area Pub.Schs.*, 323 N.W.2d 583 (Mich. Ct. App. 1982); *Salazar v. Eastin*, 890 P.2d 43 (Cal. 1995).

17 153 N.W.2d 247 (Minn. 1967).

18 640 P.2d 1000 (Okla. Ct. App. 1981).

19 161 S.E.2d 645 (N.C. 1968).

20 371 N.Y.S.2d 179 (N.Y. App. Div. 1975).

21 *King v. Manor Indep. Sch. Dist.*, No. 03–02–00473-CV, Court of Appeals of Texas, Third District, Austin, Tex. App. Lexis 6346 (2003).

22 *Hitchcock v. Garvin*, 738 S.W.2d 34 Tex. App. Dallas (1987).

23 National School Boards Association. *Newsroom.* Quoting School Bus Fleet, a school transportation publication, (2018). https://www.nsba.org/newsroom/american-school-board-journal/online-only-archive/school-transportation-outsourcing-tips

24 Florida Department of Education. *Price & Order Guide 2017.* (2017.) https://static1.squarespace.com/static/577beb319f74567384fc9f49/t/59837b266a49633397d63962/1501789006360/FDOE+Contract.pdf

25 School Transportation News. *Technology.* (2018.) https://www.stnonline.com/resources/technology

26 Florida Department of Education, *Price and Ordering Guide for School Buses.*

27 School Transportation News. "Green Bus." (2018.) https://www.stnonline.com/resources/green-bus

28 School Transportation News. *Safety & Security.* (2018.) https://www.stnonline.com/resources/safety

29 Feeding America. "Child Food Insecurity 2018." (2018.) http://www.feedingamerica.org/research/map-the-meal-gap/2016/2016-map-the-meal-gap-child-food-insecurity.pdf

30 For an excellent summary of early food service programs in U.S. schools dating back to the twentieth century, see Gordon Gunderson, *The National School Lunch: Background and Development*, www.fns.usda.gov/nslp/history

31 P.L. 74–320. The Agricultural Adjustment Act supported farmers in two major ways. First, it authorized the President to impose quotas when imports interfered with agricultural adjustment programs. Second, it also appropriated 30% of federal customs receipts to expand agricultural exports and domestic usage of surplus commodities.

32 P.L. 79–396.

33 P.L. 83–597.

34 P.L. 69–642.

35 P.L. 94–105.

36 U.S. Department of Agriculture, "Summer School Food Service Program History," www.fns.usda.gov/sfsp/program-history

37 P.L. 105–336.

38 P.L. 170–171.

39 U.S. Department of Agriculture, "Fresh Fruits and Vegetables Program History," www.fns.usda.gov/ffvp/program-history

40 P.L. 111–296.

41 New York Times. "How School Lunch Became the Latest Political Battleground." The Food Issue. (October 7, 2014.) https://www.nytimes.com/2014/10/12/magazine/how-school-lunch-became-the-latest-political-battleground.html

42 See, e.g., Townhall. "Making School Lunch Edible Again." (January 10, 2018.) https://townhall.com/columnists/kerritoloczko/2018/01/10/making-school-lunch-edible-again-n2432518

43 United States Department of Agriculture. "The School Day Just Got Healthier." (2014.) https://fns-prod.azureedge.net/sites/default/files/HHFKA_080112.pdf

44 Federal Register. "Nutrition Standards in the National School Lunch and School Breakfast Program." (2012.) https://www.fns.usda.gov/school-meals/nutrition-standards-school-meals

45 United States Department of Agriculture. "School Meal Flexibilities for SY 2017–18." (2010.) https://www.fns.usda.gov/school-meals/school-meal-flexibilities-sy-2017-18

46 United States Department of Agriculture. "School Meals, Rates of Reimbursement." (February 13, 2019.) https://www.fns.usda.gov/school-meals/rates-reimbursement

47 Federal Register. "Child Nutrition Programs: Income Eligibility Guidelines." (May 8, 2018.) https://www.federalregister.gov/documents/2018/05/08/2018-09679/child-nutrition-programs-income-eligibility-guidelines

WEB RESOURCES

Transportation

National Association for Pupil Transportation, www.napt.org

National Association of State Directors of Pupil Transportation, www.nasdpts.org/index.html

National Highway Traffic Safety Administration, "School Buses," www.nhtsa.gov/School-Buses

National School Transportation Association, www.yellowbuses.org

School Food Services

Food Research and Action Center, www.frac.org

Healthy Schools Campaign, www.healthyschoolscampaign.org

School Nutrition Association, www.asfsa.org

U.S. Department of Agriculture, Food and Nutrition Service, www.fns.usda.gov/fns

INTERACTIVE WEB RESOURCE

Use the National Center for Children in Poverty's 50-State Demographics Wizard to create custom tables of national- and state-level statistics about low income or poor children. Choose areas of interest, such as parental education, parental employment, marital status, and race/ ethnicity—among many other variables: www.nccp.org/tools/demographics.

RECOMMENDED RESOURCES

Blue, James. "Subtle Shifts in School Transportation Industry's Fuel Mix." (2018). https://www. schoolbusfleet.com/article/729882/subtle-shifts-in-school-transportation-industry-s-fuel-mix

Feeding America. "The National School Lunch Program (NSLP)." Chicago, IL (2018). https://www.feedingamerica.org/take-action/advocate/federal-hunger-relief-programs/ national-school-lunch-program

Food Research & Action Center. "National School Lunch Program". Washington, DC (2018). http://frac.org/programs/national-school-lunch-program

Gunderson, Gordon W. *The National School Lunch Background and Development.* Washington, DC: U.S. Department of Agriculture, n.d., www.fns.usda.gov/nslp/history

National Highway Traffic Safety Administration. "School Bus Safety." Washington, DC (2018). https://www.nhtsa.gov/road-safety/school-bus-safety

National Safety Council. "Buses are the Safest Mode of Transportation for School Children." (2018). https://www.nsc.org/home-safety/tools-resources/seasonal-safety/back-to-school/bus

Sackin, Barry D. "School Food Service: Outsource or Self-Op?" *Journal of Child Nutrition and Management* 1 (Spring 2006). docs.schoolnutrition.org/newsroom/jcnm/06spring/ sackin/index.asp

U.S. Department of Energy. Alternative Fuels Data Center. https://www.afdc.energy.gov/ vehicle-applications/school-transportation

CHAPTER 11

Budgeting for Legal Liability and Risk Management

CHAPTER DRIVERS

Please reflect on the following questions as you read this chapter:

- What is the relationship of schools to the law?
- How do schools derive legal authority?
- What is the origin and nature of legal liability?
- What is immunity, and how does it apply to schools?
- What is tort liability?
- What other kinds of liability arise in schools?
- What do legal liability and risk management mean in the context of school funding today?

MODERN REALITIES

The opening questions to this chapter offer a sobering view of legal liability and risk management in schools. Education, whether offered in a traditional public school or any of today's market-based competitors including charter and private schools, is no more than an arm's length away from legal liability and the resultant need for proactive and effective risk management. The range and depth of the topic is vast, as—for example—the Education Commission of the States[1] (ECS) reported in 2018 alone that 31 states considered and/or passed 66 bills addressing the single topic of school safety. More tellingly, only three pieces of proposed legislation failed to pass, i.e., 95% of all safety bills in two-thirds of the states were enacted in the year of record. Issues of liability and risk mitigation have inseparable ties to school district budgets, as the cost of insuring against liability and the costs of physical and emotional preparations are weighty. Consequently, no school finance textbook is complete without raising the level of consciousness among current and future school leaders on this life or death topic.

For the most part, applicable state statutes govern liability and risk management in public schools. To open the discussion, though, one must first consider the broadest perspective by reviewing the larger relationship of the law to schools, including how schools are granted authority and how liability enters into play. Next, the chapter examines how immunity and liability affect common school interests, such as the law of torts and contractual liability. Finally, the chapter closes by considering how legal liability and risk management affect the decisions and actions of education's stakeholders. Ultimately, this chapter provides a fitting conclusion to Part II of this textbook by warning—again—that liability represents a serious threat to a school district's financial assets.

THE LAW AND SCHOOLS

Association of the law with public schools is older than the nation itself. Earlier it was noted that the American colonies enacted laws, such as the Ye Old Deluder Satan Act of 1647 in the Massachusetts colony, requiring establishment of schools, and that the nation's first compulsory education law was enacted in that same state in 1852. Such laws were meant to compel compliance, and it stands to reason that some people still did not obey and were held accountable under the law. States enact laws in order to force individuals to conform to societal expectations partially for the betterment of the individual, while also fostering enhancement of the larger social order and for other regulatory purposes.

The relationship of law to schools today far exceeds the first colonial laws. Schools now must be especially concerned with the legal rights of children, equal access to educational programs, special programs for the economically disadvantaged, fair funding, and a host of other issues relating to constitutional and statutory protections. Legal rights have expanded to employment, with complex laws governing the rights of employees and employers so that schools are regularly engaged in legal proceedings and rulings. Also, as noted in Chapter 4, state statutes tightly control the fiscal affairs of school districts. The concept of legal liability therefore overarches all transactions and relationships in schools because it is fundamental to say that districts and every person connected to schools may be individually or severally liable for a vast array of wrongful acts and omissions.

The law and schools thus have a two-fold relationship. One piece of the relationship focuses on regulation for organizational purposes, while the other focuses on liability for acts or omissions. Much of this textbook relates to the regulatory aspect of statutes because most chapters are deeply rooted in legal prescription for carrying out the educational mission. This chapter focuses on internalizing the risks and costs of liability because the law and schools are in close partnership, with profound budget implications.

The Derivation of School Authority

Schools enjoy significant authority and control over matters that are purely educational in scope, design, and function. However, one must understand that such authority is both broadly derived and at the same time limited. Thus, it is important to identify the sources and limitations of schools' legal authority in order to gain a foundational understanding of the relationship between schools and the law.

In brief, schools derive legal authority from both constitutional and statutory roots. These sources are complex and interrelated. An overarching view notes that school authority originates in the U.S. Constitution, the U.S. Congress, the federal judiciary, the constitutions of the individual states, state statutes, state courts, and state boards of education. Each source has had a significant influence on the educational enterprise, so much so that the very existence of the local school district, its board of education, and its educational mission are derived from the combination of these powerful forces.

United States Constitution

Involvement of the federal government in education is both peripheral and influential. Starting with early federal interest through land grants to newly formed states to be used for educational purposes, federal involvement in schools has grown to be a significant force. The federal path has been indirect because the U.S. Constitution is a document of limited powers, meaning Congress cannot assume powers without specific authorization in the Constitution. As noted earlier, the Constitution is silent regarding a direct federal education role. Given the absence of authority, Congress has had to find other ways to impact education because only a Constitutional amendment could create a direct federal role in schools. In the context of this chapter, the U.S. Constitution therefore both grants authority *and* creates liability for schools by endowing certain rights to citizens relating to education, while leaving direct responsibility for education to the states.

United States Congress

Given only limited Constitutional powers, Congress itself has had to become the vehicle for federal involvement in schools. Although having no direct education role, nonetheless Congress has managed to find a path through the general welfare clause of the U.S. Constitution,[2] which Congress utilizes to pass many laws affecting schools by interpreting general welfare benevolently and broadly. Throughout the years, Congress and various federal agencies have issued grants worth billions of dollars in aid to thousands of programs in elementary and secondary schools and higher education. In related actions, Congress has found other ways to indirectly drive state and local education policy by tying seemingly unrelated federal monies to education in order to pressure states to follow federal education policy. For example, Congress has often tied federal revenue sharing for such projects as highways to Congressional education interests by threatening withdrawal of highway funds if states do not adopt federal education goals. Likewise, federal laws affecting special education and civil rights powerfully impact schools, as do other laws such as the new *Every Student Succeeds*

Act (ESSA) and all its predecessors beginning in the 1960s. In the context of this chapter, Congress both grants authority to schools *and* creates liability by enacting laws supporting federal education initiatives that result in both benefit and liability.

Federal Judiciary

A significant source of authority in schools rests with the federal courts. In a complex hierarchical legal system, federal rulings may supersede state courts, as in the familiar appeal to the U.S. Supreme Court as the court of last resort. In essence, federal courts hold great sway over education by applying federal Constitutional requirements to schools. Racial integration, special education, and countless other entitlement programs are examples of federal courts' interest in education. Congressional involvement at this level is felt, too, as Congress exerts enormous control over education through the courts by virtue of its role in approving federal judges whom Congress hopes will take a supportive view of federal interests, including federal goals for education. Similarly, Congress is responsible for writing most of the laws tested in federal courts. The upshot is that although the federal government cannot claim a direct role in education, its influence has been pervasive by its interpretation of the general welfare clause. In the context of this chapter, federal courts both grant authority *and* create liability for schools.

State Constitutions

The same authority that prevents a strong federal role in education oppositely grants plenary power over schools to the individual states. The constitutional conventions of each state almost invariably mentioned education, writing into the earliest charters an active role for states. Indeed, school finance litigation today always turns first to the states' constitutional framers' intent to test whether states are meeting their constitutional obligations. The language of a state constitution's references to education can be a powerful influence regarding educational policy, granting sweeping power to the state or significantly limiting it. In essence, states have full power over schools, subject only to higher federal protections such as Fourteenth Amendment due process. In fact, all sources of law at the state level regarding education derive from an individual state's constitutional charge to its legislature. In the context of this chapter, state constitutions both grant authority *and* create liability for schools by requiring state legislatures to devise enabling educational statutes, which in turn result in both authority and liability.

Every state has a state constitutional mandate to provide some form of public elementary and secondary education for its people. However, each state constitution is different and can only be interpreted by state courts and (ultimately) the applicable state supreme court as to the obligation that the state legislature has to offer and fund public education. Although each state constitution is different, many state constitutions have similar education clauses because in some instances the founders of the state closely copied the language from another state's constitution. But even though the words might have been the same, historical records sometimes have reflected different intent. As one U.S. Supreme Court Justice has noted, state constitutions are the "laboratories of democracy"[3] in that they may differ significantly from the U.S. Constitution as long as they are not in conflict.

State Legislatures

Consequently short of Constitutional proscription, state legislatures have the authority to write and pass any legislation they choose affecting schools, subject only to the duties and constraints interpreted by courts based on the applicable state constitution. Although such duties and constraints weigh heavily given federal and state education laws and state constitutional requirements for educational equity, state legislatures have absolute control over schools. For example, nothing in federal or state constitutions generally forbids a legislature from creating or abolishing a state department of education, consolidating or reorganizing school districts, increasing or decreasing state support for education, or a host of other far-reaching reforms.[4] Truly, the source of such power and restrictions resides in each state's constitution and in its relationship to the courts, which are obligated to interpret the constitutionality of legislative actions. In essence, states control the statutes governing schools, and states may create or abolish school structures at will, limited only by the constitutionality of their actions.

State Judiciary

The system of checks and balances in U.S. government calls for separation of the executive, legislative, and judicial branches. State courts frequently have been asked to test the limits of state legislative power, thereby creating one of the very few checks on legislative prerogative. In the context of this chapter, state courts therefore examine the legality of state acts under the state constitution, making state courts a source of authority *and* the evaluator of liability in schools.

State Boards of Education

Although state legislatures have full power over schools, nearly all states have delegated general responsibility for conducting education to a state board of education. State boards are arms of the state, usually created in statute and subject to legislative will. Alternatively, state boards may be constitutionally established, but in many cases are still under some degree of legislative control. As such, schools are legislatively based, with authority delegated to lower administrative units. In the context of this chapter, state boards both grant authority *and* create liability for schools by virtue of the rules and regulations they promulgate and administer.

Local School Authority

At the bottom of the hierarchy are local boards of education, to which states have delegated daily operation of schools. In nearly all states, school districts are not mentioned in the state constitution. As such, local districts are subject to state control and may be organized as dictated by the legislature and state board. In essence, local districts exist at the pleasure of some higher unit of government and are subject to all laws and regulations—in effect, school districts are charged with actually carrying out the state's educational duties. In the context of this chapter, local school boards function in a constitutionally limited context of state and federal laws under the watchful eye of a state legislature and state board of education—an environment that cedes significant responsibility and liability for the actual delivery of public education.

THE ORIGIN OF LIABILITY

The concept of liability is deeply rooted in this nation's history. Many excellent sources detail development of American jurisprudence, and all such sources begin by following the nation's evolution from English law. Among those imported precepts are the key elements of sovereign immunity and tort law. Although many other aspects of law, including criminal law, at times apply to public schools, issues involving torts and immunity arise most often and may place public and personal financial resources in jeopardy.

Sovereign Immunity

Sovereign immunity refers to a tenet of English law that literally argued, "the King can do no wrong." The importance is instantly apparent because law is often based on following certain logic and history to a reasonable conclusion. If courts accepted that the king could do no wrong and that a king is the head of state, then the state itself could do no wrong. The consequence is that government could have immunity against its acts or omissions, a concept aligned with other sovereign views such as the divine right of kings.

Although Americans today might spurn sovereign immunity and ask how such raw power was ever allowed, it is the case that sovereign immunity was unquestioningly transported into colonial law. The impact of English law was quickly apparent in the new nation, as the 1812 Massachusetts case of *Mower*[5] held that the state was not liable for its acts. Sovereign immunity in *Mower* and subsequent cases was based on four distinct points. One point argued that the government has limited resources so that a proliferation of lawsuits stemming from a ruling, even for limited liability, would be detrimental to the public treasury. A second point held that government must be free from fear of liability because any act of law does not carry equal benefit for each citizen. A third point held that government is the people, especially in a democracy, such that it follows that suit against government is a suit against oneself. A fourth point also held that committing an illegal act is never within the authority of government, so that a wrongful act exceeds any legal authority. This logic also became integral to many U.S. Supreme Court decisions, with the Court noting as early as 1869 that "[e]very government has an inherent right to protect itself against suits" and that "the principle is fundamental and applies to every sovereign power."[6] Presently, though, sovereign immunity is a concept almost entirely defined by state statute, particularly for public schools. Each state therefore defines the concept along a continuum from a complete lack of immunity to a few states with virtually complete immunity. Some states have established limited immunity in the sense that there are strict financial boundaries to such claims. Notwithstanding, state immunity survived nearly unquestioned in this nation until only recently.

Over time, erosion of sovereign immunity was especially aided by two related events. The first event was the Congressional enactment of the Federal Tort Claims Act[7] in 1946, which established liability for acts by the federal government. In enacting the Tort Claims Act, Congress agreed that absolute sovereign immunity was no longer viable federal policy, thereby permitting claims where previously no recourse had existed. The second event followed as states enacted similar statutes, providing at least some state-level recourse against potential abuses of government. The result of these two events led naturally to numerous suits in equity and opened the door to claims against the financial assets of federal, state, and local governments.

It is useful to think of established law as the joint product of jurisprudence (the philosophy of law) as created and confirmed through subsequent consistent case law. Such has been the course of sovereign immunity's erosion because federal and state case law is vast when tracing the assault on immunity. *Molitor*[8] illustrates the fundamental logic underlying all such claims. In this 1959 case, the state supreme court of Illinois traced the origins of sovereign immunity and its adoption into state law via *Waltham*[9] and *Kinnare*.[10] Sovereign immunity had been established in Illinois for towns and counties in *Waltham* and had been extended to school districts in *Kinnare*, wherein it was held that a school board was not liable for the death of a laborer who fell from a rooftop, even though the school district had not provided safety measures such as scaffolding. Many years later, *Molitor* reversed on the immunity ruling, as the court held a school district liable for injury to a student when a school bus hit a culvert and exploded. The court rejected the traditional argument that permitting liability required wrongful use of public funds to settle claims and further held that depletion of the state treasury was no longer a good defense. The Illinois court quoted a New Mexico case, taking that view as its own:

> The whole doctrine of governmental immunity from liability for tort rests on a rotten foundation. It is almost incredible that in this modern age of comparative sociological enlightenment, and in a republic, the medieval absolutism supposed to be implicit in the maxim "the King can do no wrong" should exempt the various branches of government from liability for their torts.[11]

Through a long and circuitous history, liability for governments has taken on new meaning. Federal, state, and local governments may now be liable under certain conditions, and employees face risk as well because acting in official capacity is no longer an automatic defense. Of particular importance are the established exceptions to sovereign immunity, as it is established precedent that liability may now apply to proprietary acts, nuisances, and Eleventh Amendment issues, along with other exposure relating to constitutional infringements. In sum, the cracks in immunity defenses have opened liability exposure for all units of government, including schools and school officials, wherein the outcome of a claim will depend on statute and facts and venue—conditions requiring careful management to guard against the financial impact of successful claims. Again, claims under federal law are significantly different than those controlled by state statutes, so that school districts may be liable under certain federal law but not under state statutes; inversely, in some instances schools may be liable under both federal and state claims.

Perhaps the best way for school leaders to think about immunity and liability is to consider whether an alleged fault was a governmental or a proprietary act. By this logic, the modern basis for any qualified immunity rests almost entirely in whether the act was part of official duties. A governmental function might be found to be an exercise of police power or a constitutional, legislative, administrative, or judicial power conferred upon federal, state, or local government and its agents. In contrast, a proprietary act is outside the primary scope of the governmental unit itself, e.g., a school district. In the context of schools, the difference comes in distinguishing educational activities from other school-sponsored events not central to the educational mission. For example, athletic events outside school time or other voluntary events may invoke a different liability threshold than class field trips. However, the school leader should recognize that rulings have not always been consistent, even given similar circumstances. Looking back over time, a spectator in *Sawaya*[12] was injured when a bleacher railing failed at a game where two school districts had rented a football stadium from a third school district. The state supreme court of Arizona held the third district liable, finding the event to be proprietary. In contrast, in the identical case of *Richards*,[13] a Michigan court found no liability, holding that the district did not intend to make a profit from the event and was merely providing an educational activity. The controlling feature seems to have been how individual state courts, within controlling state statutory language, have regarded immunity, as illustrated more recently by a Michigan court in *Ross*[14] which stated, "When a governmental agency engages in mandated or authorized activities, it is immune from tort liability unless the activity is proprietary in nature." In contrast, a Texas court wrote in *Stout*,[15] "Since a school district is purely a governmental agency … it performs no proprietary functions separate from governmental functions."

As a bottom line today, liability is still subject to interpretation of state legislative intent in abrogating immunity and further subject to state courts' attitudes toward governmental immunity and liability.

Tort Liability

With no confidence of general immunity and subjected to controlling state statutes, governmental units—including schools—now risk liability for a wide variety of acts and omissions. Most such liability arises from the law of torts, wherein a tort is a wrongful civil act for which relief may be obtained in the form of damages or an injunction. A claim for tort liability is thus broad, taking in a great many wrongs affecting nearly every aspect of human existence. A successful tort claim may carry penalties including compensation for actual losses as well as punitive damages. As a consequence, school districts and leaders need to be very concerned for individual and several liability exposures that can result in large financial consequences.

Most torts fall into one of three categories: *Intentional* torts, torts involving *negligence*, and *strict liability* torts. For the purposes of this textbook, intentional torts and negligence are most relevant to schools, along with an additional interest in contract law.

Intentional Torts

An intentional tort is an act by someone who intends to do something the law has declared wrongful. Such torts involve intent or malice, although malice may be simple indifference. Most cases in schools likely do not involve intent or malice, but there are many opportunities for intentional tort claims by alleging that some act crossed the line of intent and was accompanied by reasonable anticipation of harm.

A common intentional tort claim in schools relates to corporal punishment, as school personnel are sometimes charged with having crossed the intent line. Such cases usually allege assault and battery. Assault is any threat to inflict injury which, when coupled with a display of force, would give a victim reason to fear bodily harm. Battery is usually filed in such cases too, as it is defined as touching with threat of assault. While as a rule courts have been unwilling to outlaw corporal punishment and the U.S. Supreme Court said in *Ingraham*[16] that there is no violation of the Eighth Amendment's prohibition against cruel and unusual punishment, there is a vast record of tort claims against schools regarding this issue. These claims should give rise to considerable caution on the part of schools from both moral and legal perspectives. For example, cases have involved students who were beaten severely enough to produce medical trauma, as in *Ingraham*, which resulted in a hematoma, or as in *Mathis*[17] which claimed post-traumatic stress disorder, and other acts such as a teacher kicking a disobedient student.[18] While these cases did not find schools liable, other cases have found oppositely. For example, a teacher was convicted of assault and battery for having broken a student's arm by shaking and dropping him to the floor.[19] Likewise, a teacher was liable for breaking a pupil's collarbone upon throwing him into a wall.[20] Liability was also found when a third-grader was held upside down by her ankles while the principal struck her with a paddle.[21] Similarly, liability was found when a physical education teacher allowed a student to drown, thinking the child was joking and sending students into the water instead of rescuing the child himself.[22] Nor is it the case that liability claims have markedly diminished as a result of public awareness or opportunities for staff development,[23] as recent news reports reveal that school districts remain subject to high numbers of allegations—even in 2018.[24] While these cases seem outrageous, it is evident that common sense does not characterize everyone who works in schools. Obviously, there is a real possibility that wrongful acts in schools may also end up in criminal court—again, a concept that is not a total stranger to schools.

Negligence

Another frequent tort action in schools is a negligence claim. Negligence is defined as conduct falling below a legally established standard of care, resulting in harm. Teachers, as well as school principals, are generally regarded as highly skilled professionals given their education, training, and licensure. Still, negligence claims arise and, in examining such claims, liability depends on the facts regarding breach of duty, proximate cause, and actual harm. In many instances, the principle of strict liability (i.e., no requirement to show intent or malice in order to establish liability) may accompany negligence claims.

Duty refers to proof that the actor had a responsibility to the injured party. A duty can arise from statute or from what a reasonable person would have done in like or similar circumstances. Inadequate supervision is probably the most common allegation for breach of duty in schools, followed by claims involving lack of proper instruction and failure to maintain a safe environment. The standard most often applied is the *reasonable person* test, whereby a defendant's actions are compared to the prudence and skill expected of any reasonable person in the same or similar circumstance.

For the purposes of this chapter, the focus is how this issue relates to school-based liability: i.e., the added dimension of superior skill or knowledge is key, so that the reasonableness test takes on the crucial characteristic of the behavior of a professional under the circumstance. Proximate cause relates to whether the action, or inaction, in fact caused the injury because there is no liability if there is no unbroken chain of events leading to the defendant. Further, the negligence must be substantial; that is, negligence, while easily claimed, must meet a minimum threshold of impact.

The issue of negligence in schools arises from a duty to protect pupils from foreseeable harm. Schools are obligated to serve children's health, safety, and welfare. Under the *in loco parentis*[25] doctrine, this duty is broad, as illustrated by *Garcia*,[26] where a five-year-old boy was sexually molested when he was sent to the bathroom alone in violation of the school's written guidelines. The court found that the assault was preventable by proper supervision, which was defined as the degree of supervision a reasonable person would exercise in a comparable circumstance. Although the court agreed that a school cannot foresee and take precaution against spontaneous acts by other students and that the school had no history of similar incidents, liability still was found based on the school's knowledge of danger to unattended children— knowledge implied via the school's written security policies and via the principal's testimony acknowledging the risks to unescorted students in hallways and restrooms. Similarly, the U.S. Supreme Court spoke in *Davis*[27] of the duty of educators to guard against student violence and harassment. The victim was a fifth-grade girl who had been sexually harassed by another student. She reported the events to teachers, but the school took no action. Charges were filed, with the defendant admitting to sexual battery, whereupon the victim's mother sued the board of education and school leaders for damages under Title IX of the Education Amendments[28] of 1972. The court held for plaintiffs, stating that educators are on notice that they may be liable for failure to protect pupils from the tortious acts of third parties. The court further noted that state courts routinely uphold claims alleging that schools have been negligent in failing to protect children from their peers—notably, the court cited cases from as early as 1953 in longstanding support for its ruling.

Despite such history, case law is by no means unanimous in fixing liability on schools at the state level, in part due to the lingering question of immunity.[29] State rulings favoring immunity have led to suits in federal court, asserting that schools have a federal Constitutional duty to protect students from danger.[30] These causes of action are known as civil rights torts, or Section 1983 claims, which are actions allowing plaintiffs to seek compensatory and punitive damages when liability can be successfully established.[31]

A definitive picture of liability under law is enormously complex and far beyond the scope of this textbook. Still, a few additional cases illustrate the broader range of topics and outcomes. In *Leffal*,[32] an 18-year-old student was killed by random gunfire in a school parking lot after a school dance. The issue was whether the student's Constitutional rights were violated by the decision of the school district to sponsor the dance even after being asked by local police to stop sponsoring such events until adequate security could be provided. Only two unarmed guards were assigned to the dance, and they were unable to prevent the violence. Notwithstanding the school's prior knowledge of danger, the court noted that although students were required to attend school, they were not required to attend dances so that the school's failure to protect against violence did not violate the Constitution. The court noted that the standard under §1983 is a deliberate indifference standard where the plaintiff must show that (1) an unusually serious risk of harm existed, (2) the defendant had actual knowledge or was willfully blind to the elevated risk, and (3) the defendant failed to take obvious steps to address the risk. Similar results followed in *Rudd*[33] when a student warned his teachers that another student had brought a gun to school. Officials failed to find the weapon despite a thorough search, whereupon later in the day the suspect pulled out the gun and killed another student on his school bus. The state supreme court held that the school district was not liable under the Arkansas Civil Rights Act and further enjoyed state immunity from tort liability. The evolving saga of school mass tragedies, however, offer the opportunity for case law to continue unfolding and reshaping, as violence is coming to be viewed through a lens that includes expanded views on harassment, bullying, and much more.

The increased predilection of U.S. society to embrace litigation as first order redress has also heightened liability risks for schools, and a brief search of advocacy group interest in school legal matters instantly returns a wide array of articles and legal actions.[34] The data alone are enough to stir anxieties and to leave school leaders without a clear roadmap on how to deal with keeping schools both safe and free. The best advice continues to be to seek expert counsel and to prepare with unceasing vigilance. In generalities, school leaders should know that one line of court cases leads to the view that schools may restrict student behavior in the name of safety without fear of liability, while another line of cases warns that courts will not be sympathetic to trampling of Constitutional freedoms. As school leaders try to straddle such conflicting realities, very likely it is the middle-ground that provides the best course of action for four reasons. First, there is a strong duty to exercise the reasonable person rule, consistently applying it to all issues ranging from freedom of speech to search and seizure under reasonable suspicion of safety concerns. Second, school leaders should not fear liability when having acted affirmatively, inasmuch as they might otherwise be held liable for failing to exercise appropriate care. Third, courts generally do not hold educators liable for injuries resulting from spontaneous acts of violence if these acts were unforeseeable; however, school leaders are expected to be watchful, especially when the assailant is a student, since courts will consider a student's prior conduct because evidence of previous antisocial behavior suggests that future violent acts may be predictable. Fourth, preparedness includes evidence of sound risk management training. In essence, training in risk prevention has become a standard of care for educators.

The discussion in this section clearly indicates a strong potential for intentional and unintentional negligence claims against school districts and persons in their official and individual capacities. Whether the person was operating in his or her official capacity often tends to center upon a case-by-case factual basis. Of particular concern is that damages may apply if negligence is established. Again, damages may be compensatory or punitive, depending on whether they are awarded as compensation for actual loss or as punishment. Compensation may include medical bills and loss of earnings, and may also be given for injuries such as emotional distress or pain and suffering. Other monetary judgments may be assessed too, including exemplary damages meant to make an example of negligence in order to reduce its likelihood of recurrence. For school districts and staffs, the issue is clear: Liability represents a significant potential claim against financial assets—either by personal vulnerability or by having to budget school district monies in anticipation of potential liability claims.

Contracts

Finally but not surprisingly, school districts should be concerned for liability involving contracts. Districts in all states are authorized to enter into contracts for hiring staff, buying supplies and equipment, and carrying out facility projects. Districts are thus liable for contractual performance, including breach of contract. Liability by either party to a contract usually relates to bad faith or failure to observe one or more of the basic elements of contracts. To be valid, a contract must have mutual consent, including offer and acceptance; have consideration in the form of inducement to enter into the contract; must be entered into by competent parties; must serve a lawful purpose; and must conform to any other requirements of law. Most contracts in school districts present no problems, but some special cases involve a greater risk of liability.

Most contractual problems involving school districts arise around authority to enter into a contract, and such problems are defined by the state-specific nature of contract law. As a rule, only boards of education may enter into contracts for the district, although agency is often granted to administrators to initiate contracts on behalf of a board. Contracts by agency still must be ratified by the board, and many of the challenges involving contracts have centered on whether a contract is enforceable when a school board wishes to nullify a contract by agency. Various rulings may be found. For example, in *Community Projects*[35] the court held that only a board of education had contractual power and that an agreement to purchase goods signed by a principal was invalid. An opposite finding came in *Hebert*[36] as a court held that because the board had ultimate power to contract and had given power to a principal over extracurricular activities that led to a contract, it had granted an implied power to contract. The key to contractual authority lies in the concept of ministerial duties vs. discretionary duties of school boards. Ministerial duties are those duties of a board that it may choose not to perform for itself—for example, supervision of playgrounds and curriculum management. Discretionary duties are those other duties that the board has elected to carry out itself, such as evaluating the superintendent or approving the school district budget and the amount of local taxes. While ministerial duties may be delegated, discretionary duties cannot. Contracts by board of education agents (e.g., administrators) are controlled by this distinction, in that expenditure is a discretionary power and may not be delegated. Still, boards of education often appoint an agent to deal with contracts, therein creating a level of risk by appointing someone who does not have true legal authority to make contracts. Under these conditions, a school district is not legally bound if it refuses to ratify the contract; conversely, though, the board of education may choose to ratify an invalid contract.

Under such conditions, disputes concerning recovery arise if one party claims the other party has breached a contract. The likely scenario is that at least one party to a contract, acting on the belief that a valid contract existed, provided products or services, while the other party failed to pay the bill. Recovery may involve damages or the return of actual products. The two issues of greatest concern in such situations are whether there is an express or an implied contract and whether it can be shown that the contract itself was invalid for any reason. An express contract is one in which the duties and rights are expressly agreed upon by all parties. An implied contract is one in which at least one party has acted to read a contract into the actions of both parties, even though there was no express agreement. The difference is not trivial. In the case of an implied contract, a court must consider the value of goods or services so that a fair value can be established because—if recovery were permitted—recovery is limited to the reasonable value of goods or services. In the case of an express contract, however, recovery is controlled by the value expressly agreed to without regard for whether the amount is reasonable. In the latter instance, it is prudent to avoid contracts that are unreasonable, as courts will bind both parties to an improvident contract if the contract is determined to be both valid and express.

In some instances, however, the contract itself may be invalid. As discussed earlier, an invalid contract is one that fails to conform to all required elements. For example, no contract would exist if mutual acceptance were lacking or if one party was legally incompetent, including lack of authority to enter into a contract or when the contract's purpose is outside the law. Similarly, lack of consideration voids a contract, as gifts or free services do not meet the consideration test. Further, contracts may be invalid due to failure to follow a prescribed form. For example, a contract required to be in writing, but made orally, is invalid. These instances create particular problems under recovery claims in that services or products may have already been rendered and consumed before the dispute is known, making an equitable claim more difficult by asking a court to either relax the statutory requirement or to allow uncompensated benefit to one party. While each case is unique, the general rule has been that if all other elements of a contract were met and if the school district had express authority to contract, then it would be liable under implied contract so long as the form or requirements of the contract did not violate other statutory provisions. To some extent, the outcome depends on the court's attitude toward the question of whether equity or strict statutory application is more important when dealing with issues of the public purse.

Case law involving contract recovery is legion. One of the areas of frequent dispute involves additional work by one party beyond the expectations of the other party. This situation often arises in construction projects. For example, the court held against a school district in *Flower City*[37] where a contractor who was hired to remove asbestos from a school also cleaned up and repaired fire damage, whereon the school district refused to pay for extra services. In contrast, the court ruled for the board of education in *Owners Realty*[38] when a contractor performed additional work while removing asbestos. The court reasoned that no other recourse was available in that the written contract barred claims for additional compensation. Unless the details of the dispute are airtight and inflexible, however, courts also consider broader principles. In general, if it were found that cause exists for a claim against a public body, the first issue is whether the goods are returnable or if they have been consumed—if the goods can be returned, courts usually permit physical recovery. The second issue is whether an implied contract will be found if it is determined that no express contract existed. The third issue is equity; that is, boards of education may not abuse their power in voiding contracts, and vendors may not raid the public treasury by misusing contract law.

Contract law is complex. Yet common sense is easily applied. First, it is settled that school districts have contractual authority. Second, it is settled that the required elements of contracts apply, and it is unquestioned that boards of education are expected to protect the public treasury through economy and compliance. Third, it is clear that contract law may differ across the states, making it important to know specific state statutory requirements. Fourth, it is clear that school boards may appoint agents, but they may not delegate their discretionary duties, and it is settled that contracts and expenditure of funds are discretionary duties. Fifth, it is readily apparent that courts tend to guard the treasury at the expense of outside parties. Sixth, it is settled that school boards may not abuse their preferential treatment by taking advantage of the law's protectiveness toward the public treasury. Seventh, contracts are unassailable if in proper form. Under these conditions, schools and school leaders can avoid serious contractual problems.

WRAP-UP

The relationship between public schools and the law in the United States has been in place for centuries, with signs of growing entanglement. Educational policy and process are topics that stir public interest, and the current desire to do battle in court has accelerated what was already an adversarial relationship among the many groups taking interest in the educational enterprise. It is by no means surprising that all actions by schools, including matters involving personnel, civil rights, educational policy and practice, and constitutional responsibility have been tested in the courts.

To repeat—this chapter did not try to exhaustively review every area of risk and liability that schools may encounter, but it sought to instill instinctive awareness in school leaders. It is not necessary to be an attorney in order to obey the law and to understand that the paramount duty of schools is to assess and minimize risks and to act as a reasonable person would act under the same conditions given the same level of skill and knowledge presumed to the position. School leaders are skilled professionals as a result of their training and experience. This charge strongly asserts that school districts and individual schools should enact formal risk management plans as the very first line of defense, wherein risks are systematically predicted and reduced through well-constructed policies, procedures, and practices. Only then should risk management turn to ensuring against liability and loss; that is, insurance serves as the indispensable *second* line of defense by protecting against unforeseen risk. To underscore, districts should never substitute insurance for methodical risk prevention. In the end, planning for risk and liability is a wise act of budget stewardship—an act calling for managing the inevitable risks schools face every day.

POINT–COUNTERPOINT

POINT
Schools today have taken on many characteristics of prisons, with fences, metal detectors, guards, and remote monitoring devices that rob children of their carefree years. The ominous cloud of potential rights violations has greatly aided miscreants' free rein in schools by obstructing officials who consequently are unable to effectively deal with unacceptable behavior.

COUNTERPOINT
While schools today must be cautious in dealing with potential liability, the problem is overblown because most schools are effective sites of learning that prepare students for productive lives. Although the media may demonize schools as prisons where the students are in control, effective school leaders have sufficient power to manage the learning environment, as evidenced by the success most schools enjoy.

- Which of these viewpoints best represents your beliefs and experiences? Explain.
- What security measures exist in your school? Why were these measures enacted? How effective have these measures been? Are there areas that could be improved? If so, how?
- How can schools reduce liability risks without taking on more prison-like characteristics?

CASE STUDY

As one of the assistant principals in charge of student discipline at your high school, you are not surprised at the school administrative team meeting to hear the principal address concerns about student conduct. As in most high schools, staying on top of an energetic bunch of teenagers is always a challenge, but recent events have put student conduct high on the radar screen. The principal raised five particular cases she is concerned about. First, in the last few weeks several boys have reported instances of bullying in locker rooms and hallways. Second, several girls have indicated they are seriously considering filing sexual harassment charges against other pupils for inappropriate text messages. Third, there have been fights and vandalism at school-sponsored night activities, and the local media seems to be following these events with heightened interest. Fourth, there have been hazing rumors, with allegations that a non-school sponsored club involving all-female membership is forcing pledges to attend school wearing absurd clothing which is drawing unwanted and unwarranted comments from other students. And fifth, with a look of weariness, the principal closed with another rumor that birthday beat-downs have been occurring in allegedly unsupervised football locker rooms. The principal ended her comments with the observation that these events have attracted the attention of both the superintendent and the school board, who are worried that the types and numbers of incidents have escalated from typical daily discipline issues to a serious matter with potential legal liability for the district, which not only would be bad publicity but also could be costly.

The principal indicated that the school board will soon ask all high schools in the district to undertake a self-assessment on management of student discipline and the security and safety of students and staff during the school day and at cocurricular events. Indeed, the superintendent has already instructed principals to initiate assessments that are to result in individualized building-based risk management plans.

Since your primary job assignment deals with discipline, you fully expected to play a big part in these events. True to form, the principal asked you to head a task force to develop a building-level comprehensive risk management plan. While the principal left it to you to determine committee structure and scope of the management plan, she made it clear that the end product should be guided by best practices and should carefully assess current conditions, assess current and prospective needs, and offer actionable recommendations for site-level improvements. You know you have a big task ahead and will need to do significant research and enlist a dedicated, creative committee.

- What questions need answers before you engage other persons in this process?
- Where will you turn for information on best practices?
- What are the elements of risk assessment and risk management that should be applied to this situation?
- Who will you ask to serve on the site committee? Why?

PORTFOLIO EXERCISES

- Conduct a search of major newspapers in your state for articles involving schools, lawsuits, and liability—you may need to search several years. Using your learning from this chapter, analyze the allegations and make a judgment on the merits of the claims.
- Contact the superintendent's office or the business director in your school district to discuss how the district approaches risk management from a philosophical and operational perspective. Ask whether the district has a written risk management plan. Obtain a copy and review what the district believes is important and the preventive measures described.

- Talk to your principal about what your school does to assess risk and to protect against liability. Probe the scope of risk management and liability as understood by your principal and the general issues that are relevant on a daily basis in your school.

NOTES

1 Education Commission of the States. "State Education Policy Tracking." (2018.) https://www.ecs.org/state-education-policy-tracking/

2 The preamble states: "WE THE PEOPLE of the United States, in Order to form a more perfect Union, establish Justice, insure domestic Tranquility, provide for the common defense, promote the general Welfare, and secure the Blessings of Liberty to ourselves and our Posterity, do ordain and establish this Constitution for the United States of America." Article 1, Section 8 of the Constitution states: "The Congress shall have the Power to lay and collect Taxes, Duties, Imposts and Excises, to pay the Debts and provide for the common defense and general welfare of the United States."

3 Justice Louis Brandeis opined that a "state may, if its citizens choose, serve as a laboratory; and try novel social and economic experiments without risk to the rest of the country." *New State Ice Co. v. Liebmann*, 285 U.S.262 (1932).

4 Every state is different, as illustrated by how, in certain instances, the office of state school superintendent, state board of education and/or school districts may be created in state constitutional language whereupon the power of the legislature is much more circumscribed.

5 *Mower v. The Inhabitants of Leicester*, 9 Mass. 247 (1812).

6 *Nichols v. United States*, 74 U.S. 122 (1869).

7 See, 28 U.S.C. § 2874; 28 U.S.C. § 1346.

8 *Molitor v. Kaneland Comm. Unit Dist.*, 18 Ill.2d 11, 163 N.E.2d 89 (Ill. 1959).

9 *Town of Waltham v. Kemper*, 55 Ill. 346 (1870).

10 *Kinnare v. City of Chicago*, 171 Ill. 332, 49 N.E. 536 (1898).

11 *Barker v. City of Santa Fe*, 47 N.M. 85, 136 P.2d at 482.

12 *Sawaya v. Tucson High Sch. Dist.*, 78 Ariz. 389, 281 P.2d 105 (1955).

13 *Richards v. School Dist. of City of Birmingham*, 348 Mich. 490, 83 N.W.2d 643 (1957).

14 *Ross v. Consumers Power Co.*, 420 Mich. 567, 363 N.W.2d 641 (1984).

15 *Stout v. Grand Prairie Sch. Dist.*, 733 S.W.2d at 296 (Tex. App. 1987).

16 *Ingraham v. Wright*, 430 U.S. 651, 97 S. Ct. 1401 (1977).

17 *Mathis v. Berrien County Sch. Dist.*, 378 S.E.2d 505 (Ga. App. 1989).

18 *Thompson v. Iberville Parish Sch. Bd.*, 372 So.2d 642 (La. Ct. App. 1979), writ denied, 374 So.2d 650 (La. 1979).

19 *Frank v. Orleans Parish Sch. Bd.*, 195 So.2d 451 (La. Ct. App. 1967).

20 *Sansone v. Bechtel*, 429 A.2d 820 (Conn. 1980).

21 *Garcia v. Miera*, 817 F.2d 650 (10th Circ. 1987).

22 *Thompson v. Bagley*, 2005 Ohio 1921, 2005 WL 940872 Ohio Ct. App. (2005).

23 *Clayton v. Tate County School District,* No. 13-60608 (fifth Cir. Mar. 25, 2014), wherein the complaint alleged the child was struck three times on the buttocks with a paddle using excessive and great force to the extent that the beating "left visible bruising and welts ... which were visible for days thereafter." The complaint further alleged that the principal appeared angry and that the student fainted after being paddled and fell face first onto the floor, whereupon "he was bleeding, five of his teeth were shattered, and, it was later determined, his jaw was broken."

24 Viadero, Debra. "Nearly 100,000 K–12 Students Still Spanked or Paddled at School, Data Show." *Education Week,* (May 14, 2018). http://blogs.edweek.org/edweek/inside-school-research/2018/05/corporal_punishment_2015_16_federal_civil_rights_data.html
25 Translated as "in place of a parent."
26 *Garcia v. City of New York,* 646 N.Y.S.2d 508 (App. Div. 1996).
27 *Davis v. Monroe County Bd. of Educ.,* 119 S. Ct. 1661 (1999).
28 20 U.S.C. § 1681–1688.
29 See, e.g., *Chesshir v. Sharp,* 19 S.W.3d 502 Tex. App.—Amarillo (2000) where state statutory immunity protected a teacher when a five-year-old boy splattered hot grease on his face from a hot frying pan in the classroom.
30 See, e.g., *Graham v. Independent Sch. Dist.,* 22 F.3d 991 10th Cir. (1994).
31 42 U.S.C. § 1983.
32 *Leffal v. Dallas Indep. Sch. Dist.,* 28 F.3d 521 5th Cir. (1994).
33 *Rudd v. Pulaski County Special Sch. Dist.,* 20 S.W.3d 310 Ark. (2000).
34 Searching the American Civil Liberties Union website in late 2018 (limited to that same year) shows 418 results for the descriptor "public schools," with six lawsuits named spanning the areas of religious liberty, criminal law reform, national security, LGBT rights, and racial justice. A broader array of interests is seen in the total set of issues contained in the 418 hits. https://www.aclu.org/search/public%20schools?f%5B0%5D=field_date%3A2018
35 *Community Projects for Students v. Wilder,* 298 S.E.2d 434, 435 N.C. App. (1982).
36 *Hebert v. Livingston Parish Sch. Bd.,* 438 So.2d 1141 La. App. (1983).
37 *Flower City Insulations v. Board of Educ.,* 594 N.Y.S.2d 473 N.Y. App. Div. (1993).
38 *Owners Realty Management v. Board of Educ. of New York,* 596 N.Y.S.2d 416 N.Y. App. Div. (1993).

WEB RESOURCES

American Tort Reform Association, www.atra.org

Association of School Business Officials International, www.asbointl.org

Education Commission of the States, www.ecs.org

Education Law Association, www.educationlaw.org

National School Boards Association, www.nsba.org

Public Risk Management Association, www.primacentral.org

Public School Risk Institute, www.schoolrisk.org

Risk Management Association, www.rmahq.org

Risk Management Society, www.rims.org

School Leaders Risk Management Association, www.slrma.org

StopBullying.gov, www.stopbullying.gov

RECOMMENDED RESOURCES

Alexander, Kern and M. David Alexander. *The Law of Schools, Students, and Teachers in a Nutshell.* Sixth Edition. St. Paul, MN: West Academic Publishing, 2018.

Alliance of Schools for Cooperative Insurance Programs. *Risk Management Primer for School Districts.* 2016. http://ascip.org/wp-content/uploads/2016/06/ASCIP-Risk-Management-Primer-for-School-Districts-SIXTH-DRAFT-2016-06-20.pdf

DeAngelis, Karen J., Brian O. Brent, and Danielle Ianni. "The Hidden Cost of School Security." *Journal of Education Finance* 36, 3 (Winter, 2011): 312–337.

North Carolina Department of Public Safety. *School Risk Management: Supporting School Risk Planning, Monitoring, and Emergency Response.* Joint Legislative Emergency Oversight Committee, 2018. https://www.ncleg.net/documentsites/committees/JLEMOC/2017-2018%20Interim/January%2025,%202018/01_NCEM_SRM_JLEMOC_012518.pdf

U.S. Department of Health and Human Services. StopBullying.gov. Washington, DC (2018). https://www.stopbullying.gov

PART

III

A View of the Future

CHAPTER **12** Trends and the Future of School Funding

Trends and the Future of School Funding

THE BIG PICTURE

The overarching goal of this textbook has been to provide aspiring and practicing school leaders with a broad contextual overview of money and schools. Funding for education is complex, and making it a straightforward explanation is very difficult. Although the book has introduced many concepts at considerable depth, the topic is even deeper because both technical expertise and the unknown unfolding of politics drive every aspect of school money. Only time and experience can reveal everything there is to know, and yet there will be no end since time is eternal. But it is exactly that point which makes this book so relevant: By seeing the big picture of school money, school leaders are better prepared to be effective decision-makers in their schools, districts, communities, states, and the nation.

This final chapter tries to see into the future as best possible. The important take-aways are for readers to reflect on lessons learned and to mentally prepare for the future. Educators have too few opportunities for reflection, and reflection is priceless because it anchors leaders' understanding of how the many pieces of school funding fit together. Likewise, an eye to the future prepares leaders to proactively respond to the changes that are roiling the current landscape. Just a short decade ago, it was unthinkable to predict the political turmoil and bitter partisanship that now characterizes each day. And there is no end in sight, as traditional roles shift and as lines of authority, power, and influence become increasingly blurred and upended. Yet in all that peril, it is likely that the future also holds promise: A return, if possible, to the view of America and public schools as a cheerful prospect.[1]

WHAT ARE THE ISSUES?

A persistent theme throughout this book has been that schools and society are changing rapidly. At the outset of the first chapter, the problem seemed simple in that an equal educational opportunity is owed in full measure to every child. But the problem quickly became vexing because resolving it requires broad consensus on diverse goals and demands massive investment of new resources or at least reallocation of existing funds on a grand scale. Initially, even that seemed doable because surely everyone would agree on the aims of schooling and the nobility of equity, adequacy, efficiency, and accountability. But the early euphoria of the reader gave way to concerns like the fiscal health of the economy and disagreements regarding the extent to which equal opportunity depends on money—and even whether everyone is entitled to a basic amount or to a full cup. Every chapter so far has stayed true to those issues, leaving readers with a fuller understanding of the opportunities and barriers, but without resolution in hand. Far more likely, the reader has arrived at this final chapter with serious questions about what the future holds. And while there still can be no absolute answer, there are signs that the struggles will continue with fiery and sophisticated argumentation involving hot topics that this seventh edition relates closely to volatile emotions around the entrepreneurializing and privatizing of public schools. These aims are found particularly among market sympathizers who preach on a continuum spanning from at least increased government advocacy for return-on-investment of tax dollars via academic performance mandates, to frontal assault on democratic schooling that includes an all-out war of individualism vs. collectivism as expressed in trends like charter schools, vouchers, tax credits, and tax savings/scholarship innovations. While these trends are by no means all-inclusive, the future of school funding will be framed by these or similar debates. Without the full engagement of all education stakeholders—administrators, school boards, teachers, parents, and community members—it could portend that today's public school landscape will be only faintly recognizable.

The Persistent Landscape

Although change is rampant, many aspects of P-12 education today are likely to remain constant far into the future. Costs will continue to climb, and the federal government is unlikely to abruptly reverse course by seizing control of public schools although it will continue to aid its own interests—whatever those may become.[2] Knowing federal interests is at once simple and complex, as in the case that the federal government finds it nearly impossible to amend the U.S. Constitution in any fashion, much less in ways that would forcibly wrest control from the 50 states, including responsibility for public schools. At the same time, even the safest predictions seem tenuous, as no one could have envisioned the vast shake-up that has occurred at the federal level through Supreme Court appointments, concerted attempts at centralization of federal powers, dramatic changes to federal attitudes affecting education policy, and more. Following closely behind has been the persistence of state government as the locus of control for public education, with nearly 14,000 school districts and billions of state dollars supporting schools. Aiding this persistence has been the aggressiveness of local communities seeking to protect local control. At times seen as a struggle between equality, efficiency, and liberty,[3] all these cases portray a future in which money will be a persistent flashpoint as taxpayers try to lower their personal costs and to uniquely advantage themselves in a competitive world where the pendulum of social thought swings wildly.

The Changing Landscape

While some may find comfort in historical persistence arguments, there is other evidence of a whirlwind of change having the seeds of its own sort of persistence. At work in legislative halls is a movement to capture public monies to be used for individual benefit—a movement that has the rejection of the public ideal on the other side of its coin. It is thus a movement that has taken its cue from America's unprecedented crisis of values, ethics, and politics. At times it is hard to know if the movement's genius is top-down by cleverly manipulating street-level emotions to give the appearance of being driven by grassroots preference, or if its genius is the work of democratic government loyally responding to the governed. Whichever it is, the landscape is changing, so that—at least today and for the foreseeable future—America's sudden burst of newfound nationalism and competitiveness comprise the most nearby real threat to public schools, even greater than the chronic funding deficits that continue to plague P–12 education. Yet even that observation leads to hesitancy because a realist knows that the shortfall and all other variables are cogenerative and codependent.

The Dilemma of the Past, Present, and Future

The past, present, and future can be aptly described, i.e., public school wars are still about liberty, efficiency, and equality; social vs. individual benefits; federal and state constitutions; tax tolerance and resistance; and control of agendas/local control. These all come together under new banners that, behind the glitter, look the same as the old struggles as candidates for public office sling arrows and blood in old and new ways, and as market forces escalate the fight for control of resources in the form of school choice in all its costumes. In the end, it is still about what it was always about: Control and money. And, of course, the *control of money*. What follows in the remainder of this chapter is a few words about each. But first a caution: What the reader should not take away from the chapter are firm conclusions, either by the words spoken or by the amount of ink devoted to each topic. What matters is that the current milieu of America is being reframed with more concerted sophistication than ever before. In brief, such a world is where schoolchildren now live and will continue to live for the foreseeable future. The question is how much better will it get, and how much worse will it get? And ultimately, what can be done about it?

Liberty/Efficiency/Equality vs. Social/Individual Benefits

The wars over liberty, efficiency, and equality in the United States are headlined every day in any newspaper or media outlet. Major news networks openly brand themselves by viewer politics, and impartial journalism is scorned by many as devious and untrue. Americans increasingly have cloistered themselves into enclaves of group-think where opposing views are shouted down, and national, state and local elections often carry party labels characterized by efforts to discredit and disgrace office seekers through ideological and personal attacks. An entire industry of opposition research has been built that aims to capture control of power and money.[4] Attacks on collectivism of any stripe have enlisted the highest eschelons as illustrated by concerted governmental efforts to deconstruct any market structure other than raw competition and limited government scope.[5] Nor are these arguments newly minted—countless debates and years have gone by,[6] with struggles only worsening in outcome. For schools, a major manifestation has been wars over taxes in the classic lens seen throughout this textbook, as well as in the proliferation of the more recent school choice movement. As Americans' economic awareness and political engagement have grown, in many instances the outcome has been to take sides using foils like achievement (efficiency) and freedom (liberty), while disrespecting democratic emphasis on social justice (inequality).[7]

Federal and State Constitutions

Against this backdrop has stood the classic ideal of fiscal and educational equality for all school children. With a history spanning more than 100 years, the wars have raged, at times feeling like one step forward and two steps back.[8] As seen earlier in this textbook, federal and state constitutions have been the offensive weapons of plaintiffs and likewise the shields of defendant states, with the spoils taking various shape in the 50 states. The federal plaintiff case has been hampered by the U.S. Constitution's Tenth Amendment silence, as efforts to secure a fundamental right absent absolute deprivation have failed even as plaintiffs have continued to test that claim as a strategy to many state-level litigations. Overall, most reformers would conclude that equality has made great strides as a consequence of state constitutional language, though the battle has been long with no end in sight.[9] In looking ahead, not much has changed in the midst of great change, as the words of the states themselves (see Table 12.1) are tested and retested in court—courts that are themselves deeply embroiled in a stew of executive, legislative, and judicial limits and struggles.

Tax Tolerance and Resistance

That most Americans pay their taxes is indisputable; that they do so reluctantly with an attitude of toleration is equally true in most cases. Still others refuse to pay and, while an accurate impact is elusive, these persons are characterizable as stridently skeptical, arguing that the taxation amounts to confiscation of private property under the tyranny of government by legalized larceny.[10] Regardless of who pays, it is self-evident that successively lower units of government are seen as eminently vulnerable when it comes to rebelling against taxation and driving policy through voter behavior.

TABLE 12.1 State Education Articles

Alabama	Section 256	A liberal system of public schools throughout the state.
Alaska	Article 7	A system of public schools open to all children of the State.
Arizona	Article XI	A general and uniform public school system, which system shall include: Kindergarten schools, common schools, high schools, normal schools, industrial schools, [and] universities.
Arkansas	Article XIV	A general, suitable and efficient system of free public schools; shall adopt all suitable means to secure to the people the advantages and opportunities of education.
California	Article 9	A system of common schools.
Colorado	Article I	A thorough and uniform system of free public schools throughout the state.
Connecticut	Article XIII	Free public elementary and secondary schools in the state.
Delaware	Article X	A general and efficient system of free public schools, and may require by law that every child, not physically or mentally disabled, shall attend the public school, unless educated by other means.
Florida	Article IX	A uniform, efficient, safe, secure and high-quality system of free public schools that allows students to obtain a high-quality education.
Georgia	Article VIII	The provision of an adequate public education for the citizens shall be a primary obligation of the State of Georgia. Public education for the citizens prior to the college or postsecondary level shall be free and shall be provided for by taxation.
Hawaii	Article X	A statewide system of public schools free from sectarian control, a state university, public libraries and such other educational institutions as may be deemed desirable, including physical facilities therefor.
Idaho	Article IX	A general, uniform and thorough system of public, free common schools.
Illinois	Article X	An efficient system of high-quality public educational institutions and services.
Indiana	Article VIII	A general and uniform system of Common Schools, wherein tuition shall be without charge, and equally open to all.
Iowa	Article IX	The education of all the youths of the state, through a system of Common Schools.
Kansas	Article VI	Intellectual, educational, vocational, and scientific improvement by establishing and maintaining public schools, educational institutions, and related activities which may be organized and changed in such manner as may be provided by law.
Kentucky	Section 183	An efficient system of common schools throughout the State.
Louisiana	Article VIII	The legislature shall provide for the education of the people of the state and shall establish and maintain a public educational system.
Maine	Article VIII	The several towns to make suitable provision, at their own expense, for the support and maintenance of public schools.

(Continued)

TABLE 12.1 Continued

Maryland	Article VIII	A thorough and efficient system of free public schools.
Massachusetts	Chapter V	Cherish the interests of literature and the sciences, and all seminaries of them; especially the university at Cambridge, public schools, and grammar schools in the towns.
Michigan	Article VIII	A system of free public elementary and secondary schools as defined by law.
Minnesota	Article XIII	A general and uniform system of public schools.
Mississippi	Article 8	There shall be a state common-school fund, to be taken from the General Fund in the State Treasury, which shall be used for the maintenance and support of the common schools.
Missouri	Article IX	Free public schools for the gratuitous instruction of all persons.
Montana	Part X	A system of education which will develop the full educational potential of each person. Equality of educational opportunity is guaranteed to each person of the state ... a basic system of free quality public elementary and secondary schools.
Nebraska	Article VII	Free instruction in the common schools of this state.
Nevada	Article 11	A uniform system of common schools.
New Hampshire	Article 83	To cherish the interest of literature and the sciences, and all seminaries and public schools, to encourage private and public institutions, rewards, and immunities for the promotion of agriculture, arts, sciences, commerce, trades, manufactures, and natural history of the country.
New Jersey	Article VIII	A thorough and efficient system of free public schools for the instruction of all the children in the state.
New Mexico	Article XII	A uniform system of free public schools sufficient for the education of, and open to, all the children of school age in the state.
New York	Article XI	A system of free common schools, wherein all the children of this state may be educated.
North Carolina	Article IX	A general and uniform system of free public schools.
North Dakota	Article VIII	A uniform system of free public schools throughout the state, beginning with the primary and extending through all grades up to and including schools of higher education.
Ohio	Article VI	A thorough and efficient system of common schools throughout the state.
Oklahoma	Article XIII	Free public schools wherein all the children of the state may be educated.
Oregon	Article VIII	A uniform and general system of common schools.
Pennsylvania	Article III	A thorough and efficient system of public education to serve the needs of the Commonwealth.
Rhode Island	Article XII	Promote public schools and public libraries, and to adopt all means which it may deem necessary and proper to secure to the people the advances and opportunities of education and public library services.

(Continued)

South Carolina	Article XI	A system of free public schools open to all children in the state and shall establish, organize, and support such other public institutions of learning, as may be desirable.
South Dakota	Article VII	A general and uniform system of public schools wherein tuition shall be without charge, and equally open to all.
Tennessee	Article XI	A system of free public schools.
Texas	Article VII	An efficient system of public free schools.
Utah	Article X	The legislature shall provide for the establishment and maintenance of the state's education systems including a public education system, which shall be open to all children of the state.
Vermont	Section 68	A competent number of schools ought to be maintained in each town unless the general assembly permits other provisions for the convenient instruction of youth.
Virginia	Article VIII	A system of free public elementary and secondary schools for all children of school age throughout the Commonwealth, and shall seek to ensure that an educational program of high quality is established and continually maintained.
Washington	Article IX	The legislature shall provide for a general and uniform system of public schools.
West Virginia	Article XII	A thorough and efficient system of free schools.
Wisconsin	Article X	The establishment of district schools, which shall be as nearly uniform as practicable; and such schools shall be free and without charge for tuition
Wyoming	Article 7	A complete and uniform system of public instruction, embracing free elementary schools of every needed kind and grade.

Source: David C. Thompson, R. Craig Wood, and David S. Honeyman, *Fiscal Leadership for Schools: Concepts and Practices.* (New York: Longman, 1994), pp. 282–286. Cross-referenced and updated using Emily Parker, "50-State Review: Constitutional Obligations for Public Education." Denver, CO: Education Commission of the States (March 2016). https://www.ecs.org/wp-content/uploads/2016-Constitutional-obligations-for-public-education-1.pdf

Reports to that end are legion,[11] and the structure of any query can greatly affect the outcome. The topic is so volatile that nationally respected organizations follow trends closely, with alarmingly similar findings showing many of the nation's schools are starved for tax dollars[12] linked to ideological wars. Whether it is state legislators who drive policy emotions or whether legislators mimic the attitudes of voters seems almost immaterial since the circle is closed so tightly that it is hard to know the original sin—it is only possible to know that voters chafe under tax burdens, while other voters chafe under tax restraints in those cases when localities would choose to spend freely if permitted.[13]

Control of Agendas/Local Control

Finally, whether discussing liberty, efficiency, and equality or discussing the federal and state legal obligation to public schools, or whether discussing tax tolerance and resistance, in reality the topic is singular: i.e., control is the aim at every level. Control is how citizens frame their own existence, so that only the degree of civility with which they approach control offers any real distinction. A theme in this textbook has been that Americans historically have joined together sufficiently enough to validate an acceptable collectivism, but there are signs of deep fracture that at its core is hell-bent on rejecting even the appearance of collectivism—perhaps not infinitely greater than a few times in the past, but the loudness made possible today by relentless instant mass communication leaves an impression that fissures have become unbridgeable chasms. Americans like control, and many are tempted to define control as liberty barely restrained. Where it will go is unknown, but it is reasonable to intuit that the human condition defines equity in the eye of the beholder. If politics can be described as generational, today's American reality is one that increasingly puts the individual ahead of community. Nowhere is this more evident than in current legislative fascination with the many forms of school choice.

School Choice

The liberty, efficiency, and equality wars have opened new options for Americans who for personal reasons want alternatives to public schools. Among the inventions have been charter schools, vouchers, tax savings accounts, various tax scholarships, and individual and corporate tax credit and tax deduction plans. Numerous resources diving deeply into their bases and justification exist. Each is briefly touched on here as an important part of the changing landscape of American schools in the twenty-first century.

Charter Schools

As this textbook entered its seventh edition, charter schools existed in 44 states and the District of Columbia,[14] serving approximately three million students with expenditures of approximately $440 million.[15] While no two state charter systems are exactly alike as legislatures have built a range of designs, it is an accurate characterization to first distinguish charter schools as *private* entities supported partly or entirely by state monies. Within that framework, charter schools can be viewed as public schools that have been granted more autonomy when compared to their traditional counterparts. Generally, as long as charter schools meet state standards for health, safety, welfare, accounting and financial regulation, as well as state academic performance goals, they are allowed to operate free of most other regulation. Small wonder, then, that challenges to charter schools have arisen, alleging concerns[16] taken seriously by advocates for the public school ideal.

While charter schools currently operate in most states, they are prevalent in California, Florida, and Texas. Table 12.2 depicts the largest charter school enrollment states, revealing that these ten states enroll over 2.1 million school age children, subtracting their physical presence and financial support from the traditional K–12 system. The impact of such numbers is visible.

The lack of regulation is notable on multiple levels. The Education Commission of the States (ECS) has extensively described charter schools, saying: "Charter school laws vary from state to state and often differ on several important factors, such as who may authorize charter schools, how authorizers and charter schools are held accountable for student outcomes and whether the teachers in a charter school must

TABLE 12.2 Largest Ten States by Charter School Enrollment by Prevalence 2016–17

State	Charter Law Year	School Sites	Enrollments
California	1992	1,258	602,839
Texas	1995	750	307,716
Florida	1996	657	283,195
Arizona	1994	557	185,986
Michigan	1993	308	145,282
Pennsylvania	1997	183	133,753
New York	1998	269	128,743
Ohio	1997	365	117,075
Colorado	1993	238	115,096
North Carolina	1996	170	92,524

Source: National Alliance for Public Charter Schools (2018). www.data.publiccharters.org

be certified."[17] In some states a variety of agencies have statutory authority to authorize and create charter schools, i.e., depending on state law, authorizers may include school districts, municipalities, state or private universities and colleges, as well as specific state-created boards. The practical effect is that creation of charter schools often is executed at the local level. What is striking about this contrast is that traditional public schools are highly regulated and singular in authorization, while charter schools as shown in Table 12.3 have much freer rein to proliferate. Under these conditions, public schools face real competition—especially if the premise is accepted that charter school laws exist due to efforts to change the footprint of tax-supported education and to direct public monies to arguably private aims.

While charter schools cover nearly the entire nation, it is enrollments and numbers of actual charter schools that better define the assertion that deregulation and redesign of public education is an agenda. Table 12.3 accumulates these data, reporting in one case that 44% of eligible children are served by charter schools.[18] Generally, the impact is smaller when expressed as percentages, but Table 12.3 shows real impact in any case. And the purpose is deliberate as expressed by the National Association of Charter School Authorizers (NACSA), which in 2012 launched an ambitious campaign entitled *One Million Lives*[19] to enroll one million more children into 3,000 high-performing schools over the next five years.

Although these data are real, caution must be applied in order not to leap to wrong conclusions. In reality, each state's charter laws must be examined to know the precise effect of charter schools. For example, the data in Table 12.3 were rounded for approximation. The concentration of charter schools in certain states should be noted too: e.g., while Texas data reflect slightly more than 700 schools, that state's authorizing statute limits the actual number of charters—meaning, Texas charter school holders may operate more than one campus which can affect school site counts. Likewise, the large concentration of charter school students in the District of Columbia can give the impression that charters are everywhere, while closer examination shows that only

TABLE 12.3A Largest Charter School Authorizers by Enrollment 2016–17

Authorizer	Enrollments
Texas Education Agency	268,258
Arizona State Board for Charter Schools	176,234
Los Angeles Unified School District	156,537
North Carolina Department of Education	92,281
Utah State Charter School Board	68,705
Philadelphia School District	63,261
State University of New York Charter Schools Institute	62,948
Miami-Dade County Public Schools-Charter School Operations (FL)	62,924
Chicago Public Schools	67.015
Louisiana Board of Elementary and Secondary Education	56,640

Source: National Alliance for Public Charter Schools (2018). www.data.publiccharters.org

TABLE 12.3B Selected Charter School Facts

State	Percentage of Students in Charter Schools	Number of Charter Schools/ Percentage of Schools
Alabama	0	0
Alaska	6,000 = 5%	20–5%
Arizona	166,000 = 15%	588–28%
Arkansas	19,000 = 4%	55–4%
California	545,000 = 9%	1232–12%
Colorado	101,000 = 11%	226–12%
Connecticut	8,000 = 1%	24–2%
Delaware	11,000 = 8%	27–11%
District of Columbia	38,000 = 44%	111–50%
Florida	251,000 = 9%	656–16%
Georgia	83,000 = 5%	99–5%
Hawaii	10,000 = 6%	34–12%
Idaho	20,000 = 7%	48–7%
Illinois	62,000 + 3%	148–3%
Indiana	38,000 = 4%	91–4%
Iowa	<1,000 = <1%	2–<1%
Kansas	3,000 = 1%	10–1%
Kentucky	0	0
Louisiana	70,000 = 10%	138–9%
Maine	<1,000 = 1%	7–1%
Maryland	21,000 = 2%	53–4%
Massachusetts	37,000 = 4%	60–4%

(Continued)

Michigan	139,000 = 9%	303–8%
Minnesota	45,000 = 5%	165–7%
Mississippi	n.a.	n.a.
Missouri	20,000 = 2%	51–2%
Montana	0	0
Nebraska	0	0
Nevada	29,000 = 6%	38–6%
New Hampshire	2,600 = 1%	26–5%
New Jersey	38,000 = 3%	89–3%
New Mexico	23,000 = 7%	99–11%
New York	106,000 = 4%	257–5%
North Carolina	70,000 = 4%	161–6%
North Dakota	0	0
Ohio	124,000 = 7%	373–11%
Oklahoma	17,000 = 2%	34–2%
Oregon	30,000 = 5%	126–9%
Pennsylvania	133,000 = 7%	175–6%
Rhode Island	6,400 = 5%	24–5%
South Carolina	27,000 = 4%	67–5%
South Dakota	0	0
Tennessee	0	0
Texas	265,000 = 5%	703–8%
Utah	62,000 = 10%	119–11%
Vermont	0	0
Virginia	2.300 = <1%	9–<1%
Washington	n.a.	n.a
West Virginia	0	0
Wisconsin	43,000 = 5%	244–12%
Wyoming	500 = <1%	4–1%

Source: National Association of Charter School Authorizers (2018). www.qualitycharters.org.

a few students are enrolled in several other states. Patterns matter, though, as do total enrollments—e.g., as a percentage of traditional public school enrollments, charter schools are most prevalent in the District of Columbia, followed next by Arizona, Colorado, Louisiana, and Utah. But in terms of numbers of charter students, the most prevalent cases are in California, followed by Texas, Florida, Arizona, Michigan, Pennsylvania, Ohio, New York, and Colorado. Also, interpretation is not always straightforward inasmuch as the sheer size of school-age populations in states like California, Florida, New York, and Texas would presumptively result in large numbers of charter enrollments. In brief, charter schools have had a huge demographic, geographic, and fiscal impact; but interpreting these data requires careful analysis in order to avoid overgeneralization.

Funding Charter Schools

Charter schools throughout the nation are funded via various mechanisms, typically in similar fashion to the host state's general school aid formula. However, variations exist regarding how the local share is funded, although once again most states closely follow the general aid formula. But notable exceptions exist: For example, Texas utilizes the statewide average as the measure of local fiscal capacity. Another example is found in how some states have chosen to permit local school districts to deduct an administrative fee (typically less than 5%) for processing and administering charter school payments through the district. Also, some states grant state aid to capital outlay, and many others choose to provide aid to pupil transportation. State-by-state analysis is needed to know the relationship between charter schools and tax systems, although as a general rule charter schools are not eligible to directly sell tax-exempt government obligation bonds; however, in many states, charter schools receive substantial capital outlay grants and other awards from the state. Table 12.4 provides an excellent overview of how states fund charter schools—again, with a caution to explore in specificity any given state's complex aid relationships.

Challenges to Charter Schools

Unsurprisingly, this chapter's interest in charter schools concludes with a review of challenges to the model, as courts have examined questions of legality and appropriateness involving this use of tax dollars in a democratic society.[20]

Challenges to charter schools have often focused on claims that such schools are essentially private institutions and therefore ineligible for tax support. In *Council v. Engler*,[21] the Michigan supreme court held that charter schools were of a sufficiently public nature despite a constitutional provision stating that, "No public monies or property shall be appropriated or paid or any public credit utilized ... directly or indirectly to aid or maintain any private, denominational or other nonpublic, pre-elementary, elementary, or secondary school."[22] The court noted the legislature could revoke the charters for any number of statutory reasons and took the position that charter schools did not have to be under the total and exclusive control of the legislature. Similar logic was found by the California supreme court in *Wilson v. State Board of Education*[23] as the court viewed charter schools as part of the public education system and observed that the legislature had ultimate control of charter schools.

More recently, a specific challenge to the state's authority to create charter schools was heard by the Colorado supreme court based on plaintiffs' claim that charter schools are *inefficient and non-uniform*—i.e., in violation of two Colorado constitutional requirements for schools. The court held in *Boulder Valley v. Colorado State Board of Education*[24] that the legislature had broad and discretionary powers; that it represented the will of the people; and that it ultimately had control over the creation, operation, and existence of these schools, concluding that charter schools operated as part of the system of public education for public benefit. Similar earlier claims were also rejected by the Michigan high court in *Council of Organizations v. Governor*,[25] as the court held that charter schools, while not under the immediate and exclusive control of the state, were not required to meet such a standard because the state board of education was

TABLE 12.4 State Charter School Funding Formulas 2018

State	Funding Formula Framework
Alabama	Public charter schools receive 100% of federal funds, 100% of state funds, and up to 10 mills of local funds for each child enrolled at the public charter school. All local money above and beyond the 10-mill match remains with the local school system.
Alaska	A local school board provides an approved charter school with an annual program budget. The budget cannot be less than the amount generated by students enrolled in the charter school minus a portion for administrative costs, not to exceed 4%. The amount generated by a student enrolled in the charter school is determined in the same manner as it is for a student enrolled in another public school in that school district.
Arizona	In addition to a base support level from the state, charter schools are given equal access to all applicable categorical federal and state funding. Charter schools do not have access to local revenue from property taxes and bond measures; however, the state provides charters with "additional assistance" funds to make up for the lack of local revenues. Additionally, charter schools are eligible for results-based funding. Schools may receive funds at a rate of $250/student for schools with less than 60% of students eligible for free or reduced-price lunches, or $400/student in schools where over 60% of enrolled students qualify for free or reduced-price lunch provided the schools scored in the top 10% of all schools on statewide assessments.
Arkansas	Conversion charter schools are considered a part of the school district and receive funds equal to the amount apportioned by the district from state and local revenue per average daily membership. Open-enrollment charter schools receive funds equal to the amount that a public school would receive, as well as any other funding that the public charter school is entitled to receive, except they do not have access to local revenue from property taxes. Funding for open-enrollment charter schools is determined annually by the state board of education.
California	Charter schools receive a combination of state aid and local funds according to the same weighted student funding formula applied to traditional public schools. Charter schools are eligible for a transfer of funds from their sponsoring school districts in lieu of property taxes.
Colorado	For charter schools authorized by local school boards, 100% of the per-pupil revenue flows to charter schools, less an amount for specified administrative costs based on actual district spending as reported to the state. The administrative amount is limited to 5%. In districts with less than 500 students, charter schools receive either 100% minus the administrative fees or 85% of the district per-pupil revenue, whichever is greater. For charter schools authorized by the state charter institute, 100% of per-pupil revenue flows to charter schools, less up to 3% for the state charter school institute's administrative costs and up to 1% for the state department of education's administrative costs. Additionally, school districts were required to develop for the 2018–19 school year a plan for equitably using and distributing additional mill levy revenue to charter schools and public schools located within a district. Plans must ensure that the additional revenue is distributed to, or otherwise used for programs that benefit the schools of the participating district regardless of school type.

(Continued)

TABLE 12.4 Continued

State	Funding Formula Framework
Connecticut	For local charter schools, the school district is responsible for funding the schools at a level at least equal to the product of the per-pupil cost for the fiscal year two years prior to the fiscal year for which support will be provided and the number of students in the charter in the current fiscal year. In addition, the state board may approve a per-pupil grant not to exceed $3,000 for each student enrolled in a local charter school provided that the local or regional board of education and the representatives of the exclusive bargaining unit for certified employees mutually agree on staffing flexibility in the local charter school, and the agreement is approved by the state board. For state charter schools, the state pays a per-pupil amount to the town in which a state charter school is located; however, funding for state charter schools is directly dependent on the state's annual appropriation. Charter schools are eligible for categorical federal/state funds.
Delaware	State funding for charter schools is based on the unit funding formula used for traditional public schools. Local funding is based on the previous year's per-pupil expenditure in a student's school district of residence.
District of Columbia	State funding for charter schools is based on the unit funding formula used for traditional public schools.
Florida	Students enrolled in a charter school are funded the same as students enrolled in other public schools in the school district. Federal, state, local, discretionary lottery, and discretionary millage levy funds are allocated according to the same funding formula as funds allocated to other public schools.
Georgia	State funding for charter schools is based on the funding formula used for traditional public schools. Authorizers can deduct up to 3% of charter funding for administrative fees. Charter schools are entitled to a proportionate share of all state grants except state equalization grants. Although funding for state chartered special schools is subject to state appropriation, these schools must also be treated consistently with traditional public schools pursuant to the funding formula and grants. State-chartered special schools do not receive local tax dollars unless approved by the voters of the district.
Hawaii	General per-pupil funding for charter school students should be the same as that allocated for traditional public-school students. In addition, the state director of finance is authorized to transfer additional general fund money to charter schools as needed. Charter schools are eligible for all federal financial support to the same extent as traditional public schools. Charter schools may elect to use the traditional student funding formula or propose an alternative formula to their authorizer.
Idaho	Charter schools receive funds from the same state funding formula as traditional public schools. Funding is limited to state and federal dollars. Charter schools may qualify for alternative school support monies if they meet certain statutory requirements.
Illinois	Funding is negotiated with the sponsoring school district and specified in the charter, but must not be less than 97% or more than 103% of per-pupil funding for traditional public schools. Charter schools may apply for any grant administered by the state board that is available to school districts. The state commission can charge a charter school it authorizes up to 3% of the school's revenue to cover administration costs.
Indiana	Charter schools receive the same state and federal funding as traditional public schools. Authorizers can withhold up to 3% for administrative fees.

(Continued)

Iowa	A charter school is considered a part of the school district in which it is located for purposes of state school foundation aid. Funding is specified in the charter.
Kansas	The law does not specify how charter schools are funded, leaving it at the discretion of the school district. A petition to establish a charter school must outline the proposed school budget and include a description of how the budget will be funded if federal funds are not available.
Kentucky	Charter school funding is calculated using the state's funding formula for local school districts. A public charter school's funding is allocated in the same allocation manner as the school allocation model used by the local school district based on applicable data provided by the charter school. Charter schools do not receive local capital outlay funds that are for restricted use or other financing mechanisms for new construction and renovation projects for school facilities. Additionally, public charter schools do not receive transportation funding if the district does not provide transportation to charter schools. 3% of total funding allocated shall be retained by the authorizer.
Louisiana	Charter schools fall into five categories, with variation in funding requirements depending on the charter type. All charter schools receive a state-funded base allocation according to a weighted student membership count, and have access to local revenues and all applicable federal and state categorical funding. Authorizers can charge a 2% fee for administrative costs. New and conversion schools authorized by a local school board may agree to a lesser per-pupil amount in exchange for services provided to the charter.
Maine	State and local funding for charter schools is based on the same weighted unit funding rate used for the resident school district. In charter schools authorized by the commission with students from more than one resident school district, the weighted unit funding formula for each is applied to create a revised weighted unit average. Charter schools are not permitted to levy taxes or issue bonds. Authorizers are allowed to take a 3% authorizer fee in addition to a 1% fee that is retained by the district.
Maryland	Charter schools receive an amount of county, state, and federal money commensurate with the amount disbursed to other public schools in the local jurisdiction. In addition, the state board or the county board may give surplus educational materials, supplies, furniture and other equipment to a charter school.
Massachusetts	Horace Mann charter schools receive a tuition amount determined annually as part of their local school committee's budget process. Funding levels deemed inequitable can be appealed to the commissioner. Commonwealth charter schools receive a tuition amount which is the sum of the per-pupil amount from each district sending students to the charter school. Tuition amounts for each sending district must be adjusted to reflect, as much as practicable, the actual per-pupil spending amount that would be expended in the district if the students attended the district schools. Charter schools have equal access to all applicable categorical federal and state funding. School districts are eligible to receive full or partial reimbursement of charter school expenses from state appropriations. The reimbursement amount is equal to 100% of the increase in the year it occurs, and 25% in the 2nd, 3rd, 4th, 5th, and 6th years following. Cumulative surplus revenue in excess of 20% of a charter school's operating budget and capital costs must be returned by the charter school to the sending district or districts and the state in proportion to their share of tuition paid during the fiscal year.

(Continued)

TABLE 12.4 Continued

State	Funding Formula Framework
Michigan	Charter schools receive a base per-pupil funding equal to that of the district in which the school is located, or the state maximum charter school allocation, whichever is less. Authorizers can collect 3% of funding for monitoring and administrative expenses. Charter schools may access state/federal grants in the same manner as local districts.
Minnesota	A charter school receives general education revenue as though it were a school district. A charter school is eligible to receive other aids, grants, and revenue as though it were a school district unless a levy is required to obtain the aid, grant or revenue.
Mississippi	Charter schools receive a per-pupil amount from the state department equal to the state share for each student in the school district in which the charter school is located. The local contribution amount received is proportionate to that in the district in which the charter school student resides. Charter schools are paid a per-pupil amount equal to the ad valorem tax receipts and in-lieu payments received per-pupil for the support of the local district in which the student resides as well as pro rata ad valorem receipts and in-lieu receipts include all levies for the support of the school district. For charter schools enrolling students within the district they reside, the money comes from the local district. For charter schools enrolling students from outside of the district in which they reside, the funds come from the state department of education. The state department is required to direct the proportionate share of monies generated under federal and state categorical aid programs to charter schools serving students eligible for such aid. The state authorizer receives a 3% annual fee of each charter school's per-pupil funding.
Missouri	Charter schools receive per-pupil funding in accordance with the state funding formula as well as federal and state categorical aid. The state department of education retains 1.5% of a charter school's state and local funding (not to exceed $125,000) for administrative fees and gives the retained amount to the charter school's authorizer.
Nevada	Charter schools receive per-pupil funding in accordance with the state funding formula. Charter schools are entitled to receive a proportionate share of any other money available from federal, state, or local sources that the school or the pupils who are enrolled in the school are eligible to receive. Authorizers can deduct up to 2% of the total amount of money apportioned to the charter school for administrative fees, but charter schools meeting certain requirements can request to lower the amount retained.
New Hampshire	Charter schools authorized by a local school district receive per-pupil funding that cannot be less than 80% of the district's average cost per-pupil. All other charter schools receive the state's annual per-pupil funding amount plus adequacy and disparity aid. Charter schools are eligible for all applicable categorical funding.
New Jersey	Charter schools receive 90% of per-pupil funds budgeted for the current school year and the pre-budget year general fund tax levy per-pupil inflated by the CPI rate most recent to when the calculation is made. Charter schools also receive the federal/state categorical program funds attributed to the student. For students not included in the district's projected resident enrollment for the school year, the state pays 100% of the amount required for the first year.
New Mexico	Charter schools cannot receive less than 98% of the school-generated program costs. Authorizers may deduct up to 2% of the school-generated program cost for administrative fees. Charter schools receive all state/federal funding for which they are eligible.

(Continued)

New York	Charter schools receive basic funding according to the student's resident district per-pupil allocation. Charter schools serving students from more than one district receive basic funding according to multiple districts' per-pupil allocations. Charter schools also receive a supplemental tuition amount.
North Carolina	Charter schools receive base funds equal to the average per-pupil allocation from the district in which the school is located, with additional funds for students with disabilities and students with limited English proficiency. In addition, the school district in which a charter school student resides must transfer to the charter school an amount equal to the per-pupil share of the local current expense fund of the district for the fiscal year.
Ohio	Charter schools receive state foundation aid based on full-time enrollment and targeted assistance aid for career-technical, special education, economically disadvantaged, and limited English proficiency students. Although charter schools cannot levy taxes or issue bonds secured by tax revenues, school districts can levy taxes for charter schools sponsored by exemplary sponsors. Authorizers can retain up to 3% of the total amount of payments for operating expenses that the charter school receives for administration fees.
Oklahoma	Charter schools receive the state aid allocation and any other state-appropriated revenue generated for their students according to the same state aid funding formula as traditional public schools. Authorizers can deduct up to 5% administrative fees from the school's state aid allocation. Charter schools are eligible to receive any other aid, grants, or revenues allowed to traditional public schools. The governing body of a charter school cannot levy taxes or issue bonds.
Oregon	Charter schools authorized by the local school district receive an amount at least equal to 80% of average daily membership for students in grades K–8 and 95% for students in grades 9–12. Charter schools authorized by the state department of education or institutions of higher learning within the boundaries of local school districts receive an amount at least equal to 90% of average daily membership for students in grades K–8 and 95% for students in grades 9–12. Authorizers can retain up to 20% of funding for K–8 students and up to 5% of funding for 9–12 students for administrative fees.
Pennsylvania	Charter schools receive no less than the average district per-pupil budgeted expenditure of the previous school year, minus the budgeted expenditures for nonpublic school programs, adult education programs, community/junior college programs, student transportation services, special education programs, facilities acquisition, construction and improvement services, and other financing uses.
Rhode Island	Funding for each charter school consists of state revenue and municipal or district revenue in the same proportions that funding is provided for other schools within the sending school district. Funding is equal to a percentage of the total budgeted expenses of the sending school district, determined by dividing the number of students enrolled in the district charter school by the total resident average daily number of students in the sending school district. Funding additional to that authorized from the sending school district can be allocated to the charter school from the sending school district to the extent that the combined percentage of students eligible for free or reduced cost lunch, students with limited English proficiency, and students requiring special education exceed the combined percentage of those students in the sending school district as a whole. A charter school is eligible to receive other aids, grants, Medicaid revenue, federal aid and other revenue as though it were a school district.

(Continued)

TABLE 12.4 Continued

State	Funding Formula Framework
South Carolina	District-authorized charter schools receive state, county and district funding according to the same formula as local school districts. Charter schools authorized by the South Carolina Public Charter School District or universities are provided funding by the General Assembly. Charter schools are entitled to receive federal funds on the basis of the number of special characteristics of the students in attendance and are entitled to a proportional share of federal/state categorical aid funds for which the school qualifies.
Tennessee	District-authorized charter schools receive an amount equal to the per-pupil state and local funds received by the school district and all appropriate allocations under federal law or regulation. Allocations must be based on 100% of state and local funds received by the district, including current funds allocated for capital outlay purposes, but excluding the proceeds of debt obligations and associated debt service. Allocations to the charter school cannot be reduced by the school district for administrative, indirect, or any other category of cost or charge except as specifically provided in a charter agreement. State board-authorized charter schools receive funding according to the same provisions, except that the district in which the charter school operates pays to the department 100% of the per-pupil share of the local and federal funding that is due to the charter school, the department withholds from the district 100% of the per-pupil share of state and the federal funding in the custody of the department that is due to the charter school, and 100% of these funds are disbursed to the charter school.
Texas	Like traditional public schools, charter schools are funded through a two-tier system. Tier I allocations are determined by substituting the statewide average adjusted allotment in place of the district's calculated adjusted allotment. Tier II allocations are determined by substituting a statewide average enrichment tax rate in place of the district's calculated enrichment tax rate.
Utah	A charter school that is converted from a district school receives funding on the same basis as it did prior to its conversion. A district-authorized charter school operating in a facility owned by the school district and not paying reasonable rent to the district receives funding on the same basis as other district schools receive funding. All other charter schools receive their funds on the same basis as a school district receives funds, except with regards to student counts and weights. Subject to budget constraints, the legislature provides a per-pupil appropriation to supplement the district allocation. An additional state supplement is provided if the total district allocation and the supplement amount provided by the state is less than $1,427 per-pupil. The additional supplement is allocated among charter schools in proportion to each charter school's enrollment as a percentage of the total enrollment in charter schools. Charter schools are eligible for federal money designated for charter schools.
Virginia	The local school board establishes by contract an agreement stating the conditions for funding the charter school. Generally, funding levels are commensurate with the school-based costs of educating students in traditional public schools, unless the cost of operating the charter is less.
Washington	State funding for charter schools is intended to be distributed equitably with state funding provided to other public schools. Funding levels are based on student enrollment. The state superintendent of public instruction is tasked with calculating and distributing funds to charter schools using the state funding formula for basic education. Additionally, charter schools may receive applicable categorical funds for supplemental programs and services.

(Continued)

Wisconsin	A charter school authorized by a city, county, university, or technical college receives a per-pupil amount determined by the state. The law does not specify how charter schools authorized by the district are funded. The school funding formula is updated regularly and is used to calculate funding for charter and traditional public schools.
Wyoming	Charter schools are guaranteed 100% of foundation program funding generated by the charter school's average daily membership, less any district level amounts generated by the charter school's membership, 100% of the charter school's proportion of major maintenance payments based upon the proportion that the charter school educational building gross square footage contributes to the district educational building gross square footage, and 100% of the amount generated by the payroll of the charter school's employees in allocating any school district salary adjustment. An applicant charter school may also be funded through a specific budget mutually agreed upon by the school district and the charter school.

Source: Education Commission of the States. "How Is Charter School Funding Determined." Denver, CO (2018). (Excerpted by permission.) http://ecs.force.com/mbdata/mbquestNB2C?rep=CS1716

meeting its general responsibility in terms of leadership and overall supervision. Other cases involving unequal funding[26] have occurred, all essentially indicating that a parallel system of schools is not inherently impermissible. But the plaintiff cause has not been entirely one-sided, as in a protracted challenge where plaintiff charter schools sought remedy under several constitutional theories. Plaintiff charter schools argued that the Texas state constitution requires "A general diffusion of knowledge being essential to the preservation of liberties and rights of the people, it shall be the duty of the Legislature of the State to establish and make suitable provision for the support and maintenance of an efficient system of public free schools."[27] The state supreme court in *Morath v. Texas Taxpayers*[28] specifically addressed the funding of charter schools, saying that charter schools were created by statute and not required by the state constitution; that charter schools were viewed as a form of a contract among parties; and that charter schools were by legislative purpose to encourage different and innovative learning methods and consequently not subject to the same funding scrutiny. Conversely, though, the Louisiana supreme court in *Iberville*[29] held that charter schools were public schools within the meaning of the state constitution and entitled to local property tax revenues. These dizzying progressions of judicial thought serve to illustrate the conundrum of whether charter schools are public or private schools and how they are to be treated and funded under state-specific laws—in the end, the answer depends on the question before the courts, as well as the enabling state legislation.

Whether charter schools are proxies for privatization remains a debate that must be resolved in legislative halls. But notwithstanding, what is perfectly clear is that charter schools have become a formidable influence regardless of their underlying motivation. It is also perfectly clear that their existence—or variants thereon—are part of the foreseeable landscape.

Vouchers

While charter school organizations have dominated the landscape, other variants of school choice also have taken root. Among the options has been the school voucher movement, which has been unapologetic about its aims. *EdChoice*—a strong propo-nent of voucher plans—openly declared its purpose, saying: "School vouchers give parents the freedom to choose a private school for their children, using all or part of the public funding set aside for their children's education. Under such a program, funds typically spent by a school district would be allocated to a participating family in the form of a voucher to pay partial or full tuition for their child's private school, including both religious and non-religious options."[30]

Although less prevalent than charter schools, voucher programs exist today in 15 states and the District of Columbia.[31] Proponents proudly point to the influence, saying that nearly 200,000 schoolchildren are given an educational choice via vouch-ers, citing to a U.S. Supreme Court case upholding the legality of such programs. In *Zelman*,[32] the nation's highest court held that a voucher program created by the Ohio legislature was constitutional despite the fact that most recipients cashed their vouch-ers at parochial schools. The Court reasoned that there was no direct payment from the state to the church and therefore not in violation of separation of church and state under the U.S. Constitution. This stance was recently upheld in *Trinity*[33] as the Court ruled that a public benefit to everyone, including a church, did not violate the First Amendment—i.e., the facts of the case involved improving playgrounds across the state of Missouri, which the Court saw as a public benefit and not as direct support of religion. However, direct payment to a private religious school for the purpose of education as a public benefit under the *Trinity* standard has yet to be heard. Voucher plaintiffs, however, are resourceful—for example, if speculating that such a benefit might eventually be impermissible, it is likely that proponents would shift tactics via some vehicle like a scholarship program to devise an arm's length transaction. While such cases have yet to emerge, the certainty of continual struggle is unavoidable.

Although many voucher plans have been open primarily to students in academi-cally failing schools, some states have made vouchers more widely available. Table 12.5 later accumulates the principal forms of shifting tax support to public school competi-tors, showing that efforts have been systematic, albeit not universal in all 50 states. Importantly, it appears that every year more state legislatures are expanding vouchers in various ways. For example, in 2018 the Florida legislature passed new legislation allowing students who claim to have been bullied to become eligible for vouchers. Consequently, it is reasonable to anticipate that over the next few years increas-ingly creative avenues to vouchers and other school choices will become even more widely available.

Tax Credit/Deductions, Tax Savings/Scholarship Accounts

Still other vehicles to reach school choice ends have been adopted by various states. Individual and corporate state tax credits and deductions are one such plan. State income tax deduction plans result in tax benefits tied to individual or corporate income brackets and net tax liability (obviously, taxpayers residing in zero income tax states are unaffected by such plans). The concept is not new, as the first state income tax credit for educational purposes began in Minnesota in 1955. Key to such plans is that the U.S. Supreme Court in *Mueller*[34] in 1982 ruled this plan constitutional based on the child benefit theory, i.e., the child as the primary beneficiary.

TABLE 12.5 Additional Types of School Choice 2018

State	Program Type	Enrollment	Enrollment Rate	Eligibility	Average Funding	Public Funding	Schools
AL	Tax-Credit Scholarship	3,579	2%	183,303	$6,039	66%	162
AL	Individual Tax Credit/Deduction	122	<1%	43,876	$2,424	27%	N/A
AR	Voucher	174	<1%	71,154	$6,713	68%	22
AZ	Tax-Credit Scholarship	31,578	5%	665,587	$1,724	23%	330
AZ	Tax-Credit Scholarship	20,076	5%	387,245	$2,165	29%	242
AZ	Education Savings Account	5,409	2%	259,223	$14,518	191%	134
AZ	Tax-Credit Scholarship	20,976	2%	1,101,149	$1,360	18%	321
AZ	Tax-Credit Scholarship	936	<1%	133,456	$4,696	62%	148
DC	Voucher	1,653	9%	17,737	$9,570	46%	46
FL	Tax-Credit Scholarship	108,098	12%	872,636	$5,930	65%	1,818
FL	Voucher	31,044	8%	393,025	$7,104	78%	1,482
FL	Education Savings Account	10,153	3%	343,648	$10,312	113%	3,396
FL	Tax-Credit Scholarship	N.A.	N.A.	N.A.	$6,700	96%	N.A.
GA	Voucher	4,194	2%	200,194	$5,606	59%	235
GA	Tax-Credit Scholarship	13,243	1%	1,698,287	$3,455	36%	400
IA	Individual Tax Credit/Deduction	133,122	38%	349,173	$116	1%	N/A
IA	Tax-Credit Scholarship	10,771	7%	206,059	$1,583	14%	138
IL	Individual Tax Credit/Deduction	305,822	23%	1,342,579	$262	2%	N/A
IL	Tax-Credit Scholarship	N/A	N/A	342,439	$12,973	94%	N/A
IN	Individual Tax Credit/Deduction	54,755	29%	186,727	$1,805	19%	N/A
IN	Voucher	35,458	5%	719,319	$4,342	46%	318

(Continued)

TABLE 12.5 Continued

State	Program Type	Enrollment	Enrollment Rate	Eligibility	Average Funding	Public Funding	Schools
IN	Tax-Credit Scholarship	8,501	2%	434,594	$1,978	21%	327
KS	Tax-Credit Scholarship	292	<1%	35,248	$2,315	22%	106
LA	Individual Tax Credit/Deduction	106,549	70%	152,955	$4,060	38%	N/A
LA	Voucher	6,695	3%	257,674	$5,869	53%	120
LA	Voucher	336	2%	18,890	$2,328	21%	21
LA	Tax-Credit Scholarship	1,520	1%	226,011	$4,148	37%	165
MD	Voucher	2,659	2%	156,132	$2,294	16%	241
ME	Voucher	5,727	100%	5,727	$11,162	80%	64
MN	Individual Tax Credit/Deduction	49,952	41%	121,939	$255	2%	N/A
MN	Individual Tax Credit/Deduction	212,731	34%	613,580	$1,149	10%	N/A
MS	Voucher	165	1%	28,310	$4,980	59%	5
MS	Voucher	0		13,604	$0		0
MS	Education Savings Account	153	<1%	66,445	$6,500	77%	23
MT	Tax-Credit Scholarship	25	<1%	151,730	$500	5%	12
NC	Voucher	7,371	2%	487,330	$3,807	45%	405
NC	Voucher	1,196	1%	197,185	$6,775	79%	212
NC	Education Savings Account	300	N/A	176,759	$9,000	106%	145
NH	Tax-Credit Scholarship	332	<1%	48,227	$2,148	14%	51
NH	Voucher	N.A.	N.A.	N.A.	N.A.	N.A.	N.A.
NV	Tax-Credit Scholarship	2,133	1%	156,438	$5,114	61%	86
NV	Education Savings Account	N.A.	N.A.	453,024	$5,139	61%	N.A.
OH	Voucher	8,004	18%	44,411	$4,620	39%	42
OH	Voucher	3,522	14%	25,312	$22,748	194%	290
OH	Voucher	21,846	14%	155,692	$4,705	40%	482

OH	Voucher	4,930	2%	254,176	$9,818	84%	263
OH	Voucher	7,581	2%	396,185	$4,084	35%	474
OK	Voucher	669	1%	106,205	$6,161	76%	52
OK	Tax-Credit Scholarship	2,209	<1%	347,953	$1,765	22%	93
PA	Tax-Credit Scholarship	11,417	9%	130,044	$2,668	19%	934
PA	Tax-Credit Scholarship	30,469	5%	783,662	$1,673	12%	258
RI	Tax-Credit Scholarship	433	1%	41,116	$3,704	23%	42
SC	Tax-Credit Scholarship	1,972	2%	101,052	$5,136	52%	106
SC	Individual Tax Credit/ Deduction	N.A.	N.A.	99,101	$10,000	103%	N/A
SD	Tax-Credit Scholarship	481	1%	40,315	$603	7%	42
TN	Education Savings Account	88	<1%	18,964	$6,528	75%	14
UT	Voucher	882	1%	78,429	$5,905	87%	55
VA	Tax-Credit Scholarship	2,419	1%	325,746	$3,134	28%	169
VT	Voucher	3,350	100%	3,350	$13,152	77%	435
WI	Voucher	28,702	63%	45,504	$7,503	65%	126
WI	Voucher	3,007	32%	9,519	$7,447	65%	23
WI	Individual Tax Credit/ Deduction	36,640	31%	126,035	$4,932	42%	N/A
WI	Voucher	4,540	3%	137,920	$7,512	65%	154
WI	Voucher	246	<1%	120,677	$12,129	105%	28
Totals	Averages	1,371,207	–	16,709,986	$5,232	53%	15,257

Source: Excerpted and modified from EdChoice. "School Choice in America Dashboard." Indianapolis, IN: EdChoice (2018). By permission. https://www.edchoice.org/school-choice/school-choice-in-america/#

The potential for enacting tax credits and deductions is an ever-present legislative option in the 44 states that collect state income tax. Theoretically, taxpayers in any such state could receive tax credits for expenses such as tuition, books, supplies, computers, tutors, pupil transportation, and more. Table 12.5 indicates that 23 states now have one or more such credits or deductions, making this vehicle a meaningful player among the alternatives to traditional public schools. As with all legislative matters, it should be noted that states sometimes enact specific plans in complex detail and sometimes with restricted audiences in mind, such as South Carolina's tax credit which is aimed at special needs children as defined by federal law.[35] And needless to say, tax credits are not without argumentation, as in Illinois where litigation has accompanied legislative action by invoking First Amendment and establishment clauses of the U.S. Constitution.[36] And the consequence of such plans should not be underestimated, both for current and future impact as ideas grow and mature, sometimes in ways that can spin out of control.[37]

Table 12.5 also identifies states' interest in other school choice vehicles such as educational savings accounts. Much less widespread than charters and tax credits, the potential nonetheless has roots since six states have enacted savings accounts in some form. It is much harder to determine from Table 12.5 the impact of state sympathy for scholarship accounts, as states variously intermingle descriptions of tax credits and scholarships in ways that overlap and at times make it impossible to categorize in a discrete fashion. But as seen in Table 12.5, states have variously adopted multiple vehicles to the same intended outcome. That the stakes are meaningful is seen in the totals and averages for Table 12.5, where current enrollments in the various program types reaches nearly 1.4 million out of 16.7 million eligible students, with an average funding benefit of $5,232 and with more than 15,000 eligible sites.

In brief, many state legislatures in the past 20 years have drifted from the historical traditional public school system toward what appears to be a model of funding three separate school systems: The traditional system, a charter system, and a voucher-like system. Each system is based on the political, social, and economic philosophies of state policymakers. Traditional system values adhere to equity, fairness, and a common set of educational experiences provided to all children on an equal footing. Charter system values promote innovation, experimentation, parental choice, and shrinking educational bureaucracies. Voucher-like system values embrace maximum parental choice, freedom from regulation, and individualism. It remains to be seen whether one system will dominate or whether a hybrid will emerge; it also remains to be seen whether greater inequities or greater advances will emerge for society as a whole. Society itself will determine the fate of these policies, but it is certain that the future looks very different from the past.

Lessons from This Book

The *social, political, and economic context* of public education discussed in Chapter 1 provided a sobering lesson. In the United States, schools are a source of both cynicism and optimism. Critics of public schools point out that U.S. students continue to lag behind peers in developed, as well as some developing, nations on measures of academic achievement on international tests. At the same time, Americans over-all continue to view education as an engine for economic mobility and prosperity, even though recent research demonstrates that economic mobility is now lower in the United States than in many other developed countries, and disparities in income in the United States between the rich and the poor have reached historic highs even as the middle class shrinks. A central lesson of the chapter was that equality of educational opportunity costs money, while at the same time finite resources dictate that school leaders often have to make hard choices.

Chapter 2 transitioned to education policymaking, exploring the role of education as both an economic and social good. Education can be viewed as an investment in human capital, and research time and again has supported this investment because of the returns to the individual and society. Chapter 2 also chronicled the history of school governance in the United States, making evident that today's education system is rooted in the richness of American democracy. Part of that history has been the evolution of local, state, and federal systems of taxation from which public education draws fiscal support. The final portion of the chapter traced the quest for adequate and equitable school funding through federal and state courts, noting that the quest continues. The struggle over values in education was apparent in this chapter, as disagreements over the worth of education and who should pay for schools continue to play out in the policy arena.

Chapter 3 discussed basic school funding sources and structures. While taxes have never been popular, over time extensive federal, state, and local tax systems have nonetheless developed, from which schools derive their revenue. The chapter explored revenue structures at each of these levels and their relative contributions to school funding. Although the federal share of public education revenues currently is not insignificant, it has played only a minor role with states and local school districts shouldering around 90%. The chapter also noted that each state's school funding system is the product of its unique political, social, and economic history. The lessons learned from this chapter were twofold. First, taxes are the product of political environments where education competes with other worthy public services for limited resources. Second, although state aid formulas have the potential to provide equity and adequacy in school funding at the district level, some states have been more successful than others in achieving this goal. Additionally, school finance litigation has often provided the impetus for states to move closer to those goals.

Chapter 4 opened Part II, *operationalizing school money*, by moving from a broad policy perspective to a more detailed analysis of budgeting by examining fiscal accountability and professionalism. This chapter encouraged appreciation of the public trust placed in school leaders as fiscal stewards, emphasizing the fiduciary responsibilities of school administrators and staff and identifying how school revenues and expenditures are structured. Admittedly, these were challenging topics to present in brief form, but the overarching message was that school leaders need at least a basic knowledge of the types of money received by schools, how money can be spent, and how public funds are guarded against error, misuse, and fraud.

Chapter 5 focused on budget planning. The first part of the chapter discussed ways to organize for budgeting, including common approaches to budgeting, while the second half explored budget construction. Implicit were two key arguments. First, the central purpose of budgeting is to implement equal educational opportunity by converting dollars into program priorities. Second, budgets should be viewed as the principal planning system by which political and legal approval is secured for providing education to children; that is, budgets are more than an accounting tool. Rather, they are a tool for making informed educational decisions.

The book next turned to analyzing the major cost determinants of budgets. Chapter 6 looked at the relationship of school money to the human resource function, which represents a major portion of school budgets. Pragmatic concerns such as determining staff needs, recruitment, and selection were addressed, along with compensation and costing out salary proposals. Importantly, negotiations, due process, and alternative reward systems were also considered. With personnel-related expenses consuming on average 80% of a district budget, this chapter made clear that it is critical for school leaders to be knowledgeable about personnel budgets.

Chapter 7 moved to the heart of school budgeting by exploring instructional costs. This chapter focused on organizational options, as well as instructional budget concepts and elements. Much time was devoted to looking at district and school-based budgeting. Two key lessons emerged. First, budgeting for instruction is the most important activity in schools because it enables teaching and learning to occur. Second, instructional budgets should reflect the mission and goals of the district and individual school.

Chapter 8 turned to budgeting for student activities, an area whose importance in schools should not be underestimated. These activities were argued to be integral to students becoming well-rounded individuals. For school leaders who often have oversight of student activity funds, many opportunities and pitfalls exist in managing this important dimension of school life. This chapter focused on identifying the many activity fund accounts in a typical school district, distinguishing between student and district activity funds, and on appropriate handling of money associated with activity funds at the individual school level. Nonactivity funds like petty cash were also discussed, with caution to school leaders to develop rigorous and consistent disbursement and accounting procedures.

Chapter 9 focused on budgeting for school infrastructure. The chapter first established that the physical environment of schools is a critical factor in student success. At the same time, it is severely underfunded, with few federal resources available. State aid was shown to vary tremendously, with some states providing no aid at all. In sum, the quality of school infrastructure was demonstrated to mostly be a function of school district wealth except in states that have experienced successful litigation. The chapter then presented methods available to school districts to finance major school infrastructure projects, as well as the planning process. Finally, effective maintenance and operations practices to support a school district's infrastructure by keeping it in a condition that supports teaching and learning were surveyed.

In Chapter 10, transportation and food service were presented as essential programs supporting the educational process. While the instructional mission of schools rightly receives great attention, it was argued that equality of educational opportunity is obstructed when children are hungry or deprived of the means by which to attend school. Transportation costs were shown to vary dramatically by type of district depending upon its size and student population. Overall, school districts were seen to depend on state and local revenues to fund transportation. On the other hand, federal funding was shown to provide the bulk of revenue for school meals, but with tight regulation. However, it was emphasized that the federal government supports free and reduced-price meals for students in poverty—a major contribution to equal educational opportunity. In significant ways, the chapter held that transportation and food service require prudent fiscal leadership, as well as attention to statutory and regulatory requirements.

Chapter 11 moved to legal liability and risk management in school settings. The purpose of the chapter was to inform school leaders of broad liability principles and to encourage careful planning for risk management. Central to the chapter was the concept that leaders must understand the sources of authority enjoyed by schools; the nature and limits on immunity; the problems encountered when laws and rights are violated; and the loss of discretionary revenue resulting from liability-related fault. The overriding lesson was caution in all matters because the law and schools are constant companions.

Finally, Chapter 12 went to the heart of the future of school funding. The politics of money took center stage, with liberty, equity, efficiency, accountability, and innovation as drivers. The economy along with politics were said to be the keys to the future—a premise unchanged from all previous editions[38] of this textbook. While this new seventh edition updated facts and expanded on new developments, what remained steadfast was that the future unfolds for all eternity.

A FINAL WORD

The purpose of this book was to present a realistic assessment of the challenges facing the funding of public education and to develop skills in school leaders relating to schools and money. For over 250 years, public education has been a cornerstone of economic opportunity and upward mobility in the United States. However, the nation is still at a crossroads. With rising social and economic inequality, those on both ends of the political spectrum—conservative and liberal—have raised questions about the continued investment of tax revenues in a public education system that still trails other developed countries in academic achievement. Public education continues to be enmeshed in a complex social, economic, and political environment, and each day finds itself more deeply divided by bitter partisanship regarding the role of government.

While this book has argued that there are no simple solutions, it vehemently concludes that education needs great leaders who understand the relationship between money and educational opportunity—leaders who possess the knowledge and expertise to deploy fiscal and human resources for the benefit of every child. Schools need leaders who promote the success of all children by understanding, responding, and influencing the larger political, social, economic, legal, and cultural context in which education is embedded. In other words, money and leadership have never mattered more than today.

POINT–COUNTERPOINT

POINT

A large body of respected research demonstrates that students in poverty, as well as other students commonly defined as at risk of academic failure, need greater resources in order to be academically successful. It is clearly a matter of equity and equality of educational opportunity for states to provide the additional money for these students. If these children fail and drop out of school, they become a lifetime tax burden on the whole of society given their unemployability and burden on social services and the criminal justice system.

COUNTERPOINT

The federal government already provides significant funding for poor students as well as others categorized as at risk, e.g., funding for special education and English language learners, as well as free and reduced-price breakfast and lunch. In addition, almost every state provides extra funding for these students. With all these special aids, it is the average student who is shortchanged by being placed in large classes with little individual attention. The real problem is that schools and school districts are not using their funding efficiently.

- Given your experience and the readings in this text, which position seems more accurate? Why?
- In your view, can schools provide equal educational opportunity to all students and still be efficient? Explain.

CASE STUDY

At the start of your second year as an urban school superintendent, you were shocked to read this morning's local headline, "Parental Satisfaction with Local Schools at All Time Low." A nationally known conservative policy think tank had conducted a survey of parents in your school district unbeknownst to you and the school board, and had released a highly critical report to the media. One of the major areas of discontent, according to the news account, was what parents perceived as arbitrary assignment of their children to schools. If the media had accurately reported parental attitudes, parents were demanding not only to choose their children's school but also to have a wider array of choices, like specialty schools, alternative schools, and virtual schools.

While you would not have welcomed the news at any point, you were especially concerned about the timing of negative press. The headline had hit just as you were in the midst of your own contract renewal with the board, and the combination of these factors was unsettling because this was your first contract renewal. You knew there were tensions within the board about your performance, and you knew that several school site administrators were displeased with your focus on turning schools around through the use of incentive monies. You had undertaken that strategy very recently because—among other things—this year's student test scores had fallen for the third straight year, and as a result several schools in the district were facing state sanctions—unwelcome news that had already received unflattering local media coverage. To make matters worse, the state legislature was now considering a bill to permit vouchers in all urban school districts in the state which you feared could skim off the best and brightest students along with their engaged parents, leaving your district to educate an increasingly high cost and challenging student body.

Immediately upon arriving at your office this morning, you called an emergency senior cabinet meeting. You announced that you were creating a task force to draft a decisive response to the study, with the charge to develop low or no-cost options that would satisfy parental demands. You indicated that the task force would need to find ways around the financial barriers most urban school districts, including yours, typically face—e.g., a budget barely able to cover the necessities of instruction and a long list of problems like much needed maintenance and repairs. As you summed up the charge, you emphasized the need for thinking outside the box by saying that the district must consider some significant restructuring to meet these demands because reallocating resources was the most effective way out of this situation.

Because the headlines and your contract were hitting simultaneously, you announced that you would personally chair the task force and that you would select about a dozen individuals to serve with you. As you closed the meeting, you indicated that some members of your cabinet would be appointed to the task force and that a rigorous meeting schedule would follow because you expected to form a response in three months or less. Back in your office, you wondered about the risks inherent to your actions, but under the circumstances you knew you needed to be seen as a proactive problem-solver.

Following is a set of questions. As you respond, consider your learning throughout this book and apply your new knowledge to the situation.

- Who will you select to join you on this task force? Explain your rationale.
- Brainstorm the options you might present in your final report. Detail the costs, if any, of each option as well as the potential educational benefits.
- In addition to the task force, are there other responses or initiatives the school district might undertake to empower parents?
- Are there any assumptions or beliefs in this case study that give you cause for concern? If so, why?

PORTFOLIO EXERCISES

- Identify three major educational issues at national or state levels and provide your rationale for selecting them. Discuss how funding is associated with each and indicate whether you believe (based on your readings here and other research) that sufficient funding is available. Discuss how greater funding might be secured. Be as specific as possible, e.g., would additional funding come from local, state, or federal levels, grants, private funding, or some combination?
- Prepare a report on education policy issues in your state such as the political environment for school funding, the condition of the state economy, the impact of school choice, and demands for equity, adequacy, efficiency, and accountability. Use resources such as news articles and publications of local or state policy think tanks and stakeholder groups like teacher unions, taxpayer associations, and community organizations.

NOTES

1   Charles S. Benson. *The Cheerful Prospect: A Statement on the Future of American Education* (Boston, MA: Houghton-Mifflin, 1965).
2   Diametrically opposed political thought exists, of course, as in Henry Giroux, "The Slow and Fast Assault on Public Education." *The Boston Review* (May 14, 2018). http://bostonreview.net/education-opportunity/henry-giroux-slow-and-fast-assault-public-education. But see Laura Meckler, "The Education of Betsy DeVos: Why Her School Choice Agenda Has Not Advanced." *Washington Post* (September 4, 2018). https://www.washingtonpost.com/local/education/the-education-of-betsy-devos-why-her-school-choice-agenda-has-crashed/2018/09/04/c21119b8-9666-11e8-810c-5fa705927d54_story.html?utm_term=.4a3b0f4c3d79
3   James W. Guthrie. "Educational Accountability." Proceedings of the Academy of Political Science, *Government in the Classroom: Dollars and Power in Education* 33, 2 (1978): 24–32.
4   See, e.g., R. Craig Wood. "A Critique of the Federal Challenge to Financing Public Education Along Racial Lines in *Lynch v. Alabama*: How the Plaintiffs, the Defendants, and the Federal District Court Erred in Examining the Funding of Public Education in Alabama." *Education Law & Policy Review* 1, 1, (Spring, 2014): 123–171.
5   See, e.g., The Council of Economic Advisors. "The Opportunity Costs of Socialism." Washington, DC: Council of Economic Advisors (October 2018). www.whitehouse.gov/cea
6   See e.g., Arthur Okun, *Equality and Efficiency: The Big Trade-Off* (Washington, DC: The Brookings Institution, 1975).
7   However, see Paul Krugman, "Liberty, Equality, Efficiency." *New York Times* (March 10, 2014), arguing that reducing inequality "would probably increase, not reduce, economic growth."
8   See, e.g., David C. Thompson, Julie K. Underwood, and William E. Camp. "Equal Protection Under Law: Reanalysis and New Directions in School Finance Litigation." In *Spheres of Justice in American Education* (New York: Harper, 1990); see also R. Craig Wood and David C. Thompson. "Politics of Plaintiffs and Defendants." In *Politics of Education Law: Effects on Education Finance* (New York: Eye on Education, 2004).

9   Follow the history and developments at SchoolFunding.Info. "Daily News Roundup."
     http://schoolfunding.info

10   Romain Huret. *American Tax Resisters* (Cambridge, MA: Harvard University Press,
     2014).

11   For example, a search for "school tax" resistance yields upward of 44,000 hits.

12   See, e.g., National Public Radio series "School Money: The Cost of Opportunity."
     (2016.) A three-week series with segments on "Why America's Schools Have a Money
     Problem"; "Can More Money Fix America's Schools?"; "Is There a Better Way to Pay for
     America's Schools?" Additional segments: "Your State's Schools are in Trouble When a
     Judge Says…"; "3 School Money Updates: Chaos, Change, No Change at All"; "Taking on
     Poverty and Education in School Costs a Lot of Money"; and more. https://www.npr.org/
     series/473636949/schoolmoney

13   For example, a search for "voters wanting higher school taxes 2018" yields more than
     30 million hits, with titles reflecting yea/nay to the query.

14   Education Commission of the States. "50-State Comparison: Charter School Policies."
     (2018.) https://www.ecs.org/charter-school-policies/

15   U.S. Department of Education, National Center for Education Statistics, Common Core of
     Data (CCD), "Public Elementary/Secondary School Universe Survey," 2000–01 through
     2015–16. See Digest of Education Statistics 2016 and 2017.

16   Legal challenges involving charter schools have varied widely over the past few years. e.g.,
     authority, creation/ closing/ location, overpayments, transportation, desegregation issues,
     bond issues, National Labor Relations Board applicability, IDEA applicability, federal
     fund eligibility, separation of church and state, and more.

17   Education Commission of the States. "50-State Comparison: Charter School Policies."
     (2018.) https://www.ecs.org/charter-school-policies/

18   National Association of Charter School Authorizers (2018). https://www.qualitycharters.
     org/policy-research/state-map/district-of-columbia/

19   National Association of Charter School Authorizers (2018). www.qualitycharters.org/
     about/one-million-lives/ Also use this url's interactive map to identify charter school pres-
     ence in each state.

20   The Washington State Supreme Court was examining these issues in late 2018. See,
     Washington League of Women Voters v. State, 355 P.3d 1131 (2015). These challenges
     pertain to whether the Washington legislature could create and fund charter schools. In
     2012, voters of the state approved Measure 1240, authorizing creation of charter schools.
     Plaintiffs successfully argued before the state supreme court that charter schools were not
     common schools by the meaning of the constitution. As a result, the legislature changed
     the funding for charter schools by earmarking state lottery dollars. as opposed to gen-
     eral funds, in support of charter schools (Wash. Rev. Code § 28A.710). Plaintiffs chal-
     lenged this change, arguing that revisions were unconstitutional regardless of the funding
     method. The case was heard by the Washington Supreme Court, with a ruling expected
     in the near future (*El Centro de la Raza v. State of Washington*, No. 94269 filed July 10,
     2017; Oral Arguments May 17, 2018).

21   566 N.W.2d 208, (Mich. 1997).

22   Mich. Const. art. VIII. § 2.

23   89 Cal. Rptr. 2d 745, (Ct. App. 1999).

24   217 P.3d 918, (Colo. App. 2009).

25   566 N.W.2d 208, (1997).

26   *Craven v. Huppenthal*, 338 P.3d 324 (2014) where the court held that funding was only
     required to be adequate, not equitable. Also a series of litigations in North Carolina regard-
     ing whether charter schools had to be funded in exactly the same way as public schools—
     see, Lisa Lukasik, *Deconstructing a Decade of Charter School Funding Litigation: An
     Argument for Reform* 90 North Carolina Law Review, 1885. *See, Sugar Creek Charter
     Sch. v. Charlotte-Mecklenburg Bd. of Educ.*, 667 S.E.2d 460 (2008), (*Sugar Creek I*);

Sugar Creek Charter Sch. Inc. v. Charlotte–Mecklenburg Bd. of Educ., 655 S.E.2d 850, (2008), (*Sugar Creek II*); *Sugar Creek Charter Sch. Inc. v. Charlotte-Mecklenburg Bd. of Educ.*, 673 S.E.2d 667, (*Sugar Creek III*). See, *Thomas Jefferson Classical Acad. Charter Sch. v. Cleveland Cnty. Bd. of Educ.*, 778 S.E. 2d 295 (N.C. Ct. App. 2015), *aff'd*, 368 N.C. 900 789 S.E.2d 442 (2016).

27   Tex. Const. art. VII, §1.

28   *Morath v. Taxpayers & Students*, 490 S.W.3d 826 (2016).

29   *Iberville*, ___So. 3d ___, 2016 WL 1319404, No. 2017–C–0257, 2017–C–0633, 2017–C–0834 reversing the appellate court in *Iberville Parish Sch. Bd. v. Louisiana State Bd. of Elem. and Sec. Educ.*, 219 So. 3d 1110, (La, June 05, 2017) *cert. granted.* See also R. Craig Wood and William Thro. "Originalism and the State Education Clauses: The Louisiana Voucher Case as an Illustration," *302 Education Law Reporter.* 875 (2014).

30   EdChoice. "What Are School Vouchers?" Indianapolis, IN: EdChoice (2018). https://www.edchoice.org/school-choice/types-of-school-choice/what-are-school-vouchers-2/

31   EdChoice (2018).

32   *Zelman v. Simmons-Harris*, 536 U.S. 639 (2002).

33   *Trinity Lutheran Church of Columbia Inc. v. Comer* 137 S. Ct. 2012, (2017).

34   *Mueller v. Allen*, 463 U.S. 388.

35   S.C. Code Ann. § 59–41–20.

36   See, e.g., *Griffith v. Bower*, 747 N.E.2d 423 (5th Dist.), *appeal denied*, 755 N.E.2d 477 (Ill, 2001); *Toney v. Bower*, 744 N.E.2d 351 (4th Dist.) *appeal denied*, 195 Ill 2d 575 Ill 2001.

37   For example, tax credits to individuals can be interesting to business, e.g., if tax benefits for schooling are available to individuals, business and industry might seek the same. If a business gifts money to a school or school district, the business decreases its tax liability by some amount while thinking that the gift will decrease the need for the state to provide a like amount to schools. The underlying principle is problematic because reducing the tax liability of any entity normally results in less governmental revenue overall, *and* (in the gifting case) it directs the offsetting revenue outside the state aid formula, thereby risking disequalization. The problem is obvious unless the state aid formula takes gifts into account in ways that guard against aid supplantation and guards against fiscal imbalances if gifts are made to individual school sites. Another problem arises in that the state would have collected less revenue while not lessening its duty to fully fund the school aid formula—a case of revenue loss, along with concern for supplantation. The problem worsens when credits, deductions, and gifts to non-public schools are allowed because equity is harmed—all as a consequence of tax forgiveness at a legislature's hand.

38   Previous editions were David C. Thompson and R. Craig Wood. *Money and Schools* first ed. (New York: Eye on Education, 1998); David C. Thompson and R. Craig Wood., *Money and Schools* second ed. (New York: Eye on Education, 2001); David C. Thompson and R. Craig Wood. *Money and Schools* third ed. (New York: Eye on Education, 2005); David C. Thompson, R. Craig Wood, and Faith E. Crampton. *Money and Schools* fourth ed. (New York: Eye on Education, 2008); David C. Thompson, R. Craig Wood, and Faith E. Crampton. *Money and Schools* fifth ed. (New York: Eye on Education, 2012); Faith E. Crampton, R. Craig Wood, and David C. Thompson, *Money and Schools* sixth ed. (New York: Routledge, 2015).

WEB RESOURCES

American Legislative Exchange Council, www.alec.org

Brown Center on Education Policy at the Brookings Institution, www.brookings.edu/brown.aspx

Center on Budget and Policy Priorities, www.cbpp.org

Center on Education Policy, www.cep-dc.org

Council of the Great City Schools, www.cgcs.org

Council of State Governments, www.csg.org

Economic Policy Institute, www.epi.org

Education Commission of the States, www.ecs.org

Education Policy Analysis Archives, www.epaa.asu.edu

Heritage Foundation, www.heritage.org

Manhattan Institute for Policy Research, www.manhattan-institute.org

National Center for the Study of Privatization in Education, www.ncspe.org

National Conference of State Legislatures, www.ncsl.org

National Governors Association, www.nga.org

The Program on Education Policy and Governance at Harvard University, www.ksg.harvard.edu/pepg

The Urban Institute, www.urban.org

U.S. Government Accountability Office, www.gao.gov

RECOMMENDED RESOURCES

Alexander, Kern. "Asymmetric Information, Parental Choice, Vouchers, Charter Schools and Stiglitz." *Journal of Education Finance* 38, 2 (Fall 2012): 170–176.

American Federation of Teachers. "Take Action." Washington, DC (2018). https://www.aft.org/action

Arsen, David, Thomas DeLuca, Yongmei Ni, and Michael Bates. "Which Districts Get into Financial Trouble and Why: Michigan's Story." *Journal of Education Finance* 42, 2 (Fall 2016): 100–126.

Babington, Michael and David M. Welsch. "Open Enrollment, Competition, and Student Performance." *Journal of Education Finance* 42, 4 (Spring 2017): 414–434.

Benson, Charles S. *The Cheerful Prospect: A Statement on the Future of American Education.* Boston, MA: Houghton-Mifflin, 1965.

Bifulco, Robert and Christian Buerger. "The Influence of Finance and Accountability Policies on Location of New York State Charter Schools." *Journal of Education Finance* 40, 3 (Winter 2015): 193–221.

Callahan, Raymond. *Education and the Cult of Efficiency: A Study of the Social Forces that Have Shaped the Administration of Public Schools.* Chicago: University of Chicago Press, 1962.

Carpenter, Dick M. II. "Where Does the Money Go?: Budget Expenditure Allocations in Charter Schools." *Journal of Education Finance* 38, 4 (Spring 2013): 304–319.

Carpenter, Dick M. II and Scott L. Noller. "Measuring Charter School Efficiency: An Early Appraisal." *Journal of Education Finance* 35, 4 (Spring 2010): 397–415.

Coons, John, William Clune, and Stephen Sugarman. *Private Wealth and Public Education.* Cambridge, MA: The Belknap Press of Harvard University Press, 1970.

Cowen, Joshua M. and Marcus A. Winters. "Choosing Charters: Who Leaves Public School as an Alternative Sector Expands?" *Journal of Education Finance* 38, 3 (Winter 2013): 210–229.

De Luca, Barbara M. and R. Craig Wood. "The Charter School Movement in the United States: Financial and Achievement Evidence from Ohio." *Journal of Education Finance* 41, 4 (Spring 2016): 438–450.

Friedman, Milton. "The Role of Government in Education." In *Economics and the Public Interest*, edited by Robert A. Solo, 123–144. New Brunswick, NJ: Rutgers University Press, 1955.

Izraeli, Oded and Kevin Murphy. "An Analysis of Michigan Charter Schools: Enrollment, Revenues, and Expenditures." *Journal of Education Finance* 37, 3 (Winter 2012): 234–266.

Menifield, Charles E. "Lottery Funded Scholarships in Tennessee: Increased Access but Weak Retention for Minority Students." *Journal of Education Finance* 38, 1 (Summer 2012): 3–17.

Mills, Jonathan N. "The Achievement Impacts of Arkansas Open-Enrollment Charter Schools." *Journal of Education Finance* 38, 4 (Spring 2013): 320–342.

National Conference of State Legislatures. "Education Legislation | Bill Tracking Database." Denver, CO (2018). http://www.ncsl.org/research/education/education-bill-tracking-database.aspx

National Education Association. "Issues and Action." Washington, DC (2018). http://www.nea.org/home/IssuesAndAction.html

National Education Finance Academy (2018). https://www.nationaledfinance.com

Neher, Chris, David Patterson, John W. Duffield, and Amy Harvey. "Budgeting for the Future: The Long-Term Impacts of Short-Term Thinking in Alabama K–12 Education Funding." *Journal of Education Finance* 42, 4 (Spring 2017): 448–470.

Sutton, Lenford C. and Richard A. King. "Financial Crisis Not Wasted: Shift in State Power and Voucher Expansion." *Journal of Education Finance* 38, 4 (Spring 2013): 283–303.

Sutton, Lenford C. and Richard A. King. "School Vouchers in a Climate of Political Change." *Journal of Education Finance* 36, 3 (Winter 2011): 244–267.

Swensson, Jeff and John Ellis. "Follow the Money: On the Road to Charters and Vouchers Via the Educational-Industrial Complex." *Journal of Education Finance* 41, 4 (Spring 2016): 391–418.

Whitehead, Alfred North. *The Aims of Education and Other Essays*. New York: The Free Press (1929).

Wise, Arthur E. *Rich Schools, Poor Schools: The Promise of Equal Educational Opportunity*. Chicago: University of Chicago Press, 1968.

Wohlstetter, Priscilla, Joanna Smith, Caitlin Farrell, Guilbert C. Hentschke, and Jennifer Hirman. "How Funding Shapes the Growth of Charter Management Organizations: Is the Tail Wagging the Dog?" *Journal of Education Finance* 37, 2 (Fall 2011): 150–174.

Index

Numbers in **bold** are in tables, numbers in *italics* are in figures.

9 781138 327665